D1171977

PLOTINUS

III

LCL 442

PLOTINUS

ENNEAD III

WITH AN ENGLISH TRANSLATION BY

A. H. ARMSTRONG

HARVARD UNIVERSITY PRESS
CAMBRIDGE, MASSACHUSETTS
LONDON, ENGLAND

First published 1967
Reprinted with corrections 1980, 1993
Reprinted 1999, 2006

ISBN 0-674-99487-6

Printed on acid-free paper and bound by
Edwards Brothers, Ann Arbor, Michigan

CONTENTS

SIGLA vii

ENNEAD III

1. ON DESTINY 5
2 AND 3. ON PROVIDENCE (I) and (II) 37
4. ON OUR ALOTTED GUARDIAN SPIRIT 139
5. ON LOVE 163
6. ON THE IMPASSIBILITY OF THINGS WITHOUT BODY 205
7. ON ETERNITY AND TIME 291
8. ON NATURE AND CONTEMPLATION AND THE ONE 357
9. VARIOUS CONSIDERATIONS 403

SIGLA

A = Laurentianus 87, 3.
A′ = Codicis A primus corrector.
E = Parisinus Gr. 1976.
B = Laurentianus 85, 15.
R = Vaticanus Reginensis Gr. 97.
J = Parisinus Gr. 2082.
U = Vaticanus Urbinas Gr. 62.
S = Berolinensis Gr. 375.
N = Monacensis Gr. 215.
M = Marcianus Gr. 240.
C = Monacensis Gr. 449.
V = Vindobonensis philosophicus Gr. 226.
Q = Marcianus Gr. 242.
L = Ambrosianus Gr. 667.
D = Marcianus Gr. 209.

W = AE.
X = BRJ.
Y = USM.
Z = QL.

mg = in margine.
ac = ante correctionem.
pc = post correctionem.
γρ = γράφεται.

ORDO ENNEADVM COMPARATVR CVM ORDINE CHRONOLOGICO

Enn.	chron.	Enn.	chron.	Enn.	chron.
I 1	53	II 1	40	III 1	3
I 2	19	II 2	14	III 2	47
I 3	20	II 3	52	III 3	48
I 4	46	II 4	12	III 4	15
I 5	36	II 5	25	III 5	50
I 6	1	II 6	17	III 6	26
I 7	54	II 7	37	III 7	45
I 8	51	II 8	35	III 8	30
I 9	16	II 9	33	III 9	13

Enn.	chron.	Enn.	chron.	Enn.	chron.
IV 1	21	V 1	10	VI 1	42
IV 2	4	V 2	11	VI 2	43
IV 3	27	V 3	49	VI 3	44
IV 4	28	V 4	7	VI 4	22
IV 5	29	V 5	32	VI 5	23
IV 6	41	V 6	24	VI 6	34
IV 7	2	V 7	18	VI 7	38
IV 8	6	V 8	31	VI 8	39
IV 9	8	V 9	5	VI 9	9

ORDO CHRONOLOGICVS COMPARATVR CVM ORDINE ENNEADVM

chron.	Enn.	chron.	Enn.	chron.	Enn.
1	I 6	19	I 2	37	II 7
2	IV 7	20	I 3	38	VI 7
3	III 1	21	IV 1	39	VI 8
4	IV 2	22	VI 4	40	II 1
5	V 9	23	VI 5	41	IV 6
6	IV 8	24	V 6	42	VI 1
7	V 4	25	II 5	43	VI 2
8	IV 9	26	III 6	44	VI 3
9	VI 9	27	IV 3	45	III 7
10	V 1	28	IV 4	46	I 4
11	V 2	29	IV 5	47	III 2
12	II 4	30	III 8	48	III 3
13	III 9	31	V 8	49	V 3
14	II 2	32	V 5	50	III 5
15	III 4	33	II 9	51	I 8
16	I 9	34	VI 6	52	II 3
17	II 6	35	II 8	53	I 1
18	V 7	36	I 5	54	I 7

PLOTINUS

ENNEAD III

SVMMARIVM

Τάδε ἔνεστι Πλωτίνου φιλοσόφου ἐννεάδος τρίτης·

III. 1. ιθʹ Περὶ εἱμαρμένης.
III. 2. κʹ Περὶ προνοίας πρῶτον.
III. 3. καʹ Περὶ προνοίας δεύτερον.
III. 4. κβʹ Περι τοῦ εἰληχότος ἡμᾶς δαίμονος.
III. 5. κγʹ Περὶ ἔρωτος.
III. 6. κδʹ Περὶ ἀπαθείας τῶν ἀσωμάτων.
III. 7. κεʹ Περὶ αἰῶνος καὶ χρόνου.
III. 8. κϛʹ Περὶ φύσεως καὶ θεωρίας καὶ τοῦ ἑνός.
III. 9. κζʹ Ἐπισκέψεις διάφοροι.

ENNEAD III. 1

III. 1. ON DESTINY

Introductory Note

THIS early treatise (No. 3 in Porphyry's chronological order) is very much a conventional Platonic school discussion of its period. After a formal scholastic statement of the question to be discussed, the views of opponents of the Platonic position, Epicureans, Stoics and astrological determinists, are stated and refuted on conventional lines, and the treatise ends with a brief statement of the Platonic doctrine, with its discrimination of the parts played in the causation of human action by universal and individual souls which leaves room for human freedom within the universal order. Bréhier, in his introduction to the treatise, cites a number of parallels which show the conventional nature of the contents, and he and Harder, in the introduction to the notes on it in his second edition, have some interesting suggestions about particular opponents at whom some of the arguments may be directed. But, though the subject was well worn and the arguments here are hackneyed, the problem of reconciling human freedom with the universal divine order was an important one for Plotinus, and he treated different aspects of it more fully and originally later, in the work *On Providence* which comes next in the Third Ennead (III. 2 and 3), in the treatise on astrology (II. 3) and in his writings on the soul (especially IV. 3, 8 and 9).

Synopsis

Formal statement of the problem to be discussed, that of causation. All things have a cause except the first prin-

ciples. The Peripatetic account of the immediate causes of events accepted as true as far as it goes (ch. 1). But it is lazy and superficial not to look for higher and remoter causes, and philosophers have in fact done so. The principal non-Platonic explanations; all things, even human thought and action are caused by (*a*) atoms (the Epicureans) or (*b*) the world-soul (Stoics or stoicising Platonists; see note to ch. 4) or (*c*) the stars (astrologers) or (*d*) the universal chain of causation (Stoics) (ch. 2). Refutation of these in the same order (*a*) ch. 3, (*b*) ch. 4, (*c*) chs. 5–6, (*d*) ch. 7. Brief statement of the true Platonic doctrine; universal soul and individual souls; freedom of rational and virtuous action (chs. 8–10).

III. 1. (3) ΠΕΡΙ ΕΙΜΑΡΜΕΝΗΣ

1. Ἅπαντα τὰ γινόμενα καὶ τὰ ὄντα ἤτοι κατ' αἰτίας γίνεται τὰ γινόμενα καὶ ἔστι τὰ ὄντα, ἢ ἄνευ αἰτίας ἄμφω· ἢ τὰ μὲν ἄνευ αἰτίας, τὰ δὲ μετ' αἰτίας ἐν ἀμφοτέροις· ἢ τὰ μὲν γινόμενα μετ' αἰτίας πάντα, τὰ δὲ ὄντα τὰ μὲν αὐτῶν ἔστι μετ' αἰτίας, τὰ δ' ἄνευ αἰτίας, ἢ οὐδὲν μετ' αἰτίας· ἢ ἀνάπαλιν τὰ μὲν ὄντα μετ' αἰτίας πάντα, τὰ δὲ γινόμενα τὰ μὲν οὕτως, τὰ δὲ ἐκείνως, ἢ οὐδὲν αὐτῶν μετ' αἰτίας. Ἐπὶ μὲν οὖν τῶν ἀιδίων τὰ μὲν πρῶτα εἰς ἄλλα αἴτια ἀνάγειν οὐχ οἷόν τε πρῶτα ὄντα· ὅσα δὲ ἐκ τῶν πρώτων ἤρτηται, ἐξ ἐκείνων τὸ εἶναι ἐχέτω. Τάς τε ἐνεργείας ἑκάστων ἀποδιδούς τις ἐπὶ τὰς οὐσίας ἀναγέτω· τοῦτο γάρ ἐστι τὸ εἶναι αὐτῷ, τὸ τοιάνδε ἐνέργειαν ἀποδιδόναι. Περὶ δὲ τῶν γινομένων ἢ ὄντων μὲν ἀεί, οὐ τὴν αὐτὴν δὲ ἐνέργειαν ποιουμένων ἀεὶ κατ' αἰτίας ἅπαντα λεκτέον γίνεσθαι, τὸ δ' ἀναίτιον οὐ παραδεκτέον, οὔτε παρεγκλίσεσι κεναῖς χώραν διδόντα

---

[1] An interesting variation and expansion of *Timaeus* 28A 4–5. Plato merely says that all things that come into being

III. 1. ON DESTINY

1. All things that come into being and all things that really exist either have a cause for their coming into being (those that come to be) or for their existence (those that really exist), or have no cause:[1] or else, in both classes, some have a cause and some have not: or all things which come into being have a cause, but things which really exist have some of them a cause and some not, or none of them has a cause: or it is the other way round; all things that really exist have a cause, but things that come into being do so some this way, or some that way, or none of them has a cause. Well, then, among the eternal realities it is not possible to refer the first of them to other things which are responsible for their existence, just because they are first; but it must be admitted that all those which depend on the first realities have their being from them. And in giving an account of the activities of each of them one should refer them to their essences; for this is their being, the due output of a particular kind of activity. But as for things which come into being, or which always really exist but do not always act in the same way, we must say that all always have a cause for coming to be; nothing uncaused can be admitted; we must leave

must have a cause. Plotinus also takes into account the eternal realities, because for him even the Forms in Intellect have a cause, the One, as he indicates in the next sentence.

οὔτε κινήσει σωμάτων τῇ ἐξαίφνης, ἣ οὐδενὸς προηγησαμένου ὑπέστη, οὔτε ψυχῆς ὁρμῇ ἐμπλήκτῳ μηδενὸς κινήσαντος αὐτὴν εἰς τό τι πρᾶξαι ὧν πρότερον οὐκ ἐποίει. Ἢ αὐτῷ γε τούτῳ μείζων[1] ἄν τις ἔχοι αὐτὴν ἀνάγκη τὸ μὴ αὐτῆς εἶναι, φέρεσθαι δὲ τὰς τοιαύτας φορὰς ἀβουλήτους τε καὶ ἀναιτίους οὔσας. Ἢ γὰρ τὸ βουλητόν—τοῦτο δὲ ἢ ἔξω ἢ εἴσω—ἢ τὸ ἐπιθυμητὸν ἐκίνησεν· ἤ, εἰ μηδὲν ὀρεκτὸν ἐκίνησεν, [ἢ] οὐδ' ἂν ὅλως ἐκινήθη. Γιγνομένων δὲ πάντων κατ' αἰτίας τὰς μὲν προσεχεῖς ἑκάστῳ ῥᾴδιον λαβεῖν καὶ εἰς ταύτας ἀνάγειν· οἷον τοῦ βαδίσαι εἰς ἀγορὰν τὸ οἰηθῆναι δεῖν τινα ἰδεῖν ἢ χρέος ἀπολαβεῖν· καὶ ὅλως τοῦ τάδε ἢ τάδε ἑλέσθαι καὶ ὁρμῆσαι ἐπὶ τάδε[2] τὸ φανῆναι ἑκάστῳ ταδὶ ποιεῖν. Καὶ τὰ μὲν ἐπὶ τὰς τέχνας ἀνάγειν· τοῦ ὑγιάσαι ἡ ἰατρικὴ καὶ ὁ ἰατρός. Καὶ τοῦ πλουτῆσαι θησαυρὸς εὑρεθεὶς ἢ δόσις παρά του ἢ ἐκ πόνων ἢ τέχνης χρηματίσασθαι. Καὶ τοῦ τέκνου ὁ πατὴρ καὶ εἴ τι συνεργὸν ἔξωθεν εἰς παιδοποιίαν ἄλλο παρ' ἄλλου ἧκον· οἷον σιτία τοιάδε ἢ καὶ ὀλίγῳ προσώτερα

1 μείζων edd.: μεῖζον codd.
2 ἐπὶ τάδε Harder, H–S: ἔπειτα δὲ codd.

---

1 The famous uncaused atomic "slant" or "swerve" of Epicurus, the *clinamen* of Lucretius (II. 292; cp. Bailey's commentary on ll. 216–293 in his edition). Cicero refers to it equally impolitely in *De Fato* 23 (*commenticia declinatio*) and *De Finibus* I. 19 (*res commenticia*).

2 Cp. Aristotle, *Physics* II. 5. 196b 33-34.

3 Theiler's excellent emendation (⟨γονὴ⟩ ἢ γυνὴ for the MSS

no room for vain "slants"[1] or the sudden movement of bodies which happens without any preceding causation, or a senseless impulse of soul when nothing has moved it to do anything which it did not do before. Because of this very absence of motive a greater compulsion would hold the soul, that of not belonging to itself but being carried about by movements of this kind which would be unwilled and causeless. For either that which it willed—which could be within or outside it—or that which it desired moved the soul; or, if nothing which attracted it moved it, it would not have been moved at all. If all things have a cause for their happening it is easy to apprehend the causes which are immediately relevant to each happening and to trace it back to them: for instance, the cause of going to the market-place is that one thinks one ought to see someone or to collect a debt:[2] and in general the cause of choosing this or that or going after that is that it seemed good to the particular person involved to do that. And there are some things whose causes should be assigned to the arts; the cause of getting well is the medical art and the doctor: and the cause of getting rich is a treasure which has been found or a gift from someone, or making money by labour or skill. And the cause of the child is the father, and perhaps some external influences coming from various sources which co-operate towards the production of a child; for instance, a particular kind of diet, or, slightly remoter, seed, which flows easily for begetting, or a wife well[3]

ἡ γυνή, adopted here, is supported by the fact that it gives a verbal reminiscence of Plato, *Laws* 740D 6–7, *οἷς ἂν εὔρους ᾖ γένεσις* (though the context there is different).

εὔρους εἰς παιδοποιίαν ⟨γονὴ⟩[1] ἢ γυνὴ ἐπιτήδειος εἰς τόκους. Καὶ ὅλως εἰς φύσιν.

2. Μέχρι μὲν οὖν τούτων ἐλθόντα ἀναπαύσασθαι καὶ πρὸς τὸ ἄνω μὴ ἐθελῆσαι χωρεῖν ῥᾳθύμου ἴσως καὶ οὐ κατακούοντος τῶν ἐπὶ τὰ πρῶτα καὶ ἐπὶ τὰ ἐπέκεινα αἴτια ἀνιόντων. Διὰ τί γὰρ τῶν αὐτῶν γενομένων, οἷον τῆς σελήνης φανείσης, ὁ μὲν ἥρπασεν, ὁ δ' οὔ; Καὶ τῶν ὁμοίων ἐκ τοῦ περιέχοντος ἡκόντων ὁ μὲν ἐνόσησεν, ὁ δ' οὔ; Καὶ πλούσιος, ὁ δὲ πένης ἐκ τῶν αὐτῶν ἔργων; Καὶ τρόποι δὴ καὶ ἤθη διάφορα καὶ τύχαι ἐπὶ τὰ πόρρω ἀξιοῦσιν ἰέναι· καὶ οὕτω δὴ ἀεὶ οὐχ ἱστάμενοι οἱ μὲν ἀρχὰς σωματικὰς θέμενοι, οἷον ἀτόμους, τῇ τούτων φορᾷ καὶ πληγαῖς καὶ συμπλοκαῖς πρὸς ἄλληλα ἕκαστα ποιοῦντες καὶ οὕτως ἔχειν καὶ γίνεσθαι, ᾗ ἐκεῖνα συνέστη ποιεῖ τε καὶ πάσχει, καὶ τὰς ἡμετέρας ὁρμὰς καὶ διαθέσεις ταύτῃ ἔχειν, ὡς ἂν ἐκεῖναι ποιῶσιν, ἀνάγκην[2] ταύτην καὶ τὴν παρὰ τούτων εἰς τὰ ὄντα εἰσάγουσι. Κἂν ἄλλα δέ τις σώματα ἀρχὰς διδῷ καὶ ἐκ τούτων τὰ πάντα γίνεσθαι, τῇ παρὰ τούτων ἀνάγκῃ δουλεύειν ποιεῖ τὰ ὄντα. Οἱ δ' ἐπὶ τὴν τοῦ παντὸς ἀρχὴν ἐλθόντες ἀπ' αὐτῆς κατάγουσι πάντα, διὰ πάντων φοιτήσασαν αἰτίαν καὶ ταύτην οὐ μόνον[3] κινοῦσαν, ἀλλὰ καὶ ποιοῦσαν ἕκαστα λέγοντες, εἱμαρμένην ταύτην καὶ κυριωτάτην αἰτίαν

[1] ⟨γονὴ⟩ ἢ γυνὴ Theiler, H–S^2: ἢ J^{pc}C: ἡ wBRJ^{ac}USQ, H–S^1.
[2] ἀνάγκην A^{pc}, edd.: ἀνάγκῃ codd.
[3] οὐ μόνον A^{pc}, edd.: μόνον οὐ codd.

adapted to bearing children: and in general, one traces the cause of the child back to Nature.

2. But to come to a halt when one has reached these causes and not to want to go higher is characteristic, perhaps, of a lazy person who pays no attention to those who have ascended to the first and the transcendent causes. For why in the same circumstances, for instance when the moon shines, does one man steal and another not? And when the influences which come from the environment are similar, why does one fall ill and another not? And why does one become rich, another poor from the same activities? And different ways of behaving and characters and fortunes require us to go on to the remoter causes. So philosophers have never come to a standstill [when they have discovered the immediate causes]: some of them posit corporeal principles, for instance, atoms; they make both the way individual things exist, and the fact of their existence, depend on the movements of these, their clashings and interlockings with one another, the way in which they combine and act and are acted upon; even our own impulses and dispositions, they say, are as the atoms make them; so they introduce this compulsion which comes from the atoms into reality. And if anyone gives other bodies as principles, and says that everything comes into being from them, he makes reality the slave of the compulsion which comes from them. Others go back to the principle of the universe and derive everything from it, saying that it is a cause which penetrates all things, and one which does not only move but also makes each single thing; they posit it as fate and the

θέμενοι, αὐτὴν οὖσαν τὰ πάντα· οὐ μόνον τὰ ἄλλα, ὅσα γίνεται, ἀλλὰ καὶ τὰς ἡμετέρας διανοήσεις ἐκ τῶν ἐκείνης ἰέναι κινημάτων, οἷον ζῴου μορίων κινουμένων ἑκάστων οὐκ ἐξ αὑτῶν, ἐκ δὲ τοῦ ἡγεμονοῦντος ἐν ἑκάστῳ τῶν ζῴων. Ἄλλοι δὲ τὴν τοῦ παντὸς φορὰν περιέχουσαν καὶ πάντα ποιοῦσαν τῇ κινήσει καὶ ταῖς τῶν ἄστρων πλανωμένων τε καὶ ἀπλανῶν σχέσεσι καὶ σχηματισμοῖς πρὸς ἄλληλα, ἀπὸ τῆς ἐκ τούτων προρρήσεως πιστούμενοι, ἕκαστα ἐντεῦθεν γίνεσθαι ἀξιοῦσι. Καὶ μὴν καὶ τὴν τῶν αἰτίων ἐπιπλοκὴν πρὸς ἄλληλα καὶ τὸν ἄνωθεν εἱρμὸν καὶ τὸ ἕπεσθαι τοῖς προτέροις ἀεὶ τὰ ὕστερα καὶ ταῦτα ἐπ' ἐκεῖνα ἀνιέναι δι' αὐτῶν γενόμενα καὶ ἄνευ ἐκείνων οὐκ ἂν γενόμενα, δουλεύειν δὲ τοῖς πρὸ αὐτῶν τὰ ὕστερα, ταῦτα εἴ τις λέγοι, εἱμαρμένην ἕτερον τρόπον εἰσάγων φανεῖται. Διττοὺς δ' ἄν τις θέμενος καὶ τούτους οὐκ ἂν τοῦ ἀληθοῦς ἀποτυγχάνοι. Οἱ μὲν γὰρ ἀφ' ἑνός τινος τὰ πάντα ἀναρτῶσιν, οἱ δὲ οὐχ οὕτω. Λεχθήσεται δὲ περὶ τούτων.[1] Νῦν δ' ἐπὶ τοὺς πρώτους ἰτέον τῷ λόγῳ· εἶτ' ἐφεξῆς τὰ τῶν ἄλλων ἐπισκεπτέον.

3. Σώμασι μὲν οὖν ἐπιτρέψαι τὰ πάντα εἴτε ἀτόμοις εἴτε τοῖς στοιχείοις καλουμένοις καὶ τῇ ἐκ τούτων ἀτάκτως φορᾷ τάξιν καὶ λόγον καὶ ψυχὴν τὴν ἡγουμένην γεννᾶν ἀμφοτέρως μὲν ἄτοπον καὶ ἀδύνατον, ἀδυνατώτερον δέ, εἰ οἷόν τε[1] λέγειν, τὸ ἐξ ἀτόμων. Καὶ περὶ τούτων πολλοὶ

[1] *οἷόν τε* A^pc, edd.: *οἴονται* codd.

---

[1] In ch. 7.

supremely dominant cause, which is itself all things; they say that not only the other things which come into being but also our own thoughts come from its movements, as when the individual parts of a living creature are not moved by themselves but by the ruling principle in each living thing. Others claim that each and every thing comes to be from the universal circuit, which embraces everything and makes everything by its movement and by the positions and mutual aspects of the planets and fixed stars, relying upon the prediction which comes from them. Then, too, anyone who speaks of the mutual interweaving of causes and the chain of causation which reaches down from above, and the fact that consequents always follow antecedents and go back to them, since they come to be because of them and would not have done so without them, and says that what comes after is always enslaved to what is before, will obviously bring in fate by another way. But if one divided these philosophers, too, into two groups, one would be in accordance with the truth. For some of them make everything depend on a single principle, but others do not. We shall speak about these;[1] but now we must discuss those we mentioned first, and then consider the opinions of the others in order.

3. Well, then, to hand over the universe to bodies, whether to atoms or to what are called elements, and to generate order and reason and the ruling soul from the disorderly motion which they produce, is absurd and impossible on either view, but the more impossible, if one can say so, is the production from atoms. About these atoms many true arguments

εἴρηνται λόγοι ἀληθεῖς. Εἰ δὲ δὴ καὶ θεῖτό τις τοιαύτας ἀρχάς, οὐδ' οὕτως ἀναγκαῖον οὔτε τὴν κατὰ πάντων ἀνάγκην οὔτε τὴν ἄλλως εἱμαρμένην ἕπεσθαι. Φέρε γὰρ πρῶτον τὰς ἀτόμους εἶναι. Αὗται τοίνυν κινήσονται τὴν μὲν εἰς τὸ κάτω—ἔστω γάρ τι κάτω—τὴν δ' ἐκ πλαγίων, ὅπῃ ἔτυχεν, ἄλλαι κατ' ἄλλα. Οὐδὲν δὴ τακτῶς[1] τάξεώς γε οὐκ οὔσης, τὸ δὲ γενόμενον τοῦτο, ὅτε γέγονε, πάντως. Ὥστε οὔτε πρόρρησις οὔτε μαντικὴ τὸ παράπαν ἂν εἴη, οὔτε ἥτις ἐκ τέχνης—πῶς γὰρ ἐπὶ τοῖς ἀτάκτοις τέχνη;—οὔτε ἥτις ἐξ ἐνθουσιασμοῦ καὶ ἐπιπνοίας· δεῖ γὰρ καὶ ἐνταῦθα ὡρισμένον τὸ μέλλον εἶναι. Καὶ σώμασι μὲν ἔσται παρὰ τῶν ἀτόμων πάσχειν πληττομένοις, ἅπερ ἂν ἐκεῖναι φέρωσιν, ἐξ ἀνάγκης· τὰ δὲ δὴ ψυχῆς ἔργα καὶ πάθη τίσι κινήσεσι τῶν ἀτόμων ἀναθήσει τις; Ποίᾳ γὰρ πληγῇ[2] ἢ κάτω φερομένης ἢ ὁπουοῦν προσκρουούσης ἐν λογισμοῖς τοιοῖσδε ἢ ὁρμαῖς τοιαῖσδε ἢ ὅλως ἐν λογισμοῖς ἢ ὁρμαῖς ἢ κινήσεσιν ἀναγκαίαις εἶναι ἢ ὅλως εἶναι; Ὅταν δὲ δὴ ἐναντιῶται ψυχὴ τοῖς τοῦ σώματος παθήμασι; Κατὰ ποίας δὲ φορὰς ἀτόμων ὁ μὲν γεωμετρικὸς ἀναγκασθήσεται εἶναι, ὁ δὲ ἀριθμητικὴν καὶ ἀστρονομίαν ἐπισκέψεται, ὁ δὲ σοφὸς ἔσται; Ὅλως γὰρ τὸ ἡμέτερον ἔργον καὶ τὸ ζῴοις εἶναι ἀπολεῖται φερομένων ᾗ τὰ σώματα

[1] τακτῶς Orelli, H–S: πάντως codd.
[2] ποίᾳ γὰρ πληγῇ Harder, H–S²: ποία γὰρ πληγὴ codd.

have been brought forward. But even if one did posit principles of this kind, they would not even so necessarily entail universal compulsion or fate of a different kind. Let us start by admitting that atoms exist. Then they will be moved, some with a downward motion—let us grant that there is really a "down"—some with a sideways, just as it chances, others in other ways. Nothing will be ordered—there *is* no order—but this world which comes into existence, when it has come to be, is completely ordered. So [on the atomic theory] there would be no foretelling or divination, neither that which comes from art—for how could there be an art which deals with things without order?—nor that which comes from divine possession and inspiration;[1] for here, too, the future must be determined. And bodies will suffer, compulsorily, when they are struck by atoms, whatever the atoms may bring; but to what movements of atoms will one be able to attribute what soul does and suffers? For by what sort of atomic blow, whether the movement goes downwards or strikes against it from any direction, will the soul be engaged in reasonings or impulses of a particular kind, or any sort of reasonings or impulses or movements, necessary or not? And when the soul opposes the affections of the body? By what movements of atoms will one man be compelled to be a geometer, another study arithmetic and astronomy, and another be a philosopher? Our human activity, and our nature as living beings, will be altogether done away with if we are carried about where the [primary] bodies take

[1] This distinction between the two kinds of divination is taken from *Phaedrus* 244C.

ἄγει ὠθοῦντα ἡμᾶς ὥσπερ ἄψυχα σώματα. Τὰ αὐτὰ δὲ ταῦτα καὶ πρὸς τοὺς ἕτερα σώματα αἴτια τῶν πάντων τιθεμένους, καὶ ὅτι θερμαίνειν μὲν καὶ ψύχειν ἡμᾶς καὶ φθείρειν δὲ τὰ ἀσθενέστερα δύναται ταῦτα, ἔργον δὲ οὐδὲν τῶν ὅσα ψυχὴ ἐργάζεται παρὰ τούτων ἂν γίγνοιτο, ἀλλ' ἀφ' ἑτέρας δεῖ ταῦτα ἀρχῆς ἰέναι.

4. Ἀλλ' ἆρα μία τις ψυχὴ διὰ παντὸς διήκουσα περαίνει τὰ πάντα ἑκάστου ταύτῃ κινουμένου ὡς μέρους, ᾗ τὸ ὅλον ἄγει, φερομένων δὲ ἐκεῖθεν τῶν αἰτίων ἀκολούθων ἀνάγκη τὴν τούτων ἐφεξῆς συνέχειαν καὶ συμπλοκὴν εἱμαρμένην, οἷον εἰ φυτοῦ ἐκ ῥίζης τὴν ἀρχὴν ἔχοντος τὴν ἐντεῦθεν ἐπὶ πάντα διοίκησιν αὐτοῦ τὰ μέρη καὶ πρὸς ἄλληλα συμπλοκήν, ποίησίν τε καὶ πεῖσιν, διοίκησιν μίαν καὶ οἷον εἱμαρμένην τοῦ φυτοῦ τις εἶναι λέγοι; Ἀλλὰ πρῶτον μὲν τοῦτο τὸ σφοδρὸν τῆς ἀνάγκης καὶ τῆς τοιαύτης εἱμαρμένης αὐτὸ τοῦτο τὴν εἱμαρμένην καὶ τῶν αἰτίων τὸν εἱρμὸν καὶ τὴν συμπλοκὴν ἀναιρεῖ. Ὡς γὰρ ἐν τοῖς ἡμετέροις μέρεσι κατὰ τὸ ἡγεμονοῦν κινουμένοις ἄλογον τὸ

[1] This section (chs. 4–7 incl.) directed against the determinists has a good deal in common with the long discussion of fate in the commentary of Calcidius on the *Timaeus* (chs. 142–190), which Waszink gives quite good reasons for supposing to derive ultimately from Numenius (cp. the preface to his edition pp. lviii–lxiii). So the immediate source of Plotinus here may well be Numenius. The opponents envisaged throughout may be Stoics: there is nothing necessarily un-Stoic in this chapter,

us, as they push us along like lifeless bodies. The same objections apply against those who posit other bodies as causes of all things; and also say that these bodies can make us hot or cold and even destroy the weaker part of us; but no one of all the activities of soul can come from them, but these must come from another principle.

4. But, then, does one soul, permeating the universe, accomplish everything, each individual thing being moved as a part in the way in which the whole directs it? [1] And must we, as the consequent causes are brought into action from that one source, call their continuous ordered interweaving "destiny," as if, when a plant has its principle in the root, one were to call the direction which extends from there over all its parts and their mutual interrelation, acting and being acted upon, a single direction and, so to speak, destiny of the plant? But, first of all, this excess of necessity and of destiny so understood itself does away with destiny and the chain of causes and their interweaving. For just as with our own parts when they are moved by our ruling principle the statement

and the philosophical background of the astrological determinism criticised in 5 and 6 is Stoic. But it is odd, in this case, that Plotinus makes so clear a distinction between those who hold that all things are determined by the world-soul and those who hold that they are determined by the universal chain of causation (2. 15–26 and 31–36; 7. 5–9). There was a Platonic view which identified fate as a substantial reality with the world-soul (Ps.—Plutarch, *De Fato* 568e: Calcidius *In Tim.*, ch. 144, p. 182, 16 Waszink). And it is possible that some Platonists who held this (though not Numenius) may have adopted a Stoic-type determinism, and it is against them that Plotinus is arguing here (cp. Bréhier in his introduction to this treatise).

καθ' εἱμαρμένην λέγειν κινεῖσθαι—οὐ γὰρ ἄλλο μὲν τὸ ἐνδεδωκὸς τὴν κίνησιν, ἄλλο δὲ τὸ παραδεξάμενον καὶ παρ' αὐτοῦ τῇ ὁρμῇ κεχρημένον, ἀλλ' ἐκεῖνό ἐστι πρῶτον τὸ κινῆσαν τὸ σκέλος—τὸν αὐτὸν τρόπον εἰ καὶ ἐπὶ τοῦ παντὸς ἓν ἔσται τὸ πᾶν ποιοῦν καὶ πάσχον καὶ οὐκ ἄλλο παρ' ἄλλου κατ' αἰτίας τὴν ἀναγωγὴν ἀεὶ ἐφ' ἕτερον ἐχούσας, οὐ δὴ ἀληθὲς κατ' αἰτίας τὰ πάντα γίγνεσθαι, ἀλλ' ἓν ἔσται τὰ πάντα. Ὥστε οὔτε ἡμεῖς ἡμεῖς οὔτε τι ἡμέτερον ἔργον· οὐδὲ λογιζόμεθα αὐτοί, ἀλλ' ἑτέρου λογισμοὶ τὰ ἡμέτερα βουλεύματα· οὐδὲ πράττομεν ἡμεῖς, ὥσπερ οὐδ' οἱ πόδες λακτίζουσιν, ἀλλ' ἡμεῖς διὰ μερῶν τῶν ἑαυτῶν. Ἀλλὰ γὰρ δεῖ καὶ ἕκαστον ἕκαστον εἶναι καὶ πράξεις ἡμετέρας καὶ διανοίας ὑπάρχειν καὶ τὰς ἑκάστου καλάς τε καὶ αἰσχρὰς πράξεις παρ' αὐτοῦ ἑκάστου, ἀλλὰ μὴ τῷ παντὶ τὴν γοῦν τῶν αἰσχρῶν ποίησιν ἀνατιθέναι.

5. Ἀλλ' ἴσως μὲν οὐχ οὕτως ἕκαστα περαίνεται, ἡ δὲ φορὰ διοικοῦσα πάντα καὶ ἡ τῶν ἄστρων κίνησις οὕτως ἕκαστα τίθησιν, ὡς ἂν πρὸς ἄλληλα στάσεως ἔχῃ μαρτυρίαις καὶ ἀνατολαῖς, δύσεσί τε καὶ παραβολαῖς. Ἀπὸ τούτων γοῦν μαντευόμενοι προλέγουσι περί τε τῶν ἐν τῷ παντὶ ἐσομένων περί τε ἑκάστου, ὅπως τε τύχης καὶ διανοίας οὐχ ἥκιστα ἕξει. Ὁρᾶν δὲ καὶ τὰ ἄλλα ζῷά τε καὶ φυτὰ ἀπὸ τῆς τούτων συμπαθείας αὐξόμενά τε καὶ μειούμενα καὶ τὰ ἄλλα παρ' αὐτῶν πάσχοντα· τούς

that they are moved according to fate is unreasonable—for there is not one thing which imparts the movement and another which receives it and takes its impulse from it, but the ruling principle itself is what immediately moves the leg—in the same way if in the All the All is one thing acting and being acted upon, and one thing does not come from another according to causes which always lead back to something else, it is certainly not true that everything happens according to causes but everything will be one. So, on this assumption, we are not ourselves, nor is there any act which is our own. We do not reason, but our considered decisions are the reasonings of another. Nor do we act, any more than our feet kick; it is we who kick through parts of ourselves. But, really, each separate thing must be a separate thing; there must be actions and thoughts that are our own; each one's good and bad actions must come from himself, and we must not attribute the doing of bad actions at least to the All.

5. But perhaps particular things are not brought about in this way, but the heavenly circuit, directing everything, and the movement of the planets, arranges each and every thing according to the relative positions of the planets in their aspects and rising, settings and conjunctions. The evidence for this is that by divination from the planets people foretell what is going to happen in the All and about each individual, what sort of fortune and, in particular, what sort of thoughts he is going to have. And they say that one can see that the other animals and plants grow and diminish under the sympathetic influence of the planets, and are affected by them in other ways; and

τε τόπους τοὺς ἐπὶ γῆς διαφέροντας ἀλλήλων εἶναι κατά τε τὴν πρὸς τὸ πᾶν σχέσιν καὶ πρὸς ἥλιον μάλιστα· ἀκολουθεῖν δὲ τοῖς τόποις οὐ μόνον τὰ ἄλλα φυτά τε καὶ ζῷα, ἀλλὰ καὶ ἀνθρώπων εἴδη τε καὶ μεγέθη καὶ χρόας καὶ θυμοὺς καὶ ἐπιθυμίας ἐπιτηδεύματά τε καὶ ἤθη. Κυρία ἄρα ἡ τοῦ παντὸς πάντων φορά. Πρὸς δὴ ταῦτα πρῶτον μὲν ἐκεῖνο ῥητέον, ὅτι καὶ οὗτος ἕτερον τρόπον ἐκείνοις ἀνατίθησι τὰ ἡμέτερα, βουλὰς καὶ πάθη, κακίας τε καὶ ὁρμάς, ἡμῖν δὲ οὐδὲν διδοὺς λίθοις φερομένοις καταλείπει εἶναι, ἀλλ᾽ οὐκ ἀνθρώποις ἔχουσι παρ᾽ αὐτῶν καὶ ἐκ τῆς αὐτῶν φύσεως ἔργον. Ἀλλὰ χρὴ διδόναι μὲν τὸ ἡμέτερον ἡμῖν, ἥκειν δὲ εἰς τὰ ἡμέτερα ἤδη τινὰ ὄντα καὶ οἰκεῖα ἡμῶν ἀπὸ τοῦ παντὸς ἄττα, καὶ διαιρούμενον, τίνα μὲν ἡμεῖς ἐργαζόμεθα, τίνα δὲ πάσχομεν ἐξ ἀνάγκης, μὴ πάντα ἐκείνοις ἀνατιθέναι· καὶ ἰέναι μὲν παρὰ τῶν τόπων καὶ τῆς διαφορᾶς τοῦ περιέχοντος εἰς ἡμᾶς οἷον θερμότητας ἢ ψύξεις ἐν τῇ κράσει, ἰέναι δὲ καὶ παρὰ τῶν γειναμένων·[1] τοῖς γοῦν γονεῦσιν ὅμοιοι καὶ τὰ εἴδη ὡς τὰ πολλὰ καί τινα τῶν ἀλόγων τῆς ψυχῆς παθῶν. Οὐ μὴν ἀλλὰ καὶ ὁμοίων ὄντων τοῖς εἴδεσι παρὰ τοὺς τόπους ἔν γε τοῖς ἤθεσι πλείστη παραλλαγὴ καὶ ἐν ταῖς διανοίαις ἐνορᾶται, ὡς ἂν ἀπ᾽ ἄλλης ἀρχῆς τῶν τοιούτων ἰόντων. Αἵ τε πρὸς τὰς κράσεις τῶν σωμάτων καὶ πρὸς τὰς ἐπιθυμίας ἐναντιώσεις καὶ ἐνταῦθα πρεπόντως λέγοιντο ἄν.

the regions of the earth differ from each other according to their position in relation to the All, and particularly to the sun; and not only do the other animals and plants correspond to the regions but also the forms and sizes and colours, the tempers and desires and ways of life and characters of human beings. So the universal circuit rules all things. In answer to this we must say, first, that this man too, in a different way, attributes to those principles what is ours, acts of will and affections, vices and impulses, but gives us nothing and leaves us to be stones set rolling, but not men who have a work to do of ourselves and from our own nature. But one must give to us what is ours (though there must come to what is ours, already something and our own, a certain amount from the All), and make a distinction between what we do ourselves and what we experience of necessity and not attribute everything to those principles. And something certainly must come to us from the regions and the difference of the surrounding atmosphere, for instance, heat or coldness in our temperaments, but something also comes from our parents; at any rate, we are generally like our parents in our appearance and some of the irrational affections of our soul. Yet all the same, even when people are alike in appearance, corresponding to their regions, the greatest difference is observed in their characters and thoughts, so that things of this kind would come from another principle. Our resistances, also, to our bodily temperaments and our lusts could appropriately be mentioned here. But if, because,

[1] γειναμένων Sleeman, H–S: γι(γ)νομένων codd.

Εἰ δ' ὅτι εἰς τὴν τῶν ἄστρων σχέσιν ὁρῶντες περὶ ἑκάστων λέγουσι τὰ γινόμενα, παρ' ἐκείνων ποιεῖσθαι τεκμαίρονται, ὁμοίως ἂν καὶ οἱ ὄρνεις ποιητικοὶ ὧν σημαίνουσιν εἶεν καὶ πάντα, εἰς ἃ βλέποντες οἱ μάντεις προλέγουσιν. Ἔτι δὲ καὶ ἐκ τῶνδε ἀκριβέστερον ἄν τις περὶ τούτων ἐπισκέψαιτο. Ἅ τις ἂν ἰδὼν εἰς τὴν τῶν ἄστρων σχέσιν, ἣν εἶχον ὅτε ἕκαστος ἐγίνετο, προείποι, ταῦτά φασι καὶ γίνεσθαι παρ' αὐτῶν οὐ σημαινόντων μόνον, ἀλλὰ καὶ ποιούντων. Ὅταν τοίνυν περὶ εὐγενείας λέγωσιν ὡς ἐξ ἐνδόξων τῶν πατέρων καὶ μητέρων, πῶς ἔνι ποιεῖσθαι λέγειν ταῦτα, ἃ προυπάρχει περὶ τοὺς γονεῖς πρὶν τὴν σχέσιν γενέσθαι ταύτην τῶν ἄστρων ἀφ' ἧς προλέγουσι; Καὶ μὴν καὶ γονέων τύχας ἀπὸ τῶν παίδων τῆς γενέσεως καὶ παίδων διαθέσεις οἷαι ἔσονται καὶ ὁποίαις συνέσονται τύχαις ἀπὸ τῶν πατέρων περὶ τῶν οὔπω γεγονότων λέγουσι καὶ ἐξ ἀδελφῶν ἀδελφῶν θανάτους καὶ ἐκ γυναικῶν τὰ περὶ τοὺς ἄνδρας ἀνάπαλίν τε ἐκ τούτων ἐκεῖνα. Πῶς ἂν οὖν ἡ ἐπὶ ἑκάστου σχέσις[1] τῶν ἄστρων ποιοῖ, ἃ ἤδη ἐκ πατέρων οὕτως ἕξειν λέγεται; Ἢ γὰρ ἐκεῖνα τὰ πρότερα ἔσται τὰ ποιοῦντα, ἢ εἰ μὴ ἐκεῖνα ποιεῖ, οὐδὲ ταῦτα. Καὶ μὴν καὶ ἡ ὁμοιότης ἐν τοῖς εἴδεσι πρὸς τοὺς γονέας

[1] ἐπὶ ἑκάστου σχέσις Kirchhoff, H–S²: ἑκάστου σχέσις ἐπὶ codd.

looking at the position of the stars they announce what has happened to particular people, they adduce this as evidence that the happenings were caused by the stars, then in the same way birds would be the causes of what they indicate, and so would everything at which the soothsayers look when they foretell. Further, one could investigate these matters more exactly starting from the following observations. Whatever someone foretold, looking at the position which the stars held when a particular man was born, this, they say, was brought about by the stars, which did not only indicate but also caused the happenings. But when they talk about peoples' noble birth, that is that they come of illustrious fathers and mothers, how is it possible that the stars caused what the parents had already before the position of the stars came about from which they foretell? And they tell, too, the fortunes of parents from the nativity of their children, and what the children's dispositions are going to be and what fortunes they will meet with from the nativity of their parents speaking of children who are yet unborn, and they tell of the death of brothers from the horoscopes of their brothers, of what concerns husbands from the horoscopes of their wives and, the other way round, of wives from the horoscopes of their husbands. How, then, could the position of the stars over an individual cause what is already stated as going to occur on the evidence of the horoscope of the parents? Either those former astrological circumstances are the cause, or, if they are not, neither are those at the birth of the individual. Again, too, people's likeness in appearance to their parents declares that beauty

οἴκοθέν φησι καὶ κάλλος καὶ αἶσχος ἰέναι, ἀλλ' οὐ παρὰ φορᾶς ἄστρων. Εὔλογόν τε κατὰ τοὺς αὐτοὺς χρόνους [καὶ ἅμα] ζῷα τε παντοδαπὰ καὶ ἀνθρώπους <καὶ> ἅμα γίνεσθαι· οἷς ἅπασιν ἐχρῆν τὰ αὐτὰ εἶναι, οἷς ἡ αὐτὴ σχέσις. Πῶς οὖν ἅμα μὲν ἀνθρώπους, ἅμα δὲ τὰ ἄλλα διὰ τῶν σχημάτων;

6. Ἀλλὰ γὰρ γίγνεται μὲν ἕκαστα κατὰ τὰς αὐτῶν φύσεις, ἵππος μέν, ὅτι ἐξ ἵππου, καὶ ἄνθρωπος, ὅτι ἐξ ἀνθρώπου, καὶ τοιόσδε, ὅτι ἐκ τοιοῦδε. Ἔστω δὲ συνεργὸς καὶ ἡ τοῦ παντὸς φορὰ συγχωροῦσα τὸ πολὺ τοῖς γειναμένοις,[1] ἔστωσαν δὲ πρὸς τὰ τοῦ σώματος πολλὰ σωματικῶς διδόντες, θερμότητας καὶ ψύξεις καὶ σωμάτων κράσεις ἐπακολουθούσας, πῶς οὖν τὰ ἤθη καὶ ἐπιτηδεύματα καὶ μάλιστα οὐχ ὅσα δοκεῖ κράσει σωμάτων δουλεύειν, οἷον γραμματικὸς τίς καὶ γεωμετρικὸς καὶ κυβευτικὸς καὶ τῶνδε τίς εὑρετής; πονηρία δὲ ἤθους παρὰ θεῶν ὄντων πῶς ἂν δοθείη; καὶ ὅλως ὅσα λέγονται διδόναι κακὰ κακούμενοι, ὅτι δύνουσι καὶ ὅτι ὑπὸ γῆν φέρονται, ὥσπερ διάφορόν τι πασχόντων, εἰ πρὸς ἡμᾶς δύνοιεν, ἀλλ' οὐκ ἀεὶ ἐπὶ σφαίρας οὐρανίας φερομένων, καὶ

[1] γειναμένοις Sleeman: γινομένοις codd, H–S.

---

[1] I read here γειναμένοις (Sleeman, Class. Quart. 20, 1926, 152), for the MSS γινομένοις, because it gives a much better sense (it is difficult, indeed, to see how "the things which

and ugliness come from the family, and not from the movements of stars. It is reasonable, too, to suppose that all sorts of living creatures and men are born together; and all of them, since they have the same position of the stars, ought to have the same destiny. How, then, are at one and the same time both men and other living creatures produced by the arrangements of the stars?

6. But, in fact, all individual things come into being according to their own natures, a horse because it comes from a horse, and a man from a man, and a being of a particular kind because it comes from a being of a particular kind. Admitted that the universal circuit co-operates (conceding the main part to the parents),[1] and admitted that the stars contribute a great deal corporeally to the constituents of the body, heat and cooling and the consequent bodily temperaments; how, then, are they responsible for characters and ways of life, and especially for what is not obviously dominated by bodily temperament—becoming a man of letters, for instance, or a geometer, or a dice-player, and a discoverer in these fields? And how could a wicked character be given by the stars, who are gods? And in general, how could all the evils be given by them which they are said to give when they are brought into an evil state because they are setting and passing under the earth—as if anything extraordinary happened to them if they set from our point of view, and they were not always moving in the heavenly sphere

come into being," makes any sense at all here) and is consistent with the whole argument of the preceding lines.

πρὸς τὴν γῆν τὴν αὐτὴν ἐχόντων σχέσιν; Οὐδὲ λεκτέον, ὡς ἄλλος ἄλλον ἰδὼν τῶν θεῶν κατ' ἄλλην καὶ ἄλλην στάσιν χείρων ἢ κρείττων γίνεται· ὥστε εὐπαθοῦντας μὲν ἡμᾶς εὖ ποιεῖν, κακοῦν δέ, εἰ τἀναντία· ἀλλὰ μᾶλλον, ὡς φέρεται μὲν ταῦτα ἐπὶ σωτηρίᾳ τῶν ὅλων, παρέχεται δὲ καὶ ἄλλην χρείαν τὴν τοῦ εἰς αὐτὰ ὥσπερ γράμματα βλέποντας τοὺς τὴν τοιαύτην γραμματικὴν εἰδότας ἀναγινώσκειν τὰ μέλλοντα ἐκ τῶν σχημάτων κατὰ τὸ ἀνάλογον μεθοδεύοντας τὸ σημαινόμενον· ὥσπερ εἴ τις λέγοι, ἐπειδὴ ὑψηλὸς ὁ ὄρνις, σημαίνει ὑψηλάς τινας πράξεις.

7. Λοιπὸν δὲ ἰδεῖν τὴν ἐπιπλέκουσαν καὶ οἷον συνείρουσαν ἀλλήλοις πάντα καὶ τὸ πῶς ἐφ' ἑκάστου ἐπιφέρουσαν ἀρχὴν τιθεμένην μίαν, ἀφ' ἧς πάντα κατὰ λόγους σπερματικοὺς περαίνεται. Ἔστι μὲν οὖν καὶ αὕτη ἡ δόξα ἐγγὺς ἐκείνης τῆς πᾶσαν καὶ σχέσιν καὶ κίνησιν ἡμετέραν τε καὶ πᾶσαν ἐκ τῆς τῶν ὅλων ψυχῆς ἥκειν λεγούσης, εἰ καὶ βούλεταί τι ἡμῖν καὶ ἑκάστοις χαρίζεσθαι εἰς τὸ παρ' ἡμῶν ποιεῖν τι. Ἔχει μὲν οὖν τὴν πάντως πάντων ἀνάγκην, καὶ πάντων εἰλημμένων τῶν αἰτίων οὐκ ἔστιν ἕκαστον μὴ οὐ γίνεσθαι· οὐδὲν γὰρ ἔτι τὸ κωλῦσον ἢ ἄλλως γενέσθαι ποιῆσον, εἰ πάντα εἴληπται ἐν τῇ εἱμαρμένῃ. Τοιαῦτα δὲ ὄντα ὡς ἀπὸ μιᾶς ἀρχῆς ὡρμημένα ἡμῖν οὐδὲν καταλείψει, ἢ φέρεσθαι ὅπῃ ἂν ἐκεῖνα ὠθῇ. Αἵ τε γὰρ φαντασίαι τοῖς προηγησαμένοις αἵ τε ὁρμαὶ κατὰ ταύτας ἔσονται, ὄνομά τε μόνον

and holding the same position in relation to the earth? Nor must it be said that when one of the gods sees another in this or that position he becomes better or worse so that when they are in a good state they do good to us, but harm us when the opposite. We must rather say that the movement of the stars is for the preservation of the universe, but that they perform in addition another service; this is that those who know how to read this sort of writing can, by looking at them as if they were letters, read the future from their patterns, discovering what is signified by the systematic use of analogy—for instance, if one said that when the bird flies high it signifies some high heroic deeds.

7. It remains to look at the [theory of the] principle which interweaves and, so to speak, chains everything to everything else, and makes each individual thing be the way it is, a principle assumed to be one, from which all things come about by seminal formative principles. This opinion is close to that which says that all states and movements, both our own and all others, come from the soul of the universe, even if it does allow us, even as individuals, some room for action of our own. It certainly has in it absolute universal necessity, and when all the causes are included it is impossible for each individual thing not to happen: for there is nothing left which will hinder it or make it happen otherwise if all causes are included in fate. If they are like this, starting from a single principle, they will leave nothing for us except to move wherever they push us. For our mental images will depend on pre-existing circumstances and our impulses will follow our mental

τὸ ἐφ' ἡμῖν ἔσται· οὐ γὰρ ὅτι ὁρμῶμεν ἡμεῖς, ταύτῃ τι πλέον ἔσται τῆς ὁρμῆς κατ' ἐκεῖνα γεννωμένης· τοιοῦτόν τε τὸ ἡμέτερον ἔσται, οἷον καὶ τὸ τῶν ἄλλων ζῴων καὶ τὸ τῶν νηπίων καθ' ὁρμὰς τυφλὰς ἰόντων καὶ τὸ τῶν μαινομένων· ὁρμῶσι γὰρ καὶ οὗτοι· καὶ νὴ Δία καὶ [1] πυρὸς ὁρμαὶ καὶ πάντων ὅσα δουλεύοντα τῇ αὑτῶν κατασκευῇ φέρεται κατὰ ταύτην. Τοῦτο δὲ καὶ πάντες ὁρῶντες οὐκ ἀμφισβητοῦσιν, ἀλλὰ τῆς ὁρμῆς ταύτης ἄλλας αἰτίας ζητοῦντες οὐχ ἵστανται ὡς ἐπ' ἀρχῆς ταύτης.

8. Τίς οὖν ἄλλη αἰτία παρὰ ταύτας ἐπελθοῦσα ἀναίτιόν τε οὐδὲν καταλείψει ἀκολουθίαν τε τηρήσει καὶ τάξιν ἡμᾶς τέ τι εἶναι συγχωρήσει προρρήσεις τε καὶ μαντείας οὐκ ἀναιρήσει; Ψυχὴν δὴ δεῖ ἀρχὴν οὖσαν ἄλλην ἐπεισφέροντας εἰς τὰ ὄντα, οὐ μόνον τὴν τοῦ παντός, ἀλλὰ καὶ τὴν ἑκάστου μετὰ ταύτης, ὡς ἀρχῆς οὐ σμικρᾶς οὔσης, πλέκειν τὰ πάντα, οὐ γινομένης καὶ αὐτῆς, ὥσπερ τὰ ἄλλα, ἐκ σπερμάτων, ἀλλὰ πρωτουργοῦ αἰτίας οὔσης. Ἄνευ μὲν οὖν σώματος οὖσα κυριωτάτη τε αὑτῆς καὶ ἐλευθέρα καὶ κοσμικῆς αἰτίας ἔξω· ἐνεχθεῖσα δὲ εἰς σῶμα οὐκέτι πάντα κυρία, ὡς ἂν μεθ' ἑτέρων ταχθεῖσα. Τύχαι δὲ τὰ κύκλῳ πάντα, οἷς συνέπεσεν ἐλθοῦσα εἰς μέσον, τὰ πολλὰ ἤγαγον, ὥστε τὰ μὲν ποιεῖν διὰ ταῦτα, τὰ δὲ κρατοῦσαν αὐτὴν ταῦτα ὅπῃ ἐθέλει ἄγειν. Πλείω δὲ κρατεῖ ἡ ἀμείνων, ἐλάττω δὲ ἡ χείρων. Ἡ [2] γὰρ κράσει σώματός τι ἐνδιδοῦσα ἐπιθυμεῖν ἢ ὀργίζεσθαι

[1] καὶ Harder, H–S²: αἱ codd.
[2] ἡ Orelli H–S: ἣ codd.

images, and " what is in our power " will be a mere word; it will not exist any more just because it is we who have the impulses, if the impulse is produced in accordance with those pre-existing causes; our part will be like that of animals and babies, which go on blind impulses, and madmen, for these also have impulses—yes, by Zeus, fire has impulses too, and everything which is enslaved to its structure and moves according to it. Everyone else sees this and does not dispute it; but they look for other causes of this impulse of ours, and do not stop at this universal principle.

8. What other cause, then, occurs to us, besides these, which will leave nothing causeless, and will preserve sequence and order, and allow us to be something, and not do away with prophecies and divinations? Soul, surely, is another principle which we must bring into reality—not only the Soul of the All but also the individual soul along with it as a principle of no small importance; with this we must weave all things together, which does not itself come, like other things, from seeds but is a cause which initiates activity. Now when the soul is without body it is in absolute control of itself and free, and outside the causation of the physical universe; but when it is brought into body it is no longer in all ways in control, as it forms part of an order with other things. Chances direct, for the most part, all the things round it, among which it has fallen when it comes to this middle point, so that it does some things because of these, but sometimes it masters them itself and leads them where it wishes. The better soul has power over more, the worse over less. For the soul that gives in at all to the temperament of the body, is

ἠνάγκασται ἢ πενίαις ταπεινὴ ἢ πλούτοις χαῦνος ἢ δυνάμεσι τύραννος· ἡ δὲ καὶ ἐν τοῖς αὐτοῖς τούτοις ἀντέσχεν, ἡ ἀγαθὴ τὴν φύσιν, καὶ ἠλλοίωσεν αὐτὰ μᾶλλον ἢ ἠλλοιώθη, ὥστε τὰ μὲν ἑτεροιῶσαι, τοῖς δὲ συγχωρῆσαι μὴ μετὰ κάκης.

9. Ἀναγκαῖα μὲν οὖν ταῦτα, ὅσα προαιρέσει καὶ τύχαις κραθέντα γίνεται· τί γὰρ ἂν ἔτι καὶ ἄλλο εἴη; Πάντων δὲ ληφθέντων τῶν αἰτίων πάντα πάντως γίνεται· ἐν τοῖς ἔξωθεν δὲ καὶ εἴ τι ἐκ τῆς φορᾶς συντελεῖται. Ὅταν μὲν οὖν ἀλλοιωθεῖσα παρὰ τῶν ἔξω ψυχὴ πράττῃ τι καὶ ὁρμᾷ οἷον τυφλῇ τῇ φορᾷ χρωμένη, οὐχὶ ἑκούσιον τὴν πρᾶξιν οὐδὲ τὴν διάθεσιν λεκτέον· καὶ ὅταν αὐτὴ παρ' αὐτῆς χείρων οὖσα οὐκ ὀρθαῖς πανταχοῦ οὐδὲ ἡγεμονούσαις ταῖς ὁρμαῖς ᾖ χρωμένη. Λόγον δὲ ὅταν ἡγεμόνα καθαρὸν καὶ ἀπαθῆ τὸν οἰκεῖον ἔχουσα ὁρμᾷ, ταύτην μόνην τὴν ὁρμὴν φατέον εἶναι ἐφ' ἡμῖν καὶ ἑκούσιον, καὶ τοῦτο εἶναι τὸ ἡμέτερον ἔργον, ὃ μὴ ἄλλοθεν ἦλθεν, ἀλλ' ἔνδοθεν ἀπὸ καθαρᾶς τῆς ψυχῆς, ἀπ' ἀρχῆς πρώτης ἡγουμένης καὶ κυρίας, ἀλλ' οὐ πλάνην ἐξ ἀγνοίας παθούσης ἢ ἧτταν ἐκ βίας ἐπιθυμιῶν, αἳ προσελθοῦσαι ἄγουσι καὶ ἕλκουσι καὶ οὐκέτι ἔργα ἐῶσιν εἶναι, ἀλλὰ παθήματα παρ' ἡμῶν.

10. Τέλος δή φησιν ὁ λόγος πάντα μὲν σημαίνεσθαι καὶ γίνεσθαι κατ' αἰτίας μὲν πάντα, διττὰς δὲ ταύτας· καὶ τὰ μὲν ὑπὸ ψυχῆς, τὰ δὲ δι' ἄλλας

compelled to feel lust or anger, either abject in poverty or puffed up by wealth or tyrannical in power; but the other soul, the one which is good by nature, holds its own in these very same circumstances, and changes them rather than is changed by them; so it alters some of them and yields to others if there is no vice in yielding.

9. So all is necessary that comes about by a mixture of choice and chance; for what else could there be besides? But when all the causes are included, everything happens with complete necessity; if anything from the universal circuit makes its contribution, that, too, is counted among the external causes. When therefore, the soul is altered by the external causes, and so does something and drives on in a sort of blind rush, neither its action nor its disposition is to be called free; this applies, too, when it is worse from itself and does not altogether have its impulses right or in control. When, however, in its impulse it has as director its own pure and untroubled reason, then this impulse alone is to be said to be in our own power and free; this is our own act, which does not come from somewhere else but from within from our soul when it is pure, from a primary principle which directs and is in control, not suffering error from ignorance or defeat from the violence of the passions, which come upon it and drive and drag it about, and do not allow any acts to come from us any more but only passive responses.

10. To sum up, the argument says that all things are indicated [by the stars] and all things happen according to causes, but there are two kinds of these; and some happenings are brought about by the soul,

αἰτίας τὰς κύκλῳ. Πραττούσας δὲ ψυχὰς ὅσα πράττουσι κατὰ μὲν λόγον ποιούσας ὀρθὸν παρ' αὐτῶν πράττειν, ὅταν πράττωσι, τὰ δ' ἄλλα ἐμποδιζομένας τὰ αὐτῶν πράττειν, πάσχειν τε μᾶλλον ἢ πράττειν. Ὥστε τοῦ μὲν μὴ φρονεῖν ἄλλα αἴτια εἶναι· καὶ ταῦτα ἴσως ὀρθὸν καθ' εἱμαρμένην λέγειν πράττειν, οἷς γε καὶ δοκεῖ ἔξωθεν τὴν εἱμαρμένην αἴτιον εἶναι· τὰ δὲ ἄριστα παρ' ἡμῶν· ταύτης γὰρ καὶ τῆς φύσεώς ἐσμεν, ὅταν μόνοι ὦμεν· καὶ τούς γε σπουδαίους πράττειν, καὶ ἐπ' αὐτοῖς τὰ καλὰ πράττειν, τοὺς δὲ ἄλλους, καθ' ὅσον ἂν ἀναπνεύσωσι συγχωρηθέντες τὰ καλὰ πράττειν, οὐκ ἄλλοθεν λαβόντας τὸ φρονεῖν, ὅταν φρονῶσι, μόνον δὲ οὐ κωλυθέντας.

others through other causes, those round about it. And souls, in all that they do, when they do it according to right reason, act of themselves, whenever they do act, but in everything else are hindered in their own action and are passive rather than active. So other things [not the soul] are responsible for not thinking; and it is perhaps correct to say that the soul acts unthinkingly according to destiny, at least for people who think that destiny is an external cause; but the best actions come from ourselves; for this is the nature we are of, when we are alone; good and wise men do noble actions by their own will; but the others do their noble actions in so far as they have a breathing space and are allowed to do so, not getting their thinking from somewhere else, when they do think, but only not being hindered.

ENNEAD III. 2 AND 3

III. 2 and 3. ON PROVIDENCE

Introductory Note

THESE treatises (Nos. 47 and 48 in the chronological order) are Porphyry's divisions of a single long work on Providence which Plotinus wrote towards the end of his life. The subject was a traditional one: many Stoics and Middle Platonists had written on Providence before him: but this austere, honest and profound work is the finest of all Greek contributions to theodicy. The object of Plotinus is to explain how belief in the existence and goodness of divine providence can be justified in the face of all the apparent evils in the world: the opponents he has in view are the Epicureans, who denied providence, the Peripatetics, who denied that it extended to the world below the moon, and perhaps most of all his intimate enemies the Gnostics, who held that the material universe was the work of an evil maker. Many of the arguments he uses are traditional, taken over from the Stoics, or developed from Plato's great theodicy in Book X of the *Laws* (cp. Bréhier's introduction to the treatises). But there is much that is original in his use and elaboration of them. The work is not a systematic one: themes and arguments recur and are handled in different ways from different points of view, not always without some inconsistency. It is one of the works in which we have most vividly the impression of Plotinus thinking aloud, discussing the subject with himself as he writes.

A notable feature of the work is that Plotinus speaks in it, and it alone, of a *logos*, a rational forming principle, of the whole universe, which looks at first sight like a distinct

hypostasis, incompatible with the normal hierarchy of three and three only, the One, Intellect and Soul, on which he insists so strongly elsewhere. But Bréhier, in his introduction (pp. 18–22), is almost certainly right in understanding *logos* here, not as a distinct hypostasis, but as a way of speaking of the living formative and directive pattern, derived from Intellect through Soul in the usual way, which keeps the material universe in the best possible order and brings it into a unity-in-diversity of contrasting and clashing forces which, though far inferior to the unity of the intelligible world, is its best possible image in the sharply divided world of space and time.

Synopsis

III. 2

It is unreasonable to suppose that the world is produced by chance, but there are difficulties about universal providence which ought to be discussed. This universe is the everlasting product of the true, eternal universe of Intellect, which is at unity and peace with itself (ch. 1). This universe is not truly one: there is separation in it, and therefore conflict. It is not the result of any kind of planning or decision, but the natural product of Intellect, necessarily inferior because of its material element but with its own kind of harmony dominating its conflicts (ch. 2). It is good as a whole, and everything in it is good and seeks the Good, each in its degree (ch. 3). The destruction of one thing by another is necessary, and leads to new life. Disorder and lawlessness result from failure to attain the good, and lead inevitably and justly to punishment (ch. 4). Evils often lead to good, for the whole or the individual (ch. 5). How can we reconcile the obvious injustices of human life with providence? (ch. 6). This is a second-rate world, after all. Individual souls, too, must take their share of responsibility. But providence does

really extend to the earth (ch. 7). Man is not the best kind of creature in the universe, but midway between gods and beasts. Men get what they deserve at the hands of the wicked through their own slackness and folly. Divine providence must leave room for human initiative. Men cannot expect the gods to help them if they do not do what is necessary for their own well-being (chs. 8–9). Free-will and necessity (ch. 10). There must be inequalities in the All (chs. 11–12). It is important to take previous incarnations into account in estimating the justice of men's fates (ch. 13). The wonderful order of the universe, and man's place in it (chs. 13–14). The endless wars among animals and men (which do not affect man's true inner self) are part of the great game, incidents in the plot of the play, movements in the dance, notes in the melody of the universe, which must be as it is because it is necessarily secondary, imperfect, not fully unified (chs. 15–16). This universe is less one than its rational formative principle, the *logos*. In its clashing disunity "each man kills the thing he loves." The *logos*, in producing its play, gives human souls parts in it according to the characters they have already (ch. 17). But there are still difficulties. We must not think of the actors in our cosmic drama as improvising to fill in gaps in the play. If we take away responsibility for evil from the *logos* we shall take away responsibility for good as well. But if we give it all responsibility, even the diviner souls will count for nothing in the universe (ch. 18).

III. 3

The universal *logos* includes the *logoi* of all souls, good and bad, and each of them, while remaining itself, forms part of a complex living unity, within which strife and opposition have their place (ch. 1). The *logos* is like a general who commands the enemy's army as well as his own (ch. 2). Man's individuality and his acts of choice

are taken account of in the universal plan. It is absurd to complain because man is not better than he is: he is as good as he can be given his place in the order of things, in this universe which itself follows upon, and is less perfect than, Intellect and Soul (ch. 3). Man is not simple, but double, with a higher, free principle besides his lower self. Higher and lower providence, and higher and lower principles in man: the lower depend on and are caused by the higher. Again, we must take previous lives into account (ch. 4). The inequalities of the providential order; each individual thing in its place contributes in its own way to the single result. Fate (lower providence) and higher providence. Evil actions are not done by providence but their results are worked into the universal order. The differences in men's reactions. Their good actions are done by themselves, but according to providence (ch. 5). Divination is possible because of the universal harmony and correspondence of all things (ch. 6). Diversity, inequality and evil are necessary if there is to be any universal order at all: all things in their multiplicity grow from a single root (ch. 7).

III. 2. (47) ΠΕΡΙ ΠΡΟΝΟΙΑΣ ΠΡΩΤΟΝ

1. Τὸ μὲν τῷ αὐτομάτῳ καὶ τύχῃ διδόναι τοῦδε τοῦ παντὸς τὴν οὐσίαν καὶ σύστασιν ὡς ἄλογον καὶ ἀνδρὸς οὔτε νοῦν οὔτε αἴσθησιν κεκτημένου, δῆλόν που καὶ πρὸ λόγου καὶ πολλοὶ καὶ ἱκανοὶ καταβέβληνται δεικνύντες τοῦτο λόγοι· τὸ δὲ τίς ὁ τρόπος τοῦ ταῦτα γίνεσθαι ἕκαστα καὶ πεποιῆσθαι, ἐξ ὧν καὶ ἐνίων ὡς οὐκ ὀρθῶς γινομένων ἀπορεῖν περὶ τῆς τοῦ παντὸς προνοίας συμβαίνει, καὶ τοῖς μὲν ἐπῆλθε μηδὲ εἶναι εἰπεῖν, τοῖς δὲ ὡς ὑπὸ κακοῦ δημιουργοῦ ἐστι γεγενημένος, ἐπισκέψασθαι προσήκει ἄνωθεν καὶ ἐξ ἀρχῆς τὸν λόγον λαβόντας. Πρόνοιαν τοίνυν τὴν μὲν ἐφ' ἑκάστῳ, ἥ ἐστι λόγος πρὸ ἔργου ὅπως δεῖ γενέσθαι ἢ μὴ γενέσθαι τι τῶν οὐ δεόντων πραχθῆναι ἢ ὅπως τι εἴη ἢ μὴ εἴη ἡμῖν, ἀφείσθω· ἣν δὲ τοῦ παντὸς λέγομεν πρόνοιαν εἶναι, ταύτην ὑποθέμενοι τὰ ἐφεξῆς συνάπτωμεν. Εἰ μὲν οὖν ἀπό τινος χρόνου πρότερον οὐκ ὄντα τὸν κόσμον[1] ἐλέγομεν γεγονέναι, τὴν αὐτὴν ἂν τῷ λόγῳ ἐτιθέμεθα, οἵαν καὶ ἐπὶ τοῖς κατὰ μέρος

[1] *κόσμον* Ficinus, H–S: *χρόνον* codd.

---

[1] The Epicureans: cp. e.g. Cicero, *De Natura Deorum* I. 8. 18 and 20, 54–56.

[2] The Gnostics: cp. II. 9 [33], of which the title is given by

III. 2. ON PROVIDENCE (I)

1. To attribute the being and structure of this All to accident and chance is unreasonable and belongs to a man without intelligence or perception; this is obvious even before demonstration, and many adequate demonstrations have been set down which show it. But the way in which all these individual things here come into being and are made, some of which, on the ground that they have not rightly come into being, produce difficulties about universal providence (and it has occurred to some people to say that it does not exist at all,[1] and to others that the universe has been made by an evil maker),[2] this we ought to consider, starting our discussion from the very beginning. Let us leave out that providence [or foresight] which belongs to the individual, which is a calculation before action how something should happen, or not happen in the case of things which ought not to be done, or how we may have something, or not have it. Let us postulate what we call universal providence and connect up with it what comes after. If, then, we said that after a certain time the universe, which did not previously exist, came into being, we should in our discussion lay down that providence in the All was the same as we said it was in partial things, a

Porphyry in *Life*, ch. 24, 56–57, as "Against those who say that the maker of the universe is evil, and the universe is evil."

ἐλέγομεν εἶναι, προόρασίν τινα καὶ λογισμὸν θεοῦ, ὡς ἂν γένοιτο τόδε τὸ πᾶν, καὶ ὡς ἂν ἄριστα κατὰ τὸ δυνατὸν εἴη. Ἐπεὶ δὲ τὸ ἀεὶ καὶ τὸ οὔποτε μὴ τῷ κόσμῳ τῷδέ φαμεν παρεῖναι, τὴν πρόνοιαν ὀρθῶς ἂν καὶ ἀκολούθως λέγοιμεν τῷ παντὶ εἶναι τὸ κατὰ νοῦν αὐτὸν εἶναι, καὶ νοῦν πρὸ αὐτοῦ εἶναι οὐχ ὡς χρόνῳ πρότερον ὄντα, ἀλλ' ὅτι παρὰ νοῦ ἐστι καὶ φύσει πρότερος ἐκεῖνος καὶ αἴτιος τούτου ἀρχέτυπον οἷον καὶ παράδειγμα εἰκόνος τούτου ὄντος καὶ δι' ἐκεῖνον ὄντος καὶ ὑποστάντος ἀεί, τόνδε τὸν τρόπον· ἡ τοῦ νοῦ καὶ τοῦ ὄντος φύσις κόσμος ἐστὶν ὁ ἀληθινὸς καὶ πρῶτος, οὐ διαστὰς ἀφ' ἑαυτοῦ οὐδὲ ἀσθενὴς τῷ μερισμῷ οὐδὲ ἐλλιπὴς οὐδὲ τοῖς μέρεσι γενόμενος ἅτε ἑκάστου μὴ ἀποσπασθέντος τοῦ ὅλου· ἀλλ' ἡ πᾶσα ζωὴ αὐτοῦ καὶ πᾶς νοῦς ἐν ἑνὶ ζῶσα καὶ νοοῦσα ὁμοῦ καὶ τὸ μέρος παρέχεται ὅλον καὶ πᾶν αὐτῷ φίλον οὐ χωρισθὲν ἄλλο ἀπ' ἄλλου οὐδὲ ἕτερον γεγενημένον μόνον καὶ τῶν ἄλλων ἀπεξενωμένον· ὅθεν οὐδὲ ἀδικεῖ ἄλλο ἄλλο οὐδ' ἂν ᾖ ἐναντίον. Πανταχοῦ δὲ ὂν ἓν καὶ τέλειον ὁπουοῦν ἕστηκέ τε καὶ ἀλλοίωσιν οὐκ ἔχει· οὐδὲ γὰρ ποιεῖ ἄλλο εἰς ἄλλο. Τίνος γὰρ ἂν ἕνεκα ποιοῖ ἐλλεῖπον οὐδενί; Τί δ' ἂν λόγος λόγον ἐργάσαιτο

[1] Plotinus frequently attacks the idea that God first planned the universe and then created it, and insists that it is everlasting and not the result of divine deliberation and choice

foreseeing and calculation of God about how this All might come into existence, and how things might be as good as possible. But since we affirm that this universe is everlasting and has never not existed,[1] we should be correct and consistent in saying that providence for the All is its being according to Intellect, and that Intellect is before it, not in the sense that it is prior in time but because the universe comes from Intellect and Intellect is prior in nature, and the cause of the universe as a kind of archetype and model, the universe being an image of it and existing by means of it and everlastingly coming into existence, in this way; the nature of Intellect and Being is the true and first universe, which does not stand apart from itself and is not weakened by division and is not incomplete even in its parts, since each part is not cut off from the whole; but the whole life of it and the whole intellect lives and thinks all together in one, and makes the part the whole and all bound in friendship with itself, since one part is not separated from another and has not become merely other, estranged from the rest; and, therefore, one does not wrong another, even if they are opposites. And since it is everywhere one and complete at every point it stays still and knows no alteration; for it does not make as one thing acting upon another. For what reason could it have for making, since it is deficient in nothing? Why should a rational principle make another rational principle,

but of a spontaneous outflow of creative power without beginning or end. For a particularly notable statement of his reasons for rejecting divine planning and subsequent creation, cp. V. 8 [31] 7.

ἢ νοῦς νοῦν ἄλλον; Ἀλλὰ τὸ δι' αὐτοῦ δύνασθαί τι ποιεῖν ἦν ἄρα οὐκ εὖ ἔχοντος πάντῃ, ἀλλὰ ταύτῃ ποιοῦντος καὶ κινουμένου, καθ' ὅ τι καὶ χεῖρόν ἐστι· τοῖς δὲ πάντῃ μακαρίοις ἐν αὐτοῖς ἑστάναι καὶ τοῦτο εἶναι, ὅπερ εἰσί, μόνον ἀρκεῖ, τὸ δὲ πολυπραγμονεῖν οὐκ ἀσφαλὲς ἑαυτοὺς ἐξ αὑτῶν παρακινοῦσιν. Ἀλλὰ γὰρ οὕτω μακάριον κἀκεῖνο, ὡς ἐν τῷ μὴ ποιεῖν μεγάλα αὖ ἐργάζεσθαι, καὶ ἐν τῷ ἐφ' ἑαυτοῦ μένειν οὐ σμικρὰ ποιεῖν.

2. Ὑφίσταται γοῦν ἐκ τοῦ κόσμου τοῦ ἀληθινοῦ ἐκείνου καὶ ἑνὸς κόσμος οὗτος οὐχ εἷς ἀληθῶς· πολὺς γοῦν καὶ εἰς πλῆθος μεμερισμένος καὶ ἄλλο ἀπ' ἄλλου ἀφεστηκὸς καὶ ἀλλότριον γεγενημένον καὶ οὐκέτι φιλία μόνον, ἀλλὰ καὶ ἔχθρα τῇ διαστάσει καὶ ἐν τῇ ἐλλείψει ἐξ ἀνάγκης πολέμιον ἄλλο ἄλλῳ. Οὐ γὰρ ἀρκεῖ αὐτῷ τὸ μέρος, ἀλλὰ σῳζόμενον τῷ ἄλλῳ πολέμιόν ἐστιν ὑφ' οὗ σῴζεται. Γέγονε δὲ οὐ λογισμῷ τοῦ δεῖν γενέσθαι, ἀλλὰ φύσεως δευτέρας ἀνάγκῃ· οὐ γὰρ ἦν τοιοῦτον ἐκεῖνο οἷον ἔσχατον εἶναι τῶν ὄντων. Πρῶτον γὰρ ἦν καὶ πολλὴν δύναμιν ἔχον καὶ πᾶσαν· καὶ ταύτην τοίνυν τὴν τοῦ ποιεῖν ἄλλο ἄνευ τοῦ ζητεῖν ποιῆσαι. Ἤδη γὰρ ἂν αὐτόθεν οὐκ εἶχεν, εἰ ἐζήτει, οὐδ' ἂν ἦν ἐκ τῆς αὐτοῦ οὐσίας, ἀλλ' ἦν οἷον τεχνίτης ἀπ' αὐτοῦ τὸ ποιεῖν οὐκ ἔχων, ἀλλ' ἐπακτόν, ἐκ τοῦ μαθεῖν λαβὼν τοῦτο. Νοῦς τοίνυν δούς τι ἑαυτοῦ εἰς ὕλην ἀτρεμὴς καὶ

or an intellect another intellect? Being able to make something by itself is the characteristic of something which is not altogether in a good state but makes and moves in the direction in which it is inferior. For altogether blessed beings it is alone enough to stay still in themselves and be what they are; restless activity is unsafe for those who in it violently move themselves out of themselves. But that true All is blessed in such a way that in not making it accomplishes great works and in remaining in itself makes no small things.

2. For from that true universe which is one this universe comes into existence, which is not truly one; for it is many and divided into a multiplicity, and one part stands away from another and is alien to it, and there is not only friendship but also enmity because of the separation, and in their deficiency one part is of necessity at war with another. For the part is not self-sufficient, but in being preserved is at war with the other by which it is preserved. This universe has come into existence, not as the result of a process of reasoning that it ought to exist but because it was necessary that there should be a second nature; for that true All was not of a kind to be the last of realities. For it was the first, and had much power, indeed all power; and this is the power to produce something else without seeking to produce it. For if it had sought, it would not have had it of itself, nor would it have been of its own substance, but it would have been like a craftsman who does not have the ability to produce from himself, but as something acquired, and gets it from learning. So Intellect, by giving something of itself to matter, made all

ἥσυχος τὰ πάντα εἰργάζετο· οὗτος δὲ ὁ λόγος ἐκ νοῦ ῥυείς. Τὸ γὰρ ἀπορρέον ἐκ νοῦ λόγος, καὶ ἀεὶ ἀπορρεῖ, ἕως ἂν ᾖ παρὼν ἐν τοῖς οὖσι νοῦς. Ὥσπερ δὲ ἐν λόγῳ τῷ ἐν σπέρματι ὁμοῦ πάντων καὶ ἐν τῷ αὐτῷ ὄντων καὶ οὐδενὸς οὐδενὶ μαχομένου οὐδὲ διαφερομένου οὐδὲ ἐμποδίου ὄντος, γίνεταί τι ἤδη ἐν ὄγκῳ καὶ ἄλλο μέρος ἀλλαχοῦ καὶ δὴ καὶ ἐμποδίσειεν ἂν ἕτερον ἑτέρῳ καὶ ἀπαναλώσειεν ἄλλο ἄλλο, οὕτω δὴ καὶ ἐξ ἑνὸς νοῦ καὶ τοῦ ἀπ' αὐτοῦ λόγου ἀνέστη τόδε τὸ πᾶν καὶ διέστη καὶ ἐξ ἀνάγκης τὰ μὲν ἐγένετο φίλα καὶ προσηνῆ, τὰ δὲ ἐχθρὰ καὶ πολέμια, καὶ τὰ μὲν ἑκόντα, τὰ δὲ καὶ ἄκοντα ἀλλήλοις ἐλυμήνατο καὶ φθειρόμενα θάτερα γένεσιν ἄλλοις ειργάσατο, καὶ μίαν ἐπ' αὐτοῖς τοιαῦτα ποιοῦσι καὶ πάσχουσιν ὅμως ἁρμονίαν ἐνεστήσατο φθεγγομένων μὲν ἑκάστων τὰ αὑτῶν, τοῦ δὲ λόγου ἐπ' αὐτοῖς τὴν ἁρμονίαν καὶ μίαν τὴν σύνταξιν εἰς τὰ ὅλα ποιουμένου. Ἔστι γὰρ τὸ πᾶν τόδε οὐχ ὥσπερ ἐκεῖ νοῦς καὶ λόγος, ἀλλὰ μετέχον νοῦ καὶ λόγου. Διὸ καὶ ἐδεήθη ἁρμονίας συνελθόντος νοῦ καὶ ἀνάγκης, τῆς μὲν πρὸς τὸ χεῖρον ἑλκούσης καὶ εἰς ἀλογίαν φερούσης ἅτε οὐκ οὔσης λόγου, ἄρχοντος δὲ νοῦ ὅμως ἀνάγκης. Ὁ μὲν γὰρ νοητὸς μόνον λόγος, καὶ οὐκ ἂν γένοιτο ἄλλος

---

[1] The analogy of the seed (which in his way of thinking is superior in its concentrated unity to the full-grown plant) is a favourite one with Plotinus: cp., e.g., III. 7 [45] 11. 23–27.

[2] Plato, *Timaeus* 48A2.

things in unperturbed quietness; this something of itself is the rational formative principle flowing from Intellect. For that which flows out from Intellect is formative principle, and it flows out always, as long as Intellect is present among realities. But just as in the formative principle in a seed all the parts are together and in the same place, and none of them fights with any other or is at odds with it or gets in its way; then something comes to be in bulk, and the different parts are in different places, and then one really could get in another's way and even consume it;[1] so from Intellect which is one, and the formative principle which proceeds from it, this All has arisen and separated into parts, and of necessity some became friendly and gentle, others hostile and at war, and some did harm to each other willingly, some, too, unwillingly, and some by their destruction brought about the coming into being of others, and over them all as they acted and were acted upon in these kinds of ways they began a single melody, each of them uttering their own sounds, and the forming principle over them producing the melody and the single ordering of all together to the whole. This All of ours is not intellect and rational principle, like the All There, but participates in intellect and rational principle. Therefore, there was need of a concord in which " intellect and necessity " came together, in which necessity drags it down to what is worse and carries it away to unreason, because it is not a rational principle itself, but, all the same, " intellect controls necessity."[2] It is the intelligible universe that is nothing but rational principle, and there could not be another which is nothing but rational

μόνον λόγος· εἰ δέ τι ἐγένετο ἄλλο, ἔδει ἔλαττον ἐκείνου καὶ μὴ λόγον, μηδ' αὖ ὕλην τινά· ἄκοσμον γάρ· μικτὸν ἄρα. Καὶ εἰς ἃ μὲν λήγει, ὕλη καὶ λόγος, ὅθεν δὲ ἄρχεται, ψυχὴ ἐφεστῶσα τῷ μεμιγμένῳ, ἣν οὐ κακοπαθεῖν δεῖ νομίζειν ῥᾷστα διοικοῦσαν τόδε τὸ πᾶν τῇ οἷον παρουσίᾳ.

3. Καὶ οὐκ ἄν τις εἰκότως οὐδὲ τούτῳ μέμψαιτο ὡς οὐ καλῷ οὐδὲ τῶν μετὰ σώματος οὐκ ἀρίστῳ, οὐδ' αὖ τὸν αἴτιον τοῦ εἶναι αὐτῷ αἰτιάσαιτο πρῶτον μὲν ἐξ ἀνάγκης ὄντος αὐτοῦ καὶ οὐκ ἐκ λογισμοῦ γενομένου, ἀλλὰ φύσεως ἀμείνονος γεννώσης κατὰ φύσιν ὅμοιον ἑαυτῇ· ἔπειτα οὐδ' εἰ λογισμὸς εἴη ὁ ποιήσας, αἰσχυνεῖται τῷ ποιηθέντι· ὅλον γάρ τι ἐποίησε πάγκαλον καὶ αὔταρκες καὶ φίλον αὐτῷ καὶ τοῖς μέρεσι τοῖς αὐτοῦ τοῖς τε κυριωτέροις καὶ τοῖς ἐλάττοσιν ὡσαύτως προσφόροις. Ὁ τοίνυν ἐκ τῶν μερῶν τὸ ὅλον αἰτιώμενος ἄτοπος ἂν εἴη τῆς αἰτίας· τά τε γὰρ μέρη πρὸς αὐτὸ τὸ ὅλον δεῖ σκοπεῖν, εἰ σύμφωνα καὶ ἁρμόττοντα ἐκείνῳ, τό τε ὅλον σκοπούμενον μὴ πρὸς μέρη ἄττα μικρὰ βλέπειν. Τοῦτο γὰρ οὐ τὸν κόσμον αἰτιωμένου, ἀλλά τινα τῶν αὐτοῦ χωρὶς λαβόντος, οἷον εἰ παντὸς ζῴου τρίχα ἢ τῶν χαμαὶ δάκτυλον[1] ἀμελήσας τὸν πάντα ἄνθρωπον, δαιμονίαν τινὰ ὄψιν βλέπειν, ἢ νὴ Δία

[1] 14 λαβόντος Kirchhoff (accipientis Ficinus): λαβόντα codd. 15 δάκτυλον Kirchhoff: δακτύλων codd.

principle; but if something else did come into existence, it had to be less than that other universe, and not rational principle, nor yet some kind of matter, for that would be without beauty and order; so it had to be a mixture [of both]. Its terminal points are matter and rational principle; its starting-point is Soul presiding over the mixture, Soul which we must not think suffers any harm as it directs this All with the utmost ease by a sort of presence.

3. And it is not proper for anyone to speak ill of even this universe as not being beautiful or the best of all things which have body; nor to blame the cause of its existence when, first of all, it exists of necessity and not as the result of any process of reasoning, but of a better nature naturally producing a likeness of itself; then, even if it had been a process of reasoning which had produced it, there will be nothing to be ashamed of in its product; for it produced a whole, all beautiful and self-sufficient and friends with itself and with its parts, both the more important and the lesser, which are all equally well adapted to it. So he who blamed the whole because of the parts would be quite unreasonable in his blame; one must consider the parts in relation to the whole, to see if they are harmonious and in concord with it; and when one considers the whole one must not look at a few little parts.[1] This is not blaming the universe but taking some of its parts separately, as if one were to take a hair of a whole living being, or a toe, and neglect the whole man, a wonderful sight to see; or, really, to ignore the rest

[1] Cp. Plato, *Laws* X. 903B–C.

τὰ ἄλλα ζῷα ἀφεὶς τὸ εὐτελέστατον λαμβάνοι, ἢ τὸ ὅλον γένος παρείς, οἷον τὸ ἀνθρώπου, Θερσίτην εἰς μέσον ἄγοι. Ἐπεὶ οὖν τὸ γενόμενον ὁ κόσμος ἐστὶν ὁ σύμπας, τοῦτον θεωρῶν τάχα ἂν ἀκούσαις παρ' αὐτοῦ, ὡς «ἐμὲ πεποίηκε θεὸς κἀγὼ ἐκεῖθεν ἐγενόμην τέλειος ἐκ πάντων ζῴων καὶ ἱκανὸς ἐμαυτῷ καὶ αὐτάρκης οὐδενὸς δεόμενος, ὅτι πάντα ἐν ἐμοὶ καὶ φυτὰ καὶ ζῷα καὶ συμπάντων τῶν γενητῶν φύσις καὶ θεοὶ πολλοὶ καὶ δαιμόνων δῆμοι καὶ ψυχαὶ ἀγαθαὶ καὶ ἄνθρωποι ἀρετῇ εὐδαίμονες. Οὐ γὰρ δὴ γῆ μὲν κεκόσμηται φυτοῖς τε πᾶσι καὶ ζῴοις παντοδαποῖς καὶ μέχρι θαλάττης ψυχῆς ἦλθε δύναμις, ἀὴρ δὲ πᾶς καὶ αἰθὴρ καὶ οὐρανὸς σύμπας ψυχῆς ἄμοιρος, ἀλλ' ἐκεῖ ψυχαὶ ἀγαθαὶ πᾶσαι, ἄστροις ζῆν διδοῦσαι καὶ τῇ εὐτάκτῳ οὐρανοῦ καὶ ἀιδίῳ περιφορᾷ νοῦ μιμήσει κύκλῳ φερομένῃ ἐμφρόνως περὶ ταὐτὸν ἀεί· οὐδὲν γὰρ ἔξω ζητεῖ. Πάντα δὲ τὰ ἐν ἐμοὶ ἐφίεται μὲν τοῦ ἀγαθοῦ, τυγχάνει δὲ κατὰ δύναμιν τὴν ἑαυτῶν ἕκαστα· ἐξήρτηται γὰρ πᾶς μὲν οὐρανὸς ἐκείνου, πᾶσα δὲ ἐμὴ ψυχὴ καὶ οἱ ἐν μέρεσιν ἐμοῖς θεοί, καὶ τὰ ζῷα δὲ πάντα καὶ φυτὰ καὶ εἴ τι ἄψυχον δοκεῖ εἶναι ἐν ἐμοί. Καὶ τὰ μὲν τοῦ εἶναι μετέχειν δοκεῖ μόνον, τὰ δὲ τοῦ ζῆν, τὰ δὲ μᾶλλον ἐν τῷ αἰσθάνεσθαι, τὰ δὲ ἤδη λόγον ἔχει, τὰ δὲ πᾶσαν ζωήν. Οὐ γὰρ τὰ ἴσα ἀπαιτεῖν δεῖ τοῖς μὴ ἴσοις·

of living beings and pick out the meanest; or to pass over the whole race, say, of men and bring forward Thersites. Since, then, what has come into being is the whole universe, if you contemplate this, you might hear it say, "A god made me, and I came from him perfect above all living things, and complete in myself and self-sufficient, lacking nothing, because all things are in me, plants and animals and the nature of all things that have come into being, and many gods, and populations of spirits, and good souls and men who are happy in their virtue. It is not true that the earth is adorned with all plants and every sort of animal, and the power of soul has reached to the sea, but all the air and aether and the whole heaven is without a share of soul; but up there are all good souls, giving life to the stars and to the well-ordered everlasting circuit of the heaven, which in imitation of Intellect wisely circles round the same centre for ever; for it seeks nothing outside itself.[1] Everything in me seeks after the Good, but each attains it in proportion to its own power; for the whole heaven depends on it, and the whole of my soul, and the gods in my parts, and all animals and plants and whatever there is in me (if there is anything) which is thought to be without life. And some things appear to participate only in being, others in life, others more fully in life in that they have sense-perception, others at the next stage have reason, and others the fullness of life. One must not demand equal gifts in things which are not equal. It is not the finger's

[1] Cp. *Laws* X. 898 (especially 898A5–B3 on the likeness of the circular motion of the heavens to the activity of intellect) and XII. 967A–D.

οὐδὲ γὰρ δακτύλῳ τὸ βλέπειν, ἀλλὰ ὀφθαλμῷ τοῦτο, δακτύλῳ δὲ ἄλλο, τὸ εἶναι οἶμαι δακτύλῳ καὶ τὸ αὐτοῦ ἔχειν.»

4. Πῦρ δὲ εἰ ὑπὸ ὕδατος σβέννυται καὶ ἕτερον ὑπὸ πυρὸς φθείρεται, μὴ θαυμάσῃς. Καὶ γὰρ εἰς τὸ εἶναι ἄλλο αὐτὸ ἤγαγεν, οὐκ ἀχθὲν ὑφ᾽ αὐτοῦ ὑπ᾽ ἄλλου ἐφθάρη, καὶ ἦλθε δὲ εἰς τὸ εἶναι ὑπ᾽ ἄλλου φθορᾶς, καὶ ἡ φθορὰ δὲ αὐτῷ οὐδὲν ἂν ἡ οὕτω δεινὸν φέροι, καὶ ἀντὶ τοῦ φθαρέντος πυρὸς πῦρ ἄλλο. Τῷ μὲν γὰρ ἀσωμάτῳ οὐρανῷ ἕκαστον μένει, ἐν δὲ τῷδε τῷ οὐρανῷ πᾶν μὲν ἀεὶ ζῇ καὶ ὅσα τίμια καὶ κύρια μέρη, αἱ δὲ ἀμείβουσαι ψυχαὶ σώματα καὶ ἄλλοτε ἐν ἄλλῳ εἴδει γίγνονται, καὶ ὅταν δὲ δύνηται, ἔξω γενέσεως στᾶσα ψυχὴ μετὰ τῆς πάσης ἐστὶ ψυχῆς. Σώματα δὲ ζῇ κατ᾽ εἶδος καὶ καθ᾽ ὅλα ἕκαστα, εἴπερ ἐξ αὐτῶν καὶ ζῷα ἔσται καὶ τραφήσεται· ζωὴ γὰρ ἐνταῦθα κινουμένη, ἐκεῖ δὲ ἀκίνητος. Ἔδει δὲ κίνησιν ἐξ ἀκινησίας εἶναι καὶ ἐκ τῆς ἐν αὐτῇ ζωῆς τὴν ἐξ αὐτῆς γεγονέναι ἄλλην, οἷον ἐμπνέουσαν καὶ οὐκ ἀτρεμοῦσαν ζωὴν ἀναπνοὴν τῆς ἠρεμούσης οὖσαν. Ζῴων δὲ εἰς ἄλληλα ἀναγκαῖαι αἱ ἐπιθέσεις καὶ φθοραί· οὐδὲ γὰρ ἀίδια ἐγίνετο. Ἐγίνετο δέ, ὅτι λόγος πᾶσαν ὕλην κατελάμβανε καὶ εἶχεν ἐν αὐτῷ

[1] These individual bodies are probably the elements, earth, air, etc., which are alive and communicate their life to the living beings in them: cp. IV. 4 [28] 27, where stones are said to grow as long as they are part of the living continuous

business to see, but this is the eye's function, and the finger's is something else, to be essentially finger and to have what belongs to it."

4. But do not be surprised if fire is extinguished by water and something else is destroyed by fire. For something else brought it into existence; it did not bring itself and was then destroyed by something else; and it came to being by the destruction of something else, and its own corresponding destruction, if it comes, would bring nothing terrible to it, and there is another fire in place of the fire which was destroyed. For the incorporeal heaven, each individual part persists, but in this heaven here the whole lives for ever and all the noble and important parts, but the souls, changing their bodies, appear now in one form and now in another, and also, when it can, a soul takes its place outside the process of becoming and is with the universal soul. Bodies live by species, and individual bodies as far as they are wholes,[1] if living things both come from them and are to be nourished by them; for life is in motion here, but unmoved There. Motion had to come from stillness, and from the life which remains in itself there had to come the life which proceeds from it, which is different, like a life breathing and stirring which is the respiration of that life at rest. The attacks of living beings on each other, and their destruction of each other, are necessary; they did not come into existence to live for ever. They came into existence because the formative principle took hold of the whole of matter and had in itself all

structure of the earth, but to stop growing when they are cut away from it.

πάντα ὄντων αὐτῶν ἐκεῖ ἐν τῷ ἄνω οὐρανῷ· πόθεν γὰρ ἂν ἦλθε μὴ ὄντων ἐκεῖ; Ἀνθρώπων δὲ εἰς ἀλλήλους ἀδικίαι ἔχοιεν μὲν ἂν αἰτίαν ἔφεσιν τοῦ ἀγαθοῦ, ἀδυναμίᾳ δὲ τοῦ τυχεῖν σφαλλόμενοι ἐπ' ἄλλους τρέπονται. Ἴσχουσι δὲ ἀδικοῦντες δίκας κακυνόμενοι ταῖς ψυχαῖς ἐνεργείαις κακίας τάττονταί τε εἰς τόπον χείρονα· οὐ γὰρ μήποτε ἐκφύγῃ μηδὲν τὸ ταχθὲν ἐν τῷ τοῦ παντὸς νόμῳ. Ἔστι δὲ οὐ διὰ τὴν ἀταξίαν τάξις οὐδὲ διὰ τὴν ἀνομίαν νόμος, ὥς τις οἴεται, ἵνα γένοιτο ἐκεῖνα διὰ τὰ χείρω καὶ ἵνα φαίνοιτο, ἀλλὰ διὰ τὴν τάξιν ἐπακτὸν οὖσαν. καὶ ὅτι τάξις, ἀταξία, καὶ διὰ τὸν νόμον καὶ τὸν λόγον, καὶ ὅτι λόγος, παρανομία καὶ ἄνοια οὐ τῶν βελτιόνων τὰ χείρω πεποιηκότων, ἀλλὰ τῶν δέχεσθαι δεομένων τὰ ἀμείνω φύσει τῇ ἑαυτῶν ἢ συντυχίᾳ καὶ κωλύσει ἄλλων δέξασθαι οὐ δεδυνημένων. Τὸ γὰρ ἐπακτῷ χρώμενον τάξει τοῦτο ἂν οὐ τύχοι ἢ δι' αὐτὸ παρ' αὐτοῦ ἢ δι' ἄλλο παρ' ἄλλου· πολλὰ δὲ ὑπ' ἄλλων πάσχει καὶ ἀκόντων τῶν ποιούντων καὶ πρὸς ἄλλο ἱεμένων. Τὰ δὲ δι' αὐτὰ ἔχοντα [1] κίνησιν αὐτεξούσιον ζῷα ῥέποι ἂν ὁτὲ μὲν πρὸς τὰ βελτίω, ὁτὲ δὲ πρὸς τὰ χείρω. Τὴν δὲ πρὸς τὰ χείρω τροπὴν παρ' αὐτοῦ ζητεῖν ἴσως οὐκ ἄξιον· ὀλίγη γὰρ

[1] ἔχοντα Theodoretus: ἐχόντων codd.

---

[1] I.e. Epicurus (cp. Usener, *Epicurea* 530 ff.).

living things, because they all exist There, in the upper heaven; for where could they have come from if they did not exist There? The cause of the wrongs men do to one another might be their effort towards the Good; when they fail through their impotence to attain it, they turn against other men. But the wrongdoers pay the penalty, being corrupted in their souls by their works of wickedness, and are set in a lower place; for nothing can ever escape that which is ordained in the law of the All. But order does not exist because of disorder or law because of lawlessness, as someone thinks,[1] that these good things may exist and be manifested because of the worse ones; but disorder and lawlessness exist because of order, which is imposed from outside. It is because there is order that disorder exists, and on account of the law and formative reason, just because it is reason, that there is transgression of the law and folly; not that the better things produce the worse, but the things which ought to receive the better are unable to do so because of their own nature or because of some chance circumstance or hindrance from others. For when something has its order from outside it may fail to correspond to it either of its own accord and from itself or because of and impelled by something else; and many things are affected by others when those which act on them do not intend to do so and are aiming at something else. But living beings which have of themselves a movement under their own control might incline sometimes to what is better, sometimes to what is worse. It is probably not worth enquiring into the reason for this self-caused turning towards the worse;

τροπὴ κατ' ἀρχὰς γενομένη προϊοῦσα ταύτῃ πλέον καὶ μεῖζον τὸ ἁμαρτανόμενον ἀεὶ ποιεῖ· καὶ σῶμα δὲ σύνεστι καὶ ἐξ ἀνάγκης ἐπιθυμία· καὶ παροφθὲν τὸ πρῶτον καὶ τὸ ἐξαίφνης καὶ μὴ ἀναληφθὲν αὐτίκα καὶ αἵρεσιν εἰς ὅ τις ἐξέπεσεν εἰργάσατο. Ἕπεταί γε μὴν δίκη· καὶ οὐκ ἄδικον τοιόνδε γενόμενον ἀκόλουθα πάσχειν τῇ διαθέσει, οὐδ' ἀπαιτητέον τούτοις τὸ εὐδαιμονεῖν ὑπάρχειν, οἷς μὴ εἴργασται εὐδαιμονίας ἄξια. Οἱ δ' ἀγαθοὶ μόνοι εὐδαίμονες· διὰ τοῦτο γὰρ καὶ θεοὶ εὐδαίμονες.

5. Εἰ τοίνυν καὶ ψυχαῖς ἐν τῷδε τῷ παντὶ ἔξεστιν εὐδαίμοσιν εἶναι, εἴ τινες μὴ εὐδαίμονες, οὐκ αἰτιατέον τὸν τόπον, ἀλλὰ τὰς ἐκείνων ἀδυναμίας οὐ δυνηθείσας καλῶς ἐναγωνίσασθαι, οὗ δὴ ἆθλα ἀρετῆς πρόκειται. Καὶ μὴ θείους δὲ γενομένους θεῖον βίον μὴ ἔχειν τί δεινόν; Πενίαι δὲ καὶ νόσοι τοῖς μὲν ἀγαθοῖς οὐδέν, τοῖς δὲ κακοῖς σύμφορα·[1] καὶ ἀνάγκη νοσεῖν σώματα ἔχουσι. Καὶ οὐκ ἀχρεῖα δὲ οὐδὲ ταῦτα παντάπασιν εἰς σύνταξιν καὶ συμπλήρωσιν τοῦ ὅλου. Ὡς γὰρ φθαρέντων τινῶν ὁ λόγος ὁ τοῦ παντὸς κατεχρήσατο τοῖς φθαρεῖσιν εἰς γένεσιν ἄλλων—οὐδὲν γὰρ οὐδαμῇ ἐκφεύγει τὸ ὑπὸ τούτου καταλαμβάνεσθαι—οὕτω καὶ κακωθέντος σώματος καὶ μαλακισθείσης δὲ ψυχῆς τῆς τὰ τοιαῦτα πασχούσης τὰ[2] νόσοις καὶ κακίᾳ καταληφθέντα ὑπεβλήθη ἄλλῳ εἱρμῷ καὶ ἄλλῃ τάξει. Καὶ τὰ μὲν αὐτοῖς συνήνεγκε τοῖς παθοῦσιν, οἷον πενία καὶ νόσος, ἡ δὲ κακία

[1] σύμφορα Creuzer (utilia Ficinus): συμφορά codd.
[2] τα² A^{pc}, H–S: καὶ codd.

for a deviation which is slight to begin with, as it goes on in this way continually makes the fault wider and graver; and the body is there too, and, necessarily, its lust. And the first beginning, the sudden impulse, if it is overlooked and not immediately corrected, even produces a settled choice of that into which one has fallen. Punishment certainly follows; and it is not unjust that someone who has come to be this sort of person should suffer the consequences of his condition; people must not demand to be well off who have not done what deserves well-being. Only the good are well off; that, too, is what gives the gods their well-being.

5. If, then, it is possible for souls to be well off in this All, we must not blame the place if some are not well off, but their own incapacity, in that they have not been able to take a noble part in the contest for which the prizes of virtue are offered. Why is it disconcerting if men who have not become godlike do not have a godlike life? And poverty, too, and sickness, are nothing to the good, but advantageous to the bad; and men must fall sick if they have bodies. And even these troubles are not altogether without usefulness for the co-ordination and completion of the whole. For, just as when some things are destroyed the formative principle of the All uses them for the generation of others—for nothing anywhere escapes its grip—so, when a body is damaged, and a soul enfeebled by suffering something of this kind, what has been seized upon by sicknesses and vice is subjected to another chain of causation and another ordering. And some troubles are profitable to the sufferers themselves, poverty and sickness for

εἰργάσατό τι χρήσιμον εἰς τὸ ὅλον παράδειγμα δίκης γενομένη καὶ πολλὰ ἐξ αὐτῆς χρήσιμα παρασχομένη. Καὶ γὰρ ἐγρηγορότας ἐποίησε καὶ νοῦν καὶ σύνεσιν ἐγείρει[1] πονηρίας ὁδοῖς ἀντιτατ-τομένων, καὶ μανθάνειν δὲ ποιεῖ οἷον ἀγαθὸν ἀρετὴ παραθέσει κακῶν ὧν οἱ πονηροὶ ἔχουσι. Καὶ οὐ γέγονε τὰ κακὰ διὰ ταῦτα, ἀλλ' ὅτι χρῆται καὶ αὐτοῖς εἰς δέον, ἐπείπερ ἐγένετο, εἴρηται. Τοῦτο δὲ δυνάμεως μεγίστης, καλῶς καὶ τοῖς κακοῖς χρῆσθαι δύνασθαι καὶ τοῖς ἀμόρφοις γενομένοις εἰς ἑτέρας μορφὰς χρῆσθαι ἱκανὴν εἶναι. Ὅλως δὲ τὸ κακὸν ἔλλειψιν ἀγαθοῦ θετέον· ἀνάγκη δὲ ἔλλειψιν εἶναι ἐνταῦθα ἀγαθοῦ, ὅτι ἐν ἄλλῳ. Τὸ οὖν ἄλλο, ἐν ᾧ ἐστι τὸ ἀγαθόν, ἕτερον ἀγαθοῦ ὂν ποιεῖ τὴν ἔλλειψιν· τοῦτο γὰρ οὐκ ἀγαθὸν ἦν. Διὸ οὔτε ἀπολέσθαι τὰ κακά, ὅτι τε ἄλλα ἄλλων ἐλάττω πρὸς ἀγαθοῦ φύσιν ἕτερά τε τἆλλα[2] τοῦ ἀγαθοῦ τὴν αἰτίαν τῆς ὑποστάσεως ἐκεῖθεν λαβόντα, τοιαῦτα δὴ γενόμενα τῷ πόρρω.

6. Τὸ δὲ παρ' ἀξίαν, ὅταν ἀγαθοὶ κακὰ ἔχωσι, φαῦλοι δὲ τὰ ἐναντία, τὸ μὲν λέγειν ὡς οὐδὲν κακὸν τῷ ἀγαθῷ οὐδ' αὖ τῷ φαύλῳ ἀγαθὸν ὀρθῶς μὲν λέγεται· ἀλλὰ διὰ τί τὰ μὲν παρὰ φύσιν τούτῳ, τὰ δὲ κατὰ φύσιν τῷ πονηρῷ; Πῶς γὰρ καλῶς νέμειν οὕτω; Ἀλλ' εἰ τὸ κατὰ φύσιν οὐ

[1] εγείρει Theodoretus: ἐγεῖραι codd.
[2] τἆλλα Theiler: ἄλλα codd.

---

[1] The often-repeated quotation from Plato, *Theaetetus* 176A5, one of the cardinal texts of Plotinian Neoplatonism.

instance, and vice works something useful to the whole by becoming an example of just punishment; and also of itself it offers much that is of use. For it makes men awake and wakes up the intelligence and understanding of those who are opposed to the ways of wickedness, and makes us learn what a good virtue is by comparison with the evils of which the wicked have a share. And evils did not come into existence for these reasons, but we have explained that, when they have come into existence, the formative principle uses even them to meet a need. This belongs to the greatest power, to be able to use even the evil nobly and to be strong enough to use things which have become shapeless for making other shapes. In general, we must define evil as a falling short of good; and there must be a falling short of good here below, because the good is in something else. This something else, then, in which the good is, since it is other than good, produces the falling short; for it is not good. Therefore "evils will not be done away with,"[1] because some things are less than others in comparison with the nature of good, and the other things which have the cause of their existence from the Good are different from the Good and have certainly become the sort of things they are because of their distance from it.

6. As for people getting what they do not deserve, when the good get what is bad and the bad the opposite, it is correct to say that nothing is bad for the good man and nothing, correspondingly, good for the bad one; but why do things against nature come to the good, and things according to nature to the wicked? How can this be right distribution? But

ποιεῖ προσθήκην πρὸς τὸ εὐδαιμονεῖν, οὐδ' αὖ τὸ παρὰ φύσιν ἀφαιρεῖ τοῦ κακοῦ τοῦ ἐν φαύλοις, τί διαφέρει τὸ οὕτως ἢ οὕτως; Ὥσπερ οὐδ' εἰ ὁ μὲν καλὸς τὸ σῶμα, ὁ δὲ αἰσχρὸς ὁ ἀγαθός. Ἀλλὰ τὸ πρέπον καὶ ἀνάλογον καὶ τὸ κατ' ἀξίαν ἐκείνως ἂν ἦν, ὃ νῦν οὐκ ἔστι· προνοίας δὲ ἀρίστης ἐκεῖνο ἦν. Καὶ μὴν καὶ τὸ δούλους, τοὺς δὲ δεσπότας εἶναι, καὶ ἄρχοντας τῶν πόλεων τοὺς κακούς, τοὺς δὲ ἐπιεικεῖς δούλους εἶναι, οὐ πρέποντα ἦν, οὐδ' εἰ προσθήκην ταῦτα μὴ φέρει εἰς ἀγαθοῦ καὶ κακοῦ κτῆσιν. Καίτοι τὰ ἀνομώτατα ἂν πράξειεν ἄρχων πονηρός· καὶ κρατοῦσι δ' ἐν πολέμοις οἱ κακοὶ καὶ οἷα αἰσχρὰ δρῶσιν αἰχμαλώτους λαβόντες. Πάντα γὰρ ταῦτα ἀπορεῖν ποιεῖ, ὅπως προνοίας οὔσης γίνεται. Καὶ γὰρ εἰ πρὸς τὸ ὅλον βλέπειν δεῖ τὸν ὁτιοῦν μέλλοντα ποιεῖν, ἀλλὰ καὶ τὰ μέρη ὀρθῶς ἔχει τάττειν ἐν δέοντι αὐτῷ καὶ μάλιστα, ὅταν ἔμψυχα ᾖ καὶ ζωὴν ἔχῃ ἢ καὶ λογικὰ ᾖ, καὶ τὴν πρόνοιαν δὲ ἐπὶ πάντα φθάνειν καὶ τὸ ἔργον αὐτῆς τοῦτ' εἶναι, τὸ μηδενὸς ἠμεληκέναι. Εἰ οὖν φαμεν ἐκ νοῦ τόδε τὸ πᾶν ἠρτῆσθαι καὶ εἰς ἅπαντα ἐληλυθέναι τὴν δύναμιν αὐτοῦ, πειρᾶσθαι δεῖ δεικνύναι, ὅπῃ ἕκαστα τούτων καλῶς ἔχει.

7. Πρῶτον τοίνυν ληπτέον ὡς τὸ καλῶς ἐν τῷ μικτῷ ζητοῦντας χρὴ μὴ πάντῃ ἀπαιτεῖν ὅσον τὸ καλῶς ἐν τῷ ἀμίκτῳ ἔχει, μηδ' ἐν δευτέροις

if what is according to nature brings no addition to well-being, nor, correspondingly, does that which is contrary to nature take away anything of the evil which is in the bad, what does it matter whether it is this way or that? Just as it does not matter if the bad man is beautiful in body and the other, the good man, is ugly. But that other way, which is not the way things are now, would be proper and proportionate and according to merit; and that would be the way of the best providence. Then, again, it is not proper that the good should be slaves and the others masters, and that the wicked should be rulers of cities and decent men their slaves, even if these circumstances add nothing to the possession of good or evil. Then, too, a wicked ruler might do the most lawless things; and the bad get the upper hand in wars, and what crimes they commit when they have taken prisoners! All these things cause perplexity about how they can happen if there is a providence. For even if someone who is intending to make something must look to the whole, yet all the same it is right for him to set the parts where they ought to be, especially when they are beings with souls, and have life, or are even rational; and providence ought to reach everything, and its task ought to be just this, to leave nothing neglected. If, then, we say this All depends on Intellect, and that the power of intellect has extended to all things, we must try to show in what way each of them is excellently disposed.

7. First, then, we must understand that those who are looking for excellence in what is mixed must not demand all that excellence has in the unmixed, nor look for things of the first order among those of the

ζητεῖν τὰ πρῶτα, ἀλλ' ἐπειδὴ καὶ σῶμα ἔχει, συγχωρεῖν καὶ παρὰ τούτου ἰέναι εἰς τὸ πᾶν, ἀπαιτεῖν δὲ παρὰ τοῦ λόγου, ὅσον ἐδύνατο δέξασθαι τὸ μῖγμα, εἰ μηδὲν τούτου ἐλλείπει· οἷον, εἴ τις ἐσκόπει τὸν ἄνθρωπον τὸν αἰσθητὸν ὅστις κάλλιστος, οὐκ ἂν δήπου τῷ ἐν νῷ ἀνθρώπῳ ἠξίωσε τὸν αὐτὸν εἶναι, ἀλλ' ἐκεῖνο ἀποδεδέχθαι τοῦ ποιητοῦ, εἰ ὅμως ἐν σαρξὶ καὶ νεύροις καὶ ὀστέοις ὄντα κατέλαβε τῷ λόγῳ, ὥστε καὶ ταῦτα καλλῦναι καὶ τὸν λόγον δυνηθῆναι ἐπανθεῖν [1] τῇ ὕλῃ. Ταῦτα τοίνυν ὑποθέμενον χρὴ προιέναι τὸ ἐντεῦθεν ἐπὶ τὰ ἐπιζητούμενα· τάχα γὰρ ἂν ἐν τούτοις τὸ θαυμαστὸν ἀνεύροιμεν τῆς προνοίας καὶ τῆς δυνάμεως, παρ' οὗ ὑπέστη τὸ πᾶν τόδε. Ὅσα μὲν οὖν ἔργα ψυχῶν, ἃ δὴ ἐν αὐταῖς ἵσταται ταῖς ἐργαζομέναις τὰ χείρω, οἷον ὅσα κακαὶ ψυχαὶ ἄλλας ἔβλαψαν καὶ ὅσα ἀλλήλας αἱ κακαί, εἰ μὴ καὶ τοῦ κακὰς ὅλως αὐτὰς εἶναι τὸ προνοοῦν αἰτιῷτο, ἀπαιτεῖν λόγον οὐδὲ εὐθύνας προσήκει «αἰτία ἑλομένου» διδόντας· εἴρηται γὰρ ὅτι ἔδει καὶ ψυχὰς κινήσεις οἰκείας ἔχειν καὶ ὅτι οὐ ψυχαὶ μόνον, ἀλλὰ ζῷα ἤδη, καὶ δὴ καὶ οὐδὲν θαυμαστὸν οὔσας ὅ εἰσιν ἀκόλουθον βίον ἔχειν· οὐδὲ γάρ, ὅτι κόσμος ἦν, ἐληλύθασιν, ἀλλὰ πρὸ κόσμου τὸ κόσμου εἶναι εἶχον καὶ ἐπιμελεῖσθαι

[1] ἐπανθεῖν Theiler: ἐπανελθεῖν codd.

---

[1] From the myth of Er in *Republic* X. 617E4–5 (the soul's choice of lives).

second, but, since they also have a body, one must admit that something comes from it to the All, and demand from the rational forming principle only as much as the mixture can receive, if nothing of it is deficient: for instance, if someone was looking for the most beautiful man that we can perceive by our senses he would not, presumably, expect him to be the same as the man in Intellect, but would be satisfied with what his maker had done if he had so dominated him, even though he was held in flesh and sinews and bones, by the formative principle, that he made these material things beautiful, and the formative principle was able to come into flower upon the matter. So, then, we must take these principles as the basis of our discussion, and go on from there to our enquiries; for perhaps we may discover in them the wonder of providence and of the power from which this All came into existence. Now, as far as all the works of souls are concerned, those, that is, which remain within the souls which do wrong, for instance, the harm evil souls do to others and the harm they do to each other, unless one is to blame the providential power for their being bad at all, one has no proper reason for demanding an account or a reckoning from it, as one admits that " the blame lies with the chooser ":[1] for it has already been said that souls must have their own movements, and that they are not only souls but also already [composite] living beings, and that there is nothing surprising if, being what they are, they have a life corresponding with their nature; for they have not come into the universe because it existed but before the universe they had it in them to belong to the universe, and to care

καὶ ὑφιστάναι καὶ διοικεῖν καὶ ποιεῖν ὅστις τρόπος, εἴτε ἐφεστῶσαι καὶ διδοῦσαί τι παρ' αὐτῶν εἴτε κατιοῦσαι εἴτε αἳ μὲν οὕτως, αἳ δ' οὕτως· οὐ γὰρ ἂν τὰ νῦν περὶ τούτων, ἀλλ' ὅτι, ὅπως πότ' ἂν ᾖ, τήν γε πρόνοιαν ἐπὶ τούτοις οὐ μεμπτέον. Ἀλλ' ὅταν πρὸς τοὺς ἐναντίους τὴν παράθεσιν τῶν κακῶν τις θεωρῇ, πένητας ἀγαθοὺς καὶ πονηροὺς πλουσίους καὶ πλεονεκτοῦντας ἐν οἷς ἔχειν δεῖ ἀνθρώπους ὄντας τοὺς χείρους καὶ κρατοῦντας, καὶ ἑαυτῶν καὶ τὰ ἔθνη καὶ τὰς πόλεις; Ἆρ' οὖν, ὅτι μὴ μέχρι γῆς φθάνει; Ἀλλὰ τῶν ἄλλων γινομένων λόγῳ μαρτύριον τοῦτο καὶ μέχρι γῆς ἰέναι· καὶ γὰρ ζῷα καὶ φυτὰ καὶ λόγου καὶ ψυχῆς καὶ ζωῆς μεταλαμβάνει. Ἀλλὰ φθάνουσα οὐ κρατεῖ; Ἀλλὰ ζῴου ἑνὸς ὄντος τοῦ παντὸς ὅμοιον ἂν γένοιτο, εἴ τις κεφαλὴν μὲν ἀνθρώπου καὶ πρόσωπον ὑπὸ φύσεως καὶ λόγου γίνεσθαι λέγοι κρατοῦντος, τὸ δὲ λοιπὸν ἄλλαις ἀναθείη αἰτίαις, τύχαις ἢ ἀνάγκαις, καὶ φαῦλα διὰ τοῦτο ἢ δι' ἀδυναμίαν φύσεως γεγονέναι. Ἀλλ' οὐδὲ ὅσιον οὐδ' εὐσεβὲς ἐνδόντας τῷ μὴ καλῶς ταῦτα ἔχειν καταμέμφεσθαι τῷ ποιήματι.

8. Λοιπὸν δὴ ζητεῖν ὅπῃ καλῶς ταῦτα, καὶ ὡς τάξεως μετέχει, ἢ ὅπῃ μή. Ἢ οὐ κακῶς. Παντὸς δὴ ζῴου τὰ μὲν ἄνω, πρόσωπα καὶ

for it and bring it into existence and direct it, and, in one way or another, to make it, either by staying above it and giving something of themselves or by coming down, or some in this way and some in that; for we are not concerned with this in our present discussion; what concerns us is that, however this may be, providence ought not to be blamed for the doings of souls. But what if one considers the comparative distribution of evils to men of opposite character, that the good are poor and the wicked are rich, and the bad have more than their share of the things which those who are human beings must have, and are masters, and peoples and cities belong to them? Is it, then, because providence does not reach as far as the earth? But the fact that the other things happen in a rational pattern is evidence that it reaches the earth too; for animals and plants share in reason and soul and life. Does it, then, reach the earth, but not have full control here? But, since the All is a single living being, this would be as if someone were to say that a man's head and face had been produced by nature and a rational forming principle in full control, but should attribute the rest of the body to other causes—chances or necessities—and should say that they were inferior productions either because of this or because of the incompetence of nature. But it is neither pious or reverent to censure the work by admitting that these lower parts are not excellently disposed.

8. So it remains to enquire in what way these are excellently arranged, and how they have a share in order, and in what way not. Certainly they are not arranged badly. The upper parts of every living

κεφαλή, καλλίω, τὰ δὲ μέσα καὶ κάτω οὐκ ἴσα· ἄνθρωποι δὲ ἐν μέσῳ καὶ κάτω, ἄνω δὲ οὐρανὸς καὶ οἱ ἐν αὐτῷ θεοί· καὶ τὸ πλεῖστον τοῦ κόσμου θεοὶ καὶ οὐρανὸς πᾶς κύκλῳ, γῆ δὲ οἷα κέντρον καὶ πρὸς ἕν τι τῶν ἄστρων. Θαυμάζεται δὲ ἐν ἀνθρώποις ἀδικία, ὅτι ἄνθρωπον ἀξιοῦσιν ἐν τῷ παντὶ τὸ τίμιον εἶναι ὡς οὐδενὸς ὄντος σοφωτέρου. Τὸ δὲ κεῖται ἄνθρωπος ἐν μέσῳ θεῶν καὶ θηρίων καὶ ῥέπει ἐπ' ἄμφω καὶ ὁμοιοῦνται οἱ μὲν τῷ ἑτέρῳ, οἱ δὲ τῷ ἑτέρῳ, οἱ δὲ μεταξύ εἰσιν, οἱ πολλοί. Οἱ δὴ κακυνθέντες εἰς τὸ ἐγγὺς ζῴων ἀλόγων καὶ θηρίων ἰέναι ἕλκουσι τοὺς μέσους καὶ βιάζονται· οἱ δὲ βελτίους μέν εἰσι τῶν βιαζομένων, κρατοῦνταί γε μὴν ὑπὸ τῶν χειρόνων, ᾗ[1] εἰσι χείρους καὶ αὐτοὶ καὶ οὐκ εἰσὶν ἀγαθοὶ οὐδὲ παρεσκεύασαν αὑτοὺς μὴ παθεῖν. Εἰ οὖν παῖδες ἀσκήσαντες μὲν τὰ σώματα, τὰς δὲ ψυχὰς ὑπ' ἀπαιδευσίας τούτου χείρους γενόμενοι ἐν πάλῃ κρατοῖεν τῶν μήτε τὰ σώματα μήτε τὰς ψυχὰς πεπαιδευμένων καὶ τὰ σιτία αὐτῶν ἁρπάζοιεν καὶ τὰ ἱμάτια αὐτῶν τὰ ἁβρὰ λαμβάνοιεν, τί ἂν τὸ

[1] ᾗ A[pc], H–S[2]: ἢ codd.

---

[1] Plotinus is insisting here on the smallness and unimportance of the earth in language customary among astronomers from Aristarchus of Samos onwards: cp. his *On the Sizes and Distances of the Sun and Moon* Hypothesis 2 τὴν γῆν σημείου τε καὶ κέντρου λόγον ἔχειν πρὸς τὴν τῆς σελήνης σφαῖραν. For its use as a theme of moral and religious exhortation, to bring home the insignificance of man and the worthlessness of fame see Marcus Aurelius IV. 3. 3. (A. S. L. Farquharson in his commentary, Vol. II, p. 595, has collected a number of

thing, the face and head, are more beautiful, and the middle and lower parts are not equal to them; but men are in the middle and below, and above are heaven and the gods in it; and the greatest part of the universe is gods and all the heaven round about it; but the earth is like a central point even in comparison with only one of the stars.[1] Unrighteousness in men causes surprise, because people expect man to be the really valuable part in the All, because there is nothing wiser. But the fact is that man has the middle place between gods and beasts, and inclines now one way, now the other, and some men become like gods and others like beasts, and some, the majority, are in between. Those, then, who are corrupted, so that they come near to irrational animals and wild beasts, pull down those in the middle and do them violence; these are certainly better than those who assault them, but all the same they are mastered by the worse men, in so far as they are worse themselves too, and are not [really] good, and have not prepared themselves not to suffer wrongs. If some boys, who have kept their bodies in good training, but are inferior in soul to their bodily condition because of lack of education, win a wrestle with others who are trained neither in body or soul and grab their food and their dainty clothes, would

parallels. Cicero *Somnium Scipionis* 8 and 12 may also be compared, though the earth here is only insignificantly small, not "a point"). Geocentric cosmology did not lead the ancient astronomers and philosophers to a man-centred view of the universe, an exaggerated view of man's importance in the scheme of things. It led them rather to stress his smallness, insignificance and lowly position in the cosmic order, as Plotinus does here.

πρᾶγμα ἢ γέλως εἴη; Ἢ πῶς οὐκ ὀρθὸν καὶ τὸν νομοθέτην συγχωρεῖν ταῦτα μὲν πάσχειν ἐκείνους δίκην ἀργίας καὶ τρυφῆς διδόντας, οἳ ἀποδεδειγμένων γυμνασίων αὐτοῖς οἵδ' ὑπ' ἀργίας καὶ τοῦ ζῆν μαλακῶς καὶ ἀνειμένως περιεῖδον ἑαυτοὺς ἄρνας καταπιανθέντας λύκων ἁρπαγὰς εἶναι; Τοῖς δὲ ταῦτα ποιοῦσι πρώτη μὲν δίκη τὸ λύκοις εἶναι καὶ κακοδαίμοσιν ἀνθρώποις· εἶτα αὐτοῖς καὶ κεῖται ἃ παθεῖν χρεὼν τοὺς τοιούτους· οὐ γὰρ ἔστη ἐνταῦθα κακοῖς γενομένοις ἀποθανεῖν, ἀλλὰ τοῖς ἀεὶ προτέροις ἕπεται ὅσα κατὰ λόγον καὶ φύσιν, χείρω τοῖς χείροσι, τοῖς δὲ ἀμείνοσι τὰ ἀμείνω. Ἀλλ' οὐ παλαῖστραι τὰ τοιαῦτα· παιδιὰ γὰρ ἐκεῖ. Ἔδει γὰρ μειζόνων τῶν παίδων μετὰ ἀνοίας ἀμφοτέρων γινομένων ἀμφοτέρους μὲν ζώννυσθαι ἤδη καὶ ὅπλα ἔχειν, καὶ ἡ θέα καλλίων ἢ κατὰ πάλας γυμνάζοντι· νῦν δ' οἱ μὲν ἄοπλοι, οἱ δὲ ὁπλισθέντες κρατοῦσιν. Ἔνθα οὐ θεὸν ἔδει ὑπὲρ τῶν ἀπολέμων αὐτὸν μάχεσθαι· σῴζεσθαι γὰρ ἐκ πολέμων φησὶ δεῖν ὁ νόμος ἀνδριζομένους, ἀλλ' οὐκ εὐχομένους· οὐδὲ γὰρ κομίζεσθαι καρποὺς εὐχομένους ἀλλὰ γῆς ἐπιμελουμένους, οὐδέ γε ὑγιαίνειν μὴ ὑγείας ἐπιμελουμένους· οὐδ' ἀγανακτεῖν δέ, εἰ τοῖς φαύλοις πλείους γίνοιντο καρποὶ ἢ ὅλως αὐτοῖς γεωργοῦσιν εἴη ἄμεινον. Ἔπειτα γελοῖον τὰ μὲν ἄλλα πάντα τὰ κατὰ τὸν βίον γνώμῃ τῇ ἑαυτῶν πράττειν, κἂν μὴ ταύτῃ

---

[1] For the thought, cp. Plato, *Theaetetus* 176D–177A: "wolves" from *Republic* 566A4; Epictetus's version of this

the affair be anything but a joke? Or would it not be right for even the lawgiver to allow them to suffer this as a penalty for their laziness and luxury, these boys, who, though they were assigned training-grounds, because of laziness and soft and slack living allowed themselves to become fattened lambs, the prey of wolves? But those who do these things are punished, first by being wolves and ill-fated men; and then as well there lies before them what people like this are destined to suffer; it does not come to a stop when they have become bad here and die;[1] every time the rational and natural consequences follow what has gone before, worse for the worse, but better for the better. But this sort of thing has nothing to do with wrestling-schools; what happens there is play. For if both our sets of boys grew bigger with their folly, then they would have to gird themselves and take weapons, and it would be a finer sight than if one gave them wrestling exercise; but as things are, one set are unarmed, and those who are armed get the mastery. Here it would not be right for a god to fight in person for the unwarlike; the law says that those who fight bravely, not those who pray, are to come safe out of wars; for, in just the same way, it is not those who pray but those who look after their land who are to get in a harvest, and those who do not look after their health are not to be healthy; and we are not to be vexed if the bad get larger harvests, or if their farming generally goes better. Then again, it is ridiculous for people to do everything else in life according to their own ideas,

commonplace (IV. 1. 127) is, however, closer to the present passage than anything in Plato.

πράττωσιν, ᾖ θεοῖς φίλα, σῴζεσθαι δὲ μόνον παρὰ θεῶν οὐδὲ ταῦτα ποιήσαντας, δι' ὧν κελεύουσιν αὐτοὺς οἱ θεοὶ σῴζεσθαι. Καὶ τοίνυν οἱ θάνατοι αὐτοῖς βελτίους ἢ τὸ οὕτω ζῶντας εἶναι ὅπως ζῆν αὐτοὺς οὐκ ἐθέλουσιν οἱ ἐν τῷ παντὶ νόμοι· ὥστε τῶν ἐναντίων γινομένων, εἰρήνης ἐν ἀνοίαις καὶ κακίαις πάσαις φυλαττομένης, ἀμελῶς ἂν ἔσχε τὰ προνοίας ἐώσης κρατεῖν ὄντως τὰ χείρω. Ἄρχουσι δὲ κακοὶ ἀρχομένων ἀνανδρίᾳ· τοῦτο γὰρ δίκαιον, οὐκ ἐκεῖνο.

9. Οὐ γὰρ δὴ οὕτω τὴν πρόνοιαν εἶναι δεῖ, ὥστε μηδὲν ἡμᾶς εἶναι. Πάντα δὲ οὔσης προνοίας καὶ μόνης αὐτῆς οὐδ' ἂν εἴη· τίνος γὰρ ἂν ἔτι εἴη; Ἀλλὰ μόνον ἂν εἴη τὸ θεῖον. Τοῦτο δὲ καὶ νῦν ἐστι· καὶ πρὸς ἄλλο δὲ ἐλήλυθεν, οὐχ ἵνα ἀνέλῃ τὸ ἄλλο, ἀλλ' ἐπιόντι οἷον ἀνθρώπῳ ἦν ἐπ' αὐτῷ τηροῦσα τὸν ἄνθρωπον ὄντα· τοῦτο δέ ἐστι νόμῳ προνοίας ζῶντα, ὃ δή ἐστι πράττοντα ὅσα ὁ νόμος αὐτῆς λέγει. Λέγει δὲ τοῖς μὲν ἀγαθοῖς γενομένοις ἀγαθὸν βίον ἔσεσθαι καὶ κεῖσθαι καὶ εἰς ὕστερον, τοῖς δὲ κακοῖς τὰ ἐναντία. Κακοὺς δὲ γενομένους ἀξιοῦν ἄλλους αὐτῶν σωτῆρας εἶναι ἑαυτοὺς προεμένους οὐ θεμιτὸν εὐχὴν ποιουμένων·

---

[1] Cp. Xenophon, *Cyropaedia* I. 6. 6. As this comparison suggests, this whole passage (8. 36–9. 19) should not be taken as directed primarily against the Christians (though Plotinus may possibly have them in mind at 9. 10–12). It is a general condemnation of the unintelligent and cowardly religiosity of

even if they are not doing it in the way which the gods like, and then be merely saved by the gods without even doing the things by means of which the gods command them to save themselves.[1] And certainly death is better for them than to stay living in a way in which the universal laws do not want them to live; so that if the opposite happened, and peace was preserved in every sort of folly and vice, providence would be neglecting its duty in allowing the worse really to get the upper hand. But the wicked rule by the cowardice of the ruled; for this is just, and the opposite is not.

9. Providence ought not to exist in such a way as to make us nothing. If everything was providence and nothing but providence, then providence would not exist; for what would it have to provide for? There would be nothing but the divine. But the divine exists also as things are; and has come to something other than itself, not to destroy the other but, when a man, for instance, comes to it, it stands over him and sees to it that he is man; that is, that he lives by the law of providence, which means doing everything that its law says. But it says that those who have become good shall have a good life, now, and laid up for them hereafter as well, and the wicked the opposite. But it is not lawful for those who have become wicked to demand others to be their saviours and to sacrifice themselves in answer to

people who expect the gods to intervene to get them out of troubles into which they have got themselves by ignoring the divinely established laws of nature and of human life; an intelligent Christian would have no difficulty in agreeing with it.

οὐ τοίνυν οὐδὲ θεοὺς αὐτῶν ἄρχειν τὰ καθέκαστα ἀφέντας τὸν ἑαυτῶν βίον οὐδέ γε τοὺς ἄνδρας τοὺς ἀγαθούς, ἄλλον βίον ζῶντας τὸν ἀρχῆς ἀνθρωπίνης ἀμείνω, τούτους αὐτῶν ἄρχοντας εἶναι· ἐπεὶ οὐδ' αὐτοὶ ἐπεμελήθησάν ποτε, ὅπως ἄρχοντες ἀγαθοὶ γένοιντο τῶν ἄλλων, ὅπως αὐτοῖς ⟨εὖ⟩[1] ᾖ ἐπιμελούμενοι, ἀλλὰ φθονοῦσιν, ἐάν τις ἀγαθὸς παρ' αὐτοῦ φύηται· ἐπεὶ πλείους ἂν ἐγένοντο ἀγαθοί, εἰ τούτους ἐποιοῦντο προστάτας. Γενόμενοι τοίνυν ζῷον οὐκ ἄριστον, ἀλλὰ μέσην τάξιν ἔχον καὶ ἑλόμενον, ὅμως ἐν ᾧ κεῖται τόπῳ ὑπὸ προνοίας οὐκ ἐώμενον ἀπολέσθαι, ἀλλὰ ἀναφερόμενον ἀεὶ πρὸς τὰ ἄνω παντοίαις μηχαναῖς, αἷς τὸ θεῖον χρῆται ἐπικρατεστέραν ἀρετὴν ποιοῦν, οὐκ ἀπώλεσε τὸ λογικὸν εἶναι τὸ ἀνθρώπινον γένος, ἀλλὰ μετέχον, εἰ καὶ μὴ ἄκρως, ἐστὶ καὶ σοφίας καὶ νοῦ καὶ τέχνης καὶ δικαιοσύνης, τῆς γοῦν πρὸς ἀλλήλους ἕκαστοι· καὶ οὓς ἀδικοῦσι δέ, οἴονται δικαίως ταῦτα ποιεῖν· εἶναι γὰρ ἀξίους. Οὕτω καλόν ἐστιν ἄνθρωπος ποίημα, ὅσον δύναται καλὸν εἶναι, καὶ συνυφανθὲν εἰς τὸ πᾶν μοῖραν ἔχει τῶν ἄλλων ζῴων ὅσα ἐπὶ

[1] ⟨εὖ⟩ Beutler.

---

[1] See note on previous chapter.

[2] This may seem at first sight to contradict Plato's teaching about the duty of the philosopher to "go down again into the cave" and rule the city (*Republic* VII. 519C–521A). But, in fact, Plato makes it quite clear that philosophers in ordinary unreformed states have no such duty (520A–B). It is only in

their prayers,[1] nor, furthermore, to require gods to direct their affairs in detail, laying aside their own life, or, for that matter, good men, who live another life better than human rule, to be their rulers; for they themselves have never taken any trouble to see that there should be good rulers of the rest of mankind, who would care that it should be well with them, but they are envious if anyone naturally becomes good by himself; for more people would have become good if they had made the good their leaders.[2] Since, then, men are not the best of living creatures but the human species occupies a middle position, and has chosen it, yet all the same is not allowed by providence to perish in the place where it is set but is always being lifted up to the higher regions by all sorts of devices which the divine uses to give virtue the greater power, mankind has not lost its character of being rational but is a participant, even if not to the highest degree, in wisdom and intellect and skill, and righteousness—each and all have a share at least in the righteousness that governs their dealings with each other; and those whom they wrong, they think that they wrong rightly, because they deserve it. In this way man is a noble creation, as far as he can be noble, and, being woven into the All, has a part which is better than that of other living things, of

the ideal state, where they have been carefully trained precisely in order to be its rulers, that they have the obligation to rule. Plotinus does not advert here to the possibility of an ideal state but otherwise his thought here is quite in accordance with Plato's and he probably has this passage of the *Republic* in mind (cp. l. 14–15, with 520E4–5, and perhaps 18, ἐάν τις ἀγαθὸς παρ' αὐτοῦ φύηται, with 520B2, αὐτόματοι γὰρ ἐμφύονται).

γῆς βελτίονα. Ἐπεὶ καὶ τοῖς ἄλλοις ὅσα ἐλάττω ζῷα αὐτοῦ κόσμον γῇ φέροντα μέμφεται οὐδεὶς νοῦν ἔχων. Γελοῖον γάρ, εἴ τις μέμφοιτο, ὅτι τοὺς ἀνθρώπους δάκνοι, ὡς δέον αὐτοὺς ζῆν κοιμωμένους. Ἀνάγκη δὲ καὶ ταῦτα εἶναι· καὶ αἱ μὲν πρόδηλοι παρ' αὐτῶν ὠφέλειαι, τὰς δὲ οὐ φανερὰς ἀνεῦρε πολλὰς ὁ χρόνος· ὥστε μηδὲν αὐτῶν[1] μάτην μηδὲ ἀνθρώποις εἶναι. Γελοῖον δὲ καὶ ὅτι ἄγρια πολλὰ αὐτῶν μέμφεσθαι γινομένων καὶ ἀνθρώπων ἀγρίων· εἰ δὲ μὴ πεπίστευκεν ἀνθρώποις, ἀλλὰ ἀπιστοῦντα ἀμύνεται, τί θαυμαστόν ἐστιν;

10. Ἀλλ' εἰ ἄνθρωποι ἄκοντές εἰσι κακοὶ καὶ τοιοῦτοι οὐχ ἑκόντες, οὔτ' ἄν τις τοὺς ἀδικοῦντας αἰτιάσαιτο, οὔτε τοὺς πάσχοντας ὡς δι' αὐτοὺς ταῦτα πάσχοντας. Εἰ δὲ δὴ καὶ ἀνάγκη οὕτω κακοὺς γίνεσθαι εἴτε ὑπὸ τῆς φορᾶς εἴτε τῆς ἀρχῆς διδούσης τὸ ἀκόλουθον ἐντεῦθεν, φυσικῶς οὕτως. Εἰ δὲ δὴ καὶ ὁ λόγος αὐτός ἐστιν ὁ ποιῶν, πῶς οὐκ ἄδικα οὕτως; Ἀλλὰ τὸ μὲν ἄκοντες, ὅτι ἁμαρτία ἀκούσιον· τοῦτο δὲ οὐκ ἀναιρεῖ τὸ αὐτοὺς τοὺς πράττοντας παρ' αὐτῶν εἶναι, ἀλλ'

[1] αὐτῶν Theodoretus Graec. affect. cur. vi. 71, H–S[2]: αὐτοῖς codd.

---

[1] The reference to Plato, *Laws* V. 731C, given by Henry-Schwyzer, Bréhier, and Beutler-Theiler can be misleading here. The *Laws* passage is stating the familiar Socratic–Platonic doctrine, πᾶς ὁ ἄδικος οὐχ ἑκὼν ἄδικος (C2–3): wrongdoing is error because nobody who knew what he was doing would deliberately choose the worst of evils for his most valuable

all, that is, which live on the earth. And besides, no one of any intelligence complains of all the other creatures, lower than himself, which ornament the earth. It would be ridiculous if someone complained of their biting men, as if men ought to pass their lives asleep. No, it is necessary that these, too, should exist; and some of the benefits which come from them are obvious, and those which are not evident, many of them time discovers; so that none of them exist without good purpose, even for men. But it is absurd, too, to complain that many of them are savage, when there are savage men as well; and if they do not trust men but in their distrust attack to keep them off, what is there surprising in that?

10. But if men are unwillingly wicked,[1] and are the sort of people they are, not by their own free will, one could neither blame the wrongdoers nor those who suffer wrong because they suffer it by their agency. But if there is a necessity that they should become wicked in this way, brought about either by the heavenly circuit or by the first principle determining the consequences that necessarily follow it, then their being wicked in this way is natural. But then surely, if it is the rational forming principle itself which makes them wicked, things are unjust in this way? But " unwilling " means that the error is unwilling; and this does not do away with the fact that it is men themselves who act of themselves

part, the soul. Plotinus, no doubt, has the Platonic formula in mind here; but what he is really concerned with is not to maintain that wrongdoing is error but that the control and ordering of all things by Providence still leaves room for human moral responsibility.

ὅτι αὐτοὶ ποιοῦσι, διὰ τοῦτο καὶ αὐτοὶ ἁμαρτάνουσιν· ἢ οὐδ' ἂν ὅλως ἥμαρτον μὴ αὐτοὶ οἱ ποιοῦντες ὄντες. Τὸ δὲ τῆς ἀνάγκης οὐκ ἔξωθεν, ἀλλ' ὅτι πάντως. Τὸ δὲ τῆς φορᾶς οὐχ ὥστε μηδὲν ἐφ' ἡμῖν εἶναι· καὶ γὰρ εἰ ἔξωθεν τὸ πᾶν, οὕτως ἂν ἦν, ὡς αὐτοὶ οἱ ποιοῦντες ἐβούλοντο· ὥστε οὐκ ἂν αὐτοῖς ἐναντία ἐτίθεντο ἄνθρωποι οὐδ' ἂν ἀσεβεῖς, εἰ θεοὶ ἐποίουν. Νῦν δὲ παρ' αὐτῶν τοῦτο. Ἀρχῆς δὲ δοθείσης τὸ ἐφεξῆς περαίνεται συμπαραλαμβανομένων εἰς τὴν ἀκολουθίαν καὶ τῶν ὅσαι εἰσὶν ἀρχαί· ἀρχαὶ δὲ καὶ ἄνθρωποι. Κινοῦνται γοῦν πρὸς τὰ καλὰ οἰκείᾳ φύσει καὶ ἀρχὴ αὕτη αὐτεξούσιος.

11. Πότερα δὲ φυσικαῖς ἀνάγκαις οὕτως ἕκαστα καὶ ἀκολουθίαις καὶ ὅπῃ δυνατὸν καλῶς; Ἢ οὔ, ἀλλ' ὁ λόγος ταῦτα πάντα ποιεῖ ἄρχων καὶ οὕτω βούλεται καὶ τὰ λεγόμενα κακὰ αὐτὸς κατὰ λόγον ποιεῖ οὐ βουλόμενος πάντα ἀγαθὰ εἶναι, ὥσπερ ἂν εἴ τις τεχνίτης οὐ πάντα τὰ ἐν τῷ ζῴῳ ὀφθαλμοὺς ποιεῖ· οὕτως οὐδ' ὁ λόγος πάντα θεοὺς εἰργάζετο, ἀλλὰ τὰ μὲν θεούς, τὰ δὲ δαίμονας, δευτέραν φύσιν, εἶτα ἀνθρώπους καὶ ζῷα ἐφεξῆς, οὐ φθόνῳ, ἀλλὰ λόγῳ ποικιλίαν νοερὰν ἔχοντι. Ἡμεῖς δέ, ὥσπερ οἱ ἄπειροι γραφικῆς τέχνης αἰτιῶνται, ὡς οὐ καλὰ τὰ χρώματα πανταχοῦ, ὁ δὲ ἄρα τὰ προσήκοντα

but it is because they themselves do the deed that they themselves err; if they were not themselves the doers, they would not have erred at all. But as for the necessity, this does not mean that it comes in from outside but only that it is universally so. And as for the heavenly circuit, it does not work so that nothing is in our power; for if the All was external to us, it would be just as its makers wished, so that, if it was gods who made it, men, even impious ones, would do nothing opposed to them. But as it is, this [the power of free action] originates in men. Given a first principle, it accomplishes what follows with the inclusion in the chain of causation of all the principles there are; but men, too, are principles; at any rate, they are moved to noble actions by their own nature, and this is an independent principle.

11. But are all individual things as they are by natural necessities and causal sequences, and excellently disposed in every way that can be? No, but the rational forming principle makes all these things as their sovereign, and wishes them to be as they are, and makes the things which are called bad according to reason, because it does not wish that all should be good, just like a craftsman who does not make everything eyes in his picture; in the same way the formative principle did not make everything gods but some gods, some spirits (a nature of the second rank), then men and animals after them in order, not out of grudging meanness but by a reason containing all the rich variety of the intelligible world. But we are like people who know nothing about the art of painting and criticise the painter because the colours are not beautiful everywhere, though he has

ἀπέδωκεν ἑκάστῳ τόπῳ· καὶ αἱ πόλεις δὲ οὐκ ἐξ ἴσων, καὶ αἳ εὐνομίᾳ[1] χρῶνται· ἢ εἴ τις δρᾶμα μέμφοιτο, ὅτι μὴ πάντες ἥρωες ἐν αὐτῷ, ἀλλὰ καὶ οἰκέτης καί τις ἀγροῖκος καὶ φαύλως φθεγγόμενος· τὸ δὲ οὐ καλόν ἐστιν, εἴ τις τοὺς χείρους ἐξέλοι, καὶ ἐκ τούτων συμπληρούμενον.

12. Εἰ μὲν οὖν αὐτὸς ὁ λόγος ἐναρμόσας ἑαυτὸν εἰς ὕλην ταῦτα εἰργάσατο τοῦτο ὢν οἷός ἐστιν, ἀνόμοιος τοῖς μέρεσιν, ἐκ τοῦ πρὸ αὐτοῦ τοῦτο ὤν, καὶ τοῦτο τὸ γενόμενον οὕτω γενόμενον μὴ ἂν ἔσχε κάλλιον ἑαυτοῦ ἄλλο. Ὁ δὲ λόγος ἐκ πάντων ὁμοίων καὶ παραπλησίων οὐκ ἂν ἐγένετο καὶ οὗτος ὁ τρόπος μεμπτός· πάντα ὄντος κατὰ μέρος ἕκαστον ἄλλος. Εἰ δὲ ἔξω ἑαυτοῦ ἄλλα εἰσήγαγεν, οἷον ψυχάς, καὶ ἐβιάσατο παρὰ τὴν αὐτῶν φύσιν ἐναρμόσαι τῷ ποιήματι πρὸς τὸ χεῖρον πολλάς, πῶς ὀρθῶς; Ἀλλὰ φατέον καὶ τὰς ψυχὰς οἷον μέρη αὐτοῦ εἶναι καὶ μὴ χείρους ποιοῦντα ἐναρμόττειν, ἀλλ' ὅπου προσῆκον αὐταῖς καταχωρίζειν κατ' ἀξίαν.

13. Ἐπεὶ οὐδὲ ἐκεῖνον ἀποβλητέον τὸν λόγον, ὃς οὐ πρὸς τὸ παρὸν ἑκάστοτέ φησι βλέπειν, ἀλλὰ

[1] καὶ αἳ εὐνομίᾳ Theiler, H–S²: καὶ αἱ εὐνομίαι A^{ac}ExyQ: ταῖς εὐνομίαις A^{pc}.

---

[1] Cp. Plato, *Republic* IV. 420C–D. The ignorant critic in Plato does not blame the painter for not making "everything

really distributed the appropriate colours to every place;[1] and cities are not composed of citizens with equal rights, even those which have good laws and constitutions; or we are like someone who censures a play because all the characters in it are not heroes but there is a servant and a yokel who speaks in a vulgar way; but the play is not a good one if one expels the inferior characters, because they too help to complete it.

12. If, then, the rational formative principle itself has, by fitting itself into matter, done these works, being the thing that it is, unlike in its parts, and deriving its being this from the principle before it, then this that has come into existence, since it has come into existence in this way, would have nothing else nobler than itself. If the rational formative principle had been composed of parts which were all alike and equal, it would not have come into existence and [if it had] this manner of construction would be worthy of blame; since it is all things, it is different in every part. But if it brought in other things outside itself, souls for instance, and forced them, against their own nature, to fit into its creation, making many of them worse in doing so, how is this rightly done? But we must say that the souls, too, are in a way parts of it, and it does not fit them in by making them worse but puts them in places appropriate to them according to their worth.

13. Then we must not discard that argument, either, which says that the rational principle does not

eyes" but for painting the eyes ugly black instead of beautiful crimson. So the reference is better placed here than where Henry-Schwyzer placed it at l. 5–6.

πρὸς τὰς πρόσθεν περιόδους καὶ αὖ τὸ μέλλον, ὥστε ἐκεῖθεν τάττειν τὴν ἀξίαν καὶ μετατιθέναι ἐκ δεσποτῶν τῶν πρόσθεν δούλους ποιοῦντα, εἰ ἐγένοντο κακοὶ δεσπόται, καὶ ὅτι σύμφορον αὐτοῖς οὕτω, καὶ εἰ κακῶς ἐχρήσαντο πλούτῳ, πένητας—καὶ ἀγαθοῖς οὐκ ἀσύμφορον [1] πένησιν εἶναι—καὶ φονεύσαντας ἀδίκως φονευθῆναι ἀδίκως μὲν τῷ ποιήσαντι, αὐτῷ δὲ δικαίως τῷ παθόντι, καὶ τὸ πεισόμενον συναγαγεῖν εἰς τὸ αὐτὸ τῷ ἐπιτηδείῳ ποιῆσαι, ἃ παθεῖν ἐχρῆν ἐκεῖνον. Μὴ γὰρ δὴ κατὰ συντυχίαν δοῦλον μηδὲ αἰχμάλωτον ὡς ἔτυχε μηδὲ ὑβρισθῆναι εἰς σῶμα εἰκῇ, ἀλλ' ἦν ποτε ταῦτα ποιήσας, ἃ νῦν ἐστι πάσχων· καὶ μητέρα τις ἀνελὼν ὑπὸ παιδὸς ἀναιρεθήσεται γενόμενος γυνή, καὶ βιασάμενος γυναῖκα ἔσται, ἵνα βιασθῇ. Ὅθεν καὶ θείᾳ φήμῃ Ἀδράστεια· αὕτη γὰρ ἡ διάταξις Ἀδράστεια ὄντως καὶ ὄντως Δίκη καὶ σοφία θαυμαστή. Τεκμαίρεσθαι δὲ δεῖ τοιαύτην τινὰ εἶναι τὴν τάξιν ἀεὶ τῶν ὅλων ἐκ τῶν ὁρωμένων ἐν τῷ παντί, ὡς εἰς ἅπαν χωρεῖ καὶ ὅ τι μικρότατον, καὶ ἡ τέχνη θαυμαστὴ οὐ μόνον ἐν τοῖς θείοις, ἀλλὰ καὶ ὧν ἄν τις ὑπενόησε καταφρονῆσαι ὡς μικρῶν τὴν πρόνοιαν, οἷα καὶ ἐν τοῖς τυχοῦσι

[1] ἀσύμφορον A^{pc}, H–S: ἀσύμφοροι codd.

---

[1] The thought here follows Plato closely. For the reincarnation of the matricide cp. *Laws* IX. 872E; for the "law of Adrasteia" applied to reincarnation, cp. *Phaedrus* 248C2.

look only at the present on each occasion but at the cycles of time before, and also at the future, so as to determine men's worth from these, and to change their positions, making slaves out of those who were masters before, if they were bad masters (and also because it is good for them this way); and, if men have used wealth badly, making them poor (and for the good, too, it is not without advantage to be poor); and causing those who have killed unjustly to be killed in their turn, unjustly as far as the doer of the deed is concerned, but justly as far as concerns the victim; and it brings that which is to suffer together to the same point with that which is fit and ready to execute what that unjust killer is fated to endure. There is certainly no accident in a man's becoming a slave, nor is he taken prisoner in war by chance, nor is outrage done on his body without due cause, but he was once the doer of that which he now suffers; and a man who made away with his mother will be made away with by a son when he has become a woman, and one who has raped a woman will be a woman in order to be raped. Hence comes, by divine declaration, the name Adrasteia: for this world-order is truly Adrasteia [the Inescapable] and truly Justice and wonderful wisdom.[1] We must conclude that the universal order is for ever something of this kind from the evidence of what we see in the All, how this order extends to everything, even to the smallest, and the art is wonderful which appears, not only in the divine beings but also in the things which one might have supposed providence would have despised for their smallness, for example, the workmanship which produces wonders in rich variety in ordinary animals,

ζῴοις ἡ ποικίλη θαυματουργία καὶ τὸ μέχρι τῶν ἐμφύτων καρποῖς καὶ ἔτι φύλλοις τὸ εὐειδὲς καὶ τὸ ῥᾷστα εὐανθὲς καὶ ῥαδινὸν καὶ ποικίλον, καὶ ὅτι οὐ πεποίηται ἅπαξ καὶ ἐπαύσατο, ἀλλ' ἀεὶ ποιεῖται τῶν ὑπεράνω φερομένων κατὰ ταῦτα οὐχ ὡσαύτως. Μετατίθεται τοίνυν τὰ μετατιθέμενα οὐκ εἰκῇ μετατιθέμενα οὐδ' ἄλλα σχήματα λαμβάνοντα, ἀλλ' ὡς καλόν, καὶ ὡς πρέποι ἂν δυνάμεσι θείαις ποιεῖν. Ποιεῖ γὰρ πᾶν τὸ θεῖον ὡς πέφυκε· πέφυκε δὲ κατὰ τὴν αὐτοῦ οὐσίαν· οὐσία δὲ αὐτῷ, ἣ τὸ καλὸν ἐν ταῖς ἐνεργείαις αὐτοῦ καὶ τὸ δίκαιον συνεκφέρει. Εἰ γὰρ μὴ ἐκεῖ ταῦτα, ποῦ ἂν εἴη;

14. Ἔχει τοίνυν ἡ διάταξις οὕτω κατὰ νοῦν, ὡς ἄνευ λογισμοῦ εἶναι, οὕτω δὲ εἶναι, ὡς, εἴ τις ἄριστα δύναιτο λογισμῷ χρῆσθαι, θαυμάσαι, ὅτι μὴ ἂν ἄλλως εὗρε λογισμὸς ποιῆσαι, ὁποῖόν τι γινώσκεται καὶ ἐν ταῖς καθ' ἕκαστα φύσεσι, γινομένων εἰς ἀεὶ νοερώτερον ἢ κατὰ λογισμοῦ διάταξιν. Ἐφ' ἑκάστου μὲν οὖν τῶν γινομένων ἀεὶ γενῶν οὐκ ἔστιν αἰτιᾶσθαι τὸν ποιοῦντα λόγον, εἴ τις μὴ ἀξιοῖ ἕκαστον οὕτω γενονέναι χρῆναι, ὡς τὰ μὴ γεγονότα, ἀίδια δέ, ἔν τε νοητοῖς ἔν τε αἰσθητοῖς ἀεὶ κατὰ ταὐτὰ [1] ὄντα, προσθήκην αἰτῶν

[1] κατὰ ταὐτὰ Dodds, H–S^2: καὶ αὐτὰ codd.

and the beauty of appearance which extends to the fruits and even the leaves of plants, and their beauty of flower which comes so effortlessly, and their delicacy and variety, and that all this has not been made once and come to an end but is always being made as the powers above move in different ways over this world. So the things which are changing change, not changing and taking new shapes without due cause but in a way which is excellent and appropriate to their making by divine powers. For all that is divine makes according to its nature; but its nature corresponds to its substance, and its substance is that which brings forth together beauty and justice in its workings; for if beauty and justice are not in it, where could they be?

14. The ordering of the universe, then, corresponds with Intellect in such a way that it exists without rational planning,[1] but exists so that if anyone could plan rationally as well as possible, he would wonder at it because planning could not have found out another way to make it; something of this is observed even in individual natures, which come into being continually more conformed to Intellect than they could be by an ordering which depended on rational planning. With each, therefore, of the kinds of things which continually come into existence it is not possible to blame the rational principle which makes them, unless someone should demand that they ought to have come into existence just like the things which have not come into existence, but are eternal, existing always in the same way both in the intelligible world and in the world of sense, asking for a further

[1] Cp. note on ch. 1. 1. 20–21.

ἀγαθοῦ πλείονα, ἀλλ' οὐ τὸ δοθὲν ἑκάστῳ εἶδος αὔταρκες ἡγούμενος, οἷον τῷδε, ὅτι μὴ καὶ κέρατα, οὐ σκοπούμενος ὅτι ἀδύνατον ἦν λόγον μὴ οὐκ ἐπὶ πάντα ἐλθεῖν, ἀλλ' ὅτι ἔδει ἐν τῷ μείζονι τὰ ἐλάττω καὶ ἐν τῷ ὅλῳ τὰ μέρη καὶ οὐκ ἴσα δυνατὸν εἶναι· ἢ οὐκ ἂν ἦν μέρη. Τὸ μὲν γὰρ ἄνω πᾶν πάντα, τὰ δὲ κάτω οὐ πάντα ἕκαστον. Καὶ ἄνθρωπος δή, καθ' ὅσον μέρος, ἕκαστος,[1] οὐ πᾶς. Εἰ δέ που ἐν μέρεσί τισι καὶ ἄλλο τι, ὃ οὐ μέρος, τούτῳ κἀκεῖνο πᾶν. Ὁ δὲ καθ' ἕκαστα, ᾗ τοῦτο, οὐκ ἀπαιτητέος τέλεος εἶναι εἰς ἀρετῆς ἄκρον· ἤδη γὰρ οὐκέτ' ἂν μέρος. Οὐ μὴν οὐδὲ τῷ ὅλῳ τὸ μέρος κοσμηθὲν εἰς μείζονα ἀξίαν ἐφθόνηται· καὶ γὰρ κάλλιον τὸ ὅλον ποιεῖ κοσμηθὲν ἀξίᾳ μείζονι. Καὶ γὰρ γίνεται τοιοῦτον ἀφομοιωθὲν τῷ ὅλῳ καὶ οἷον συγχωρηθὲν τοιοῦτον εἶναι καὶ συνταχθὲν οὕτως, ἵνα καὶ κατὰ τὸν ἀνθρώπου τόπον ἐκλάμπῃ τι ἐν αὐτῷ, οἷον καὶ κατὰ τὸν θεῖον οὐρανὸν τὰ ἄστρα, καὶ ᾖ[2] ἐντεῦθεν ἀντίληψις οἷον ἀγάλματος μεγάλου καὶ καλοῦ εἴτε ἐμψύχου εἴτε καὶ τέχνῃ Ἡφαίστου γενομένου, ᾧ ⟨εἴ⟩σι[3] μὲν καὶ κατὰ τὸ πρόσωπον ἐπιστίλβοντες ἀστέρες

[1] ἕκαστος A^pc, H–S²: ἕκαστον codd.
[2] ᾖ Dodds, H–S: ἡ codd.

addition of good, but not thinking the form given to each thing sufficient, for instance, thinking that the form given to this particular animal is insufficient because it has not horns as well, and not considering that it was impossible for the formative principle not to reach to all things, but that there must be lesser things in the greater and parts in the whole and that they cannot be equal to the whole or they would not be parts. In the world above every thing is all things, but the things below are not each of them all things. Even man, in so far as he is a part, is an individual, not all. But if somewhere among parts there is something else which is not a part, in virtue of this that thing below, too, is all. But man in his individuality, in so far as he is an individual being, cannot be required to be perfect to the point of reaching the summit of virtue; for if he did he would no longer be a part. But there would certainly not be any grudging by the whole if the part did gain in beauty and order so as to make it of greater worth; for it makes the whole more beautiful when it has become of greater value by its gain in beauty and order. For it becomes of this kind by being made like the whole and, so to speak, being allowed to be like this and given such a place that in the region of man, too, something may shine in him as the stars shine in the heaven of the gods; a place from which there may be a perception of something like a great and beautiful image of a god—whether a living one or one made by the art of Hephaestus—in which there are stars flashing on the face, and in the

[3] ᾧ ⟨εἶ⟩σι Theiler, H–S: ὦσι codd.

καὶ ἐν τοῖς στήθεσι δὲ ἄλλοι καὶ ᾗ[1] ἔμελλεν ἐπιπρέψειν ἄστρων θέσις κειμένων.

15. Τὰ μὲν οὖν ἕκαστα αὐτὰ ἐφ' ἑαυτῶν θεωρούμενα οὕτως· ἡ συμπλοκὴ δὲ ἡ τούτων γεννηθέντων καὶ ἀεὶ γεννωμένων ἔχοι ἂν τὴν ἐπίστασιν καὶ ἀπορίαν κατά τε τὴν ἀλληλοφαγίαν τῶν ἄλλων ζῴων καὶ τὰς ἀνθρώπων εἰς ἀλλήλους ἐπιθέσεις, καὶ ὅτι πόλεμος ἀεὶ καὶ οὐ μήποτε παῦλαν οὐδ' ἂν ἀνοχὴν λάβοι, καὶ μάλιστα εἰ λόγος πεποίηκεν οὕτως ἔχειν, καὶ οὕτω λέγεται καλῶς ἔχειν. Οὐ γὰρ ἔτι τοῖς οὕτω λέγουσιν ἐκεῖνος ὁ λόγος βοηθεῖ, ὡς καλῶς κατὰ τὸ δυνατὸν ἔχειν, αἰτίᾳ ὕλης οὕτως ἐχόντων ὡς ἐλαττόνως ἔχειν, καὶ ὡς οὐ δυνατὸν τὰ κακὰ ἀπολέσθαι εἴπερ οὕτως ἐχρῆν ἔχειν, καὶ καλῶς οὕτω, καὶ οὐχ ἡ ὕλη παρελθοῦσα κρατεῖ, ἀλλὰ παρήχθη, ἵνα οὕτω, μᾶλλον δὲ ἦν καὶ αὐτὴ αἰτίᾳ λόγου οὕτως. Ἀρχὴ οὖν λόγος καὶ πάντα λόγος καὶ τὰ γινόμενα κατ' αὐτὸν καὶ συνταττόμενα ἐπὶ τῇ γενέσει πάντως οὕτως. Τίς οὖν ἡ τοῦ πολέμου τοῦ ἀκηρύκτου ἐν ζῴοις καὶ ἐν ἀνθρώποις ἀνάγκη; Ἢ ἀλληλοφαγίαι μὲν ἀναγκαῖαι, ἀμοιβαὶ ζῴων οὖσαι οὐ δυναμένων, οὐδ' εἴ τις μὴ κτιννύοι αὐτά,

[1] ᾗ F^{3mg} (= Ficinus), H–S²: εἰ codd.

---

[1] The thought seems to be: the physical universe is the great star-decked image of the intelligible divinity (cp. Plato, *Timaeus* 37C 6–7); and because man can contemplate it he gains in beauty and order; he is conformed by his contemplation to the starry heaven, and something of its splendour shines in him.

breast others, and a setting of stars placed where it will be clearly seen.[1]

15. So it is, then, with individual things when they are considered separately. But the weaving together into a pattern of these things which have been and are always being produced might hold obstacles and difficulties, because the other animals eat each other, and men attack each other, and there is always war with never a pause or armistice; and this is particularly difficult if it is the rational forming principle of the world which has brought it about that this is so, and if it is said to be well that it is so. That argument is no longer any help to the people who say this which maintains that all is as well as it can be, and that it is the fault of matter when things are so disposed as to be less than good, and that " evils cannot be done away with "; [2] if, that is, it is really true that things had to be so, and that it is well that they should be so, and matter does not come along and dominate but was brought along so that things should be in this state, or rather is itself, too, caused to be as it is by the rational principle. The rational principle, then, is the origin, and all things are reason, both those which are brought into being according to the principle and those which, in their coming to birth, are altogether ranged in this common order. What, then, is the necessity of the undeclared war among animals and among men? It is necessary that animals should eat each other; these eatings are transformations into each other of animals which could not stay as they are for ever, even if no one

[2] The familiar quotation, repeated again and again by Plotinus, from Plato, *Theaetetus* 176A5.

οὕτω μένειν εἰς ἀεί. Εἰ δὲ ἐν ᾧ χρόνῳ δεῖ ἀπελθεῖν οὕτως ἀπελθεῖν ἔδει, ὡς ἄλλοις γενέσθαι χρείαν παρ' αὐτῶν, τί φθονεῖν ἔδει; Τί δ' εἰ βρωθέντα ἄλλα ἐφύετο; Οἷον εἰ ἐπὶ σκηνῆς τῶν ὑποκριτῶν ὁ πεφονευμένος ἀλλαξάμενος τὸ σχῆμα ἀναλαβὼν πάλιν εἰσίοι ἄλλου πρόσωπον. Ἀλλὰ τέθνηκεν ἀληθῶς οὗτος. Εἰ οὖν καὶ τὸ ἀποθανεῖν ἀλλαγή ἐστι σώματος, ὥσπερ ἐσθῆτος ἐκεῖ, ἢ καί τισιν ἀποθέσεις σώματος, ὥσπερ ἐκεῖ ἔξοδος ἐκ τῆς σκηνῆς παντελὴς τότε, εἰσύστερον πάλιν ἥξοντος ἐναγωνίσασθαι, τί ἂν δεινὸν εἴη ἡ τοιαύτη τῶν ζῴων εἰς ἄλληλα μεταβολὴ πολὺ βελτίων οὖσα τοῦ μηδὲ τὴν ἀρχὴν αὐτὰ γενέσθαι; Ἐκείνως μὲν γὰρ ἐρημία ζωῆς καὶ τῆς ἐν ἄλλῳ οὔσης ἀδυναμία· νῦν δὲ πολλὴ οὖσα ἐν τῷ παντὶ ζωὴ πάντα ποιεῖ καὶ ποικίλλει ἐν τῷ ζῆν καὶ οὐκ ἀνέχεται μὴ ποιοῦσα ἀεὶ καλὰ καὶ εὐειδῆ ζῶντα παίγνια. Ἀνθρώπων δὲ ἐπ' ἀλλήλους ὅπλα θνητῶν ὄντων ἐν τάξει εὐσχήμονι μαχομένων, οἷα ἐν πυρρίχαις παίζοντες ἐργάζονται, δηλοῦσι τάς τε

[1] The comparison of life to a play was a commonplace of Cynic, Stoic and Stoic-influenced moralists from Bion of Borysthenes and Teles onwards (cp. *Teles* 16, 4 Hense). The finest example is Marcus Aurelius XII. 36.

[2] Plotinus, here and in what follows, probably has Plato's description of man as God's toy, playing to please him, in mind (*Laws* VII. 803C–D; θεοῦ τι παίγνιον (C4–5)). But there is an important difference in the thought. For Plato, in this passage at least, man is wholly and entirely God's toy, and his "play" is the most serious and important thing in his life—though he is not really worth taking seriously at all; only

killed them. And if, at the time when they had to depart, they had to depart in such a way that they were useful to others, why do we have to make a grievance out of their usefulness? And what does it matter if, when they are eaten, they come alive again as different animals? It is like on the stage, when the actor who has been murdered changes his costume and comes on again in another character.[1] But [in real life, not on the stage,] the man is really dead. If, then, death is a changing of body, like changing of clothes on the stage, or, for some of us, a putting off of body, like in the theatre the final exit, in that performance, of an actor who will on a later occasion come in again to play, what would there be that is terrible in a change of this kind, of living beings into each other? It is far better than if they had never come into existence at all. For that way there would be a barren absence of life and no possibility of a life which exists in something else; but as it is a manifold life exists in the All and makes all things, and in its living embroiders a rich variety and does not rest from ceaselessly making beautiful and shapely living toys.[2] And when men, mortal as they are, direct their weapons against each other, fighting in orderly ranks, doing what they do in sport in their

God is *πάσης μακαρίου σπουδῆς ἄξιον* (C2–3). For Plotinus, as the rest of this chapter shows clearly, it is only man's lower, external life which is "play." His true, inner self is serious and important. For Plato man's best game is the religious dance, at once play, worship and education, in which he attains all the seriousness he is capable of. For Plotinus man's game is the grim one of killing and being killed, which the wise man will not take seriously and cry over like a child, because it only affects his unimportant lower self.

ἀνθρωπίνας σπουδὰς ἁπάσας παιδιὰς οὔσας τούς τε θανάτους μηνύουσιν οὐδὲν δεινὸν εἶναι, ἀποθνῄσκειν δ' ἐν πολέμοις καὶ ἐν μάχαις ὀλίγον προλαβόντας τοῦ γινομένου ἐν γήρᾳ θᾶττον ἀπιόντας καὶ πάλιν ἰόντας. Εἰ δ' ἀφαιροῖντο ζῶντες χρημάτων, γινώσκοιεν ἂν μηδὲ πρότερον αὐτῶν εἶναι καὶ τοῖς ἁρπάζουσιν αὐτοῖς γελοίαν εἶναι τὴν κτῆσιν ἀφαιρουμένων αὐτοὺς ἄλλων· ἐπεὶ καὶ τοῖς μὴ ἀφαιρεθεῖσι χεῖρον γίνεσθαι τῆς ἀφαιρέσεως τὴν κτῆσιν. Ὥσπερ δ' ἐπὶ τῶν θεάτρων ταῖς σκηναῖς, οὕτω χρὴ καὶ τοὺς φόνους θεᾶσθαι καὶ πάντας θανάτους καὶ πόλεων ἁλώσεις καὶ ἁρπαγάς, μεταθέσεις πάντα καὶ μετασχηματίσεις καὶ θρήνων καὶ οἰμωγῶν ὑποκρίσεις. Καὶ γὰρ ἐνταῦθα ἐπὶ τῶν ἐν τῷ βίῳ ἑκάστων οὐχ ἡ ἔνδον ψυχή, ἀλλ' ἡ ἔξω ἀνθρώπου σκιὰ καὶ οἰμώζει καὶ ὀδύρεται καὶ πάντα ποιεῖ ἐν σκηνῇ τῇ ὅλῃ γῇ πολλαχοῦ σκηνὰς ποιησαμένων. Τοιαῦτα γὰρ ἔργα ἀνθρώπου τὰ κάτω καὶ τὰ ἔξω μόνα ζῆν εἰδότος καὶ ἐν δακρύοις καὶ σπουδαίοις ὅτι παίζων ἐστὶν ἠγνοηκότος. Μόνῳ γὰρ τῷ σπουδαίῳ σπουδαστέον ἐν σπουδαίοις τοῖς ἔργοις, ὁ δ' ἄλλος ἄνθρωπος παίγνιον. Σπουδάζεται δὲ καὶ τὰ παίγνια τοῖς σπουδάζειν οὐκ εἰδόσι καὶ τοῖς αὐτοῖς οὖσι παιγνίοις. Εἰ δέ τις συμπαίζων αὐτοῖς τὰ τοιαῦτα πάθοι, ἴστω παραπεσὼν παίδων παιδιᾷ τὸ περὶ αὐτὸν ἀποθέμενος παίγνιον. Εἰ δὲ δὴ καὶ παίζοι

war-dances, their battles show that all human concerns are children's games, and tell us that deaths are nothing terrible, and that those who die in wars and battles anticipate only a little the death which comes in old age—they go away and come back quicker. But if their property is taken away while they are still alive, they may recognise that it was not theirs before either, and that its possession is a mockery to the robbers themselves when others take it away from them; for even to those who do not have it taken away, to have it is worse than being deprived of it. We should be spectators of murders, and all deaths, and takings and sackings of cities, as if they were on the stages of theatres, all changes of scenery and costume and acted wailings and weepings. For really here in the events of our life it is not the soul within but the outside shadow of man which cries and moans and carries on in every sort of way on a stage which is the whole earth where men have in many places set up their stages. Doings like these belong to a man who knows how to live only the lower and external life and is not aware that he is playing in his tears, even when they are serious tears. For only the seriously good part of man is capable of taking serious doings seriously; the rest of man is a toy. But toys, too, are taken seriously by those who do not know how to be serious and are toys themselves. But if anyone joins in their play and suffers their sort of sufferings, he must know that he has tumbled into a children's game and put off the play-costume in which he was dressed.[1] And even if Socrates, too,

[1] I.e. if he is killed it is all part of the game, and the body which he puts off is only a toy.

Σωκράτης, παίζει τῷ ἔξω Σωκράτει. Δεῖ δὲ κἀκεῖνο ἐνθυμεῖσθαι, ὡς οὐ δεῖ τεκμήρια τοῦ κακὰ εἶναι τὸ δακρύειν καὶ θρηνεῖν τίθεσθαι, ὅτι δὴ καὶ παῖδες ἐπὶ οὐ κακοῖς καὶ δακρύουσι καὶ ὀδύρονται.

16. Ἀλλ᾽ εἰ καλῶς ταῦτα λέγεται, πῶς ἂν ἔτι πονηρία; Ποῦ δ᾽ ἀδικία; Ἁμαρτία δὲ ποῦ; Πῶς γὰρ ἔστι καλῶς γινομένων ἁπάντων ἀδικεῖν ἢ ἁμαρτάνειν τοὺς ποιοῦντας; Κακοδαίμονες δὲ πῶς, εἰ μὴ ἁμαρτάνοιεν μηδὲ ἀδικοῖεν; Πῶς δὲ τὰ μὲν κατὰ φύσιν, τὰ δὲ παρὰ φύσιν φήσομεν εἶναι, τῶν γινομένων ἁπάντων καὶ δρωμένων κατὰ φύσιν ὄντων; Πῶς δ᾽ ἂν καὶ πρὸς τὸ θεῖον ἀσέβειά τις εἴη τοιούτου ὄντος τοῦ ποιουμένου; Οἷον εἴ τις ἐν δράμασι λοιδορούμενον ποιητὴς ὑποκριτὴν ποιήσαιτο καὶ κατατρέχοντα τοῦ ποιητοῦ τοῦ δράματος. Πάλιν οὖν σαφέστερον λέγωμεν τίς ὁ λόγος καὶ ὡς εἰκότως τοιοῦτός ἐστιν. Ἔστι τοίνυν οὗτος ὁ λόγος—τετολμήσθω γάρ· τάχα δ᾽ ἂν καὶ τύχοιμεν—ἔστι τοίνυν οὗτος οὐκ ἄκρατος νοῦς οὐδ᾽ αὐτονοῦς οὐδέ γε ψυχῆς καθαρᾶς τὸ γένος, ἠρτημένος δὲ ἐκείνης καὶ οἷον ἔκλαμψις ἐξ ἀμφοῖν, νοῦ καὶ ψυχῆς καὶ ψυχῆς κατὰ νοῦν διακειμένης γεννησάντων τὸν λόγον τοῦτον ζωὴν λόγον τινὰ ἡσυχῇ ἔχουσαν. Πᾶσα δὲ ζωὴ ἐνέργεια, καὶ ἡ φαύλη· ἐνέργεια δὲ οὐχ ὡς τὸ πῦρ ἐνεργεῖ, ἀλλ᾽ ἡ ἐνέργεια αὐτῆς, κἂν μὴ αἴσθησίς τις παρῇ, κίνησίς τις οὐκ εἰκῇ. Οἷς γοῦν ἐὰν μὴ παρῇ καὶ μετάσχῃ ὁπωσοῦν ὁτιοῦν, εὐθὺς λελόγωται, τοῦτο

may play sometimes, it is by the outer Socrates that he plays. But we must consider this further point, too, that one must not take weeping and lamenting as evidence of the presence of evils, for children, too, weep and wail over things that are not evils.

16. But if this is well said, how can there still be wickedness? Where is injustice? Where is error? For how, if all things are well done, can the doers act unjustly or err? And how can they be ill-fated, if they do not err or act unjustly? And how can we assert that some things are according to nature, but others against nature, if all things that happen and are done are according to nature? And how could there be any blasphemy against the divine when that which is made is made like this? It is just as if a poet in his plays wrote a part for an actor insulting and depreciating the author of the play. Let us, then, again, and more clearly, explain what the rational forming principle of our universe is and that it is reasonable for it to be like this. This rational principle, then, is—let us take the risk! We might even, perhaps succeed [in describing it]—it is not pure intellect or absolute intellect; it is not even of the kind of pure soul but depends on soul, and is a sort of outshining of both; intellect and soul (that is, soul disposed according to intellect) generated this rational principle as a life which quietly contains a rationality. All life, even worthless life, is activity; activity not in the way that fire acts; but its activity, even if there is no perception there, is a movement which is not random. For with living things when there is no perception present and any one of them has any share in life, it is immediately enreasoned, that

δέ ἐστι μεμόρφωται, ὡς τῆς ἐνεργείας τῆς κατὰ τὴν ζωὴν μορφοῦν δυναμένης καὶ κινούσης οὕτως ὡς μορφοῦν. Ἡ τοίνυν ἐνέργεια αὐτῆς τεχνική, ὥσπερ ἂν ὁ ὀρχούμενος κινούμενος εἴη· ὁ γὰρ ὀρχηστὴς τῇ οὕτω τεχνικῇ ζωῇ ἔοικεν αὐτὸς καὶ ἡ τέχνη αὐτὸν κινεῖ καὶ οὕτω κινεῖ, ὡς τῆς ζωῆς αὐτῆς τοιαύτης πως οὔσης. Ταῦτα μὲν οὖν εἰρήσθω τοῦ οἵαν δεῖ καὶ τὴν ἡντινοῦν ζωὴν ἡγεῖσθαι ἕνεκα. Ἥκων τοίνυν οὗτος ὁ λόγος ἐκ νοῦ ἑνὸς καὶ ζωῆς μιᾶς πλήρους ὄντος ἑκατέρου οὐκ ἔστιν οὔτε ζωὴ μία οὔτε νοῦς τις εἷς οὔτε ἑκασταχοῦ πλήρης οὐδὲ διδοὺς ἑαυτὸν οἷς δίδωσιν ὅλον τε καὶ πάντα. Ἀντιθεὶς δὲ ἀλλήλοις τὰ μέρη καὶ ποιήσας ἐνδεᾶ πολέμου καὶ μάχης σύστασιν καὶ γένεσιν εἰργάσατο καὶ οὕτως ἐστὶν εἷς πᾶς, εἰ μὴ ἓν εἴη. Γενόμενον γὰρ ἑαυτῷ τοῖς μέρεσι πολέμιον οὕτως ἕν ἐστι καὶ φίλον, ὥσπερ ἂν εἰ δράματος λόγος· εἷς ὁ τοῦ δράματος ἔχων ἐν αὐτῷ πολλὰς μάχας. Τὸ μὲν οὖν δρᾶμα τὰ μεμαχημένα οἷον εἰς μίαν ἁρμονίαν ἄγει σύμφωνον οἷον διήγησιν τὴν πᾶσαν τῶν μαχομένων ποιούμενος· ἐκεῖ δὲ ἐξ ἑνὸς λόγου ἡ τῶν διαστατῶν μάχη· ὥστε μᾶλλον ἄν τις τῇ ἁρμονίᾳ τῇ ἐκ μαχομένων εἰκάσειε, καὶ ζητήσει διὰ τί τὰ μαχόμενα ἐν τοῖς λόγοις. Εἰ οὖν καὶ ἐνταῦθα ὀξὺ καὶ βαρὺ ποιοῦσι

is informed, since the activity which is proper to life is able to form it and moves it in such way that its movement is a forming. So the activity of life is an artistic activity, like the way in which one who is dancing is moved; for the dancer himself is like the life which is artistic in this way and his art moves him, and moves in such a way that the actual life is somehow of this [artistic] kind. This, then, should be enough to show how we should think of any sort of life. Now the rational forming principle of this universe, which comes from a single Intellect and a single life, both of them complete, is not a single life nor any kind of single intellect, and is not at every point complete, nor does it at every point give itself whole and entire to the things to which it does give itself. But by setting the parts against each other and making them deficient it generates and maintains war and battle, and so it is one as a whole even if it is not one single thing. For though it is at war with itself in its parts it is one thing and on good terms with itself in the same way that the plot of a play might be; the plot of the play is one though it contains in itself many battles. Of course, the play brings the conflicting elements into a kind of harmonious concordance, by composing the complete story of the persons in conflict; but in the universe the battle of conflicting elements springs from a single rational principle; so that it would be better for one to compare it to the melody which results from conflicting sounds, and one will then enquire why there are the conflicting sounds in the rational proportions [of musical scales]. If, then, in music the laws of rational proportion make high and low notes

λόγοι καὶ συνίασιν εἰς ἕν, ὄντες ἁρμονίας λόγοι, εἰς αὐτὴν τὴν ἁρμονίαν, ἄλλον λόγον μείζονα, ὄντες ἐλάττους αὐτοὶ καὶ μέρη, ὁρῶμεν δὲ καὶ ἐν τῷ παντὶ τὰ ἐναντία, οἷον λευκὸν μέλαν, θερμὸν ψυχρόν, καὶ δὴ πτερωτὸν ἄπτερον, ἄπουν ὑπόπουν, λογικὸν ἄλογον, πάντα δὲ ζῴου ἑνὸς τοῦ σύμπαντος μέρη, καὶ τὸ πᾶν ὁμολογεῖ ἑαυτῷ τῶν μερῶν πολλαχοῦ μαχομένων, κατὰ λόγον δὲ τὸ πᾶν, ἀνάγκη καὶ τὸν ἕνα τοῦτον λόγον ἐξ ἐναντίων λόγον εἶναι ἕνα, τὴν σύστασιν αὐτῷ [1] καὶ οἷον οὐσίαν τῆς τοιαύτης ἐναντιώσεως φερούσης. Καὶ γὰρ εἰ μὴ πολὺς ἦν, οὐδ' ἂν ἦν πᾶς, οὐδ' ἂν λόγος· λόγος δὲ ὢν διάφορός τε πρὸς αὑτόν ἐστι καὶ ἡ μάλιστα διαφορὰ ἐναντίωσίς ἐστιν· ὥστε εἰ ἕτερον ὅλως, τὸ δὲ ἕτερον ποιεῖ, καὶ μάλιστα ἕτερον, ἀλλ' οὐχ ἧττον ἕτερον ποιήσει· ὥστε ἄκρως ἕτερον ποιῶν καὶ τὰ ἐναντία ποιήσει ἐξ ἀνάγκης καὶ τέλεος ἔσται, οὐκ εἰ διάφορα μόνον, ἀλλ' εἰ καὶ ἐναντία ποιοῖ εἶναι ἑαυτόν.

17. Ὢν δὴ τοιοῦτος οἷος καὶ πάντως ποιεῖ, πολὺ μᾶλλον τὰ ποιούμενα ποιήσει ἐναντία, ὅσῳ καὶ διέστηκε μᾶλλον· καὶ ἧττον ἓν ὁ κόσμος ὁ αἰσθητὸς ἢ ὁ λόγος αὐτοῦ, ὥστε καὶ πολὺς μᾶλλον καὶ ἡ ἐναντιότης μᾶλλον καὶ ἡ τοῦ ζῆν ἔφεσις μᾶλλον ἑκάστῳ καὶ ὁ ἔρως τοῦ εἰς ἓν μᾶλλον.

[1] αὐτῷ A^pc, H–S²: αὐτῶν codd.

and come together into a unity—being the proportional laws of melody they come together into the melody itself, which is another greater law of proportion, while they are lesser ones and part of it; in the universe, too, we see the opposites, for instance, white-black, hot-cold, and, too, winged-wingless, footless-footed, rational-irrational, but all are parts of the single universal living being, and the All agrees with itself; the parts are in conflict in many places, but the All is in accordance with its rational formative pattern, and it is necessary that this one formative pattern should be one pattern made out of opposites, since it is opposition of this kind which gives it its structure, and, we might say, its existence. For certainly, if it was not many it would not be all, and would not therefore be rational pattern [of the universe]; but, since it is rational pattern it has distinctions in itself, and the extreme distinction is opposition; so that if in general it makes one thing different from another, it will also make them different in the extreme, and not different in a lesser degree; so by making one thing different from another in the highest degree it will necessarily make the opposites, and will be complete if it makes itself not only into different things but into opposite things.

17. Since its nature corresponds to its whole productive activity, the more it is differentiated the more opposed will it make the things it makes; and the universe perceived by the senses is less of a unity than its rational formative principle, so that it is more of a manifold and there is more opposition in it, and each individual in it has a greater urge to live, and there is a greater passion for unification.

Φθείρει δὲ καὶ τὰ ἐρῶντα τὰ ἐρώμενα πολλάκις εἰς τὸ αὐτῶν ἀγαθὸν σπεύδοντα, ὅταν φθαρτὰ ᾖ, καὶ ἡ ἔφεσις δὲ τοῦ μέρους πρὸς τὸ ὅλον ἕλκει εἰς αὐτὸ ὃ δύναται. Οὕτως οὖν καὶ οἱ ἀγαθοὶ καὶ οἱ κακοί, ὥσπερ παρὰ τῆς αὐτῆς τέχνης ὀρχουμένου τὰ ἐναντία· καὶ αὐτοῦ τὸ μέν τι μέρος ἀγαθόν, τὸ δὲ κακὸν φήσομεν, καὶ οὕτω καλῶς ἔχει. Καίτοι οὐδὲ κακοὶ ἔτι. Ἢ τὸ μὲν κακοὺς εἶναι οὐκ ἀναιρεῖται, ἀλλ' ἢ μόνον ὅτι μὴ παρ' αὐτῶν τοιοῦτοι. Ἀλλὰ ἴσως συγγνώμη τοῖς κακοῖς, εἰ μὴ καὶ τὸ τῆς συγγνώμης καὶ μὴ ὁ λόγος ποιεῖ· ποιεῖ δὲ ὁ λόγος μηδὲ συγγνώμονας ἐπὶ τοῖς τοιούτοις εἶναι. Ἀλλ' εἰ τὸ μὲν μέρος αὐτοῦ ἀγαθὸς ἀνήρ, τὸ δὲ ἄλλο πονηρός, καὶ πλείω μέρη ὁ πονηρός, ὥσπερ ἐν δράμασι τὰ μὲν τάττει αὐτοῖς ὁ ποιητής, τοῖς δὲ χρῆται οὖσιν ἤδη· οὐ γὰρ αὐτὸς πρωταγωνιστὴν οὐδὲ δεύτερον οὐδὲ τρίτον ποιεῖ, ἀλλὰ διδοὺς ἑκάστῳ τοὺς προσήκοντας λόγους ἤδη ἀπέδωκεν ἑκάστῳ εἰς ὃ τετάχθαι δέον· οὕτω τοι καὶ ἔστι τόπος ἑκάστῳ ὁ μὲν τῷ ἀγαθῷ, ὁ δὲ τῷ κακῷ πρέπων. Ἑκάτερος οὖν κατὰ φύσιν καὶ κατὰ λόγον εἰς ἑκάτερον καὶ τὸν πρέποντα χωρεῖ τὸν τόπον ἔχων, ὃν εἵλετο. Εἶτα φθέγγεται καὶ

But those that love passionately often destroy the objects of their passion, when they are perishable, in the pursuit of their own good; and the urgent straining of the part towards the whole draws to itself what it can. So, then, there are good men and wicked men, like the opposed movements of a dancer inspired by one and the same art; and we shall call one part of his performance "good" and another "wicked," and in this way it is a good performance.[1] But, then, the wicked are no longer wicked. No, their being wicked is not done away with, only their being like that does not originate with themselves. But there might perhaps be some sympathy for the wicked, except that it is the rational formative principle which is responsible for our sympathising or not; and the rational principle does not make us disposed to sympathise with people of this sort. But if one part of it is a good man, and another a villain—and villainous humanity forms the larger class—it is like in the production of a play; the author gives each actor a part, but makes use of their characteristics which are there already. He does not himself rank them as leading actor or second or third, but gives each man suitable words and so assigns him to the position which is proper to him. So there is a place for every man, one to fit the good and one to fit the bad. Each kind of man, then goes according to nature and the rational principle to the place that suits him, and holds the position he has chosen. There one speaks blasphemies and does

[1] The dancer is a *pantomimus*, who represents different characters, good and bad, in the course of his one-man ballet or mime, as Harder saw (cp. his note *ad loc.*).

ποιεῖ ὁ μὲν ἀσεβεῖς λόγους καὶ ἔργα πονηρῶν,[1] ὁ δὲ τὰ ἐναντία· ἦσαν γὰρ καὶ πρὸ τοῦ δράματος οἱ τοιοῦτοι ὑποκριταὶ διδόντες ἑαυτοὺς τῷ δράματι. Ἐν μὲν οὖν τοῖς ἀνθρωπίνοις δράμασιν ὁ μὲν ποιητὴς ἔδωκε τοὺς λόγους, οἱ δὲ ἔχουσι παρ' αὐτῶν καὶ ἐξ αὐτῶν τό τε καλῶς καὶ τὸ κακῶς ἕκαστος—ἔστι γὰρ καὶ ἔργον αὐτοῖς μετὰ τὰς ῥήσεις τοῦ ποιητοῦ· ἐν δὲ τῷ ἀληθεστέρῳ ποιήματι, ὅ τι μιμοῦνται κατὰ μέρος ἄνθρωποι ποιητικὴν ἔχοντες φύσιν, ψυχὴ μὲν ὑποκρίνεται, ἃ δ' ὑποκρίνεται λαβοῦσα παρὰ τοῦ ποιητοῦ, ὥσπερ οἱ τῇδε ὑποκριταὶ τὰ προσωπεῖα, τὴν ἐσθῆτα, τοὺς κροκωτοὺς καὶ τὰ ῥάκη, οὕτω καὶ ψυχὴ αὐτὴ τὰς τύχας οὐ λαβοῦσα εἰκῇ· κατὰ λόγον δὲ καὶ αὗται· καὶ ἐναρμοσαμένη ταύτας σύμφωνος γίνεται καὶ συνέταξεν ἑαυτὴν τῷ δράματι καὶ τῷ λόγῳ παντί· εἶτα οἷον φθέγγεται τὰς πράξεις καὶ τὰ ἄλλα, ὅσα ἂν ψυχὴ κατὰ τρόπον τὸν ἑαυτῆς ποιήσειεν, ὥσπερ τινὰ ᾠδήν. Καὶ ὡς ὁ φθόγγος καὶ τὸ σχῆμα παρ' αὐτοῦ καλὸν ἢ αἰσχρὸν καὶ ἢ κόσμον προσέθηκεν, ὡς δόξειεν ἄν, εἰς τὸ ποίημα ἢ προσθεὶς τὴν αὐτοῦ τῆς φωνῆς κάκην οὐκ ἐποίησε μὲν τὸ δρᾶμα ἕτερον ἢ οἷον ἦν, αὐτὸς δὲ ἀσχήμων ἐφάνη, ὁ δὲ ποιητὴς τοῦ δράματος ἀπέπεμψε κατ' ἀξίαν ἀτιμάσας καὶ τοῦτο ἔργον ποιῶν ἀγαθοῦ κριτοῦ, τὸν δὲ ἤγαγεν εἰς μείζους τιμὰς καί, εἰ ἔχοι, ἐπὶ τὰ καλλίω δράματα, τὸν δ' ἕτερον, εἴ που εἶχε χείρονα, τοῦτον τὸν τρόπον εἰσελθοῦσα εἰς τόδε τὸ πᾶν ποίημα καὶ μέρος ἑαυτὴν ποιησαμένη τοῦ δράματος εἰς

[1] πονηρῶν Theiler, H–S²: ποιῶν codd.

crimes, the other speaks and acts the opposite; for the actors, good and bad, existed before the play and bring their own selves to it. Now in human plays the author provides the words, but the actors, each and every one of them, are responsible by themselves and from themselves for the good or bad acting of their parts—for there is action, too, which is their business, following from the speeches written by the author; but in the truer poetic creation, which men who have a poetic nature imitate in part, the soul acts, receiving the part which it acts from the poet creator; just as the actors here get their parts and their costumes, the saffron robes and the rags, so the soul, too, itself gets its fortunes, and not by random chance; these fortunes, too, are according to the rational principle; and by fitting these into the pattern it becomes in tune itself and puts itself into its proper place in the play and the universal rational pattern; then it makes its actions sound out, we may say, and everything else that a soul might produce according to its character, like a song. And as the sound of the voice and the gestures of the actor are beautiful or ugly as he makes them, and either adorn the poet's creation further, as one might think, or by adding the badness of the actor's own voice, do not make the play other than what it was, but the actor makes a grotesque exhibition of himself, and the author of the play sends him off in deserved disgrace, behaving in this like a good judge of acting, but promotes the good actor to higher rank, and, if he has any, to finer plays, but puts the bad actor into any worse play that he has; in this way the soul, coming on the stage in this universal poetic creation and

ὑπόκρισιν τὸ εὖ ἢ τὸ κακῶς εἰσενεγκαμένη παρ' αὐτῆς καὶ ἐν τῇ εἰσόδῳ συνταχθεῖσα καὶ τὰ ἄλλα πάντα χωρὶς ἑαυτῆς καὶ τῶν ἔργων αὐτῆς λαβοῦσα δίκας τε καὶ τιμὰς αὖ ἔχει. Πρόσεστι δέ τι τοῖς ὑποκριταῖς ἅτε ἐν μείζονι τόπῳ ἢ κατὰ σκηνῆς μέτρον ὑποκρινομένοις, καὶ τοῦ ποιητοῦ παντὸς τούτους ποιοῦντος κυρίους, καὶ δυνάμεως οὔσης μείζονος ἐπὶ πολλὰ ἰέναι εἴδη τόπων τιμὰς καὶ ἀτιμίας ὁρίζουσι, κατὰ[1] τὸ συνεπιλαμβάνειν καὶ αὐτοὺς ταῖς τιμαῖς καὶ ἀτιμίαις, ἁρμόζοντος ἑκάστου τόπου τοῖς ἤθεσιν, ὡς συμφωνεῖν τῷ τοῦ παντὸς λόγῳ, ἐναρμοζομένου κατὰ δίκην ἑκάστου τοῖς μέρεσι τοῖς δεξομένοις, ὥσπερ χορδῆς ἑκάστης εἰς τὸν οἰκεῖον καὶ προσήκοντα τόπον ταττομένης κατὰ λόγον τὸν τοῦ φθέγγεσθαι, ὁποῖόν ἐστιν αὐτῇ τὸ τῆς δυνάμεως εἰς τοῦτο. Καὶ γὰρ ἐν τῷ ὅλῳ τὸ πρέπον καὶ τὸ καλόν, εἰ ἕκαστος οὗ δεῖ τετάξεται φθεγγόμενος κακὰ ἐν τῷ σκότῳ καὶ τῷ ταρτάρῳ· ἐνταῦθα γὰρ καλὸν τὸ οὕτω φθέγγεσθαι· καὶ τὸ ὅλον τοῦτο καλόν, οὐκ εἰ Λίνος[2] εἴη ἕκαστος, ἀλλ' εἰ τὸν φθόγγον τὸν αὐτοῦ εἰσφερόμενος συντελεῖ εἰς μίαν ἁρμονίαν ζωὴν καὶ αὐτὸς φωνῶν, ἐλάττω

[1] κατὰ Harder, H–S²: καὶ codd.
[2] Λίνος Sleeman, H–S: λίθος codd.

---

[1] I accept, with Henry-Schwyzer and Beutler-Theiler, the brilliant emendation of Sleeman (C. Q. 20, 1926, 153) Λίνος

making itself a part of the play, supplies of itself the good or the bad in its acting; it is put in its proper place on its entrance and receives everything except itself and its own works, and so is given punishments or rewards. But the actors [in the universal drama] have something extra, in that they act in a greater space than that within the limits of a stage, and the author makes them masters of the All, and they have a greater possibility of going to many kinds of places and determining honours and dishonours, as they contribute themselves to their honours and dishonours; for each place is fitted to their characters, so as to be in tune with the rational principle of the universe, since each individual is fitted in, according to justice, in the parts of the universe designed to receive him; just as each string is set in its own proper place according to the rational proportion which governs the sounding of notes, of whatever quality its power of producing a note is. For there is fitness and beauty in the whole only if each individual is stationed where he ought to be—the one who utters evil sounds in darkness and Tartarus: for there to make these sounds is beautiful; and this whole is beautiful, not if each is Linus[1] but if each by contributing his own sound helps towards the perfection of a single melody, himself, too, sounding the note of

for λίθος because it seems to fit the context better. The idea is, clearly, that the universal melody needs bad singers who make horrible noises, as well as good ones, like the mythical Linus, for its completion (contrast I. 6 [1] 1, 26–30). But, as Cilento points out (see his note *ad loc.*), Plotinus is fond of the image of the "dead stone" (cp. VI. 2 [43] 6, 6; VI. 5 [23] 11, 5–14) and λίθος (all MSS, and cp. Aeneas of Gaza, *Theophrastus*, p. 23, Boiss.) may be right.

δὲ καὶ χείρω καὶ ἀτελεστέραν· ὥσπερ οὐδ' ἐν σύριγγι φωνὴ μία, ἀλλὰ καὶ ἐλάττων τις οὖσα καὶ ἀμυδρὰ πρὸς ἁρμονίαν τῆς πάσης σύριγγος συντελεῖ, ὅτι μεμέρισται ἡ ἁρμονία εἰς οὐκ ἴσα μέρη καὶ ἄνισοι μὲν οἱ φθόγγοι πάντες, ὁ δὲ τέλεος εἷς ἐκ πάντων. Καὶ δὴ καὶ ὁ λόγος ὁ πᾶς εἷς, μεμέρισται δὲ οὐκ εἰς ἴσα· ὅθεν καὶ τοῦ παντὸς διάφοροι τόποι, βελτίους καὶ χείρους, καὶ ψυχαὶ οὐκ ἴσαι ἐναρμόττουσιν οὕτω τοῖς οὐκ ἴσοις, καὶ οὕτω καὶ ἐνταῦθα συμβαίνει καὶ τοὺς τόπους ἀνομοίους καὶ τὰς ψυχὰς οὐ τὰς αὐτάς, ἀλλ' ἀνίσους οὔσας καὶ ἀνομοίους τοὺς τόπους ἐχούσας, οἷον κατὰ σύριγγος ἤ τινος ἄλλου ὀργάνου ἀνομοιότητας, ἐν τόποις [τε] [1] πρὸς ἄλληλα διαφέρουσιν εἶναι καθ' ἕκαστον τόπον τὰ αὑτῶν συμφώνως καὶ τοῖς τόποις καὶ τῷ ὅλῳ φθεγγομένας. Καὶ τὸ κακῶς αὐταῖς ἐν καλῷ κατὰ τὸ πᾶν κείσεται καὶ τὸ παρὰ φύσιν τῷ παντὶ κατὰ φύσιν καὶ οὐδὲν ἧττον φθόγγος ἐλάττων. Ἀλλ' οὐ χεῖρον πεποίηκε τὸ ὅλον οὕτω φθεγγομένη, ὥσπερ οὐδὲ ὁ δήμιος πονηρὸς ὢν χείρω πεποίηκε τὴν εὐνομουμένην πόλιν, εἰ δεῖ καὶ ἄλλῃ χρῆσθαι εἰκόνι. Δεῖ γὰρ καὶ τούτου ἐν πόλει—δεῖ δὲ καὶ ἀνθρώπου τοιούτου πολλάκις—καὶ καλῶς καὶ οὗτος κεῖται.

18. Χείρους δὲ καὶ βελτίους ψυχαὶ αἱ μὲν καὶ δι' ἄλλας αἰτίας, αἱ δὲ οἷον ἐξ ἀρχῆς οὐ πᾶσαι ἴσαι· ἀνὰ λόγον γὰρ καὶ αὗται τῷ λόγῳ μέρη οὐκ ἴσα,

[1] τε del. Theiler.

life, but a lesser, worse, and more incomplete life; just as in a pan-pipe there is not one note only but a note which is weaker and duller contributes to the melody of the whole pan-pipe, because the melody is divided into parts which are not equal, and all the notes of the pipe are unequal, but the melody is complete, made up of all. So, too, the universal rational principle is one, but is divided into parts which are not equal; for this reason there are different regions of the universe, better and worse ones, and souls which are not equal fit in this way into unequal places; and so in the universe, too, it happens that there are places which are unlike each other and souls which are not the same but are unequal and occupy the unlike places, just like the unlikenesses of a pan-pipe or any other instrument, and are in places which differ from each other and in each place utter their own sounds in harmony with the places and with the whole. And their evil-sounding singing will be beautifully disposed from the point of view of the All, and their unnatural sounds will be for the All according to nature, and none the less, the sound itself will be worse. But it does not make the whole worse by making a sound like this, just as (if we should use another image as well) the public executioner, who is a scoundrel, does not make his well governed city worse. For the executioner is needed in a city—and a man of his kind is often needed [for other purposes]—and so he, too, is well placed.

18. But souls are better or worse, some from other causes and some because they were not all equal, as we may say, from the beginning; for they, too, in the same way as the rational principle, are unequal parts

ἐπείπερ διέστησαν. Χρὴ δὲ ἐνθυμεῖσθαι καὶ τὰ δεύτερα καὶ τὰ τρίτα καὶ τὸ μὴ τοῖς αὐτοῖς ἐνεργεῖν ἀεὶ μέρεσι ψυχήν. Ἀλλὰ πάλιν αὖ καὶ ὧδε λεκτέον· πολλὰ γὰρ ἐπιποθεῖ εἰς σαφήνειαν ὁ λόγος. Μὴ γὰρ οὐδὲν δεῖ ἐπεισάγειν τοιούτους ὑποκριτάς, οἳ ἄλλο τι φθέγγονται ἢ τὰ τοῦ ποιητοῦ, ὥσπερ ἀτελοῦς παρ' αὐτοῦ τοῦ δράματος ὄντος αὐτοὶ ἀποπληροῦντες τὸ ἐλλεῖπον καὶ τοῦ ποιήσαντος διὰ μέσου κενοὺς ποιήσαντος [τοὺς][1] τόπους, ὡς τῶν ὑποκριτῶν οὐχ ὑποκριτῶν ἐσομένων, ἀλλὰ μέρος τοῦ ποιητοῦ, καὶ προειδότος ἃ φθέγξονται, ἵν' οὕτω τὰ λοιπὰ συνείρων καὶ τὰ ἐφεξῆς οἷός τε ᾖ. Καὶ γὰρ τὰ ἐφεξῆς ἐν τῷ παντὶ καὶ ἑπόμενα τοῖς κακοῖς τῶν ἔργων οἱ λόγοι καὶ κατὰ λόγον· οἷον ἐκ μοιχείας καὶ αἰχμαλώτου ἀγωγῆς παῖδες κατὰ φύσιν καὶ βελτίους ἄνδρες, εἰ τύχοι, καὶ πόλεις ἄλλαι ἀμείνους τῶν πεπορθημένων ὑπὸ ἀνδρῶν πονηρῶν. Εἰ οὖν ἄτοπος ἡ εἰσαγωγὴ τῶν ψυχῶν, αἳ δὴ[2] τὰ πονηρά, αἱ δὲ τὰ χρηστὰ ἐργάσονται—ἀποστερήσομεν γὰρ τὸν λόγον καὶ τῶν χρηστῶν ἀφαιροῦντες αὐτοῦ τὰ πονηρά—τί κωλύει καὶ τὰ τῶν ὑποκριτῶν ἔργα μέρη ποιεῖν, ὥσπερ τοῦ δράματος ἐκεῖ, οὕτω καὶ τοῦ ἐν τῷ παντὶ λόγου, καὶ ἐνταῦθα καὶ τὸ καλῶς καὶ τὸ ἐναντίον, ὥστε εἰς ἕκαστον τῶν ὑποκριτῶν οὕτω παρ' αὐτοῦ τοῦ λόγου, ὅσῳ τελειότερον τοῦτο τὸ

[1] τοὺς in A expunctum del. Volkmann.
[2] δὴ Kirchhoff, H–S: δὲ codd.

as a consequence of their separation. But one must consider, too, the second and third parts of the soul, and the fact that soul is not always active in the same parts. But, again, on the other side we must say this too—the argument still needs a great deal more before it attains clearness. We ought certainly not to introduce actors of a kind who say something else besides the words of the author, as if the play was incomplete in itself and they filled in what was wanting, and the writer had left blank spaces in the middle; the actors, then, would not be just actors but a part of the author, and an author who foreknew what they were going to say, so that he might in this way be able to bring the rest of the play and the consequences of their interventions into a coherent whole. For certainly in the All the rational principles bring into a connected whole the consequences and results which follow upon those deeds which are evil, and do so rationally; for instance, from adultery, or the carrying off of a captive, children may come according to nature and better men, it may happen, and other better cities than those sacked by wicked men. If, then, it is absurd to bring in souls, some of which do the wicked deeds in the world, and some the good—for we shall deprive the rational principle of the good deeds, too, if we take the wicked ones away from it—what prevents us from making the deeds of the actors parts, as they are of the play in our example, so also of the rational principle in the universe, and attributing good performance and the opposite to it, so that in this way it comes to each individual actor from the rational principle itself—and all the more in proportion as this play is more perfect, and every-

δρᾶμα καὶ πάντα παρ' αὐτοῦ; Ἀλλὰ τὸ κακὸν ποιῆσαι ἵνα τί; καὶ αἱ ψυχαὶ δὲ οὐδὲν ἔτι ἐν τῷ παντὶ αἱ θειότεραι, ἀλλὰ μέρη λόγου πᾶσαι; καὶ ἢ οἱ λόγοι πάντες ψυχαί, ἢ διὰ τί οἱ μὲν ψυχαί, οἱ δὲ λόγοι μόνον παντὸς ψυχῆς τινος ὄντος;

thing comes from it? But what is the point of doing evil? And do the diviner souls count for nothing any more in the universe, but are all of them parts of the rational principle? And are all rational principles souls, or why are some souls and some only rational principles, when every one of them belongs to some soul?

III. 3. (48) ΠΕΡΙ ΠΡΟΝΟΙΑΣ ΔΕΥΤΕΡΟΝ

1. Τί τοίνυν δοκεῖ περὶ τούτων; Ἢ καὶ τὰ πονηρὰ καὶ τὰ χρηστὰ λόγος περιείληφεν ὁ πᾶς, οὗ μέρη καὶ ταῦτα· οὐ γὰρ ὁ πᾶς λόγος γεννᾷ ταῦτα, ἀλλ᾽ ὁ πᾶς ἐστι μετὰ τούτων. Ψυχῆς γάρ τινος πάσης ἐνέργεια οἱ λόγοι, τῶν δὲ μερῶν τὰ μέρη· μιᾶς δὲ διάφορα ἐχούσης μέρη ἀνὰ λόγον καὶ οἱ λόγοι, ὥστε καὶ τὰ ἔργα ἔσχατα ὄντα γεννήματα. Σύμφωνοι δὲ αἵ τε ψυχαὶ πρὸς ἀλλήλας τά τε ἔργα· σύμφωνα δὲ οὕτως, ὡς ἓν ἐξ αὐτῶν, καὶ εἰ ἐξ ἐναντίων. Ἐκ γὰρ ἑνός τινος ὁρμηθέντα πάντα εἰς ἓν συνέρχεται φύσεως ἀνάγκῃ, ὥστε καὶ διάφορα ἐκφύντα καὶ ἐναντία γενόμενα τῷ ἐξ ἑνὸς εἶναι συνέλκεται ὅμως εἰς σύνταξιν μίαν· ὥσπερ γὰρ καὶ ἐφ᾽ ἑκάστων ζῴων· ἓν ἵππων γένος,[1] κἂν μάχωνται κἂν δάκνωσιν ἀλλήλους κἂν φιλονεικῶσι κἂν ζήλῳ θυμῶνται, καὶ τὰ ἄλλα καθ᾽ ἓν γένη ὡσαύτως· καὶ δὴ οὕτω καὶ ἀνθρώπους θετέον. Συναπτέον τοίνυν αὖ πάλιν πάντα τὰ εἴδη ταῦτα εἰς ἓν «τὸ ζῷον» γένος· εἶτα καὶ τὰ

[1] ἓν ἵππων γένος MacKenna, Cilento, H–S[2]: ἐν ἵππων γένει codd.

III. 3. ON PROVIDENCE (II)

1. What, then, do we think about these questions? Now the universal rational principle includes both good and evil things; evil things are parts of it too. It is not that the universal rational principle produces them but that it is the universal principle with them included. The rational principles are an activity of an universal soul, and their parts of soul-parts; but, as the one soul has differing parts, so correspondingly do the rational principles differ, with the result that the works also differ which are their ultimate products. The souls and the works are in harmony with each other; in harmony in such a way that a unity comes from them, even if it is a unity produced from opposites. For all things sprung from a unity come together into a unity by natural necessity, so that, though they grow out different and come into being as opposites they are, all the same, drawn together into a single common order by the fact that they come from a unity. For, just as in the case of particular kinds of living creatures there is one genus of horses, even if they fight and bite each other, and are pugnacious and furiously jealous, and the same applies to all the other individual genera, so, certainly, men must be considered like this too. Then, again, all these kinds must be brought together under the one genus "living creature"; then also the things which are not living creatures must be

μὴ ζῷα κατ᾽ εἴδη αὖ· εἶτα εἰς ἓν « τὸ μὴ ζῷον »· εἶτα ὁμοῦ, εἰ βούλει, εἰς τὸ εἶναι· εἶτα εἰς τὸ παρέχον τὸ εἶναι. Καὶ πάλιν ἐπὶ τούτῳ ἐκδήσας κατάβαινε διαιρῶν καὶ σκιδνάμενον τὸ ἓν ὁρῶν τῷ ἐπὶ πάντα φθάνειν καὶ ὁμοῦ περιλαμβάνειν συντάξει μιᾷ, ὡς διακεκριμένον ἓν εἶναι ζῷον πολὺ ἑκάστου πράττοντος τῶν[1] ἐν αὐτῷ τὸ κατὰ φύσιν ἑαυτοῦ ἐν αὐτῷ τῷ ὅλῳ ὅμως ὄντος, οἷον πυρὸς μὲν καίοντος, ἵππου τὰ ἵππου ἔργα, ἄνθρωποι δὲ τὰ αὑτῶν ἕκαστοι ᾗ πεφύκασι καὶ διάφορα οἱ διάφοροι. Καὶ ἕπεται κατὰ τὰς φύσεις καὶ τὰ ἔργα καὶ τὸ ζῆν τὸ εὖ καὶ τὸ κακῶς.

2. Αἱ δὲ συντυχίαι οὐ κύριαι τοῦ εὖ, ἀκολουθοῦσι δὲ καὶ αὗται συμφώνως τοῖς πρὸ αὐτῶν καὶ ἴασιν ἀκολουθίᾳ[2] ἐμπλεκεῖσαι. Συμπλέκει δὲ πάντα τὸ ἡγούμενον συμφερομένων τῶν ἐφ᾽ ἑκάτερα κατὰ φύσιν, οἷον ἐν στρατηγίαις ἡγουμένου μὲν τοῦ στρατηγοῦ, συμπνεόντων δὲ τῶν συντεταγμένων. Ἐτάχθη δὲ τὸ πᾶν προνοίᾳ στρατηγικῇ ὁρώσῃ καὶ τὰς πράξεις καὶ τὰ πάθη καὶ ἃ δεῖ παρεῖναι, σιτία καὶ ποτὰ καὶ δὴ καὶ ὅπλα πάντα καὶ μηχανήματα, καὶ ὅσα ἐξ αὐτῶν συμπλεκομένων προεώραται, ἵνα τὸ ἐκ τούτων συμβαῖνον ἔχῃ χώραν τοῦ

[1] τῶν Creuzer: τὴν codd.
[2] ἀκολουθίᾳ Kirchhoff, H–S²: ἀκολουθίαι codd.

classed by their kinds, and then included in the one genus " non-living "; then both together, if you like, must be included in being; and then in that which makes being possible. Then, having attached everything to this, go down again, dividing and seeing the one dispersed by reaching to all things and including them together in a single common order, so that it is a single multiplex living thing with distinct parts, and each of the things in it acts according to its own nature while being all the same in the whole, for instance, fire burns, a horse does the things which belong to a horse, and individual men do their own things in the way in which they have been disposed by nature, and different men different things. And what is done, and living well or badly, follows according to their natures.

2. Chance circumstances are not responsible for the good life, but they, too, follow harmoniously on the causes before them, and proceed woven into the chain of causation by so following. The ruling principle weaves all things together, while individual things co-operate on one side or the other according to their nature, as in military commands the general gives the lead and his subordinates work in unity with him.[1] The universe is ordered by the generalship of providence which sees the actions and experiences and what must be ready to hand, food and drink, and all weapons and devices as well; everything which results from their interweaving is foreseen, in order that this result may have room to be

[1] The source of this military analogy for the cosmic order is Aristotle, *Metaphysics* Λ 1075a, 13 ff.; cp. the pseudo-Aristotelian *De Mundo* 399b, 3 ff., for a rhetorical elaboration of it.

τεθῆναι εὖ, καὶ ἐλήλυθε πάντα τρόπον τινὰ εὐμήχανον παρὰ τοῦ στρατηγοῦ, καίτοι ἔξωθεν ἦν ὅσα ἔμελλον δράσειν οἱ ἐναντίοι. Εἰ δὲ οἷόν τε ἦν κἀκείνου ἄρχειν τοῦ στρατοπέδου, εἰ δὲ δὴ ὁ μέγας ἡγεμὼν εἴη, ὑφ᾽ ᾧ πάντα, τί ἂν ἀσύντακτον, τί δὲ οὐκ ἂν συνηρμοσμένον εἴη;

3. Καὶ γὰρ « εἰ ἐγὼ κύριος τοῦ τάδε ἑλέσθαι ἢ τάδε »; Ἀλλ᾽ ἃ [1] αἱρήσει συντέτακται, ὅτι μὴ ἐπεισόδιον τὸ σὸν τῷ παντί, ἀλλ᾽ ἠρίθμησαι ὁ τοιόσδε. Ἀλλὰ πόθεν ὁ τοιόσδε; Ἔστι δὴ δύο, ἃ ὁ λόγος ζητεῖ, τὸ μέν, εἰ ἐπὶ τὸν ποιήσαντα, εἴ τις ἐστίν, ἀνενεγκεῖν δεῖ τοῦ ποιοῦ τοῦ ἐν τοῖς ἤθεσιν ἑκάστου τὴν αἰτίαν ἢ ἐπὶ τὸ γενόμενον αὐτό· ἢ ὅλως οὐκ αἰτιατέον, ὥσπερ οὐδὲ ἐπὶ φυτῶν γενέσεως, ὅτι μὴ αἰσθάνεται, ἢ ἐπὶ ζῴων τῶν ἄλλων, ὅτι μὴ ὡς ἄνθρωποι ἔχουσι· ταὐτὸν γὰρ τούτῳ « διὰ τί ἄνθρωποι οὐχ ὅπερ θεοί; » Διὰ τί γὰρ ἐνταῦθα οὔτε αὐτὰ οὔτε τὸν ποιήσαντα εὐλόγως αἰτιώμεθα, ἐπὶ δὲ ἀνθρώπων, ὅτι μὴ κρεῖττον ἢ τοῦτο; Εἰ μὲν γάρ, ὅτι ἐδύνατο τοῦτο κάλλιον εἶναι, εἰ μὲν παρ᾽ αὐτοῦ προστιθέντος τι

[1] ἀλλ᾽ ἃ Harder, H–S: ἀλλὰ codd.

---

[1] Plato, *Phaedrus* 246E4.

[2] Cp. Plato's treatment of the same question in *Laws* X. 904B–C. Plotinus here, at the end of the chapter, gives the same answer as Plato, that the blame should fall upon individual men, not on their Maker; but he shows himself, here as elsewhere, a good deal more conscious of the difficulties

well placed, and all things come in a well-planned way from the general—though what his enemies planned to do is out of his control. But if it was possible for him to command the enemy force as well, if he was really "the great leader"[1] to whom all things are subject, what would be unordered, what would not be fitted into his plan?

3. Suppose you say "I have power to choose this or that"? But the things that you will choose are included in the universal order, because your part is not a mere casual interlude in the All but you are counted in as just the person you are. But for what reason is a man the sort of person he is? There are two questions which the argument seeks to settle here, one, whether the blame should rest on the maker, if there is one, who determined the moral character of the individual, or on the being which has come into existence itself:[2] rather, we should not attribute blame at all, just as there is no blame attaching to the production of plants because they have no sense-perception, nor in the case of the other animals because they are not like men; to blame anyone for this would be the same as asking, "Why are men not what gods are?" Why then, where plants and animals are concerned, is it unreasonable for us to blame them or their creator, but reasonable in the case of men, because man is not a better thing than he is? For if it is because he was able to be something nobler than he is, if he was able to add

raised by the presence of bad men in a divinely ordered universe than Plato is; this is no doubt because of the centuries of debate about Providence which came between him and his master.

εἰς τὸ κρεῖττον, αὐτὸς αἴτιος ἑαυτῷ ὁ μὴ ποιήσας· εἰ δὲ μὴ παρ' αὐτοῦ, ἀλλ' ἔδει ἔξωθεν προσεῖναι παρὰ τοῦ γεννητοῦ, ἄτοπος ὁ τὸ πλέον ἀπαιτῶν τοῦ δοθέντος, ὥσπερ εἰ καὶ ἐπὶ τῶν ἄλλων ζῴων ἀπαιτοῖ καὶ τῶν φυτῶν. Δεῖ γὰρ οὐ ζητεῖν, εἰ ἔλαττον ἄλλου, ἀλλ' εἰ ὡς αὐτὸ αὐτάρκως· οὐ γὰρ πάντα ἴσα ἔδει. Ἆρ' οὖν μετρήσαντος αὐτοῦ προαιρέσει τοῦ μὴ δεῖν πάντα ἴσα; Οὐδαμῶς· ἀλλ' οὕτω κατὰ φύσιν εἶχε γενέσθαι. Ἀκόλουθος γὰρ οὗτος ὁ λόγος ψυχῇ ἄλλῃ, ἀκόλουθος δὲ ψυχὴ αὕτη νῷ, νοῦς δὲ οὐ τούτων τι ἕν, ἀλλὰ πάντα· τὰ δὲ πάντα πολλά· πολλὰ δὲ ὄντα καὶ οὐ ταὐτὰ τὰ μὲν πρῶτα, τὰ δὲ δεύτερα, τὰ δὲ ἐφεξῆς καὶ τῇ ἀξίᾳ ἔμελλεν εἶναι. Καὶ τοίνυν καὶ τὰ γενόμενα ζῷα οὐ ψυχαὶ μόνον, ἀλλὰ ψυχῶν ἐλαττώσεις, οἷον ἐξίτηλον ἤδη προϊόντων. Ὁ γὰρ τοῦ ζῴου λόγος, κἂν ἔμψυχος ᾖ, ἑτέρα ψυχή, οὐκ ἐκείνη, ἀφ' ἧς ὁ λόγος, καὶ ὁ σύμπας οὗτος ἐλάττων δὴ γίνεται σπεύδων εἰς ὕλην, καὶ τὸ γενόμενον ἐξ αὐτοῦ ἐνδεέστερον. Σκόπει δὴ ὅσον ἀφέστηκε τὸ γενόμενον καὶ ὅμως ἐστὶ θαῦμα. Οὐ τοίνυν, εἰ τοιοῦτον τὸ γενόμενον, καὶ τὸ πρὸ αὐτοῦ τοιοῦτον·

something to make himself better, he is responsible to himself for not doing it; but if it was not from himself that the addition had to come but it was necessary for it to come from outside, from his producer, then it is absurd to ask for more than was given, as it would be in the case of the other animals and of plants. For one ought not to enquire whether one thing is less than another but whether it is, as itself, sufficient; for all things ought not to have been equal. Is this then so, because the creator measured them out with the deliberate intention that all things ought not to be equal? Not at all; but it was according to nature for things to come about so. For the rational forming principle of this universe follows upon another soul, and this soul follows upon Intellect, and Intellect is not some one of the things here but all things; but all things means many things; but if there are many things, and not the same, some of them were going to be first, some second, and some of successive lower ranks, in value too. Then, again, the living creatures which have come into being are not only souls but diminutions of souls, a kind of fading away as the living things move on further from their origins. For the formative principle of the living thing, even if it is ensouled, is another soul, not that from which the formative principle comes, and this whole principle becomes less as it hastens to matter, and that which comes into being from it is more deficient. See how far what has come into being stands from its origin, and yet, it is a wonder! If, then, that which has come into being is of a particular kind, it does not follow that what is before it is also of that kind: for

ἔστι γὰρ παντὸς κρεῖττον τοῦ γενομένου καὶ ἔξω αἰτίας καὶ μᾶλλον θαυμάσαι, ὅτι ἔδωκέ τι μετ' αὐτὸ καὶ τὰ ἴχνη αὐτοῦ τοιαῦτα. Εἰ δὲ δὴ καὶ πλέον ἔδωκεν ἢ ὅσον ἔχουσι κτήσασθαι, ἔτι μᾶλλον ἀποδεκτέον· ὥστε κινδυνεύειν τὴν αἰτίαν ἐπὶ τοὺς γενομένους ἰέναι, τὸ δὲ τῆς προνοίας μειζόνως ἔχειν.

4. Ἁπλοῦ μὲν γὰρ ὄντος τοῦ ἀνθρώπου—λέγω δὲ ἁπλοῦ ὡς τοῦτο ὃ πεποίηται μόνον ὄντος καὶ κατὰ ταῦτα ποιοῦντος καὶ πάσχοντος—ἀπῆν αἰτία ἡ κατὰ τὴν ἐπιτίμησιν, ὥσπερ ἐπὶ τῶν ζῴων τῶν ἄλλων. Νῦν δὲ ἄνθρωπος μόνον ἐν ψόγῳ ὁ κακὸς καὶ τοῦτο ἴσως εὐλόγως. Οὐ γὰρ μόνον ὃ πεποίηταί ἐστιν, ἀλλ' ἔχει ἀρχὴν ἄλλην ἐλευθέραν οὐκ ἔξω τῆς προνοίας οὖσαν οὐδὲ τοῦ λόγου τοῦ ὅλου· οὐ γὰρ ἀπήρτηται ἐκεῖνα τούτων, ἀλλ' ἐπιλάμπει τὰ κρείττω τοῖς χείροσι καὶ ἡ τελεία πρόνοια τοῦτο· καὶ λόγος ὁ μὲν ποιητικός, ὁ δὲ συνάπτων τὰ κρείττω τοῖς γενομένοις, κἀκεῖνα πρόνοια ἡ ἄνωθεν, ἡ δὲ ἀπὸ τῆς ἄνω, ὁ ἕτερος λόγος συνημμένος ἐκείνῳ, καὶ γίνεται ἐξ ἀμφοῖν πᾶν πλέγμα καὶ πρόνοια ἡ πᾶσα. Ἀρχὴν μὲν οὖν ἔχουσιν ἄλλην ἄνθρωποι, οὐ πάντες δὲ πᾶσιν οἷς ἔχουσι χρῶνται, ἀλλ' οἱ μὲν τῇ ἑτέρᾳ, οἱ δὲ τῇ ἑτέρᾳ ἢ ταῖς ἑτέραις ταῖς χείροσι χρῶνται. Πάρεισι δὲ

it is better than all that has come into being, and beyond blame; one should rather wonder at it because it has given something [to what comes] after it and its traces are of such a quality. But if indeed it has given more than they are able to appropriate, it ought to be approved still more; so that it seems likely that blame should fall upon the men who have come into being, and that what belongs to providence is on a higher level.

4. For if man was simple—I mean, simple in the sense that he was nothing but what he was made and his actions and experiences corresponded to this—there would be no blame in the sense of moral reproach, just as there is none in the case of other living creatures. But, as it is, man, the bad man, is uniquely subject to blame, perhaps reasonably. For he is not only what he was made but has another free principle, which is not outside providence or the rational principle of the whole; for those higher principles are not separated from these here but the better illuminate the worse, and this is perfect providence; and there is one rational principle which is creative, and another which connects the better principles with the things which have come into being, and those higher principles are providence which acts from above, but there is another providence derived from that which is above, the other rational principle connected with that higher one, and the whole interweaving and total providence results from both. So then, men have another principle, but not all men use all that they have but some use one principle, some the other, or rather a number of others, the worse ones. But those higher

κἀκεῖναι οὐκ ἐνεργοῦσαι εἰς αὐτούς, οὔ τι γε αὐταὶ ἀργοῦσαι· πράττει γὰρ ἕκαστον τὸ ἑαυτοῦ. Ἀλλʼ εἰς τούτους οὐκ ἐνεργοῦσιν αἰτίᾳ τίνος, εἴποι τις ἄν, παροῦσαι; Ἢ οὐ πάρεισι; Καίτοι πάντῃ φαμὲν παρεῖναι καὶ οὐδὲν ἔρημον. Ἢ οὐ τούτοις, ἐν οἷς μὴ εἰς αὐτοὺς ἐνεργεῖ. Διὰ τί οὖν οὐκ ἐνεργεῖ εἰς πάντας, εἴπερ μέρη καὶ ταῦτα αὐτῶν; Λέγω δὲ τὴν ἀρχὴν τὴν τοιαύτην. Ἐπὶ μὲν γὰρ τῶν ἄλλων ζῴων οὐκ αὐτῶν ἡ ἀρχὴ αὕτη, ἐπὶ δὲ ἀνθρώπων οὐκ ἐπὶ πάντων. Ἆρʼ οὖν οὐκ ἐπὶ πάντων οὐ μόνον ἥδε; Ἀλλὰ διὰ τί οὐ μόνη; Ἐφʼ ὧν δὲ μόνη, καὶ κατὰ ταύτην τὸ ζῆν, τὰ δʼ ἄλλα ὅσον ἀνάγκη. Εἴτε γὰρ ἡ σύστασις τοιαύτη, ὡς οἷον εἰς θολερὸν ἐμβάλλειν, εἴτε ἐπιθυμίαι κρατοῦσιν, ὅμως ἀνάγκη λέγειν ἐν τῷ ὑποκειμένῳ τὸ αἴτιον εἶναι. Ἀλλὰ πρῶτον μὲν δόξει οὐκέτι ἐν τῷ λόγῳ, ἀλλὰ μᾶλλον ἐν τῇ ὕλῃ, καὶ ἡ ὕλη, οὐχ ὁ λόγος κρατήσει, εἶτα τὸ ὑποκείμενον ὡς πέπλασται. Ἢ τὸ ὑποκείμενον τῇ ἀρχῇ ὁ λόγος ἐστὶ καὶ τὸ ἐκ τοῦ λόγου γενόμενον καὶ ὂν κατὰ τὸν λόγον· ὥστε οὐχ ἡ ὕλη κρατήσει, εἶτα ἡ πλάσις. Καὶ τὸ τοιόνδε εἶναι ἐπὶ τὴν προτέραν

[1] This brings out clearly an important point in the psychology of Plotinus, that the duality or cleavage in man is for him not between matter and spirit, or even body and soul, but between higher and lower self: cp. I. 1 [53] 10; II. 9 [33] 2; IV. 4 [28] 18; VI. 4 [22] 14–15. Free will can only be exercised by the true, higher self in so far as it transcends and makes itself independent of the lower "composite" self, which is part

principles are there, but not acting upon them, though certainly not inactive in themselves; for each one of them does its own work. But, someone might say, what is to blame for their not working on these men when they are present? Or are they not present? But we assert that they are present everywhere and nothing is deprived of them. Surely they are not present in those people on whom they do not act. Why, then, do they not act upon all, if these, too, are parts of them?—I mean the principle of this higher kind. As far as the other living creatures are concerned, this principle is not their own; as for men, it does not act on all of them. Is this then not the only principle which does not act on all? But why should it not be the only one? But in those in whom it is the only one, their life is conformed to it, and the other forces only enter into it as far as necessity requires. For whether the man's constitution is of a kind to plunge him, so to speak, into troubled waters, or his lusts dominate him, it is alike necessary to say that the cause lies in the substratum. But at first this would appear to mean that the cause is no more in the rational principle, but rather in the matter, and the matter, not the rational principle will be dominant, and the substrate in so far as it is formed will come second to it. In fact, the substrate to the free principle is the rational form, and that which has come into existence from the rational form and exists according to it; so that the matter will not be dominant and the formation come second.[1] Further, one might refer the being

of and dominated by the order of the physical universe; cp. II. 3 [52] 15. 17 ff.

βιοτὴν ἀνάγοι τις, οἷον γινομένου ἐκ τῶν προτέρων ἀμυδροῦ ὡς πρὸς τὸν πρὸ αὐτοῦ τοῦ λόγου, οἷον ψυχῆς ἀσθενεστέρας γενομένης· ὕστερον δὲ καὶ ἐκλάμψει. Καὶ ὁ λόγος δὲ λεγέσθω ἔχειν καὶ τὸν λόγον αὖ ἐν αὐτῷ τῆς ὕλης, ἣν αὐτῷ ἐργάσεται ποιώσας καθ' αὑτὸν τὴν ὕλην ἢ σύμφωνον εὑρών. Οὐ γὰρ ὁ τοῦ βοὸς λόγος ἐπ' ἄλλης ἢ βοὸς ὕλης· ὅθεν καὶ εἰς τὰ ἄλλα ζῷά φησιν εἰσκρίνεσθαι οἷον ἄλλης τῆς ψυχῆς γενομένης καὶ ἑτεροιωθέντος τοῦ λόγου, ἵνα γένηται ψυχὴ βοός, ἣ πρότερον ἦν ἄνθρωπος· ὥστε κατὰ δίκην ὁ χείρων. Ἀλλ' ἐξ ἀρχῆς διὰ τί ὁ χείρων ἐγένετο καὶ πῶς ἐσφάλη; Πολλάκις εἴρηται, ὡς οὐ πρῶτα πάντα, ἀλλ' ὅσα δεύτερα καὶ τρίτα ἐλάττω τὴν φύσιν τῶν πρὸ αὐτῶν ἔχει, καὶ σμικρὰ ῥοπὴ ἀρκεῖ εἰς ἔκβασιν τοῦ ὀρθοῦ. Καὶ ἡ συμπλοκὴ δὲ ἡ πρὸς ἄλλο ἄλλου ὥσπερ τις σύγκρασίς ἐστιν, ἑτέρου ἐξ ἀμφοῖν γενομένου, καὶ οὐκ ὄντος ἠλάττωσεν· ἀλλὰ ἐγένετο ἐξ ἀρχῆς ἔλαττον τὸ ἔλαττον καὶ ἔστιν ὃ ἐγένετο κατὰ φύσιν τὴν αὐτοῦ ἔλαττον, καί, εἰ τὸ ἀκόλουθον πάσχει, πάσχει τὸ κατ' ἀξίαν. Καὶ εἰς τὰ προβεβιωμένα δὲ ἀναπέμπειν δεῖ τὸν λογισμὸν ὡς κἀκεῖθεν ἠρτημένων τῶν ἐφεξῆς.

5. Γίνεται τοίνυν ἡ πρόνοια ἐξ ἀρχῆς εἰς τέλος κατιοῦσα ἄνωθεν οὐκ ἴση οἷον κατ' ἀριθμόν, ἀλλὰ

---

[1] *Timaeus* 42C 3.

this or that kind of man to the previous life, as if the rational principle became dim in comparison to that prior to it as the result of previous happenings, as if the soul had become weaker; but it will shine out again later. And the rational principle must be said to contain within itself the rational principle of the matter as well, the matter which it will make suitable for itself, either giving it qualities corresponding to itself or finding it already consonant. For the rational principle of an ox does not impose itself on any other matter than that of an ox. Hence, Plato says [1] that the soul enters into other living beings, in the sense that the soul becomes different and the rational principle is altered, in order that what was formerly the soul of a man may become the soul of an ox; so that the worse being is justly dealt with. But how did he originally become worse, and how did he fall? It has often been said that all things are not of the first rank but all things which are second and third class have a lesser nature than those before them, and a light tilting of the balance is enough to turn them out of the right way. And the interweaving of one thing with another is like a sort of mixture; another thing results from both, and the interweaving does not diminish a thing's being; but the inferior became inferior from its beginning, and is what it became, inferior by its nature, and, if it suffers the consequences of its inferiority, it suffers what it deserves. And one must carry back the reckoning to what happened in previous lives, because what happens afterwards depends on that too.

5. Providence, then, which in its descent from above reaches from the beginning to the end, is not

κατ᾽ ἀναλογίαν ἄλλη ἐν ἄλλῳ τόπῳ, ὥσπερ ἐπὶ ζῴου ἑνὸς εἰς ἔσχατον ἐξ ἀρχῆς ἠρτημένου, ἑκάστου τὸ οἰκεῖον ἔχοντος, τοῦ μὲν βελτίονος τὸ βέλτιον τῆς ἐνεργείας, τοῦ δὲ πρὸς τὸ κάτω ἤδη ἐνεργοῦντός τε τοῦ αὐτοῦ καὶ πάσχοντος τὰ ὅσα αὐτῷ οἰκεῖα παθήματα πρὸς αὐτό τε καὶ πρὸς τὴν σύνταξιν τὴν πρὸς ἄλλο. Καὶ δὴ καὶ οὑτωσὶ πληγέντα οὕτως ἐφθέγξατο τὰ φωνήεντα, τὰ δὲ σιωπῇ πάσχει καὶ κινεῖται τὰ ἀκόλουθα, καὶ ἐκ τῶν φθόγγων ἁπάντων καὶ ἐκ τῶν παθημάτων καὶ ἐνεργημάτων μία τοῦ ζῴου οἷον φωνὴ καὶ ζωὴ καὶ βίος· καὶ γὰρ καὶ τὰ μόρια διάφορα ὄντα καὶ διάφορον τὴν ἐνέργειαν ἔχοντα· ἄλλο γὰρ ποιοῦσι πόδες, ὀφθαλμοὶ δ᾽ ἄλλο, διάνοια δὲ ἄλλο καὶ νοῦς ἄλλο. Ἓν δὲ ἐκ πάντων καὶ πρόνοια μία· εἱμαρμένη δὲ ἀπὸ τοῦ χείρονος ἀρξαμένη, τὸ δὲ ὑπεράνω πρόνοια μόνον. Τὰ μὲν γὰρ ἐν τῷ κόσμῳ τῷ νοητῷ πάντα λόγος καὶ ὑπὲρ λόγον· νοῦς γὰρ καὶ ψυχὴ καθαρά· τὸ δὲ ἐντεῦθεν ἤδη ὅσον μὲν ἔρχεται ἐκεῖθεν, πρόνοια, καὶ ὅσον ἐν ψυχῇ καθαρᾷ καὶ ὅσον ἐντεῦθεν εἰς τὰ ζῷα. Ἔρχεται δὲ μεριζόμενος ὁ λόγος οὐκ ἴσα· ὅθεν οὐδ᾽ ἴσα ποιεῖ, ὥσπερ καὶ ἐν ζῴῳ ἑκάστῳ. Τὸ δὲ ἐντεῦθεν ἤδη ἀκόλουθα μὲν τὰ δρώμενα καὶ προνοίᾳ ἑπόμενα, εἴ τις δρῴη θεοῖς φίλα· ἦν γὰρ θεοφιλὴς ὁ λόγος

[1] This distinction between higher providence and lower fate is common in Middle Platonism; cp. Pseudo-Plutarch, *De Fato* 9. 572F–573B; Apuleius, *De Platone* I. 12; and C. de Vogel, *Greek Philosophy* III. 1279d (p. 343).

equal as in a numerical distribution but differs in different places according to a law of correspondence, just as in a single living creature, which is dependent on its principle down to its last and lowest part, each part having its own, the better part having the better part of the activity, and that which is at the lower limit still active in its own way and undergoing the experiences which are proper to it as regards its own nature and its co-ordination with anything else. Yes, and if the parts are struck in a particular way, the speaking parts give out a corresponding sound, and others receive the blow in silence and make the movements which result from it; and from all the sounds and passive experiences and activities come a kind of single voice of the living creature, a single life and way of living; for the organs are different and have activities which are different; for the feet do one thing, the eyes another, the discursive reason one thing and the intuitive intellect another. But one thing results from all, and there is one providence; but it is " fate " beginning from the lower level; the upper is providence alone.[1] For in the intelligible world all things are rational principle and above rational principle; for all are intellect and pure soul; what comes from there, all that comes from intellect, is providence, both all that is in pure soul and all that comes from it to living things. But the rational principle as it comes is divided into unequal parts; hence the things it does are not equal either, as also in each individual living creature. From this point the things which are done are consequences, and follow upon providence if a man does things which are pleasing to the gods; for the rational forming

ὁ προνοίας. Συνείρεται μὲν οὖν καὶ τὰ τοιαῦτα τῶν ἔργων, πεποίηται δὲ οὐ προνοίᾳ, ἀλλὰ γενόμενα ἢ παρὰ ἀνθρώπων τὰ γενόμενα ἢ παρ' ὁτουοῦν ἢ ζῴου ἢ ἀψύχου, εἴ τι ἐφεξῆς τούτοις χρηστόν, πάλιν κατείληπται προνοίᾳ, ὡς πανταχοῦ ἀρετὴν κρατεῖν καὶ μετατιθεμένων καὶ διορθώσεως τυγχανόντων τῶν ἡμαρτημένων, οἷον ἐν ἑνὶ σώματι ὑγιείας δοθείσης κατὰ πρόνοιαν τοῦ ζῴου, γενομένης τομῆς[1] καὶ ὅλως τραύματος, πάλιν ἐφεξῆς ὁ λόγος ὁ διοικῶν συνάπτοι καὶ συνάγοι καὶ ἰῷτο καὶ διορθοῖτο τὸ πονῆσαν. Ὥστε τὰ κακὰ ἑπόμενα εἶναι, ἐξ ἀνάγκης δέ· καὶ γὰρ παρ' ἡμῶν κατ' αἰτίας οὐχ ὑπὸ τῆς προνοίας ἠναγκασμένων, ἀλλ' ἐξ αὐτῶν συναψάντων μὲν τοῖς τῆς προνοίας καὶ ἀπὸ προνοίας ἔργοις, τὸ δὲ ἐφεξῆς συνεῖραι κατὰ βούλησιν ἐκείνης οὐ δυνηθέντων, ἀλλὰ κατὰ τὴν τῶν πραξάντων ἢ κατ' ἄλλο τι τῶν ἐν τῷ παντί, μηδ' αὐτοῦ κατὰ πρόνοιαν πεπραχότος ἢ πεποιηκότος τι ἐν ἡμῖν πάθος. Οὐ γὰρ τὸ αὐτὸ ποιεῖ πᾶν προσελθὸν παντί, ἀλλὰ τὸ αὐτὸ πρὸς ἄλλο καὶ ἄλλο πρὸς ἄλλο· οἷον καὶ τὸ τῆς Ἑλένης κάλλος πρὸς μὲν τὸν Πάριν ἄλλο εἰργάζετο, Ἰδομενεὺς δὲ ἔπαθεν οὐ τὸ αὐτό· καὶ ἀκόλαστος ἀκολάστῳ

[1] τομῆς Creuzer, H–S: τόλμης codd.

---

[1] For Idomeneus, a frequent visitor to the house of Menelaus who did not seduce Helen, see *Iliad* III. 230–233.

principle of providence is dear to the gods. Then, too, these kind of actions [the kind which cause our difficulties about providence, i.e. evil actions] are linked up with the good ones, but they are not done by providence but the things which have happened, whether they have happened as a result of human action or of the action of anything else, living or lifeless, if anything which follows from them is good, are taken up again by providence, so that virtue has everywhere the mastery, and the things which have gone wrong are changed and corrected, as in a single body, where health is given by the providence of the living thing, when a cut or injury of any kind occurs, the directing rational principle again afterwards joins it and closes the wound and heals and sets right the suffering part. So the evil deeds are consequences, but follow from necessity; they come from us (i.e. we cause them), and we are not compelled by providence but we connect them, of our own accord, with the works of providence or works derived from providence, but are not able to link up what follows according to the will of providence but do so according to the will of the people who act or according to something else in the universe, which itself is acting or producing some effect in us in a way not according to the will of providence. For everything does not always produce the same effect when it encounters everything else, but it produces the same effect when it encounters one thing and a different effect when it encounters another; as, for instance, the beauty of Helen produced one effect on Paris, but Idomeneus [1] was not affected in the same way; and when one thoroughly dissolute man happens upon

καλὸς καλῷ συμπεσὼν ἄλλο, ὁ δὲ σώφρων καλὸς ἄλλο πρὸς σώφρονα τοιοῦτον· ἢ πρὸς ἀκόλαστον ἄλλο ὁ αὐτός, ὁ δ' ἀκόλαστος πρὸς αὐτὸν ἄλλο. Καὶ παρὰ μὲν τοῦ ἀκολάστου τὸ πραχθὲν οὔτε ὑπὸ προνοίας οὔτε κατὰ πρόνοιαν, τὸ δ' ὑπὸ τοῦ σώφρονος ἔργον οὐχ ὑπὸ προνοίας μέν, ὅτι ὑπ' αὐτοῦ, κατὰ πρόνοιαν δέ· σύμφωνον γὰρ τῷ λόγῳ, ὥσπερ καὶ ὃ ὑγιεινῶς πράξειεν ἄν τις αὐτὸς πράξας κατὰ λόγον τὸν τοῦ ἰατροῦ. Τοῦτο γὰρ καὶ ὁ ἰατρὸς παρὰ τῆς τέχνης ἐδίδου εἴς τε τὸ ὑγιαῖνον εἴς τε τὸ κάμνον. Ὃ δ' ἄν τις μὴ ὑγιαῖνον ποιῇ, αὐτός τε ποιεῖ καὶ παρὰ τὴν πρόνοιαν τοῦ ἰατροῦ εἰργάσατο.

6. Πόθεν οὖν καὶ τὰ χείρω μάντεις προλέγουσι καὶ εἰς τὴν τοῦ παντὸς φορὰν ὁρῶντες πρὸς ταῖς ἄλλαις μαντείαις προλέγουσι ταῦτα; Ἢ δῆλον ὅτι τῷ συμπεπλέχθαι πάντα τὰ ἐναντία, οἷον τὴν μορφὴν καὶ τὴν ὕλην· οἷον ἐπὶ ζῴου συνθέτου ὄντος ὅ τι τὴν μορφὴν καὶ τὸν λόγον θεωρῶν καὶ τὸ μεμορφωμένον θεωρεῖ. Οὐ γὰρ ὡσαύτως ζῷον νοητὸν καὶ ζῷον σύνθετον θεωρεῖ, ἀλλὰ λόγον ζῴου ἐν τῷ συνθέτῳ μορφοῦντα τὰ χείρω. Ζῴου δὴ ὄντος τοῦ παντὸς ὁ τὰ ἐν αὐτῷ γινόμενα

another, and both are beautiful, the effect is different from what follows when one chaste beauty meets another; and something different again happens to the chaste beauty when he meets the dissolute man, and again something different to the dissolute one when he meets the chaste. And the action which proceeds from the dissolute man is done neither by providence nor according to providence, but what is done by the chaste man is not done by providence, because it is done by the man himself, but is done according to providence; for it is in tune with the rational principle, just as, too, what a man might do to promote his health would be his own action according to the rational plan of his doctor. For this is what the doctor prescribed, from the resources of his skill, both in health and sickness. But whatever anyone does that is unhealthy, he does it himself and it is an act which goes against the providence of the doctor.

6. What is the reason, then, that diviners foretell the worse sort of actions, and by looking at the circuit of the heavens foretell these as well as their other prophecies? Obviously because all opposites are entwined together, form and matter, for instance; as, for example, in the case of a living thing which is composite, one who in any way contemplates the form and the rational principle also contemplates the formed thing. For he does not contemplate an intelligible living thing and a composite living thing in the same way, but in the composite he contemplates the rational principle of the living thing forming what is worse. Now, since the universe is a living thing, one who contemplates the things which come to be

θεωρῶν θεωρεῖ ἅμα καὶ ἐξ ὧν ἐστι καὶ τὴν πρόνοιαν τὴν ἐπ' αὐτῷ· τέταται δὴ ἐπὶ πάντα καὶ τὰ γινόμενα· τὰ δ' ἐστὶ καὶ ζῷα καὶ πράξεις αὐτῶν καὶ διαθέσεις κραθεῖσαι, λόγῳ καὶ ἀνάγκῃ μεμιγμέναι· μεμιγμένα οὖν θεωρεῖ καὶ διηνεκῶς μιγνύμενα· καὶ διακρίνειν μὲν αὐτὸς οὐ δύναται πρόνοιαν καὶ τὸ κατὰ πρόνοιαν χωρὶς καὶ αὖ τὸ ὑποκείμενον ὅσα δίδωσιν εἰς τὸ [ὑποκείμενον] [1] παρ' αὐτοῦ. Ἀλλ' οὐδὲ ἀνδρὸς τοῦτο ποιεῖν ἢ σοφοῦ τινος καὶ θείου· ἢ θεὸς ἂν ἔχοι, φαίη τις ἄν, τοῦτο τὸ γέρας. Καὶ γὰρ οὐ τοῦ μάντεως τὸ διότι, ἀλλὰ τὸ ὅτι μόνον εἰπεῖν, καὶ ἡ τέχνη ἀνάγνωσις φυσικῶν γραμμάτων καὶ τάξιν δηλούντων καὶ οὐδαμοῦ πρὸς τὸ ἄτακτον ἀποκλινόντων, μᾶλλον δὲ καταμαρτυρούσης τῆς φορᾶς καὶ εἰς φῶς ἀγούσης καὶ πρὶν παρ' αὐτῶν φανῆναι, οἷος ἕκαστος καὶ ὅσα. Συμφέρεται γὰρ καὶ ταῦτα ἐκείνοις κἀκεῖνα τούτοις συντελοῦντα ἅμα πρὸς σύστασιν καὶ ἀιδιότητα κόσμου, ἀναλογίᾳ δὲ σημαίνοντα τὰ ἄλλα τῷ τετηρηκότι· ἐπεὶ καὶ αἱ ἄλλαι μαντικαὶ τῷ ἀναλόγῳ. Οὐ γὰρ ἔδει ἀπηρτῆσθαι ἀλλήλων τὰ πάντα, ὡμοιῶσθαι δὲ πρὸς ἄλληλα ἀμῃγέπῃ. Καὶ τοῦτ' ἂν ἴσως εἴη τὸ λεγόμενον ὡς συνέχει τὰ πάντα ἀναλογία. Ἔστι

[1] ὑποκείμενον del. Bréhier, H–S[2].

---

[1] Plato, *Timaeus* 47E5–48A1.
[2] Simonides, quoted by Plato *Protagoras* 341E3.
[3] Cp. II. 3 [52] 7. 4–6.
[4] Cp. *Timaeus* 31C3 and 32C2. But Plato's ἀναλογία is

in it contemplates at the same time its origins and the providence which watches over it; this certainly extends over all things, including the things which come to be; and these are both living things and their actions and mixed dispositions, "compounded of reason and necessity":[1] so he contemplates things which are mixed and continually go on being mixed; and he cannot himself distinguish providence and what is according to providence clearly on the one side, and on the other the substrate and all that it gives to what results from it. This discrimination is not for a man, except a wise and godlike man: or one might say that "a god alone could have this privilege."[2] In fact, it is not for the diviner to tell the "because" but only the "that"; his art is a reading of letters written in nature,[3] declaring an order and never deviating into disorder, or rather of the heavenly circuit which proclaims and brings to light what each individual is like and all his characteristics even before they appear in the people themselves. For these things here below are carried along with those things in heaven, and those in heaven with these on earth, and both together contribute to the consistency and everlastingness of the universe, and by correspondence indicate the others to the observer; for other forms of divination, too, work by correspondence. For it would not have been right for all things to be cut off from each other but they had to be made like each other, in some way at least. Perhaps this might be the meaning of the saying that correspondence holds all things together.[4] And

mathematical proportion. As usual, Plotinus pays little attention to the mathematical side of Plato's thought.

δὲ τοιοῦτον ἡ ἀναλογία, ὥστε καὶ τὸ χεῖρον πρὸς τὸ χεῖρον ὡς τὸ βέλτιον πρὸς τὸ βέλτιον, οἷον ὡς ὄμμα πρὸς ὄμμα καὶ πους πρὸς πόδα, θάτερον πρὸς θάτερον, καί, εἰ βούλει, ὡς ἀρετὴ πρὸς δικαιοσύνην καὶ κακία πρὸς ἀδικίαν. Εἰ τοίνυν ἀναλογία ἐν τῷ παντί, καὶ προειπεῖν ἔνι· καὶ εἰ ποιεῖ δὲ ἐκεῖνα εἰς ταῦτα, οὕτω ποιεῖ, ὡς καὶ τὰ ἐν παντὶ ζῴῳ εἰς ἄλληλα, οὐχ ὡς θάτερον γεννᾷ θάτερον—ἅμα γὰρ γεννᾶται—ἀλλ' ὡς, ᾗ πέφυκεν ἕκαστον, οὕτω καὶ πάσχει τὸ πρόσφορον εἰς τὴν αὑτοῦ φύσιν, καὶ ὅτι τοῦτο τοιοῦτον, καὶ τὸ τοιοῦτον τοῦτο· οὕτω γὰρ καὶ λόγος εἷς.

7. Καὶ ὅτι δὲ τὰ βελτίω, καὶ τὰ χείρω. Ἐπεὶ πῶς ἂν εἴη τι χεῖρον ἐν πολυειδεῖ μὴ ὄντος βελτίονος, ἢ πῶς τὸ βέλτιον μὴ χείρονος; Ὥστε οὐκ αἰτιατέον τὸ χεῖρον ἐν τῷ βελτίονι, ἀλλὰ ἀποδεκτέον τὸ βέλτιον, ὅτι ἔδωκεν ἑαυτοῦ τῷ χείρονι. Ὅλως δὲ οἱ ἀναιρεῖν ἀξιοῦντες τὸ χεῖρον ἐν τῷ παντὶ ἀναιροῦσι πρόνοιαν αὐτήν. Τίνος γὰρ ἔσται; Οὐ γὰρ δὴ αὐτῆς οὐδὲ τοῦ βελτίονος· ἐπεὶ καὶ τὴν ἄνω πρόνοιαν ὀνομάζοντες πρὸς τὸ κάτω λέγομεν. Τὸ μὲν γὰρ εἰς ἓν πάντα ἀρχή, ἐν ᾗ ὁμοῦ πάντα καὶ ὅλον πάντα. Πρόεισι δὲ ἤδη ἐκ ταύτης ἕκαστα μενούσης ἐκείνης ἔνδον οἷον ἐκ ῥίζης μιᾶς ἑστώσης αὐτῆς ἐν αὐτῇ· τὰ δὲ ἐξήνθησεν εἰς

[1] For the plant-image applied to the physical universe; cp. IV. 4 [28] 11. 9–11.

correspondence is of this kind, that the worse is related to the worse as the better is to the better, for instance, as eye is to eye, so is foot to foot, the one to the other; or, if you like, as virtue is to justice, so is vice to injustice. If, then, there is correspondence in the All, prediction is possible; and if the heavenly bodies act on the things here below, they act in the way in which the parts in every living thing work on each other, not that one thing produces another—they are produced together—but that each thing in accordance with what it naturally is experiences what is suitable to its own nature; because this thing is of this kind, this experience is of this kind too; for so the formative pattern remains one.

7. And because there are better things, there must be worse as well. Or how could there be anything worse in a multiform thing if there was not something better, and how could there be anything better if there was not something worse? So one should not blame the worse when one finds it in the better but approve the better because it has given something of itself to the worse. And altogether, those who make the demand to abolish evil in the All are abolishing providence itself. For what would it be providence of? Certainly not of itself or of the better; for when we speak of providence above, we are using the term of its relation to what is below. For the gathering together of all things into one is the principle, in which all are together and all make a whole. And individual things proceed from this principle while it remains within; they come from it as from a single root which remains static in itself,[1] but they flower out into a divided multiplicity, each

πλῆθος μεμερισμένον εἴδωλον ἕκαστον ἐκείνου φέρον, ἄλλο δὲ ἐν ἄλλῳ ἐνταῦθα ἤδη ἐγίγνετο καὶ ἦν τὰ μὲν πλησίον τῆς ῥίζης, τὰ δὲ προιόντα εἰς τὸ πόρρω ἐσχίζετο καὶ μέχρις οἷον κλάδων καὶ ἄκρων καὶ καρπῶν καὶ φύλλων· καὶ τὰ μὲν ἔμενεν ἀεί, τὰ δὲ ἐγίνετο ἀεί, οἱ καρποὶ καὶ τὰ φύλλα· καὶ τὰ γινόμενα ἀεὶ εἶχε τοὺς τῶν ἐπάνω λόγους ἐν αὐτοῖς οἷον μικρὰ δένδρα βουληθέντα εἶναι, καὶ εἰ ἐγέννησε πρὶν φθαρῆναι, τὸ ἐγγὺς ἐγέννα μόνον. Τὰ δὲ διάκενα οἷον τῶν κλάδων ἐπληροῦτο ἐκ τῶν αὖ ἐκ τῆς ῥίζης καὶ αὐτῶν ἄλλον τρόπον πεφυκότων, ἐξ ὧν καὶ ἔπασχε τὰ ἄκρα τῶν κλάδων, ὡς ἐκ τοῦ πλησίον οἴεσθαι τὸ πάθος ἰέναι μόνον· τὸ δὲ κατὰ τὴν ἀρχὴν αὖ τὸ μὲν ἔπασχε, τὸ δὲ ἐποίει, ἡ δὲ ἀρχὴ ἀνήρτητο καὶ αὐτή. Πόρρωθεν μὲν γὰρ ἐλθόντα ἄλλα τὰ ποιοῦντα εἰς ἄλληλα, ἐξ ἀρχῆς δὲ ἀπὸ τοῦ αὐτοῦ, οἷον εἰ ἀδελφοὶ δρῷέν τι ἀλλήλους ὅμοιοι γενόμενοι ἐκ τῶν αὐτῶν ὁρμηθέντες τῶν πεποιηκότων.

one bearing an image of that higher reality, but when they reach this lower world one comes to be in one place and one in another, and some are close to the root and others advance farther and split up to the point of becoming, so to speak, branches and twigs and fruits and leaves; and those that are closer to the root remain for ever, and the others come into being for ever, the fruits and the leaves; and those which come into being for ever have in them the rational forming principles of those above them, as if they wanted to be little trees; and if they produce before they pass away, they only produce what is near to them. And what are like empty spaces between the branches are filled with shoots which also grow from the root, these, too, in a different way; and the twigs on the branches are also affected by these, so that they think the effect on them is only produced by what is close to them; but in fact the acting and being acted upon are in the principle, and the principle itself, too, is dependent.[1] The principles which act on each other are different because they come from a far-off origin, but in the beginning they come from the same source, as if brothers were to do something to each other who are alike because they originate from the same parents.

[1] The imagery in this sentence is remarkably obscure, but perhaps Plotinus is thinking of apparently disorderly and unplanned shoots which grow between the spaced branches of a well-pruned fruit tree and affect them adversely; these, too, grow from the root and are produced by the growth-principle of the whole tree.

ENNEAD III. 4

III. 4. ON OUR ALLOTTED GUARDIAN SPIRIT

Introductory Note

THIS treatise is No. 15 in the chronological order: it was written, therefore, before Porphyry came to Rome (*Life* ch. 4). Porphyry seems to think that its writing was connected (his language is, perhaps deliberately, vague) with an incident which he records in ch. 10 of the *Life*. An Egyptian priest offered to conjure up the guardian spirit of Plotinus; when the conjuration took place in the temple of Isis at Rome, a god appeared instead of a spirit (on this episode see E. R. Dodds, *The Greeks and the Irrational*, Appendix II, iii, pp. 289–291). But, whatever the connection between this and the writing of the treatise may have been, the doctrine which Plotinus expounds here has little to do with the superstitions of his time or even with the theology of spirits which is to be found in his Platonist predecessors and successors (Proclus criticises Plotinus's interpretation of Plato in his *Commentary on the Alcibiades*, pp. 383–385 Cousin, paras. 75–76 Westerink). Plotinus is concerned to reconcile the various statements which Plato makes about guardian spirits in the myths of the *Phaedo*, *Republic* X and *Timaeus*, and to interpret them in a way which fits his own version of Platonism. He does this by means of his doctrine that each soul is a " universe " (chs. 3 and 6) containing many different levels of reality, on any one of which we may choose to live; the principle, then, on the level above that on which we choose to live, next above the principle which is dominant in us in any particular life, is our " guardian spirit ": if we live

well we may rise to its level in our next life, and so have an even higher being for our "spirit." So the perfectly good and wise man, who lives entirely on the level of Intellect, will have that which is above Intellect, the Good, for his guardian (ch. 6).

Synopsis

Soul has the power of growth, present in us too, but dominant, because isolated, in plants; it gives form to body, its last expression in the world below (ch. 1). The human soul has all powers down to the lowest, and can live on the level of any one of them; its life in its next incarnation, plant, animal or man, will depend on the level it chooses to live on in this one (ch. 2). Man's spirit is the principle on the level above that on which he lives; each of us is an "intelligible universe" (ch. 3). Universal soul and body; the universe has no perceptions or sensations (ch. 4). The "choice of lives" in *Republic* X; the individual is responsible for choosing: the guardian spirit is "ours and not ours": explanation of *Timaeus* 90A (ch. 5). The good man, who lives on the level of Intellect, has the God beyond Intellect for his guardian spirit. Spirits stay with their souls during the intervals between incarnations; at their next incarnation the souls get a new spirit, bad or good according to their deserts. Some souls may ascend to the stars, and these have star-gods for their guardian spirits; we are not only an intelligible universe but have powers in us akin to those of the world-soul, and go to the star appropriate to the power which worked in us. Some go outside the visible world altogether, taking with them the lower soul which desires birth; in what sense this lower soul is divisible. When the soul comes again to the lower world it embarks in it with its spirit as in a ship, and the circuit of the universe carries it on the voyage of life; what happens to it then depends partly on the motion of the universe, partly on itself (ch. 6).

III. 4. (15) ΠΕΡΙ ΤΟΥ ΕΙΛΗΧΟΤΟΣ ΗΜΑΣ ΔΑΙΜΟΝΟΣ

1. Τῶν μὲν αἱ ὑποστάσεις γίνονται μενόντων ἐκείνων, ἡ δὲ ψυχὴ κινουμένη ἐλέγετο γεννᾶν καὶ αἴσθησιν τὴν ἐν ὑποστάσει καὶ φύσιν καὶ μέχρι φυτῶν. Καὶ γὰρ ἔχει αὐτὴν καὶ ἐν ἡμῖν οὖσα, κρατεῖ δὲ μέρος οὖσαν·[1] ὅταν δὲ ἐν φυτοῖς γένηται, αὕτη κρατεῖ οἷον μόνη γενομένη. Αὕτη μὲν οὖν οὐδὲν γεννᾷ; Γεννᾷ πάντη ἕτερον αὑτῆς· οὐκέτι γὰρ ζωὴ μετὰ ταύτην, ἀλλὰ τὸ γεννώμενον ἄζων. Τί οὖν; Ἤ, ὥσπερ πᾶν, ὅσον πρὸ τούτου ἐγεννᾶτο, ἀμόρφωτον ἐγεννᾶτο, εἰδοποιεῖτο δὲ τῷ ἐπιστρέφεσθαι πρὸς τὸ γεννῆσαν οἷον ἐκτρεφόμενον, οὕτω δὴ καὶ ἐνταῦθα τὸ γεννηθὲν οὐ ψυχῆς ἔτι εἶδος—οὐ γὰρ ἔτι ζῇ—ἀλλ' ἀοριστίαν εἶναι παντελῆ. Εἰ μὲν γὰρ κἀν τοῖς προτέροις ἡ ἀοριστία, ἀλλ' ἐν εἴδει· οὐ γὰρ πάντη ἀόριστον, ἀλλ' ὡς πρὸς τὴν τελείωσιν αὐτοῦ· τὸ δὲ νῦν πάντη. Τελειούμενον δὲ γίνεται σῶμα μορφὴν λαβὸν τὴν τῇ δυνάμει

[1] οὖσαν Kirchhoff: οὖσα codd.

---

[1] Cp. Plato, *Phaedo* 107D6–7 . . . τελευτήσαντα ἕκαστον ὁ ἑκάστου δαίμων, ὅσπερ ζῶντα εἰλήχει, οὗτος ἄγειν ἐπιχειρεῖ . . .

[2] The reference is to V. 2 [11] 1. 18–21.

III. 4. ON OUR ALLOTTED GUARDIAN SPIRIT[1]

1. The expressions of some realities come into existence while the realities themselves remain unmoved, but soul has been already said to be in motion when it generates the sense-perception which is its expressed form and the power of growth which extends also to plants.[2] For soul has the power of growth when it exists in us, too, but it dominates it because it is only a part; but when it comes to be in plants, this power of growth dominates because it has, so to speak, become isolated. Does this power of growth, then, produce nothing? It produces a thing altogether different from itself; for after it there is no more life, but what is produced is lifeless. What is it then? Just as everything which was produced before this was produced shapeless, but was formed by turning towards its producer and being, so to speak, reared to maturity by it, so here, too, that which is produced is not any more a form of soul—for it is not alive—but absolute indefiniteness. For even if there is indefiniteness in the things before it, it is nevertheless indefiniteness within form; the thing is not absolutely indefinite but only in relation to its perfection; but what we are dealing with now is absolutely indefinite. When it is perfected it becomes a body, receiving the form appropriate to its

πρόσφορον, ὑποδοχὴ[1] τοῦ γεννήσαντος καὶ ἐκθρέψαντος· καὶ μόνον τοῦτο ἐν σώματι ἔσχατον τῶν ἄνω ἐν ἐσχάτῳ τοῦ κάτω.

2. Καὶ τὸ «ψυχὴ πᾶσα ἐπιμελεῖται τοῦ ἀψύχου» ἐπὶ ταύτης μάλιστα· αἱ δ' ἄλλαι ἄλλως. Πάντα δὲ οὐρανὸν περιπολεῖ ἄλλοτε ἐν ἄλλοις εἴδεσιν, ἢ ἐν αἰσθητικῷ εἴδει ἢ ἐν λογικῷ ἢ ἐν αὐτῷ τῷ φυτικῷ. Τὸ γὰρ κρατοῦν αὐτῆς μόριον τὸ ἑαυτῷ πρόσφορον ποιεῖ, τὰ δ' ἄλλα ἀργεῖ· ἔξω γάρ. Ἐν δὲ ἀνθρώπῳ οὐ κρατεῖ τὰ χείρω, ἀλλὰ σύνεστιν· οὐδέ γε τὸ κρεῖττον ἀεί· ἔστι γὰρ καὶ ταῦτα χώραν τινὰ ἔχοντα. Διὸ καὶ ὡς αἰσθητικοί· ἔστι γὰρ καὶ ὄργανα αἰσθήσεως· καὶ πολλὰ ὡς φυτά· ἔστι γὰρ σῶμα αὐξόμενον καὶ γεννῶν· ὥστε πάντα συνεργεῖ, κατὰ δὲ τὸ κρεῖττον τὸ ὅλον εἶδος ἄνθρωπος. Ἐξελθοῦσα δέ, ὅ τι περ ἐπλεόνασε, τοῦτο γίνεται. Διὸ φεύγειν δεῖ πρὸς τὸ ἄνω, ἵνα μὴ εἰς τὴν αἰσθητικὴν ἐπακολουθοῦντες τοῖς αἰσθητοῖς εἰδώλοις, μηδὲ εἰς τὴν φυτικὴν ἐπακολουθοῦντες τῇ ἐφέσει τοῦ γεννᾶν καὶ ἐδωδῶν λιχνείαις, ἀλλ' εἰς τὸ νοερὸν καὶ νοῦν καὶ θεόν. Ὅσοι μὲν οὖν τὸν ἄνθρωπον ἐτήρησαν, πάλιν ἄνθρωποι. Ὅσοι δὲ αἰσθήσει μόνον ἔζησαν, ζῷα· ἀλλ' εἰ μὲν αἰσθήσεις μετὰ

[1] ὑποδοχὴ Kirchhoff: ὑποδοχὴν codd.

---

[1] These two quotations are from Plato, *Phaedrus* 246B6–7.

[2] Again the favourite passage from Plato, *Theaetetus*, 176A8–B1.

[3] The phrase is taken from *Republic* VII. 519B1–2.

potentiality, a receiver for the principle which produced it and brought it to maturity. And only this form in body is the last representative of the powers above in the last depth of the world below.

2. And the text "All soul cares for that which is without soul" applies to this [the power of growth] in particular; other kinds of soul [care for the inanimate] in other ways. "It traverses the whole universe in different forms at different times,"[1] either in the perceptive form or the rational or in this very growth-form. For the dominant part of it makes the thing appropriate to itself, but the other parts do nothing, for they are outside. In man, however, the inferior parts are not dominant but they are also present; and in fact the better part does not always dominate; the other parts exist and have a certain place. Therefore we also live like beings characterised by sense-perception, for we, too, have sense-organs; and in many ways we live like plants, for we have a body which grows and produces; so that all things work together, but the whole form is man in virtue of its better part. But when it goes out of the body it becomes what there was most of in it. Therefore one must "escape"[2] to the upper world, that we may not sink to the level of sense-perception by pursuing the images of sense, or to the level of the growth-principle by following the urge for generation and the "gluttonous love of good eating,"[3] but may rise to the intelligible and intellect and God. Those, then, who guarded the man in them, become men again. Those who lived by sense alone become animals; but if their sense-perceptions have been accompanied by passionate

θυμοῦ, τὰ ἄγρια, καὶ ἡ διαφορὰ ἡ ἐν τούτοις τὸ διάφορον τῶν τοιούτων ποιεῖ· ὅσοι δὲ μετ' ἐπιθυμίας καὶ τῆς ἡδονῆς τοῦ ἐπιθυμοῦντος, τὰ ἀκόλαστα τῶν ζῴων καὶ γαστρίμαργα. Εἰ δὲ μηδ' αἰσθήσει μετὰ τούτων, ἀλλὰ νωθείᾳ αἰσθήσεως μετ' αὐτῶν, καὶ φυτά· μόνον γὰρ τοῦτο ἢ μάλιστα ἐνήργει τὸ φυτικόν, καὶ ἦν αὐτοῖς μελέτη δενδρωθῆναι. Τοὺς δὲ φιλομούσους μέν, καθαρίους δὲ τὰ ἄλλα, εἰς τὰ ᾠδικά· τοὺς δὲ ἀλόγως βασιλέας αἰετούς, εἰ μὴ ἄλλη κακία παρείη· μετεωρολόγους δὲ ἄνευ φρονήσεως εἰς τὸν οὐρανὸν ἀεὶ αἰρομένους εἰς ὄρνεις μετεώρους ταῖς πτήσεσιν. Ὁ δὲ τὴν πολιτικὴν ἀρετὴν ἄνθρωπος· ὁ δ' ἧττον ἀρετῆς πολιτικῆς μετέχων πολιτικὸν ζῷον, μέλιττα ἢ τὰ τοιαῦτα.

3. Τίς οὖν δαίμων; ὁ καὶ ἐνταῦθα. Τίς δὲ θεός; ἢ ὁ ἐνταῦθα. Τὸ γὰρ ἐνεργῆσαν τοῦτο ἕκαστον[1] ἄγει, ἅτε καὶ ἐνταῦθα ἡγούμενον. Ἆρ' οὖν τοῦτό

[1] ἕκαστον AB Harder: ἑκάστου ERJ y Q.

---

[1] For reincarnation in appropriate animal forms see Plato, *Phaedo* 81E–82B, *Republic* X. 620, and *Timaeus* 91–92. The lowest form of life to which a human soul can sink in Plato is that of an oyster (*Timaeus* 92B6–7), but reincarnation as a plant appears in Empedocles (Frs. 117, 127 Diels-Kranz). In spite of the somewhat light-hearted way in which Plotinus (following Plato) touches on the future of stupid kings (is there perhaps a disrespectful allusion here to the formality of releasing an eagle from the imperial pyre?) and unphilosophic

temper they become wild animals, and the difference in temper in them makes the differences between the animals of this kind; those whose sense-perceptions went with desires of the flesh and the delight of the desiring part of the soul become lustful and gluttonous animals.[1] But if they did not even live by sense along with their desires but coupled them with dullness of perception, they even turn into plants; for it was this, the growth-principle which worked in them, alone or predominantly, and they were taking care to turn themselves into trees. Those who loved music but were in other ways respectable turn into song-birds; kings who ruled stupidly into eagles, if they had no other vices; astronomers who were always raising themselves to the sky without philosophic reflection turn into birds which fly high. The man who practised community virtue becomes a man again; but one who has a lesser share of it a creature that lives in community, a bee or something of the sort.

3. Who, then, becomes a spirit? He who was one here too. And who a god? Certainly he who was one here. For what worked in a man leads him[2] [after death], since it was his ruler and guide here

astronomers, there is no doubt that he took Plato's statements about animal reincarnation literally and seriously; cp. e.g., VI. 7 [38] 6. 20 ff. Porphyry disagreed with his master on this point (Augustine *De Civ. Dei* X. 30). On the differing opinions held by Platonists on animal reincarnation see H. Dörrie *Kontroverse um die Seelenwanderung im kaiserzeitlichen Platonismus*, *Hermes* 85. 4 (Dec. 1957), pp. 414–435.

[2] ἑκάστου printed by Henry-Schwyzer here, seems to me impossible. I adopt ἕκαστον which appears in the MSS A and B, and which Dr. Schwyzer now considers necessary.

ἐστιν ὁ δαίμων, ὅσπερ ζῶντα εἰλήχει; Ἢ οὔ, ἀλλὰ τὸ πρὸ αὐτοῦ· τοῦτο γὰρ ἐφέστηκεν ἀργοῦν, ἐνεργεῖ δὲ τὸ μετ' αὐτόν. Καὶ εἰ μὲν τὸ ἐνεργοῦν ᾗ αἰσθητικοί, καὶ ὁ δαίμων τὸ λογικόν· εἰ δὲ κατὰ τὸ λογικὸν ζῴημεν, ὁ δαίμων τὸ ὑπὲρ τοῦτο ἐφεστὼς ἀργὸς συγχωρῶν τῷ ἐργαζομένῳ. Ὀρθῶς οὖν λέγεται ἡμᾶς αἱρήσεσθαι. Τὸν γὰρ ὑπερκείμενον κατὰ τὴν ζωὴν αἱρούμεθα. Διὰ τί οὖν αὐτὸς ἄγει; Ἢ τὸν βιοτεύσαντα οὐκ ἔστιν ἄγειν, ἀλλὰ πρὸ τοῦ μὲν ἄγειν, ὅτε ἔζη, παυσάμενον δὲ τοῦ ζῆν ἄλλῳ παραχωρεῖν τὴν ἐνέργειαν τεθνηκότα τὴν αὐτοῦ κατ' ἐνέργειαν ζωήν. Ὁ μὲν οὖν ἐθέλει ἄγειν καὶ κρατήσας ζῇ αὐτὸς ἄλλον καὶ αὐτὸς ἔχων δαίμονα· εἰ δὲ βαρύνοιτο τῇ ῥώσει τοῦ χείρονος ἤθους, ἔχει ἐκεῖνο τὴν δίκην. Ταύτῃ καὶ ὁ κακὸς ἐπὶ τὸ χεῖρον βρίσαντος πρὸς τὴν ὁμοιότητα τοῦ ἐνεργήσαντος ἐν τῇ ζωῇ εἰς βίον θήρειον. Εἰ δὲ ἕπεσθαι δύναιτο τῷ δαίμονι τῷ ἄνω αὐτοῦ, ἄνω γίνεται ἐκεῖνον ζῶν καὶ ἐφ' ὃ ἄγεται κρεῖττον μέρος αὐτοῦ ἐν προστασίᾳ θέμενος καὶ μετ' ἐκεῖνον ἄλλον ἕως ἄνω. Ἔστι γὰρ καὶ πολλὰ ἡ ψυχὴ καὶ πάντα καὶ τὰ ἄνω καὶ τὰ κάτω αὖ μέχρι πάσης

---

[1] See note on title of this treatise.

[2] *Republic* X. 617E1. [3] *Phaedo* 107D7.

too. Is this, then, "the spirit to whom he was allotted while he lived"?[1] No, but that which is before the working principle; for this presides inactive over the man, but that which comes after it acts. If the working principle is that by which we have sense-perception, the spirit is the rational principle; but if we live by the rational principle, the spirit is what is above this, presiding inactive and giving its consent to the principle which works. So it is rightly said that "we shall choose."[2] For we choose the principle which stands above us according to our choice of life. Why, then, does the spirit "lead"[3] us? It is not possible for the principle which led the man in life to lead [after death], but only before, when the man lived; when he ceases to live the principle must hand over its activity to another, since he has died in the life which corresponded to that spirit's activity. This [other principle], then, wants to lead, and when it has become dominant lives itself and has itself, too, a different spirit; but if it is weighed down by the force of its bad character, this weighing down contains in itself the penalty. In this way, too, the wicked man, since the principle which worked in him during his life has pressed him down to the worse, towards what is like itself, enters into the life of a beast. But if a man is able to follow the spirit which is above him, he comes to be himself above, living that spirit's life, and giving the pre-eminence to that better part of himself to which he is being led; and after that spirit he rises to another, until he reaches the heights. For the soul is many things, and all things, both the things above and the things below down to the limits

ζωῆς, καὶ ἐσμὲν ἕκαστος κόσμος νοητός, τοῖς μὲν κάτω συνάπτοντες τῷδε, τοῖς δὲ ἄνω καὶ τοῖς κόσμου τῷ νοητῷ, καὶ μένομεν τῷ μὲν ἄλλῳ παντὶ νοητῷ ἄνω, τῷ δὲ ἐσχάτῳ αὐτοῦ πεπεδήμεθα τῷ κάτω οἷον ἀπόρροιαν ἀπ᾽ ἐκείνου διδόντες εἰς τὸ κάτω, μᾶλλον δὲ ἐνέργειαν, ἐκείνου οὐκ ἐλαττουμένου.

4. Ἆρ᾽ οὖν ἀεὶ ἐν σώματι τοῦτο; Ἢ οὔ· ἐὰν γὰρ στραφῶμεν, συνεπιστρέφεται καὶ τοῦτο. Τί οὖν ἡ τοῦ παντός; Ἀποστήσεται καὶ τὸ αὐτῆς μέρος στραφείσης; Ἢ οὐδὲ συνένευσε τῷ μέρει αὐτῆς τῷ ἐσχάτῳ· οὐδὲ γὰρ ἦλθεν οὐδὲ κατῆλθεν, ἀλλὰ μενούσης προσάπτεται τὸ σῶμα τοῦ κόσμου καὶ οἷον καταλάμπεται, οὐκ ἐνοχλοῦν οὐδὲ [1] παρέχον μερίμνας, ἐν ἀσφαλεῖ τοῦ κόσμου κειμένου. Τί οὖν; Οὐκ αἰσθάνεταί τινα αἴσθησιν; Ὅρασιν οὐκ ἔχει, φησίν, ὅτι μηδὲ ὀφθαλμούς· οὐδὲ ὦτα οὐδὲ ῥῖνας δηλονότι οὐδὲ γλῶτταν. Τί οὖν; Συναίσθησιν ὥσπερ ἡμεῖς τῶν ἐντὸς ἡμῶν; Ἢ ὁμοίως κατὰ φύσιν ἐχόντων ἠρέμησις. Οὐδὲ ἡδονή. Πάρεστιν οὖν καὶ τὸ φυτικὸν οὐ παρὸν καὶ τὸ αἰσθητικὸν ὡσαύτως. Ἀλλὰ περὶ μὲν τοῦ

[1] οὐκ ἐνοχλοῦν οὐδὲ Müller, H–S²: οὐκ ἐνοχλουμένου δὲ codd.

---

[1] This sentence shows very clearly how Plotinus thinks of soul as a rich, complex unity capable of existing on many levels and operating in many ways, which can be distinguished but must not be separated. This was a way of thinking which was quite unacceptable to the later Neoplatonists, with their

of all life, and we are each one of us an intelligible universe, making contact with this lower world by the powers of soul below, but with the intelligible world by its powers above and the powers of the universe; and we remain with all the rest of our intelligible part above, but by its ultimate fringe we are tied to the world below, giving a kind of outflow from it to what is below, or rather an activity, by which that intelligible part is not itself lessened.[1]

4. Is this lower part, then, always in body? No; if we turn, this, too, turns with us to the upper world. What, then, about the soul of the universe? Will its [lower] part leave the body when it turns? No; it has not even inclined with its lower part to the last depth; for it did not come or come down but as it abides the body of the universe attaches itself to it and is, as it were, illumined, not annoying the soul or causing it any worries, for the universe lies in safety. What, has it then no kind of perception? Plato says that it has no sight, because it has no eyes either; nor ears nor nostrils either, obviously, nor tongue.[2] Well, then, has it an immanent sensation as we have of what goes on inside us? No, for things which are uniformly in accord with nature are quiet. It has no pleasure either. So the principle of growth is present in it without being present, and the principle of sense in the same way. But we deal with the universe in

passion for sharp distinction and separation, and desire to put and keep man in his proper place low down in the elaborate hierarchy of being. Proclus sharply criticises this passage of Plotinus in his Commentary on *Parmenides* 134A (V, p. 948, 14–20; ed. Cousin 1864); see P. Henry *États du Texte de Plotin*, pp. 220–221.

[2] Cp. *Timaeus* 33C.

κόσμου ἐν ἄλλοις· νῦν δὲ ὅσον ἐφήπτετο ἡ ἀπορία αὐτοῦ εἴρηται.

5. Ἀλλ᾽ εἰ ἐκεῖ αἱρεῖται τὸν δαίμονα καὶ εἰ τὸν βίον, πῶς ἔτι τινὸς κύριοι; Ἢ καὶ ἡ αἵρεσις ἐκεῖ ἡ λεγομένη τὴν τῆς ψυχῆς προαίρεσιν καὶ διάθεσιν καθόλου καὶ πανταχοῦ αἰνίττεται. Ἀλλ᾽ εἰ ἡ προαίρεσις τῆς ψυχῆς κυρία καὶ τοῦτο κρατεῖ, ὃ ἂν πρόχειρον ἔχῃ μέρος ἐκ τῶν προβεβιωμένων, οὐκέτι τὸ σῶμα αἴτιον οὐδενὸς κακοῦ αὐτῷ· εἰ γὰρ προτερεῖ τὸ τῆς ψυχῆς ἦθος τοῦ σώματος καὶ τοῦτ᾽ ἔχει, ὃ εἵλετο, καὶ τὸν δαίμονα, φησίν, οὐκ ἀλλάττεται, οὐδὲ ὁ σπουδαῖος ἐνταῦθα γίγνεται οὐδ᾽ ὁ φαῦλος. Ἆρ᾽ οὖν δυνάμει ἐστὶν ἑκάτερος, ἐνεργείᾳ δὲ γίγνεται; Τί οὖν, εἰ φαύλου σώματος ὁ τὸ ἦθος σπουδαῖος τύχοι, ὁ δὲ τἀναντία; Ἢ δύναται μᾶλλον καὶ ἧττον τὰ τῆς ψυχῆς ἑκατέρας ἑκάτερα τὰ σώματα παρέχεσθαι, ἐπεὶ καὶ αἱ ἄλλαι ἔξωθεν τύχαι τὴν ὅλην προαίρεσιν οὐκ ἐκβιβάζουσιν. Ὅταν δὲ λέγηται, ὡς πρῶτον οἱ κλῆροι, εἶτα τὰ τῶν βίων παραδείγματα, †ἔπειτα ταῖς τύχαις†[1] καὶ ὡς ἐκ τῶν παρόντων τοὺς βίους,

[1] ἔπειτα ⟨τὰ ἐν⟩ ταῖς τύχαις Creuzer, sed locus nondum sanatus.

---

[1] Cp. *Republic* X. 620D8–E1.

[2] The text here is clearly corrupt. Plotinus is commenting on the description of the choice of lives in *Republic* X. 617E–620D. If Creuzer's insertion ἔπειτα ⟨τὰ ἐν⟩ ταῖς τύχαις is accepted, it is just possible to see in these words an obscure allusion to 619B–C, the case of the man who chose the biggest tyranny he could find, neglecting to observe that there was contained in it the fate that he should eat his children and suffer many other evils, and the remarks that follow on the

other treatises; now we have said as much about it as is relevant to our problem.

5. But if the soul chooses its guardian spirit and chooses its life there in the other world, how have we still [in this world] any power of decision? The choice in the other world which Plato speaks of is really a riddling representation of the soul's universal and permanent purpose and disposition. But if the soul's purpose is decisive, and that part of it dominates which lies ready to hand as the result of its previous lives, the body is no longer responsible for any evil which may affect the man. For if the soul's character exists before the body, and has what it chose, and, Plato says, does not change its guardian spirit,[1] then the good man does not come into existence here below, and neither does the worthless one. Is man, then, one or the other potentially [in the other world] and does he become actually good or bad [in this world]? What, then, if a man who is good in character happens to get a bad body, and a bad man meets the opposite fortune? The powers of either kind of soul, can, more or less, make their bodies of either kind, since other external chances, too, cannot turn aside the whole purpose of the soul. But when it is said that first come the "lots," then "the examples of lives," then what lies in the fortunes of the lives,[2] then that they choose their lives from those

mistakes in choosing made by the inexperienced and unintelligently virtuous: there does seem here a distinction implicit in Plato's text between the "examples of lives" and "what lies in the fortunes of the lives," between the general type of life and the particular fortunes or misfortunes contained in it. I have translated Creuzer's text on this assumption, but am not at all certain that this is the right solution.

κατὰ τὰ ἤθη τὸ κύριον μᾶλλον δίδωσι ταῖς ψυχαῖς διατιθείσαις τὰ δοθέντα πρὸς τὰ αὐτῶν ἤθη. Ὅτι γὰρ ὁ δαίμων οὗτος οὐ παντάπασιν ἔξω—ἀλλ' οὕτως ὡς μὴ συνδεδεμένος—οὐδ' ἐνεργῶν, ἡμέτερος δέ, ὡς ψυχῆς πέρι εἰπεῖν, οὐχ ὁ ἡμέτερος δέ, εἰ ὡς ἄνθρωποι τοιοίδε τὴν ὑπ' αὐτὸν ζωὴν ἔχοντες, μαρτυρεῖ τὰ ἐν τῷ Τιμαίῳ· ἃ εἰ μὲν οὕτω ληφθείη, οὐδεμίαν ἕξει μάχην σχόντα ἄν τινα ἀσυμφωνίαν, εἰ ἄλλως ὁ δαίμων ληφθείη. Τὸ δὲ ἀποπληρωτὴν ὧν τις εἵλετο καὶ αὐτὸ σύμφωνον. Οὔτε γὰρ πολὺ κατωτέρω ἐᾷ ἐλθεῖν εἰς τὸ χεῖρον ὑπερκαθήμενος, ἀλλ' ἐκεῖνο ἐνεργεῖ μόνον τὸ ὑπ' αὐτόν, οὔτε ὑπεράνω αὐτοῦ οὔτε εἰς ἴσον· οὐ γὰρ δύναται ἄλλο γενέσθαι ἢ ᾗ ἐστι.

6. Τί οὖν ὁ σπουδαῖος; Ἢ ὁ τῷ βελτίονι ἐνεργῶν. Ἢ οὐκ ἂν ἦν σπουδαῖος συνεργοῦντα ἑαυτῷ τὸν δαίμονα ἔχων. Νοῦς γὰρ ἐνεργεῖ ἐν τούτῳ. Ἢ οὖν δαίμων αὐτὸς ἢ κατὰ δαίμονα καὶ δαίμων τούτῳ θεός. Ἆρ' οὖν καὶ ὑπὲρ νοῦν; Εἰ τὸ ὑπὲρ νοῦν δαίμων αὐτῷ, διὰ τί οὐκ ἐξ ἀρχῆς; Ἢ διὰ τὸν θόρυβον τὸν ἐκ τῆς γενέσεως. Ὑπάρχει δὲ ὅμως καὶ πρὸ λόγου ἡ κίνησις ἡ ἔνδοθεν ὀρεγομένη τῶν αὐτῆς. Πάντως οὖν κατορθοῖ;

---

[1] *Timaeus* 90A, the passage where the *δαίμων* is identified with the highest part of our soul, the immortal reason.

[2] *Republic* X. 620E1.

[3] Cp. *Timaeus* 43A6–44B7.

presented to them according to their characters, Plato gives the power of decision rather to the souls, which adapt what is given to them to their own characters. For that this guardian spirit is not entirely outside but only in the sense that he is not bound to us, and is not active in us but is ours, to speak in terms of soul, but not ours if we are considered as men of a particular kind who have a life which is subject to him, is shown by what is said in the *Timaeus*;[1] if the passage is taken in this way it will contain no contradiction, but it would have some disaccord if the spirit was understood otherwise. And the " fulfiller of what one has chosen "[2] is also in accord. For the spirit sits above us, and does not let us go down much lower into evil, but that alone acts in us which is under the spirit, not above him or on a level with him; for it is impossible for the spirit to become something else than [a being appropriate to the place] where he is.

6. What, then, is the nobly good man? He is the man who acts by his better part. He would not have been a good man if he had the guardian spirit as a partner in his own activity. For intellect is active in the good man. He is, then, himself a spirit or on the level of a spirit, and his guardian spirit is God. Is it, then, even above intellect? If that which is above intellect is his guardian spirit, why, then, is he not a man of noble goodness from the beginning? It is because of the " disturbance " which comes from birth.[3] But all the same, even before reason there is in him the inward movement which reaches out towards its own. Does the spirit, then, always and in every way accomplish its task successfully? Not

Ἢ οὐ πάντως, εἴπερ οὕτως ἡ ψυχὴ διαθέσεως ἔχει, ὡς ἐν τούτοις τοῖς τοιοῖσδε τοιάδε οὖσα τοῦτον ἔχειν βίον καὶ ταύτην προαίρεσιν. Ὁ μέντοι δαίμων οὗτος, ὃν λέγομεν, ἀγαγὼν λέγεται εἰς Ἅιδου οὐκέτι ὁ αὐτὸς μένειν, ἐὰν μὴ τὰ αὐτὰ ἕληται πάλιν. Πρὸ δὲ τοῦ πῶς; Τὸ δὴ ἀγαγεῖν εἰς τὴν κρίσιν τὸ εἰς τὸ αὐτὸ σχῆμα ἐλθεῖν μετὰ τὴν ἀπογένεσιν, ὃ εἶχε πρὸ τῆς γενέσεως· εἶτα ὥσπερ ἀπ' ἀρχῆς ἄλλης τὸν μεταξὺ τῆς ὕστερον γενέσεως χρόνον ταῖς κολαζομέναις πάρεστιν. Ἢ οὐδὲ βίος αὐταῖς, ἀλλὰ δίκη. Τί δὲ ταῖς εἰς θήρεια σώματα εἰσιούσαις; ἔλαττον ἢ δαίμων; Ἢ πονηρός γε ἢ εὐήθης. Ταῖς δὲ ἄνω; Ἢ τῶν ἄνω αἱ μὲν ἐν αἰσθητῷ, αἱ δὲ ἔξω. Αἱ μὲν οὖν ἐν αἰσθητῷ ἢ ἐν ἡλίῳ ἢ ἐν ἄλλῳ τῶν πλανωμένων, αἱ δ' ἐν τῇ ἀπλανεῖ, ἑκάστη καθὸ λογικῶς ἐνήργησεν ἐνταῦθα· χρὴ γὰρ οἴεσθαι καὶ κόσμον εἶναι ἐν τῇ ψυχῇ ἡμῶν μὴ μόνον νοητόν, ἀλλὰ καὶ ψυχῆς τῆς κόσμου ὁμοειδῆ διάθεσιν· νενεμημένης οὖν κἀκείνης εἴς τε τὴν ἀπλανῆ καὶ τὰς πλανωμένας κατὰ δυνάμεις διαφόρους ὁμοειδεῖς ταύταις ταῖς δυνάμεσι καὶ τὰς παρ' ἡμῖν εἶναι καὶ ἐνέργειαν εἶναι παρ' ἑκάστης καὶ ἀπαλλαγείσας ἐκεῖ γίνεσθαι

---

[1] Cp. *Phaedo* 107D7–E4.

[2] Here, and in what follows, Plotinus is basing his thought on *Timaeus* 41D6–42D1, where the Demiurge at his original making of souls which are to be born into this word allots each of them to a star, and promises them that they will each return to their appropriate star if they overcome the disturbances and temptations of mortal life.

[3] Cp. *Timaeus* 41D4–7.

altogether, since the soul is of such a disposition that it is of a particular kind in particular circumstances and so has a life and a purpose corresponding to its kind and circumstances. Now this spirit of whom we are speaking is said, when it has led the soul to Hades,[1] no longer to remain the same, unless the soul chooses again the same type of life. But what happens before [the choice of lives]? The leading to judgement means that the spirit comes to the same form after the soul's departure from this life as it had before the soul's birth; then, as if from a different starting-point, it is present to the souls which are being punished during the time which intervenes before their next birth—this is not a life for them, but an expiation. But what about the souls which enter into the bodies of brutes? Is their guardian something less than a spirit? It *is* a spirit, a wicked or stupid one. And what about those in the upper world? Of those in the upper world, some are in the visible region and some outside. Those, then, in the visible region are in the sun or in another of the moving stars, and some of them in the sphere of the fixed stars, each according to his rational activity here:[2] for one must think that there is a universe in our soul, not only an intelligible one but an arrangement like in form to that of the soul of the world:[3] so, as that, too, is distributed according to its diverse powers into the sphere of the fixed stars and those of the moving stars,[4] the powers in our soul also are of like form to these powers, and there is an activity proceeding from each power, and when the souls are

[4] Cp. *Timaeus* 38C–40B.

πρὸς ἄστρον τὸ σύμφωνον τῷ ἐνεργήσαντι καὶ ζήσαντι ἤθει καὶ δυνάμει· καὶ τοιούτῳ θεῷ καὶ δαίμονί γε ἢ αὐτῷ τούτῳ χρήσεται ἢ τῷ ὑπὲρ ταύτην τὴν δύναμιν· σκεπτέον δὲ τοῦτο βέλτιον. Τὰς δ' ἔξω γενομένας τὴν δαιμονίαν φύσιν ὑπερβεβηκέναι καὶ πᾶσαν εἱμαρμένην γενέσεως καὶ ὅλως ⟨τὸ⟩[1] ἐν τῷδε τῷ ὁρατῷ, ἕως ἐστὶν ἐκεῖ, συνανενεχθείσης καὶ τῆς ἐν αὐτῇ φιλογενέσεως οὐσίας, ἣν εἴ τις λέγοι ταύτην εἶναι τὴν περὶ τὰ σώματα γινομένην μεριστὴν συμπληθύουσαν ἑαυτὴν καὶ συμμερίζουσαν τοῖς σώμασιν, ὀρθῶς λέξει. Μερίζεται δὲ οὐ μεγέθει· τὸ γὰρ αὐτὸ ἐν πᾶσιν ὅλον καὶ πάλιν ἕν· καὶ ἐξ ἑνὸς ζῴου ἀεὶ πολλὰ γεννᾶται ταύτης μεριζομένης οὕτως, ὥσπερ καὶ ἐκ τῶν φυτῶν· περὶ τὰ σώματα γὰρ καὶ αὕτη μεριστή. Καὶ ὁτὲ μὲν μένουσα ἐπὶ τοῦ αὐτοῦ δίδωσιν, οἷον ἡ ἐν τοῖς φυτοῖς· ὅπου δὲ ἀπελθοῦσα πρὶν ἀπελθεῖν ἔδωκεν, οἷον καὶ ἐν τοῖς ἀνῃρημένοις φυτοῖς ἢ ἐν ζῴοις ἀποθανοῦσιν ἐκ σήψεως πολλῶν ἐξ ἑνὸς γεννηθέντων. Συνεργεῖν δὲ καὶ [τὴν][2] ἐκ τοῦ παντὸς τὴν τοιαύτην δύναμιν ἐνταῦθα τὴν αὐτὴν οὖσαν.

Πάλιν δὲ ἐὰν ἴῃ ἡ ψυχὴ ἐνταῦθα, ἢ τὸν αὐτὸν ἢ

[1] ⟨τὸ⟩ Kirchhoff, H–S.
[2] τὴν del. Kirchhoff, H–S[2].

[1] Plotinus may be thinking here of Plato, *Laws* X. 898E–899A, where Plato leaves it open whether the soul which

set free they come there to the star which is in harmony with the character and power which lived and worked in them; and each will have a god of this kind as its guardian spirit, either the star itself or the god set above this power; but this requires more accurate investigation.[1] But those which have come to be outside have transcended the nature of spirits and the whole destiny of birth, and altogether what is in this visible world; as long as the soul is there, the substance in it which desires birth is taken up with it; if anyone should say that this substance is "the soul which has come to be among bodies and is divisible,"[2] multiplying and dividing itself with its bodies, he will speak correctly. But it is not divided quantitatively, for it is the same thing in all, a whole and again one; and since this soul is in process of division in this way, many animals are always produced from one, as happens also with plants, for this [the plant-soul], too, is also divisible among bodies. And sometimes the soul remains in the same living thing and gives [life to others], like the soul in plants; but sometimes when it goes away it gives before it goes, as with plants which have been pulled up or dead animals, when from their corruption many are generated from one. And the soul-power from the All co-operates, the particular power which is the same here too.

But if the soul comes here again, it has either the same or another guardian spirit according to the life

governs the sun is related to it as our soul is to our body, or directs it in some quite different way.

[2] *Timaeus* 35 A 2–3; cp. the fuller discussions of the "divisibility" of the soul, with reference to this passage of the *Timaeus* in IV. 9 [8] and IV. 3 [27] 19.

ἄλλον ἔχει δαίμονα κατὰ τὴν ζωήν, ἣν ποιήσεται. Ἐπιβαίνει οὖν μετὰ τούτου τοῦ δαίμονος ὥσπερ σκάφους τοῦδε τοῦ παντὸς πρῶτον, εἶτα παραλαβοῦσα ἡ τοῦ ἀτράκτου λεγομένη φύσις κατέταξεν ὥσπερ ἐν νηὶ εἴς τινα ἕδραν τύχης. Περιαγούσης δὲ τῆς περιφορᾶς ὥσπερ πνεύματος τὸν ἐπὶ τῆς νεὼς καθήμενον ἢ καὶ φερόμενον πολλαὶ καὶ ποικίλαι γίνονται καὶ θέαι καὶ μεταθέσεις καὶ συμπτώματα, καὶ ὥσπερ ἐν αὐτῇ τῇ νηὶ ἢ παρὰ τοῦ σάλου τῆς νεὼς ἢ παρ' αὐτοῦ κινηθέντος ὁρμῇ οἰκείᾳ, ἣν ἂν σχοίη τῷ ἐπὶ νεὼς εἶναι παρὰ τὸν ἑαυτοῦ τρόπον. Οὐ γὰρ ὁμοίως ἐν τοῖς αὐτοῖς πᾶς κινεῖται ἢ βούλεται ἢ ἐνεργεῖ. Γίνεται οὖν διάφορα διαφόροις ἢ ἐκ τῶν αὐτῶν ἢ διαφόρων προσπεσόντων, ἢ τὰ αὐτὰ ἄλλοις, κἂν διάφορα τὰ προσπεσόντα· τοιοῦτον γὰρ ἡ εἱμαρμένη.

which it is going to make for itself. It embarks, then, with this spirit first of all in this universe as if in a boat, then the nature which has the name of the "Spindle"[1] takes it over and sets it, just as in a ship, in some seat of fortune. And as the circuit of heaven, like a wind, carries round the man sitting, or even moving about, on the ship, there occur many and various sights and changes and incidents, and, just as in the actual ship, [they occur because] he is moved either by the tossing of the ship or by himself, of his own impulse, whatever it may be, which he has because he is on the ship precisely in his own way. For everyone is not moved and does not will or act alike in the same circumstances. So different things happen to different people as a result of the same or different occurrences, or the same things to others even if the circumstances they encounter are different; for that is what destiny is like.

[1] Cp. *Republic* X. 616C4 ff.

ENNEAD III. 5

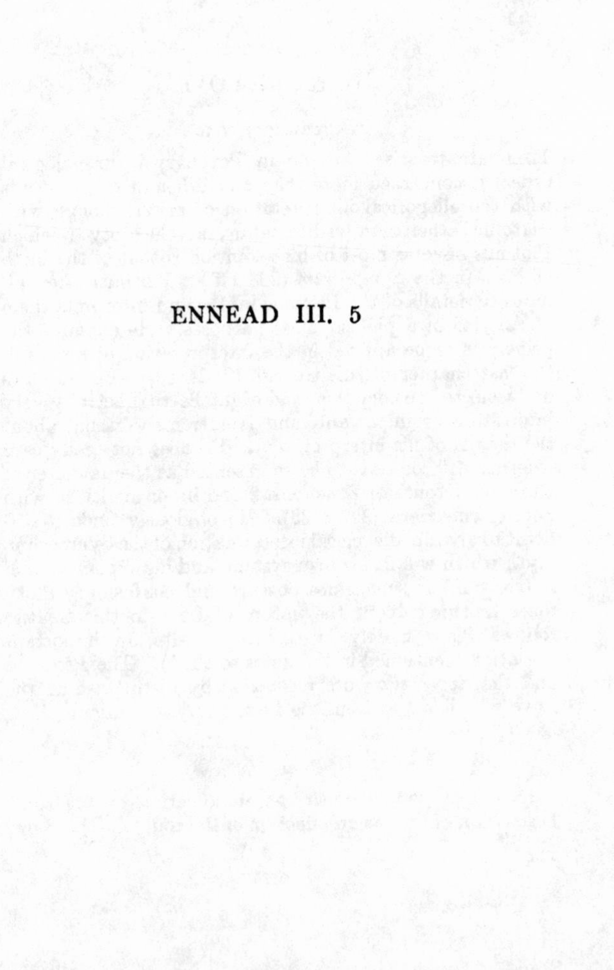

III. 5. ON LOVE

Introductory Note

THIS late treatise (No. 50 in Porphyry's chronological order) is concerned more than any other in the Enneads with the allegorical interpretation of myth, though with Platonic rather than traditional myth: the story to which Plotinus devotes most of his attention is that of the birth of Eros in the *Symposium* (203B ff.). Plotinus often alludes to details of the Platonic myths and interprets them to suit his own philosophical purposes. He explains the principles to be applied in the interpretation of myths in the last chapter of this treatise (9. 24–29). But he does not seem to consider this kind of intellectual activity very interesting or important, and is extremely casual about the details of his interpretation. He does not really care whether Aphrodite is to be represented as the daughter of Ouranos, Kronos or Zeus (chs. 2 and 8), or identified with Zeus's wife Hera (8. 22–23). He obviously finds it difficult to give an allegorical interpretation of the Symposium myth which will fit his own system, and his explanation of it (ch. 6 ff.) is sometimes obscure and confusing. Plotinus's teaching about the nature of Love in this treatise follows Plato closely in essentials (with an important variation mentioned in the notes to ch. 1). The *Phaedrus* and the *Symposium* are reconciled by distinguishing the Love who is a god from the Love who is a daimon (ch. 4, 23–25).

Synopsis

Is love a god, a spirit, or an affection of the soul? Discussion of love as an affection of the soul (ch. 1). Love

as a god. Is he born from or with Aphrodite? The two Aphrodites, the heavenly one and the goddess of marriage: the heavenly Aphrodite is the most divine kind of soul and produces the appropriate Love (ch. 2). Love is a substantial reality; how he comes into existence from the soul's seeing. The lower Aphrodite is the soul of the universe, and produces her own Love (ch. 3). Each individual soul has its own love, related to the universal Love as individual souls are to universal Soul: the higher Love is a god, the lower a spirit (ch. 4). The Love who is a spirit is not the physical universe, as some think (ch. 5). Interpretation of the myth of the birth of Love in the *Symposium:* first, how spirits (*daimones*) differ from gods, being subject to affections and passions through participating in intelligible matter (ch. 6). The parents of Love: Plenty is an intelligible reality, Poverty is intelligible matter, indefinite and so giving unbounded desire to Love. All spirits have this double origin: perverse loves, like false thoughts, are not substantial realities but passive affections of the soul (ch. 7). Zeus and Aphrodite are Intellect and Soul (ch. 8). Plenty, his drunkenness with nectar, and the "garden," all represent in different ways the glorifying outflow of *Logoi* from Intellect into Soul. Principles for the interpretation of myths: their application to this one (ch. 9).

III. 5. (50) ΠΕΡΙ ΕΡΩΤΟΣ

1. Περὶ ἔρωτος, πότερα θεός τις ἢ δαίμων ἢ πάθος τι τῆς ψυχῆς, ἢ ὁ μὲν θεός τις ἢ δαίμων, τὸ δέ τι καὶ πάθος, καὶ ποῖόν τι ἕκαστον, ἐπισκέψασθαι ἄξιον τάς τε τῶν ἄλλων ἀνθρώπων ἐπινοίας ἐπιόντας, καὶ ὅσαι ἐν φιλοσοφίᾳ ἐγένοντο περὶ τούτων, καὶ μάλιστα ὅσα ὑπολαμβάνει ὁ θεῖος Πλάτων, ὃς δὴ καὶ πολλὰ πολλαχῇ τῶν ἑαυτοῦ περὶ ἔρωτος ἔγραψεν· ὃς δὴ οὐ μόνον ἐν ταῖς ψυχαῖς ἐγγιγνόμενόν τι πάθος εἴρηκεν εἶναι, ἀλλὰ καὶ δαίμονά φησιν αὐτὸν καὶ περὶ γενέσεως αὐτοῦ διεξῆλθεν, ὅπως καὶ ὅθεν ἐστὶ γεγενημένος. Περὶ μὲν οὖν τοῦ πάθους οὗ τὸν ἔρωτα αἰτιώμεθα, ὅτι ἐγγίνεται ἐν ψυχαῖς ἐφιεμέναις καλῷ τινι συμπλακῆναι, καὶ ὡς ἡ ἔφεσις αὕτη ἡ μέν ἐστι παρὰ σωφρόνων αὐτῷ τῷ κάλλει οἰκειωθέντων, ἡ δὲ καὶ τελευτᾶν ἐθέλει εἰς αἰσχροῦ τινος πρᾶξιν, οὐδεὶς ἀγνοεῖ δήπου· ὅθεν δὲ τὴν ἀρχὴν ἔχει ἑκάτερος, τὸ ἐντεῦθεν ἐπισκοπεῖν διὰ φιλοσοφίας προσήκει. Ἀρχὴν δὲ εἴ τις θεῖτο τὴν αὐτοῦ κάλλους πρότερον

III. 5. ON LOVE

1. Our enquiry concerns love, whether it is a god or a spirit or an affection of the soul, or whether one kind is a god or spirit and another also an affection, and what sort of god or spirit or affection each of these is; it is worth while considering the ideas about it which have occurred to the rest of mankind and all the teachings of philosophy on this subject, and in particular all the opinions of that godlike man Plato, who has, of course, written much about love in many places in his works. He has said that love is not only an affection occurring in souls but asserts that it is also a spirit, and has described its origin, how and from what source it came to be. Now about the affection of soul for which we make love responsible,[1] there is no one, I suppose, who does not know that it occurs in souls which desire to embrace some beauty, and that this desire has two forms, one which comes from the chaste who are akin to absolute beauty, and one which wants to find its fulfilment in the doing of some ugly act; but it is appropriate to go on from there to a philosophical consideration of the source from which each of them originates. And if someone assumed that the origin of love was the longing for beauty itself which was there before in men's souls, and their recog-

[1] That is Love as a substantial superhuman reality, a god or a spirit, who is responsible for producing the affection of love in the human soul.

ἐν ταῖς ψυχαῖς ὄρεξιν καὶ ἐπίγνωσιν καὶ συγγένειαν καὶ οἰκειότητος ἄλογον σύνεσιν, τυγχάνοι ἄν, οἶμαι, τοῦ ἀληθοῦς τῆς αἰτίας. Τὸ μὲν γὰρ αἰσχρὸν ἐναντίον καὶ τῇ φύσει καὶ τῷ θεῷ. Καὶ γὰρ ἡ φύσις πρὸς τὸ καλὸν βλέπουσα ποιεῖ καὶ πρὸς τὸ ὡρισμένον βλέπει, ὅ ἐστιν ἐν τῇ τοῦ ἀγαθοῦ συστοιχίᾳ· τὸ δὲ ἀόριστον αἰσχρὸν καὶ τῆς ἑτέρας συστοιχίας. Τῇ δὲ φύσει γένεσις ἐκεῖθεν ἐκ τοῦ ἀγαθοῦ καὶ δηλονότι τοῦ καλοῦ. Ὅτῳ δέ τις ἄγαται καί ἐστι συγγενής, τούτου ᾠκείωται καὶ πρὸς τὰς εἰκόνας. Εἰ δέ τις ταύτην τὴν αἰτίαν ἀνέλοι, ὅπῃ τὸ πάθος γίνεται καὶ δι' ἃς αἰτίας οὐχ ἕξει λέγειν οὐδ' ἐπ' αὐτῶν τῶν διὰ μῖξιν ἐρώντων.[1] Καὶ γὰρ οὗτοι τίκτειν βούλονται ἐν καλῷ· ἐπείπερ ἄτοπον βουλομένην τὴν φύσιν καλὰ ποιεῖν ἐν αἰσχρῷ γεννᾶν βούλεσθαι. Ἀλλὰ γὰρ τοῖς μὲν τῇδε γεννᾶν κινουμένοις ἀρκεῖ τὸ τῇδε καλὸν ἔχειν, ὅπερ πάρεστιν ἐν εἰκόσι καὶ σώμασιν, ἐπεὶ μὴ τὸ ἀρχέτυπον αὐτοῖς πάρεστιν, ὅ ἐστιν αἴτιον αὐτοῖς τοῦ καὶ τοῦδε ἐρᾶν. Καὶ εἰς ἀνάμνησιν μὲν ἐκείνου ἀπὸ τοῦδε ἐλθοῦσιν ἀγαπᾶται τοῦτο ὡς εἰκών, μὴ ἀναμνησθεῖσι δὲ ὑπ' ἀγνοίας τοῦ πάθους ἀληθὲς τοῦτο φαντάζεται.

[1] ἐρώντων Harder: ἐρώτων codd.

---

[1] For this thoroughly Hellenic notion of the natural affinity of the soul to beauty and its natural repulsion from ugliness; cp. I. 6 [1] 2. 1–6. Both passages derive from Plato, *Symposium* 206D 1–2.

[2] The phrase is taken, with a slight but significant alteration (τοῦ ἀγαθοῦ singular for τῶν ἀγαθῶν plural) from Aristotle,

nition of it and kinship with it and unreasoned awareness that it is something of their own, he would hit, I think, on the truth about its cause. For the ugly is opposed to nature and to God.[1] For nature when it creates looks towards beauty, and it looks towards the definite, which is " in the column of the good "; [2] but the indefinite is ugly and belongs to the other column. And nature has its origin from above, from the Good and, obviously, from Beauty. But if anyone delights in something and is akin to it, he has an affinity also with its images. But if anyone rejects this cause, he will be unable to say how and for what reasons the emotion of love occurs even in those lovers who aim at sexual intercourse. For these certainly want to " bring forth in beauty ": [3] for it would be absurd for nature, when it wants to create beautiful things, to want to generate in ugliness. It is true, certainly, that those who are moved to generation here below are content to have the beauty here below, the beauty which is present in images and bodies, since the archetype is not present to them which is responsible for their loving even this beauty here below. And if they come from this beauty here to the recollection of that archetype, this earthly beauty still satisfies them as an image; but if they do not recollect, then, because they do not know what is happening to them, they fancy this is the true

Nicomachean Ethics A6 1096b6; cp. *Metaphysics* A5. 986a22–26. The reference is to the columns or tables of ten pairs of basic opposites which some Pythagoreans, according to Aristotle drew up, which included *πέρας καὶ ἄπειρον* and *ἀγαθὸν καὶ κακόν*. *ἀόριστον* (for *ἄπειρον*) is a Platonic rather than a Pythagorean term.

[3] *Symposium* 206C 4–5.

Καὶ σώφροσι μὲν οὖσιν ἀναμάρτητος ἡ πρὸς τὸ τῇδε καλὸν οἰκείωσις, ἡ δὲ πρὸς μῖξιν ἔκπτωσις ἁμαρτία. Καὶ ὅτῳ μὲν καθαρὸς ὁ τοῦ καλοῦ ἔρως, ἀγαπητὸν τὸ κάλλος μόνον εἴτε ἀναμνησθέντι εἴτε καὶ μή, ὅτῳ δὲ μέμικται καὶ ἄλλη τοῦ ἀθάνατον εἶναι ὡς ἐν θνητῷ ἐπιθυμία, οὗτος ἐν τῷ ἀειγενεῖ καὶ ἀιδίῳ τὸ καλὸν ζητεῖ καὶ κατὰ φύσιν μὲν ἰὼν σπείρει καὶ γεννᾷ ἐν καλῷ, σπείρων μὲν εἰς τὸ ἀεί, ἐν καλῷ δὲ διὰ συγγένειαν τοῦ καλοῦ. Καὶ γὰρ καὶ τὸ ἀίδιον συγγενὲς τῷ καλῷ καὶ ἡ ἀίδιος φύσις τὸ πρώτως τοιοῦτον καὶ τὰ ἀπ᾿ αὐτῆς τοιαῦτα πάντα. Τὸ μὲν οὖν μὴ γεννᾶν ἐθέλον μᾶλλον αὐταρκέστερον τῷ καλῷ, τὸ δὲ ἐφιέμενον ποιῆσαι καλόν τε ἐθέλει ποιεῖν ὑπ᾿ ἐνδείας καὶ οὐκ αὔταρκες· καί, εἴπερ τοιοῦτον ποιήσει, οἴεται, εἰ ἐν καλῷ γεννήσεται. Οἳ δ᾿ ἂν ἐν παρανόμῳ καὶ παρὰ τὴν φύσιν ἐθέλωσι γεννᾶν, ἐκ τῆς κατὰ φύσιν πορείας ποιησάμενοι τὰς ἀρχὰς γενόμενοι παράφοροι ἐκ ταύτης οἷον ὁδοῦ ὀλισθήσαντες κεῖνται πεσόντες οὔτε ἔρωτα γνόντες ἐφ᾿ ὃ ἦγεν αὐτοὺς οὔτε ἔφεσιν γεννήσεως οὔτε χρῆσιν κάλλους εἰκόνος οὔτε ὅ τι ἐστὶ κάλλος αὐτό. Ἀλλ᾿ οὖν οἵ τε σωμάτων καλῶν καὶ διὰ μῖξιν ἐρῶντες, ὅτι καλά ἐστιν ἐρῶσιν, οἵ τε τὸν λεγόμενον μικτὸν

---

[1] Throughout this passage Plotinus is trying to follow closely the doctrine of Plato (*Symposium* 206C ff.), but he has, in fact, introduced an important change by distinguishing so sharply between the pure love of beauty which does not desire to generate and that which is mixed with desire for perpetuity and so seeks to generate, which he regards as inferior. In

beauty. If they remain chaste there is no error in their intimacy with the beauty here below, but it is error to fall away into sexual intercourse. And the man whose love of the beautiful is pure will be satisfied with beauty alone, if he recollects the archetype or even if he does not, but the man whose love is mixed with another desire of " being immortal as far as a mortal may," seeks the beautiful in that which is everlasting and eternal; and as he goes the way of nature he sows and generates in beauty, sowing for perpetuity, and in beauty because of the kinship of perpetuity and beauty. The eternal is certainly akin to the beautiful, and the eternal nature is that which is primarily beautiful and the things which spring from it are all beautiful too. That, therefore, which does not want to generate suffices more to itself in beauty, but that which desires to create wants to create beauty because of a lack and is not self-sufficient; and, if it does create something of the sort, it thinks it is self-sufficient if it generates in beauty.[1] But those who want to generate unlawfully and against nature take their starting-point from the course which accords with nature but diverge from it and slip, as we may say, out of the way and lie fallen, having failed to recognise where love was leading them, or the impulse of generating, or the right use of an image of beauty, or what absolute beauty is. But to return to the main point; those who love beautiful bodies, also with a view to sexual intercourse, love them because they are beautiful, and so do those who love with the mixed love of which

Plato all love up to the highest is essentially productive (cp. *Symposium* 212A). In Plotinus it is not.

ἔρωτα, γυναικῶν μέν, ἵνα καὶ τὸ ἀεί, μὴ τοιούτων δέ, σφαλλόμενοι· οἱ δὲ ἀμείνους· σωφρονοῦσι μὲν ἄμφω. Ἀλλ' οἱ μὲν καὶ τὸ τῇδε κάλλος σέβουσιν ἀρκούμενοι, οἱ δὲ κἀκεῖνο, ὅσοι ἀνεμνήσθησαν, καὶ οὐκ ἀτιμάζουσιν οὐδὲ τοῦτο ὡς ἂν καὶ ἀποτέλεσμά τι ὂν ἐκείνου καὶ παίγνιον. Οὗτοι μὲν οὖν περὶ τὸ καλὸν αἰσχροῦ ἄνευ, οἱ δὲ καὶ διὰ τὸ καλὸν εἰς αἰσχρὸν πεσόντες· καὶ γὰρ ἡ ἀγαθοῦ ἔφεσις ἔχει εἰς κακὸν τὴν ἔκπτωσιν πολλάκις. Καὶ ταῦτα μὲν τῆς ψυχῆς τὰ παθήματα.

2. Περὶ δὲ τοῦ ὃν θεὸν τίθενται οὐ μόνον οἱ ἄλλοι ἄνθρωποι, ἀλλὰ καὶ θεολόγοι καὶ Πλάτων πολλαχοῦ Ἀφροδίτης Ἔρωτα λέγων καὶ ἔργον αὐτῷ εἶναι καλῶν τε ἔφορον παίδων καὶ κινητικὸν τῶν ψυχῶν πρὸς τὸ ἐκεῖ κάλλος, ἢ καὶ ἐπαύξειν τὴν ἤδη γενομένην πρὸς τὸ ἐκεῖ ὁρμήν, περὶ τούτου μάλιστα φιλοσοφητέον· καὶ δὴ καὶ ὅσα ἐν Συμποσίῳ εἴρηται παραληπτέον, ἐν οἷς οὐκ ⟨Ἀφροδίτης φησὶν αὐτὸν γενέσθαι, ἀλλ' ἐν⟩[1] Ἀφροδίτης γενεθλίοις ἐκ τῆς Πενίας καὶ τοῦ Πόρου. Ἔοικε δὲ ὁ λόγος καὶ περὶ τῆς Ἀφροδίτης ἀπαιτήσειν τι εἰπεῖν, εἴτ' οὖν ἐξ ἐκείνης εἴτε μετ' ἐκείνης γεγονέναι λέγεται ὁ Ἔρως. Πρῶτον

[1] ⟨*Ἀφροδίτης . . . ἐν*⟩ Kirchhoff.

---

[1] *Phaedrus* 242D9.
[2] *Phaedrus* 265C2–3.
[3] *Symposium* 203B–C.

we have spoken; they love women in order to perpetuate themselves, but if the women are not beautiful they fail in their purpose [of " generating in beauty "]; but the first group [those who love without thought of self-perpetuation, with a pure love of beauty] are better; both are chaste. But some lovers even worship earthly beauty, and it is enough for them, but others, those who have recollected the archetype, venerate that higher beauty too, and do not treat this earthly beauty, either, with disrespect, since they see in it the creation and plaything of that other. These lovers, then, are concerned about beauty without any ugliness, but there are others who fall into ugliness and they too do so because of beauty; for in fact the desire of good often involves the fall into evil. So much, then, for the affections of the soul [produced by love].

2. But the Love whom we ought to make the main object of our philosophical discourse is the one whom not only the rest of mankind but those also who give accounts of the gods, and especially Plato, make a god; Plato in many places speaks of " Love son of Aphrodite," [1] and says that his work is to be " guardian of beautiful boys " [2] and mover of the soul towards the beauty of the higher world, or also to increase the impulse towards that world which is already there; we must also take into account all that is said in the *Banquet*, in which he says that Love is not born of Aphrodite but " from Poverty and Plenty at Aphrodite's birthday party." [3] But our discussion seems to require us to say something about Aphrodite, whether Love is said to have been born from her or with her. First, then, who is Aphrodite?

οὖν τίς ἡ Ἀφροδίτη; Εἶτα πῶς ἢ ἐξ αὐτῆς ἢ σὺν αὐτῇ ἢ τίνα τρόπον ἔχει τὸν αὐτὸν τὸ ἐξ αὐτῆς τε ἅμα καὶ σὺν αὐτῇ. Λέγομεν δὴ τὴν Ἀφροδίτην εἶναι διττήν, τὴν μὲν οὐρανίαν Οὐρανοῦ λέγοντες εἶναι, τὴν δὲ ἐκ Διὸς καὶ Διώνης, τὴν τῶν τῇδε ἐφαπτομένην ἔφορον γάμων· ἀμήτορα δὲ ἐκείνην καὶ ἐπέκεινα γάμων, ὅτι μηδ' ἐν οὐρανῷ γάμοι. Τὴν δὲ οὐρανίαν λεγομένην ἐκ Κρόνου νοῦ ὄντος ἐκείνου ἀνάγκη ψυχὴν θειοτάτην εἶναι εὐθὺς ἐξ αὐτοῦ ἀκήρατον ἀκηράτου μείνασαν ἄνω, ὡς μηδὲ εἰς τὰ τῇδε ἐλθεῖν μήτε ἐθελήσασαν μήτε δυναμένην [ὅτι ἦν φύσεως] [1] μὴ κατὰ τὰ κάτω φῦσαν βαίνειν χωριστὴν οὖσάν τινα ὑπόστασιν καὶ ἀμέτοχον ὕλης οὐσίαν—ὅθεν αὐτὴν τούτῳ ᾐνίττοντο, τῷ ἀμήτορα εἶναι—ἣν δὴ καὶ θεὸν ἄν τις δικαίως, οὐ δαίμονα εἴποι ἄμικτον οὖσαν καὶ καθαρὰν ἐφ' ἑαυτῆς μένουσαν. Τὸ γὰρ εὐθὺς ἐκ νοῦ πεφυκὸς καθαρὸν καὶ αὐτό, ἅτε ἰσχύον καθ' ἑαυτὸ τῷ ἐγγύθεν, ἅτε καὶ τῆς ἐπιθυμίας οὔσης αὐτῇ καὶ τῆς ἱδρύσεως πρὸς τὸ γεννῆσαν ἱκανὸν ὂν κατέχειν ἄνω· ὅθεν οὐδ' ἂν ἐκπέσοι ψυχὴ νοῦ ἐξηρτημένη πολὺ μᾶλλον ἢ ἥλιος ἂν ἔχοι ἐξ ἑαυτοῦ ὅσον αὐτὸν περιλάμπει φῶς τὸ ἐξ αὐτοῦ εἰς αὐτὸν συνηρτημένον. Ἐφεπο-

[1] ὅτι ἦν φύσεως del. Volkmann, H–S.

---

[1] This allegorisation of the cult-titles Οὐρανία and Πάνδημος and the different mythical accounts of the birth of Aphrodite (which has no basis in actual Greek religious practice), appears in the speech of Pausanias in the *Symposium* (180D) and in Xenophon's *Symposium* viii, 9–10. Plato himself does not appear to take it very seriously, and it plays no important part

Next, we must ask how Love is either born from her or with her, or in what way it applies to the same Love that he is at the same time from her and with her. Now we say that Aphrodite is double; one, the heavenly, we say is the " daughter of Heaven," and the other, the one " born of Zeus and Dione," takes charge of earthly marriages as their guardian; but that other is " motherless " and above marriages, because there are no marriages in heaven.[1] The heavenly one, since she is said to be the child of Kronos, and he is Intellect, must be the most divine kind of soul, springing directly from him, pure from the pure, remaining above, as neither wanting nor being able to descend to the world here below, since it is not according to her nature to come down, since she is a separate reality and a substance without part in matter—for which reason they spoke of her riddlingly in this way, that she was " motherless "; one would be right in speaking of her as a goddess, not as a spirit, since she is unmixed and remains pure by herself. For that which derives its nature immediately from Intellect is itself, too, pure, since it is strong in itself by its nearness, since, too, Soul's desire and its abiding-place are close to its parent principle which is strong enough to hold it above; for which reason Soul which is immediately dependent on Intellect could not fall away; it is much more firmly held than the sun holds the light which shines out from himself around him, which comes from him and is closely joined to him. Now since Aphrodite follows upon Kronos—

in the development of his thought about Love in the *Symposium.* Plotinus finds it useful because it can be made to fit his distinction between higher and lower Soul.

μένη δὴ τῷ Κρόνῳ ἤ, εἰ βούλει, τῷ πατρὶ τοῦ Κρόνου Οὐρανῷ ἐνήργησέ τε πρὸς αὐτὸν καὶ ᾠκειώθη καὶ ἐρασθεῖσα Ἔρωτα ἐγέννησε καὶ μετὰ τούτου πρὸς αὐτὸν βλέπει, καὶ ἡ ἐνέργεια αὐτῆς ὑπόστασιν καὶ οὐσίαν εἰργάσατο, καὶ ἄμφω ἐκεῖ βλέπει, καὶ ἡ γειναμένη καὶ ὁ καλὸς Ἔρως ὁ γεγενημένος ὑπόστασις πρὸς ἄλλο καλὸν ἀεὶ τεταγμένη καὶ τὸ εἶναι ἐν τούτῳ ἔχουσα μεταξὺ ὥσπερ ποθοῦντος καὶ ποθουμένου, ὀφθαλμὸς ὁ τοῦ ποθοῦντος παρέχων μὲν τῷ ἐρῶντι δι' αὐτοῦ τὸ ὁρᾶν τὸ ποθούμενον, προτρέχων δὲ αὐτὸς καὶ πρὶν ἐκείνῳ παρασχεῖν τὴν τοῦ ὁρᾶν δι' ὀργάνου δύναμιν αὐτὸς πιμπλάμενος τοῦ θεάματος, πρότερος μέν, οὐ μὴν ὁμοίως ὁρῶν τῷ ἐνστηρίζειν μὲν ἐκείνῳ τὸ ὅραμα, αὐτὸν δὲ καρποῦσθαι τὴν θέαν τοῦ καλοῦ αὐτὸν παραθέουσαν.

3. Ὑπόστασιν δὲ εἶναι καὶ οὐσίαν ἐξ οὐσίας ἐλάττω μὲν τῆς ποιησαμένης, οὖσαν δὲ ὅμως, ἀπιστεῖν οὐ προσήκει. Καὶ γὰρ ἡ ψυχὴ ἐκείνη οὐσία ἦν γενομένη ἐξ ἐνεργείας τῆς πρὸ αὐτῆς [καὶ ζῶσα] καὶ τῆς τῶν ὄντων οὐσίας καὶ πρὸς ἐκεῖνο ὁρῶσα, ὃ πρώτη ἦν οὐσία, καὶ σφόδρα ὁρῶσα.[1]

[1] καὶ ζῶσα (glossa) del. Theiler. ὁρῶσα Bréhier: ὁρώσης codd.

---

[1] This shows clearly how little real importance Plotinus attached to myths and their allegorical interpretation. According to Hesiod (*Theogony* 188 ff.) Aphrodite sprang from the foam round the severed genitals of Ouranos when they fell into the sea after his castration by Kronos—a story which Plato particularly disliked (cp. *Republic* II 377E–378A, and

or, if you like, the father of Kronos, Heaven[1]—she directed her activity towards him and felt affinity with him, and filled with passionate love for him brought forth Love, and with this child of hers she looks towards him; her activity has made a real substance, and the two of them look on high, the mother who bore him and the beautiful Love who has come into existence as a reality always ordered towards something else beautiful, and having its being in this, that it is a kind of intermediary between desiring and desired, the eye of the desiring which through its power gives to the lover the sight of the object desired; but Love himself runs on ahead and, before he gives the lover the power of seeing through the organ [of bodily sight], he fills himself with gazing, seeing before the lover but certainly not in the same way, because he fixes the sight firmly in the lover, but himself plucks the fruit of the vision of beauty as it speeds past him.

3. We ought not to disbelieve that Love is a reality and a substance sprung from a substance, less than that which made it, but all the same substantially existent. For that higher soul was, certainly, a substance, which came into being from the activity which existed before it, and from the substance of the world of real beings, which also looks towards that which was the first substance, and looks towards it with great intensity. This was its first vision, and

Euthyphro 6A–B), which may be one reason why Plotinus shifts the parentage of Aphrodite here: his main reason, however, is that Kronos is his normal mythical equivalent for Intellect (cp. V. 1 [10] 4), on which Aphrodite as divine Soul must follow immediately.

Καὶ πρῶτον ἦν ὅραμα αὐτῇ τοῦτο καὶ ἑώρα ὡς πρὸς ἀγαθὸν αὐτῆς καὶ ἔχαιρεν ὁρῶσα, καὶ τὸ ὅραμα τοιοῦτον ἦν, ὡς μὴ πάρεργον ποιεῖσθαι τὴν θέαν τὸ ὁρῶν, ὡς τῇ οἷον ἡδονῇ καὶ τάσει τῇ πρὸς αὐτὸ καὶ σφοδρότητι τῆς θέας γεννῆσαί τι παρ' αὐτῆς ἄξιον αὐτῆς καὶ τοῦ ὁράματος. Ἐξ οὖν τοῦ ἐνεργοῦντος συντόνως περὶ τὸ ὁρώμενον καὶ ἐκ τοῦ οἷον ἀπορρέοντος ἀπὸ τοῦ ὁρωμένου ὄμμα πληρωθέν, οἷον μετ' εἰδώλου ὅρασις, Ἔρως ἐγένετο τάχα που καὶ τῆς προσηγορίας ἐντεῦθεν μᾶλλον αὐτῷ γεγενημένης, ὅτι ἐξ ὁράσεως τὴν ὑπόστασιν ἔχει· ἐπεὶ τό γε πάθος ἀπὸ τούτου ἔχοι ἂν τὴν ἐπωνυμίαν,[1] εἴπερ πρότερον οὐσία μὴ οὐσίας—καίτοι τό γε πάθος « ἐρᾶν » λέγεται—καὶ εἴπερ « ἔρως αὐτὸν ἔχει τοῦδε », ἁπλῶς δὲ οὐκ ἂν λέγοιτο ἔρως. Ὁ μὲν δὴ τῆς ἄνω ψυχῆς Ἔρως τοιοῦτος ἂν εἴη, ὁρῶν καὶ αὐτὸς ἄνω, ἅτε ὀπαδὸς ὢν ἐκείνης καὶ ἐξ ἐκείνης καὶ παρ' ἐκείνης γεγενημένος καὶ θεῶν ἀρκούμενος θέᾳ. Χωριστὴν δὲ ἐκείνην τὴν ψυχὴν λέγοντες τὴν πρώτως ἐλλάμπουσαν τῷ οὐρανῷ, χωριστὸν καὶ τὸν Ἔρωτα τοῦτον θησόμεθα—εἰ καὶ ὅτι μάλιστα οὐρανίαν τὴν ψυχὴν εἴπομεν· ἐπεὶ καὶ ἐν ἡμῖν λέγοντες τὸ ἐν ἡμῖν ἄριστον εἶναι χωριστὸν ὅμως τιθέμεθα αὐτὸ εἶναι—

[1] ἐπωνυμίαν Creuzer, H–S: ἐπιθυμίαν codd.

---

[1] Ἔρως from ὅρασις.

[2] The higher soul is called "Heavenly" because it "illuminates" (i.e. is the immediate source of the forms in) the visible heaven, but it is not immanent in heaven but trans-

it looked towards it as to its own good, and rejoiced in its looking, and the vision was of a kind which made it impossible for the visionary to make its gaze a secondary activity; so that the soul by a kind of delight and intense concentration on the vision and by the passion of its gazing generates something from itself which is worthy of itself and of the vision. So from the power which is intensely active about the object of vision, and from a kind of outflow from that object, Love came to be as an eye filled with its vision, like a seeing that has its image with it; and, I suppose, his name most likely came to him from this, because he derives his real existence from seeing;[1] for the emotion of love must take its name from him, on the assumption that substance is prior to non-substance—after all it is an emotion that is called " falling in love "—and if we say " love for this particular person possesses him," but love would not be spoken of without any particular qualification. The Love which belongs to the higher soul, then, would be of this kind, himself, too, looking on high, since he is that soul's follower and has come into being from her and by her, and satisfies himself with the contemplation of the gods. But since we say that that higher soul which primarily illuminates heaven is separate, we shall also make this Love separate—however much we call this soul " heavenly ": for, though we say, too, that the best in us men is " in " us, all the same we give it a separate existence.[2]

cends the material universe altogether. In the same way the highest, intellectual, element in us is not really " we " but separate and transcendent; cp. the nearly contemporary treatise V. 3 [49] 3.

μόνον ἐκεῖ ἔστω, οὗ ἡ ψυχὴ ἡ ἀκήρατος. Ἐπεὶ δὲ καὶ τοῦδε τοῦ παντὸς ψυχὴν εἶναι ἔδει, ὑπέστη μετὰ ταύτης ἤδη καὶ ὁ ἄλλος Ἔρως ὄμμα καὶ ταύτης, ἐξ ὀρέξεως καὶ αὐτὸς[1] γεγενημένος. Τοῦ δὲ κόσμου οὖσα ἡ Ἀφροδίτη αὕτη καὶ οὐ μόνον ψυχὴ οὐδὲ ἁπλῶς ψυχὴ καὶ τὸν ἐν τῷδε τῷ κόσμῳ Ἔρωτα ἐγεννήσατο ἐφαπτόμενον ἤδη καὶ αὐτὸν γάμων καί, καθʼ ὅσον ἐφάπτεται καὶ αὐτὸς τῆς ὀρέξεως τῆς ἄνω, κατὰ τοσοῦτον κινοῦντα καὶ τὰς τῶν νέων ψυχὰς καὶ τὴν ψυχὴν ᾗ συντέτακται ἀναστρέφοντα, καθʼ ὅσον καὶ αὐτὴ εἰς μνήμην ἐκείνων πέφυκεν ἰέναι. Πᾶσα γὰρ ἐφίεται τοῦ ἀγαθοῦ καὶ ἡ μεμιγμένη καὶ ἡ τινὸς γενομένη· ἐπεὶ καὶ αὕτη ἐφεξῆς ἐκείνῃ καὶ ἐξ ἐκείνης.

4. Ἆρʼ οὖν καὶ ἑκάστη ψυχὴ ἔχει ἔρωτα τοιοῦτον ἐν οὐσίᾳ καὶ ὑποστάσει; Ἢ διὰ τί ἡ μὲν ὅλη ἕξει καὶ ἡ τοῦ παντὸς ὑποστατὸν ἔρωτα, ἡ δὲ ἑκάστου ἡμῶν οὔ, πρὸς δὲ καὶ ἡ ἐν τοῖς ἄλλοις ζῴοις ἅπασι; Καὶ ἆρα ὁ ἔρως οὗτός ἐστιν ὁ δαίμων, ὅν φασιν ἑκάστῳ συνέπεσθαι, ὁ αὐτοῦ ἑκάστου ἔρως; Οὗτος γὰρ ἂν εἴη καὶ ὁ ἐμποιῶν τὰς ἐπιθυμίας κατὰ φύσιν ἑκάστης τῆς ψυχῆς ὀριγνωμένης ἀνάλογον ἑκάστης πρὸς τὴν αὑτῆς φύσιν καὶ τὸν ἔρωτα γεννώσης εἴς τε ἀξίαν καὶ πρὸς οὐσίαν. Ἐχέτω δὴ ἡ μὲν ὅλη ὅλον, αἱ δʼ ἐν μέρει τὸν αὑτῆς ἑκάστη. Καθʼ ὅσον δὲ ἑκάστη πρὸς τὴν ὅλην ἔχει οὐκ ἀποτετμημένη, ἐμπεριεχομένη δέ, ὡς εἶναι πάσας μίαν, καὶ ὁ ἔρως ἕκαστος

[1] αὐτὸς Creuzer: αὐτῆς codd.

So he must exist only there above, where the soul which is pure abides. But since this universe, too, had to have a soul, the other Love came to be at once along with it, and is also the eye of this soul, himself, too, produced from desire. And because this Aphrodite belongs to the universe and is not only soul or simply soul, she produced the Love in this universe, who himself, too, immediately takes charge of marriages and, in so far as he, too, possesses the desire for what is above, in the same degree moves the souls of the young, and turns the soul with which he is ranked to higher things, in so far as it, too, is naturally able to come to remembrance of them. For every soul seeks the good, the mixed soul, too, and the individual soul: since it, too, follows upon that higher soul and derives from it.

4. Does, then, each individual soul have a love like itself which has a real substantial existence? Now why should the universal soul and the soul of the All have a real love, but not the soul of each of us, and the soul in all other living things as well? And is this love the spirit which, they say, accompanies each of us, the love, that is, that belongs to each of us? For this would be the love which implants the desires appropriate to the nature of each individual soul; the individual soul longs for what corresponds to its own nature, and produces a love which accords with its value and is proportioned to its being. Let us grant, then, that the universal soul has a universal love, and each of the partial souls its own particular love. But in so far as each individual soul in its relation to the whole is not in a state of being completely cut off, but of inclusion in it so that all souls

πρὸς τὸν πάντα ἂν ἔχοι· συνεῖναι δ' αὖ καὶ τὸν ἐν μέρει τῇ ἐν μέρει καὶ τῇ ὅλῃ τὸν μέγαν ἐκεῖνον καὶ τὸν ἐν τῷ παντὶ τῷ παντὶ πανταχοῦ αὐτοῦ· καὶ πολλοὺς αὖ τὸν ἕνα τοῦτον γίνεσθαι καὶ εἶναι, φαινόμενον πανταχοῦ τοῦ παντὸς οὗ ἂν θέλῃ, σχηματιζόμενον μέρεσιν ἑαυτοῦ καὶ φανταζόμενον, εἰ θέλοι. Οἴεσθαι δὲ χρὴ καὶ Ἀφροδίτας ἐν τῷ ὅλῳ πολλάς, δαίμονας ἐν αὐτῷ γενομένας μετ' Ἔρωτος, ῥυείσας ἐξ Ἀφροδίτης τινὸς ὅλης, ἐν μέρει πολλὰς ἐκείνης ἐξηρτημένας μετὰ ἰδίων ἐρώτων, εἴπερ ψυχὴ μήτηρ ἔρωτος, Ἀφροδίτη δὲ ψυχή, ἔρως δὲ ἐνέργεια ψυχῆς ἀγαθοῦ ὀριγνωμένης. Ἄγων τοίνυν ἑκάστην οὗτος ὁ ἔρως πρὸς τὴν ἀγαθοῦ φύσιν ὁ μὲν τῆς ἄνω θεὸς ἂν εἴη, ὃς ἀεὶ ψυχὴν ἐκείνῳ συνάπτει, δαίμων δ' ὁ τῆς μεμιγμένης.

5. Ἀλλὰ τίς ἡ δαίμονος καὶ ὅλως ἡ δαιμόνων φύσις, περὶ ἧς καὶ ἐν Συμποσίῳ λέγεται, ἥ τε τῶν ἄλλων καὶ ἡ αὐτοῦ τοῦ Ἔρωτος, ὡς ἐκ Πενίας καὶ Πόρου Μήτιδός ἐστι γεγενημένος ἐν τοῖς Ἀφροδίτης γενεθλίοις; Τὸ μὲν οὖν τὸν κόσμον ὑπονοεῖν λέγεσθαι τόνδε τῷ Πλάτωνι τὸν Ἔρωτα, ἀλλὰ μὴ

---

[1] For the unity of individual souls in the one soul, see IV. 3 [27] 8, IV. 9 [8], VI. 4 [22] 14.

[2] By this distinction Plotinus reconciles the *Phaedrus*, where Eros is a god, with the *Symposium*, where he is a daemon: and also keeps Plato's insight that ἔρως is not just desire (which must disappear with satisfaction) but something which persists when the lover attains to full fruition and union with the beloved.

[3] The identification of the god Eros with the whole universe is found in Cornutus (*Theologiae Graecae Compendium*, ch. 25 (p. 48, 5–9 Lang)): it may be Stoic. Plutarch applies it

are one,[1] so the individual love, too, is related to the universal love; so, then, the partial love accompanies the partial soul, and that great Love accompanies the universal soul, and the love in the All accompanies the All, and is everywhere in it; and, again, this one love becomes and is many loves, appearing everywhere that he wishes in the All, taking shape and assuming appearances in its parts if he wants to. But one must think that there are many Aphrodites in the All, which have come into being in it as spirits along with Love, flowing from an universal Aphrodite, many partial ones depending from that universal one, with their own particular loves—if one assumes, that is, that soul is the mother of love, and Aphrodite is soul, and love is the activity of soul reaching out after good. So this love here leads each individual soul to the Good, and the love which belongs to the higher soul is a god, who always keeps the soul joined to the Good, but the love of the mixed soul is a spirit.[2]

5. But what is the nature of this spirit, and of spirits in general, about which Plato speaks also in the *Banquet*, the nature of the other spirits, and of Love himself; how is he born of Poverty and Plenty, son of Cunning, at Aphrodite's birthday party? The interpretation that Plato means this universe by Love,[3] but not a part of the universe, the Love that

to the interpretation of the *Symposium* myth in *De Iside et Osiride*, ch. 57, 374D–E, where he identifies the parents of Love, Plenty and Poverty, with intelligible reality and matter, which unite to form the universe, and assimilates the three to the Egyptian triad Osiris, Isis, and Horus. Plotinus, though rejecting the identification of Love with the universe, retains something from this older allegorical interpretation of his parents.

τοῦ κόσμου τὸν ἐν αὐτῷ ἐκφύντα Ἔρωτα, πολλὰ τὰ ἐναντιούμενα τῇ δόξῃ ἔχει, τοῦ μὲν κόσμου λεγομένου εὐδαίμονος θεοῦ καὶ αὐτάρκους εἶναι, τοῦ δὲ Ἔρωτος τούτου ὁμολογουμένου τῷ ἀνδρὶ οὔτε θεοῦ οὔτε αὐτάρκους, ἀεὶ δὲ ἐνδεοῦς εἶναι. Εἶτα ἀνάγκη, εἴπερ ὁ κόσμος ἐστὶν ἐκ ψυχῆς καὶ σώματος, ἡ δὲ ψυχὴ τοῦ κόσμου ἡ Ἀφροδίτη ἐστὶν αὐτῷ, μέρος τὸ κύριον τοῦ Ἔρωτος τὴν Ἀφροδίτην εἶναι· ἤ, εἰ κόσμος ἡ ψυχή ἐστιν αὐτοῦ, ὥσπερ καὶ ἄνθρωπος ἡ ἀνθρώπου ψυχή, τὸν Ἔρωτα τὴν Ἀφροδίτην εἶναι. Εἶτα διὰ τί οὗτος μὲν δαίμων ὢν ὁ κόσμος ἔσται, οἱ δ' ἄλλοι δαίμονες—δῆλον γὰρ ὅτι ἐκ τῆς αὐτῆς οὐσίας εἰσίν—οὐ καὶ αὐτοὶ ἔσονται; Καὶ ὁ κόσμος ἔσται σύστασις αὐτὸ τοῦτο ἐκ δαιμόνων. Ὁ δὲ ἔφορος καλῶν παίδων λεχθεὶς εἶναι πῶς ἂν ὁ κόσμος εἴη; Τὸ δὲ ἄστρωτον καὶ ἀνυπόδητον καὶ ἄοικον πῶς ἂν ἐφαρμόσειε μὴ οὐ γλίσχρως καὶ ἀπᾳδόντως;

6. Ἀλλὰ τί δὴ χρὴ λέγειν περὶ τοῦ Ἔρωτος καὶ τῆς λεγομένης γενέσεως αὐτοῦ; Δῆλον δὴ ὅτι δεῖ λαβεῖν τίς ἡ Πενία καὶ τίς ὁ Πόρος, καὶ πῶς ἁρμόσουσιν οὗτοι γονεῖς εἶναι αὐτῷ. Δῆλον δὲ ὅτι δεῖ καὶ τοῖς ἄλλοις δαίμοσι τούτους ἁρμόσαι, εἴπερ δεῖ φύσιν εἶναι καὶ οὐσίαν μίαν καθὸ δαίμονες δαιμόνων, εἰ μὴ κοινὸν ὄνομα ἕξουσι μόνον. Λάβωμεν τοίνυν πῇ ποτε διορίζομεν θεοὺς δαιμόνων, καὶ εἰ πολλάκις καὶ δαίμονας θεοὺς λέγομεν εἶναι, ἀλλ' ὅταν γε τὸ μὲν ἕτερον, τὸ δὲ ἕτερον

grows up naturally within it, contains in itself many contradictions; Plato says that the universe is a " blessed god " and self-sufficient, but he admits that this Love is not a god and not self-sufficient, but always in need. Then again it is necessary, if the universe is composed of soul and body, and Aphrodite is for Plato the soul of the universe, that Aphrodite should be the most important part of Love, or, if its soul is the universe, as man's soul is man, that Love must be Aphrodite. Then again, why should he, who is a spirit, be the universe, but the other spirits—for it is obvious that they are of the same substance—not be the universe, themselves too? And the universe then would be nothing but a conglomeration of spirits. And how could a being who is called " guardian of beautiful boys " be the universe? And how would Plato's " bedless " and " shoeless " and " houseless "[1] fit this interpretation without being mean and inharmonious?

6. But what, then, are we to say about Love and the account of his birth? It is obvious that we must understand who Poverty is, and who Plenty is, and how they will be appropriate parents for him. It is obvious, too, that these must be appropriate for the other spirits, assuming that spirits as spirits have one single nature and substance—otherwise they will merely have the name in common. Let us, then, understand how we distinguish gods from spirits (even if we do often call spirits gods), at any rate on the occasions when we do speak of each kind of being as

[1] *Symposium* 203D 1–2.

λέγωμεν αὐτῶν εἶναι γένος. Τὸ μὲν δὴ θεῶν ἀπαθὲς λέγομεν καὶ νομίζομεν γένος, δαίμοσι δὲ προστίθεμεν πάθη, ἀιδίους λέγοντες ἐφεξῆς τοῖς θεοῖς, ἤδη πρὸς ἡμᾶς, μεταξὺ θεῶν τε καὶ τοῦ ἡμετέρου γένους. Πῇ δὴ οὖν οὐκ ἔμειναν ἀπαθεῖς οὗτοι, πῇ δὲ κατέβησαν τῇ φύσει πρὸς τὸ χεῖρον; Καὶ δὴ καὶ τοῦτο σκεπτέον, πότερα δαίμων ἐν τῷ νοητῷ οὐδὲ εἷς καὶ αὖ ἐν τῷ κόσμῳ τῷδε δαίμονες μόνον, θεὸς δὲ ἐν τῷ νοητῷ ἀφορίζεται, ἢ εἰσὶ καὶ ἐνταῦθα θεοὶ καὶ ὁ κόσμος θεός, ὥσπερ σύνηθες λέγειν, τρίτος καὶ οἱ μέχρι σελήνης ἕκαστος θεός. Βέλτιον δὲ μηδένα ἐν τῷ νοητῷ δαίμονα λέγειν, ἀλλὰ καὶ εἰ αὐτοδαίμων, θεὸν καὶ τοῦτον εἶναι, καὶ αὖ ἐν τῷ αἰσθητῷ τοὺς μέχρι σελήνης θεοὺς τοὺς ὁρατοὺς θεοὺς δευτέρους μετ᾽ ἐκείνους καὶ κατ᾽ ἐκείνους τοὺς νοητούς, ἐξηρτημένους ἐκείνων, ὥσπερ αἴγλην περὶ ἕκαστον ἄστρον. Τοὺς δὲ δαίμονας τί; Ἆρά γε ψυχῆς ἐν κόσμῳ γενομένης τὸ ἀφ᾽ ἑκάστης ἴχνος; Διὰ τί δὲ τῆς ἐν κόσμῳ; Ὅτι ἡ καθαρὰ θεὸν γεννᾷ, καὶ θεὸν ἔφαμεν τὸν ταύτης ἔρωτα. Πρῶτον δὴ διὰ τί οὐ πάντες οἱ δαίμονες ἔρωτες; Εἶτα πῶς οὐ καθαροὶ καὶ οὗτοι ὕλης; Ἢ ἔρωτες μέν, οἳ γεννῶνται ψυχῆς ἐφιεμένης τοῦ ἀγαθοῦ καὶ καλοῦ, καὶ

---

[1] The use of the name *δαίμονες* for supernatural beings of inferior rank to the gods goes back to Hesiod (*Works and Days* 122–126). But it was Plato, and still more Xenocrates and the Middle Platonists taking up and developing his ideas, who defined the characteristics of these intermediate beings and worked out a regular daemonology, whose main lines Plotinus follows in this chapter.

different from the other.[1] Now we speak and think of the race of gods as without affections or passions, but we attribute affections and passions to the spirits; we say that they are eternal next after the gods, but already inclining towards us, between the gods and our race. In what way, then, did they not stay passionless, and in what way did they come down in their nature to a lower level? Then, too, we must consider this question whether there is no spirit at all in the intelligible world, and, on the other hand, nothing but spirits in this universe, whether godhead is confined to the intelligible world, or " there are gods here too " and the universe is, as we are used to say, a " third god," [2] and each of the beings down to the moon is a god. But it is better not to call any being in the intelligible world a spirit, but, even if there is an Idea of spirit, to call this a god, and, on the other side, to say that the gods in the universe of sense down to the moon, the visible ones, are secondary gods which come after and correspond to those higher intelligible gods and depend upon them, like the radiance around every star. But what are the spirits? Are they the trace left by each soul when it enters the universe? But why only of the soul in the universe? Because the pure soul produces a god, and we have affirmed already that its love is a god. Well, then, first of all why are not all spirits loves? Then how does it happen that they, too, are not undefiled by matter? Those are loves who are produced by the soul desiring the good and beautiful, and all the souls in the universe produce this

[2] The phrase comes from Numenius (Test. 24 Leemans = Proclus, *In Tim.* 303, 27–304, 1).

γεννῶσι πᾶσαι τοῦτον τὸν δαίμονα αἱ ἐν τῷδε· οἱ δὲ ἄλλοι δαίμονες ἀπὸ ψυχῆς μὲν καὶ οὗτοι τῆς τοῦ παντός, δυνάμεσι δὲ ἑτέραις γεννώμενοι κατὰ χρείαν τοῦ ὅλου συμπληροῦσι καὶ συνδιοικοῦσι[1] τῷ παντὶ ἕκαστα. Ἔδει γὰρ ἀρκεῖν τὴν ψυχὴν τοῦ παντὸς τῷ παντὶ γεννήσασαν δυνάμεις δαιμόνων καὶ προσφόρους τῷ ἑαυτῆς ὅλῳ. Ἀλλὰ πῶς καὶ τίνος ὕλης μετέχουσιν; Οὐ γὰρ δὴ τῆς σωματικῆς, ἢ ζῷα αἰσθητὰ ἔσται. Καὶ γὰρ εἰ σώματα προσλαμβάνουσιν ἀέρινα ἢ πύρινα, ἀλλὰ δεῖ γε πρότερον διάφορον αὐτῶν τὴν φύσιν εἶναι, ἵνα καὶ μετάσχωσι σώματος· οὐ γὰρ εὐθὺς τὸ καθαρὸν πάντῃ σώματι μίγνυται· καίτοι πολλοῖς δοκεῖ ἡ οὐσία τοῦ δαίμονος καθ' ὅσον δαίμων μετά τινος σώματος ἢ ἀέρος ἢ πυρὸς εἶναι. Ἀλλὰ διὰ τί ἡ μὲν σώματι μίγνυται, ἡ δὲ οὔ, εἰ μή τις εἴη τῇ μιγνυμένῃ αἰτία; Τίς οὖν ἡ αἰτία; Ὕλην δεῖ νοητὴν ὑποθέσθαι, ἵνα τὸ κοινωνῆσαν ἐκείνης ἥκῃ καὶ εἰς ταύτην τὴν τῶν σωμάτων δι' αὐτῆς.

7. Διὸ καὶ ἐν τῇ γενέσει τοῦ Ἔρωτος ὁ Πλάτων φησὶ τὸν Πόρον τὴν μέθην ἔχειν τοῦ νέκταρος οἴνου οὔπω ὄντος, ὡς πρὸ τοῦ αἰσθητοῦ

[1] συμπληροῦσι καὶ συνδιοικοῦσι Kirchhoff: συμπληροῦσαν καὶ συνδιοικοῦσαν codd.

---

[1] For daemonic bodies made of the very best air, see Apuleius, *De Deo Socratis*, ch. 11 (the whole treatise is one of the best examples of vulgar Platonic daemonology); also Por-

spirit. But the other spirits come, they, too, from the soul of the All, but are produced by other powers according to the need of the All; they help to complete it, and along with the All govern individual things. For the soul of the All had to provide adequately for the All by producing powers which are those of spirits and beneficial to its totality. But how do they participate in matter, of any sort at all? Obviously not in bodily matter, or they will be perceptible living creatures. Even if they do take as well bodies of air or fire,[1] their nature must certainly have been different before, to give them any possibility of participating in body. For that which is altogether pure does not directly combine with body; though many people think that a body of air or fire is included in the substantial nature of a spirit in so far as it is a spirit. But why does one substance combine with body and another not, unless there is something responsible for the combination in the case of one that combines? What, then, is responsible? One must suppose an intelligible matter, in order that a being which has a share in it may come to this matter here of bodies by means of it.[2]

7. Therefore, too, in the story of the birth of Love Plato says that Plenty "was drunk with nectar, as wine did not yet exist," meaning that Love came

phyry, *De Abstinentia* II. 39. Belief in these bodies was general among Platonists of the 2nd century A.D. and later, and may ultimately derive from Posidonius.

[2] This idea that participation in "intelligible matter" is an intermediate stage between complete incorporeality and material embodiment is unparalleled in Plotinus. For his normal thought on the subject see especially II. 4 [12] 3–5 and 15.

τοῦ Ἔρωτος γενομένου καὶ τῆς Πενίας μετεχούσης φύσεως νοητοῦ, ἀλλ' οὐκ εἰδώλου νοητοῦ οὐδ' ἐκεῖθεν ἐμφαντασθέντος, ἀλλ' ἐκεῖ γενομένης καὶ συμμιχθείσης ὡς ἐξ εἴδους καὶ ἀοριστίας, ἣν ⟨ἣν⟩[1] ἔχουσα ἡ ψυχὴ πρὶν τυχεῖν τοῦ ἀγαθοῦ, μαντευομένη δέ τι εἶναι κατὰ ἀόριστον καὶ ἄπειρον φάντασμα, τὴν ὑπόστασιν τοῦ Ἔρωτος τεκούσης. Λόγος οὖν γενόμενος ἐν οὐ λόγῳ, ἀορίστῳ δὲ ἐφέσει καὶ ὑποστάσει ἀμυδρᾷ, ἐποίησε τὸ γενόμενον οὐ τέλεον οὐδὲ ἱκανόν, ἐλλιπὲς δέ, ἅτε ἐξ ἐφέσεως ἀορίστου καὶ λόγου ἱκανοῦ γεγενημένον. Καὶ ἔστι λόγος οὗτος οὐ καθαρός, ἅτε ἔχων ἐν αὑτῷ ἔφεσιν ἀόριστον καὶ ἄλογον καὶ ἄπειρον· οὐ γὰρ μήποτε πληρώσεται ἕως ἂν ἔχῃ ἐν αὑτῷ τὴν τοῦ ἀορίστου φύσιν. Ἐξήρτηται δὲ ψυχῆς ὡς ἐξ ἐκείνης μὲν γενόμενος ὡς ἀρχῆς, μῖγμα δὲ ὢν ἐκ λόγου οὐ μείναντος ἐν αὑτῷ, ἀλλὰ μιχθέντος ἀοριστίᾳ, οὐκ αὐτοῦ ἀνακραθέντος ἐκείνῃ, ἀλλὰ τοῦ ἐξ αὐτοῦ ἐκείνῃ. Καὶ ἔστιν ὁ ἔρως οἷον οἶστρος ἄπορος τῇ ἑαυτοῦ φύσει· διὸ καὶ τυγχάνων ἄπορος πάλιν· οὐ γὰρ ἔχει πληροῦσθαι διὰ τὸ μὴ ἔχειν

[1] ⟨ἣν⟩ H–S².

[1] The conception of intelligible matter here is much closer to Plotinus's normal thought than that remarked on in the last chapter. The idea that the soul's Love has a radical incompleteness, a permanent incapacity to be satisfied, because of the "material" element in it goes rather beyond anything else in the *Enneads* (it is, of course, unavoidable if the *Symposium* is to be interpreted in this way). It has, however, something in common with the account of the "restless power" in soul which produces time in III. 7 [45] 11.

into existence before the world of sense, and that Poverty had intercourse with an intelligible nature, not merely with an image of the intelligible or an imagination derived from it, but she was there in the intelligible and united with it, and bore the substance of Love made from form and indefiniteness, the indefiniteness which the soul had before it attained the Good, while it was divining that there was something there by an indefinite, unlimited imagination. Therefore, since a rational principle came to be in something which was not rational, but an indefinite impulse and an obscure expression, what it produced was something not complete or sufficient, but defective, since it came into being from an indefinite impulse and a sufficient rational principle. So Love is not a pure rational principle, since he has in himself an indefinite, irrational, unbounded impulse; for he will never be satisfied, as long as he has in him the nature of the indefinite.[1] He depends on soul in such a way that he comes from it as his origin, but is a mixture of a rational principle which did not stay in itself but was mingled with indefiniteness—it was not the rational principle itself which was mixed with it but that which came from it. And Love is like a "sting,"[2] without resources in his own nature; therefore, even when he attains his object he is without resources again;[3] he cannot be satisfied because

[2] *Phaedrus* 240D 1.

[3] Intellect, on the other hand, "always desires and always attains"; and the One neither desires, for it has nothing to desire, nor attains (*ὥστε ἐν μὲν τῷ νῷ ἡ ἔφεσις καὶ ἐφιέμενος ἀεὶ καὶ ἀεὶ τυγχάνων, ἐκεῖνος δὲ οὔτε ἐφιέμενος—τίνος γάρ; οὔτε τυγχάνων*, III. 8 [30] 11, 23–25).

τὸ μῖγμα· μόνον γὰρ πληροῦται ἀληθῶς, ὅτιπερ καὶ πεπλήρωται τῇ ἑαυτοῦ φύσει· ὁ δὲ διὰ τὴν συνοῦσαν ἔνδειαν ἐφίεται, κἂν παραχρῆμα πληρωθῇ, οὐ στέγει· ἐπεὶ καὶ τὸ ἀμήχανον[1] αὐτῷ διὰ τὴν ἔνδειαν, τὸ δὲ ποριστικὸν διὰ τὴν τοῦ λόγου φύσιν.

Δεῖ δὲ καὶ πᾶν τὸ δαιμόνιον τοιοῦτον νομίζειν καὶ ἐκ τοιούτων· καὶ γὰρ ἕκαστον ἐφ' ᾧ τέτακται ποριστικὸν ἐκείνου καὶ ἐφιέμενον ἐκείνου καὶ συγγενὲς καὶ ταύτῃ τῷ Ἔρωτι καὶ οὐ πλῆρες οὐδ' αὐτό, ἐφιέμενον δέ τινος τῶν ἐν μέρει ὡς ἀγαθῶν. Ὅθεν καὶ τοὺς ἐνταῦθα ἀγαθούς, ὃν ἔχουσιν ἔρωτα, τοῦ ἁπλῶς ἀγαθοῦ καὶ τοῦ ὄντως ἔχειν οὐκ ἔρωτά τινα ἔχοντας· τοὺς δὲ κατ' ἄλλους δαίμονας τεταγμένους κατ' ἄλλον καὶ ἄλλον δαίμονα τετάχθαι ὃν ἁπλῶς εἶχον ἀργὸν ἀφέντας, ἐνεργοῦντας δὲ κατ' ἄλλον δαίμονα, ὃν εἵλοντο κατὰ τὸ σύμφωνον μέρος τοῦ ἐνεργοῦντος ἐν αὐτοῖς, ψυχῆς. Οἱ δὲ κακῶν ἐφιέμενοι ταῖς κακαῖς ἐγγενομέναις ἐπιθυμίαις ἐπέδησαν πάντας τοὺς ἐν αὐτοῖς ἔρωτας, ὥσπερ καὶ λόγον τὸν ὀρθόν, ὅστις σύμφυτος, κακαῖς ταῖς ἐπιγενομέναις δόξαις. Οἱ μὲν οὖν φύσει ἔρωτες καὶ κατὰ φύσιν καλοί· καὶ οἱ μὲν

[1] ἀμήχανον Kirchhoff: εὐμήχανον codd, H–S.

---

[1] I read here ἀμήχανον with Kirchhoff and other editors, including Harder[2] (see Theiler's note *ad loc.*). Henry-Schwyzer retain the MSS εὐμήχανον and remark *sollertem, non inhabilem facit indigentia.* But this would make both parents provide Love with essentially the same quality, ability to get what he wanted, instead of with two opposed qualities, as the sense requires; and in the allusion to the myth in III. 6 [26] 14,

the mixed thing cannot be; only that is truly satisfied which has already attained full satisfaction in its own nature; but Love because of his intimate deficiency is impelled to longing, and even if he is for the moment satisfied, he does not hold what he has received, since his powerlessness comes from his deficiency,[1] but his ability to provide for himself from his rational nature.

But one must consider that the whole race of spirits is like this and comes from parents of this kind; for every spirit is able to provide himself with that to which he is ordered, and impelled by desire for it, and akin to Love in this way too, and is like him, too, in not being satisfied but impelled by desire for one of the partial things which he regards as goods. For this reason we must consider, too, that the love which good men in this world have is a love for that which is simply and really good, not just any kind of love; but that those who are ordered under other spirits are ordered under different ones at different times, leaving their love of the simply good inoperative, but acting under the control of other spirits, whom they chose according to the corresponding part of that which is active in them, the soul. But those who are impelled by desire for evil things have fettered all the loves in them with the evil passions that have grown up in their souls, just as they have fettered their right reason, which is inborn in them, with the evil opinions which have grown upon them. So, then, the loves which are natural and according to nature are fair and good; and the

it is Plenty who is πρᾶγμα εὐμήχανον (l. 17). (Dr. Schwyzer now agrees.)

ἐλάττονος ψυχῆς ἐλάττους εἰς ἀξίαν καὶ δύναμιν, οἱ δὲ κρείττους, πάντες ἐν οὐσίᾳ. Οἱ δὲ παρὰ φύσιν σφαλέντων πάθη ταῦτα καὶ οὐδαμῇ οὐσία οὐδὲ ὑποστάσεις οὐσιώδεις οὐ παρὰ ψυχῆς ἔτι γεννώμενα, ἀλλὰ συνυφιστάμενα κακίᾳ ψυχῆς ὅμοια γεννώσης ἐν διαθέσεσι καὶ ἕξεσιν ἤδη. Καὶ γὰρ ὅλως κινδυνεύει τὰ μὲν ἀγαθὰ τὰ ἀληθῆ κατὰ φύσιν ψυχῆς ἐνεργούσης ἐν ὡρισμένοις οὐσία εἶναι, τὰ δ' ἄλλα οὐκ ἐξ αὐτῆς ἐνεργεῖν, οὐδὲν δ' ἄλλο ἢ πάθη εἶναι· ὥσπερ ψευδῆ νοήματα οὐκ ἔχοντα τὰς ὑπ' αὐτὰ οὐσίας, καθάπερ τὰ ἀληθῆ ὄντως καὶ ἀίδια καὶ ὡρισμένα ὁμοῦ τὸ νοεῖν καὶ τὸ νοητὸν καὶ τὸ εἶναι ἔχοντα οὐ μόνον ἐν τῷ ἁπλῶς, ἀλλὰ καὶ ἐν ἑκάστῳ περὶ τὸ νοητὸν ὄντως καὶ νοῦν τὸν ἐν ἑκάστῳ, εἰ δεῖ[1] καὶ ἐν ἑκάστῳ ἡμῶν τίθεσθαι καθαρῶς νόησιν καὶ νοητόν—καὶ μὴ ὁμοῦ καὶ ἡμῶν τοῦτο καὶ ἁπλῶς—ὅθεν καὶ τῶν ἁπλῶν ἡμῖν ὁ ἔρως· καὶ γὰρ αἱ νοήσεις· καὶ εἴ τινος τῶν ἐν μέρει, κατὰ συμβεβηκός, ὥσπερ, εἰ τόδε τὸ τρίγωνον, δύο ὀρθὰς θεωρεῖ, καθ' ὅσον ἁπλῶς τρίγωνον.

8. Ἀλλὰ τίς ὁ Ζεύς, οὗ τὸν κῆπον λέγει, εἰς ὃν εἰσῆλθεν ὁ Πόρος, καὶ τίς ὁ κῆπος οὗτος;

[1] εἰ δεῖ Dodds, H–S²: εἴδει codd.

---

[1] This example is taken from Aristotle, who uses it frequently, e.g. *Metaphysics* Δ 30. 1025a, 32.

[2] *Symposium* 203B 5–6.

loves of a lesser soul are less in worth and power, but those [of a better soul] are more; both are real substantial loves. But the loves which are against nature, these are passive affections of the perverted and are not in any way substance or expressions of substantial realities, and are not any longer products of the soul but have come into existence together with the vice of a soul which now produces things like itself in its dispositions and states. For it is likely in general that the true goods, which are in accordance with the nature of a soul active among things defined and limited, are substance, but the others [evils] are not acts which the soul produces from itself but are nothing else but passive affections; they are like false thoughts which have no substantial realities as their bases, as really true thoughts which are everlasting and definite have thinking and object of thought and existence all together, not only in the act of thought taken simply and absolutely, but in each individual act concerned with the real object of thought and the mind in each individual; if, indeed, we are to assume that in each one of us thinking and object of thought exist in a pure state—and yet they are not together and this state [of unity of thought and object of thought] does not belong to us and our thinking is not simple: hence our love is of simple realities, for so are our thoughts; and if we love one of the partial things this is incidental, just as, if according to the theorem this particular triangle has the sum of its angles equal to two right angles, it is in so far as it is simply a triangle.[1]

8. But who is Zeus, whose "garden" Plato says it is "into which Plenty came,"[2] and what is this

Ἡ μὲν γὰρ Ἀφροδίτη ψυχὴ ἦν ἡμῖν, λόγος δὲ ἐλέγετο τῶν πάντων ὁ Πόρος. Ταῦτα δὲ τί δεῖ τίθεσθαι, τὸν Δία καὶ τὸν κῆπον αὐτοῦ; Οὐδὲ γὰρ ψυχὴν δεῖ τίθεσθαι τὸν Δία τὴν Ἀφροδίτην τοῦτο θέντας. Δεῖ δὴ λαβεῖν καὶ ἐνταῦθα παρὰ Πλάτωνος τὸν Δία ἐκ μὲν Φαίδρου ἡγεμόνα μέγαν λέγοντος αὐτοῦ τοῦτον τὸν θεόν, ἐν ἄλλοις δὲ τρίτον, οἶμαι, τοῦτον· σαφέστερον δὲ ἐν τῷ Φιλήβῳ, ἡνίκ' ἂν φῇ ἐν τῷ Διὶ εἶναι βασιλικὴν μὲν ψυχήν, βασιλικὸν δὲ νοῦν. Εἰ οὖν ὁ Ζεὺς νοῦς ἐστι μέγας καὶ ψυχὴ καὶ ἐν τοῖς αἰτίοις τάττεται, κατὰ δὲ τὸ κρεῖττον δεῖ τάττειν διά τε τὰ ἄλλα καὶ ὅτι αἴτιον καὶ τὸ βασιλικὸν δὲ καὶ τὸ ἡγούμενον, ὁ μὲν ἔσται κατὰ τὸν νοῦν, ἡ δὲ Ἀφροδίτη αὐτοῦ οὖσα καὶ ἐξ αὐτοῦ καὶ σὺν αὐτῷ κατὰ τὴν ψυχὴν τετάξεται κατὰ τὸ καλὸν καὶ ἀγλαὸν καὶ τὸ τῆς ψυχῆς ἄκακον καὶ ἁβρὸν Ἀφροδίτη λεχθεῖσα. Καὶ γὰρ εἰ κατὰ μὲν τὸν νοῦν τοὺς ἄρρενας τάττομεν τῶν θεῶν, κατὰ δὲ τὰς ψυχὰς αὐτῶν τὰς θηλείας λέγομεν, ὡς νῷ ἑκάστῳ ψυχῆς συνούσης, εἴη ἂν καὶ ταύτῃ ἡ ψυχὴ τοῦ Διὸς ἡ Ἀφροδίτη πάλιν μαρτυρούντων τούτῳ τῷ λόγῳ ἱερέων καὶ θεολόγων, οἳ εἰς ταὐτὸν Ἥραν καὶ Ἀφροδίτην ἄγουσι καὶ τὸν τῆς Ἀφροδίτης ἀστέρα ἐν οὐρανῷ Ἥρας λέγουσιν.

---

[1] *Phaedrus* 246E4.

[2] *Letter* II. 312E4 (this passage, one of the foundations of Plotinus's interpretation of Plato, is quoted in full in the next treatise in the chronological order, I. 8 [51] 2. 28–32).

[3] *Philebus* 30D 1–2.

garden? Now Aphrodite was for us the soul, and we said that Plenty was the rational principle of all things. But what are we to make of these, Zeus and his garden? For we must not make Zeus the soul, since this is what we have made Aphrodite. Here too, certainly, we must take our understanding of Zeus from Plato, from the *Phaedrus* where he says that this god is a " great leader,"[1] but elsewhere he says, I think, that Zeus is the third:[2] but he is clearer in the *Philebus*, when he says that there is in Zeus " a royal soul and a royal intellect."[3] If, then, Zeus is a great intellect and soul and is ranked among the causes, and we must rank him on the higher level, for other reasons and particularly because the epithets " royal " and " leading " mean " cause," he will be on the level of Intellect,[4] and Aphrodite, who is his daughter and comes from him and is with him, will be ranked on the level of soul, being called Aphrodite because of the beauty and brightness and innocence and delicacy of soul. And, then, if we rank the male gods on the level of Intellect, and speak of the female gods as being their souls, since each intellect is accompanied by a soul, in this way, too, Aphrodite would be the soul of Zeus; and, again, priests and theologians bear witness to this interpretation, who make Hera and Aphrodite one and the same and call the star of Aphrodite in heaven the star of Hera.[5]

[4] In ch. 2 of this treatise, and elsewhere, Kronos is Intellect. This passage shows again how little real importance Plotinus attaches to the interpretation of myths, and also how closely, at times, he is prepared to assimilate higher Soul to Intellect.

[5] Cp. [Aristotle], *De Mundo* 392a 27–28.

9. Ὁ οὖν Πόρος λόγος ὢν τῶν ἐν τῷ νοητῷ καὶ νῷ καὶ μᾶλλον κεχυμένος καὶ οἷον ἁπλωθεὶς περὶ ψυχὴν ἂν γένοιτο καὶ ἐν ψυχῇ. Τὸ γὰρ ἐν νῷ συνεσπειραμένον, καὶ οὐ παρὰ ἄλλου εἰς αὐτόν, τούτῳ δὲ μεθύοντι ἐπακτὸν τὸ τῆς πληρώσεως. Τὸ δ' ἐκεῖ πληρούμενον[1] τοῦ νέκταρος τί ἂν εἴη ἢ λόγος ἀπὸ κρείττονος ἀρχῆς πεσὼν εἰς ἐλάττονα; Ἐν οὖν τῇ ψυχῇ ἀπὸ νοῦ ὁ λόγος οὗτος, ὅτε ἡ Ἀφροδίτη λέγεται γεγονέναι, εἰσρυεὶς εἰς τὸν κῆπον αὐτοῦ. Κῆπος δὲ πᾶς ἀγλάισμα καὶ πλούτου ἐγκαλλώπισμα. Ἀγλαΐζεται δὲ τὰ τοῦ Διὸς λόγῳ, καὶ τὰ καλλωπίσματα αὐτοῦ τὰ παρὰ τοῦ νοῦ αὐτοῦ εἰς τὴν ψυχὴν ἐλθόντα ἀγλαΐσματα. Ἢ τί ἂν εἴη ὁ κῆπος τοῦ Διὸς ἢ τὰ ἀγάλματα αὐτοῦ καὶ τὰ ἀγλαΐσματα; Τί δ' ἂν εἴη τὰ ἀγλαΐσματα αὐτοῦ καὶ τὰ κοσμήματα ἢ οἱ λόγοι οἱ παρ' αὐτοῦ ῥυέντες; Ὁμοῦ δὲ οἱ λόγοι ὁ Πόρος, ἡ εὐπορία καὶ ὁ πλοῦτος τῶν καλῶν, ἐν ἐκφάνσει ἤδη· καὶ τοῦτό ἐστι τὸ μεθύειν τῷ νέκταρι. Τί γὰρ θεοῖς νέκταρ ἢ ὃ τὸ θεῖον κομίζεται; Κομίζεται δὲ τὸ ὑποβεβηκὸς νοῦ λόγον· νοῦς δὲ ἑαυτὸν ἔχει

[1] πληρούμενον Kirchhoff: πληροῦν codd. H–S.

---

[1] For the "contraction" or concentrated unity of Intellect as contrasted with the relative diffusion of Soul or the λόγος in Soul cp. III. 7 [45] 11. 23 ff., and III. 2 [47] 2. 17 ff. In this passage Plotinus shows the same care to distinguish between pure Intellect and the intellectual in Soul that he does in the nearly contemporary treatise V. 3 [49].

9. Plenty, then, since he is a rational principle in the intelligible world and in Intellect, and since he is more diffused and, as it were, spread out, would be concerned with soul and in soul. For that which is in Intellect is contracted together,[1] and nothing comes to it from anything else, but when Plenty was drunk his state of being filled was brought about from outside. But what could that which is filled [2] with nectar in the higher world be except a rational principle which has fallen from a higher origin to a lesser one? So this principle is in Soul and comes from Intellect, flowing into his garden when Aphrodite is said to have been born. And every garden is a glory and decoration of wealth; and the property of Zeus is glorified by rational principle, and his decorations are the glories that come from Intellect itself into the soul. Or what could the garden of Zeus be but his images in which he takes delight and his glories? And what could his glories and adornments be but the rational principles which flow from him? The rational principles all together are Plenty, the plenitude and wealth of beauties, already manifested; and this is the being drunk with nectar. For what is nectar for the gods but that which the divinity acquires? And that which is on the level below Intellect acquires rational principle; but Intellect

[2] I read here Kirchhoff's πληρούμενον (adopted by Cilento and Harder [2]) which the sense plainly seems to require. Henry-Schwyzer retain the MSS πληροῦν which the free paraphrase in Ambrose (*De Bono Mortis* 5. 19, *divitiis horti in quo repletus potu iaceret Porus qui nectar effunderet*), on the whole seems to support. It is just possible that πληροῦν may have been a slip by Plotinus himself.

ἐν κόρῳ καὶ οὐ μεθύει ἔχων. Οὐ γὰρ ἐπακτόν τι ἔχει. Ὁ δὲ λόγος νοῦ γέννημα καὶ ὑπόστασις μετὰ νοῦν καὶ οὐκέτι αὐτοῦ ὤν, ἀλλ' ἐν ἄλλῳ, ἐν τῷ τοῦ Διὸς κήπῳ λέγεται κεῖσθαι τότε κείμενος, ὅτε ἡ Ἀφροδίτη ἐν τοῖς οὖσιν ὑποστῆναι λέγεται.

Δεῖ δὲ τοὺς μύθους, εἴπερ τοῦτο ἔσονται, καὶ μερίζειν χρόνοις ἃ λέγουσι, καὶ διαιρεῖν ἀπ' ἀλλήλων πολλὰ τῶν ὄντων ὁμοῦ μὲν ὄντα, τάξει δὲ ἢ δυνάμεσι διεστῶτα, ὅπου καὶ οἱ λόγοι καὶ γενέσεις τῶν ἀγεννήτων ποιοῦσι, καὶ τὰ ὁμοῦ ὄντα καὶ αὐτοὶ διαιροῦσι, καὶ διδάξαντες ὡς δύνανται τῷ νοήσαντι ἤδη συγχωροῦσι συναιρεῖν. Ἡ δὲ συναίρεσις· ψυχὴ νῷ συνοῦσα καὶ παρὰ νοῦ ὑποστᾶσα καὶ αὖ λόγων πληρωθεῖσα καὶ καλὴ καλοῖς κοσμηθεῖσα καὶ εὐπορίας πληρωθεῖσα, ὡς εἶναι ἐν αὐτῇ ὁρᾶν πολλὰ ἀγλαίσματα καὶ τῶν καλῶν ἁπάντων εἰκόνας, Ἀφροδίτη μέν ἐστι τὸ πᾶν, οἱ δὲ ἐν αὐτῇ λόγοι πάντες εὐπορία καὶ Πόρος ἀπὸ τῶν ἄνω ῥυέντος[1] τοῦ ἐκεῖ νέκταρος· τὰ δὲ ἐν αὐτῇ ἀγλαίσματα ὡς ἂν ἐν ζωῇ κείμενα κῆπος Διὸς λέγεται, καὶ εὕδειν ἐκεῖ ὁ Πόρος οἷς ἐπληρώθη βεβαρημένος. Ζωῆς δὲ φανείσης καὶ

[1] ῥυέντος Kirchhoff, H–S[2]: ῥυέντες codd.

---

[1] Plotinus is prepared to apply this penetrating observation of the closeness of metaphysical and mythical discourses

possesses itself in satiety and is not drunk with the possession. For it does not possess anything from outside. But the rational principle, the product and expression of Intellect, coming after Intellect and no longer belonging to it, but being in something else, is said to lie in the garden of Zeus, lying there at the time when it is said that Aphrodite came into existence in the realm of being.

But myths, if they are really going to be myths, must separate in time the things of which they tell, and set apart from each other many realities which are together, but distinct in rank or powers, at points where rational discussions, also, make generations of things ungenerated, and themselves, too, separate things which are together;[1] the myths, when they have taught us as well as they can, allow the man who has understood them to put together again that which they have separated. Here is the putting together [of the myth of Eros]: Soul, which is with Intellect and has come into existence from Intellect, and then again been filled with rational principles and, itself beautiful, adorned with beauties and filled with plenitude, so that there are in it many glories and images of all beautiful things, is as a whole Aphrodite, and the rational principles in it are all plenitude and Plenty, as the nectar there flows from the regions above; and the glories in it, since they are set in life, are called the " garden of Zeus," and it is said[2] that Plenty " sleeps " there, " weighed down " by the principles with which he was filled.

(λόγοι and μῦθοι) to each other to his own metaphysical discussions: cp. VI. 7 [38] 35, 27–30.

[2] *Symposium* 203B 5–7.

οὔσης ἀεὶ ἐν τοῖς οὖσιν ἑστιᾶσθαι οἱ θεοὶ λέγονται ὡς ἂν ἐν τοιαύτῃ μακαριότητι ὄντες. Ἀεὶ δὲ οὕτως ὑπέστη ὅδε ἐξ ἀνάγκης ἐκ τῆς ψυχῆς ἐφέσεως πρὸς τὸ κρεῖττον καὶ ἀγαθόν, καὶ ἦν ἀεί, ἐξ οὗπερ καὶ ψυχή, Ἔρως. Ἔστι δ' οὗτος μικτόν τι χρῆμα μετέχον μὲν ἐνδείας, ᾗ πληροῦσθαι θέλει, οὐκ ἄμοιρον δὲ εὐπορίας, ᾗ οὗ ἔχει τὸ ἐλλεῖπον ζητεῖ· οὐ γὰρ δὴ τὸ πάμπαν ἄμοιρον τοῦ ἀγαθοῦ τὸ ἀγαθὸν ἄν ποτε ζητήσειεν. Ἐκ Πόρου οὖν καὶ Πενίας λέγεται εἶναι, ᾗ ἡ ἔλλειψις καὶ ἡ ἔφεσις καὶ τῶν λόγων ἡ μνήμη ὁμοῦ συνελθόντα ἐν ψυχῇ ἐγέννησε τὴν ἐνέργειαν τὴν πρὸς τὸ ἀγαθόν, ἔρωτα τοῦτον ὄντα. Ἡ δὲ μήτηρ αὐτῷ Πενία, ὅτι ἀεὶ ἡ ἔφεσις ἐνδεοῦς. Ὕλη δὲ ἡ Πενία, ὅτι καὶ ἡ ὕλη ἐνδεὴς τὰ πάντα, καὶ τὸ ἀόριστον τῆς τοῦ ἀγαθοῦ ἐπιθυμίας—οὐ γὰρ μορφή τις οὐδὲ λόγος ἐν τῷ ἐφιεμένῳ τούτου—ὑλικώτερον τὸ ἐφιέμενον καθ' ὅσον ἐφίεται ποιεῖ. Τὸ δὲ πρὸς αὐτὸ εἶδός ἐστι μόνον ἐν αὐτῷ μένον· καὶ δέξασθαι δὲ ἐφιέμενον ὕλην τῷ ἐπιόντι τὸ δεξόμενον παρασκευάζει. Οὕτω τοι ὁ Ἔρως ὑλικός τίς ἐστι, καὶ δαίμων οὗτός ἐστιν ἐκ ψυχῆς, καθ' ὅσον ἐλλείπει τῷ ἀγαθῷ, ἐφίεται δέ, γεγενημένος.

And since life has appeared, and is always there, in the world of realities, the gods are said to " feast "[1] since they are in a state of blessedness appropriate to the word. And so this being, Love, has from everlasting come into existence from the soul's aspiration towards the higher and the good, and he was there always, as long as Soul, too, existed. And he is a mixed thing, having a part of need, in that he wishes to be filled, but not without a share of plenitude, in that he seeks what is wanting to that which he already has; for certainly that which is altogether without a share in the good would not ever seek the good. So he is said to be born of Plenty and Poverty, in that the lack and the aspiration and the memory of the rational principles coming together in the soul, produced the activity directed towards the good, and this is Love. But his mother is Poverty, because aspiration belongs to that which is in need. And Poverty is matter, because matter, too, is in every way in need, and because the indefiniteness of the desire for the good—for there is no shape or rational forming principle in that which desires it—makes the aspiring thing more like matter in so far as it aspires. But the good, in relation to that which aspires to it, is form only, remaining in itself; and that which aspires to receive it prepares its receptive capacity as matter for the form which is to come upon it. So Love is a material kind of being, and he is a spirit produced from soul in so far as soul falls short of the good but aspires to it.

[1] *Symposium* 203B 2.

ENNEAD III. 6

III. 6. ON THE IMPASSIBILITY OF THINGS WITHOUT BODY

Introductory Note

THIS treatise is No. 26 in Porphyry's chronological order, and so comes immediately before the great treatise *On The Problems of the Soul* (divided by Porphyry into two, IV. 3 [27] and IV. 4 [28].) Plotinus was, it seems, at this time much concerned with questions of psychology, and in the first part of the treatise (chs. 1–5) he sets out to show that the soul is not subject to affections or modifications. In the second part (chs. 6–19), he turns to consider a very different kind of impassibility, that of matter. The two parts of the treatise appear at first sight to have little connection with each other. But there is no doubt that Plotinus himself composed them as parts of a single work, as he refers back to the first part in the second (9. 6). And there is more connection between them than may appear at first sight. What Plotinus is primarily concerned with in this treatise is to work out and display the implications of incorporeality, to exclude from philosophy ways of speaking and thinking about incorporeal things as subject to impressions, modifications or contaminations which really imply that they are corporeal (like the Stoic God and soul). And matter, for both Platonists and Aristotelians, is, of course, incorporeal. In the first part, where Plotinus is concerned to show that soul is impassible because incorporeal, he is able to use Aristotelian ideas in combating Stoic corporealism. But in the second part he differs sharply from Aristotle and goes, as far as we can tell, well beyond any earlier Platonists (and certainly beyond his own earlier discussion of matter in II. 4 [12]) in

his assertion that matter is absolutely impassible in the sense that it is not affected, modified or changed in any way by the forms which enter it, which are themselves, he maintains, mere ghosts of form, powerless to act on it. Here again there is a connection of thought with the first part of the treatise. Plotinus's assertion of the impassibility of incorporeal soul is an essential part of his general assertion of the primacy and radical independence of soul, his insistence that it is solely responsible for such reality as there is in this world, and is always active in and never passive to and affected by bodies; this is fundamental to his whole way of thinking about man and how he ought to live. And the presentation of matter as radically impassible, totally unaffected by form, carries with it the converse, that matter is utterly powerless in any way to affect or capture form. And the picture of the physical world as a world of ghosts in a vacuum, where phantoms of form flit in and out like reflections in a non-existent mirror serves to emphasise its inability to affect soul in any way. (Soul and matter are several times compared and contrasted in the second part of the treatise.) Some readers may feel, by the time they reach the end of the treatise, that Plotinus has made matter not only impassible but impossible; that is, that his elimination of even the idea of positive potency has left the concept without any content at all, has made " matter " only a meaningless word. But not only in this treatise but to the end of his life (see the treatise *On What are and Whence Come Evils* I. 8 [51]) he insists on the necessity of postulating matter, mainly in order that, by its utter negativity and total incapacity to receive any degree of good, it may provide an explanation of evil.

Synopsis

A. The impassibility of soul. General statement of the position to be maintained: soul, being incorporeal, cannot

be affected or modified like a body, though difficulties arise about vice and error (ch. 1). Discussion of vice: rejection of the theory that virtue and vice are just harmony and disharmony of the different parts of the soul: each part must have its own virtue, which is, essentially, seeing reason: the passage from virtue to vice and vice to virtue involves no intrinsic alteration in the soul-parts (ch. 2). Discussion of emotions: distinction between the body-element and the soul-element; the soul moves itself, but is not moved or affected by the emotions (ch. 3). The part of the soul subject to affections: relation between opinions, mental images and bodily disturbances: soul is form, and form is not affected or disturbed by what goes on in that which it informs (ch. 4). What, then, is meant by philosophical purification, freeing the soul from affections? Waking up the soul from its bad dreams, freeing it from distracting mental pictures and turning from the things below to those above (ch. 5).

B. The impassibility of matter. Matter, too, is something incorporeal. Real being is immaterial, eternal, unchanging, living intellect. Resistance, obstruction, hardness, aggressive corporeality are signs of lack of being and life: and the more a thing is a body, the more it is affected. To think that bodies are real is an illusion, a dream from which we should wake up (ch. 6). Matter is truly non-being, nothing but a ghost; and the forms which pass through it are ghosts too; they cannot act, and it is not acted on (ch. 7). Things which are affected are affected by their opposites, and affection is the way to destruction: but matter is indestructible (ch. 8). If a thing is present in or to something else it does not necessarily affect it: matter has no opposite, and is therefore not affected by anything (ch. 9). If matter was altered or affected it would no longer be able to receive all forms (ch. 10). Exegesis of *Timaeus* 50 B–C. How the forms are in matter without altering it and making it beautiful and

good instead of ugly and bad (ch. 11). Plato's real thought, rather cursorily expressed, is that matter is not affected by form in any way at all, receives neither shape nor size nor anything else, because it is not a body (ch. 12). What is meant by saying that matter " tries to escape " from form, and that it is " the receptacle and nurse of all becoming." The ghostly forms in the falsity of matter are like reflections in an invisible and formless mirror (ch. 13). Matter is the medium in which images of real being quasi-exist, the " Poverty " of the *Symposium*, always begging for what it can never really have, like a reflecting surface which concentrates rays on its outside (ch. 14). Analogies, and differences, between the mental pictures in soul and the phantoms in matter; soul is something, and has its own power to deal with its images, matter is nothing and has no power (ch. 15). Matter and size: size comes with form and is form; matter has only false size, not true size (chs. 16–18). Matter like soul contains all forms, but not all together, like soul, but divided (ch. 18). The forms do matter neither harm nor good. Matter is only a " mother " in a manner of speaking, for it brings forth nothing and is only a passive receptacle (as the mother is according to one theory). The ithyphallic Hermes is a symbol of the generative power of the *logos*; the eunuchs who accompany the Great Mother symbolise the sterility of matter (ch. 19).

III. 6. (26) ΠΕΡΙ ΤΗΣ ΑΠΑΘΕΙΑΣ ΤΩΝ ΑΣΩΜΑΤΩΝ

1. Τὰς αἰσθήσεις οὐ πάθη λέγοντες εἶναι, ἐνεργείας δὲ περὶ παθήματα καὶ κρίσεις, τῶν μὲν παθῶν περὶ ἄλλο γινομένων, οἷον τὸ σῶμα φέρε τὸ τοιόνδε, τῆς δὲ κρίσεως περὶ τὴν ψυχήν, οὐ τῆς κρίσεως πάθους οὔσης—ἔδει γὰρ αὖ ἄλλην κρίσιν γίνεσθαι καὶ ἐπαναβαίνειν ἀεὶ εἰς ἄπειρον—εἴχομεν οὐδὲν ἧττον καὶ ἐνταῦθα ἀπορίαν, εἰ ἡ κρίσις ᾗ κρίσις οὐδὲν ἔχει τοῦ κρινομένου. Ἢ, εἰ τύπον ἔχοι, πέπονθεν. Ἦν δ' ὅμως λέγειν καὶ περὶ τῶν καλουμένων τυπώσεων, ὡς ὁ τρόπος ὅλως ἕτερος ἢ ὡς ὑπείληπται, ὁποῖος καὶ ἐπὶ τῶν νοήσεων ἐνεργειῶν καὶ τούτων οὐσῶν γινώσκειν ἄνευ τοῦ παθεῖν τι δυναμένων· καὶ ὅλως ὁ λόγος ἡμῖν καὶ τὸ βούλημα μὴ ὑποβαλεῖν[1] τροπαῖς καὶ ἀλλοιώσεσι τὴν ψυχὴν τοιαύταις, ὁποῖαι αἱ θερμάνσεις καὶ ψύξεις σωμάτων. Καὶ τὸ παθητικὸν δὲ λεγόμενον αὐτῆς ἔδει ἰδεῖν καὶ ἐπισκέψασθαι, πότερα καὶ

[1] ὑποβαλεῖν Ficinus, H–S: ὑπολαβεῖν codd.

---

[1] By the Stoics: cp., e.g., *Stoicorum Veterum Fragmenta* I. 141 and 484; II. 55.

III. 6. ON THE IMPASSIBILITY OF THINGS WITHOUT BODY

1. We say that sense-perceptions are not affections but activities and judgements concerned with affections; affections belong to something else, say, for instance, to the body qualified in a particular way, but the judgement belongs to the soul, and the judgement is not an affection—for if it was, there would have to be yet another judgement, and we should have to go back for ever to infinity. None the less we had a problem at this point, whether the judgement in so far as it is a judgement has nothing in it of what is judged. If it has an impression of it, then it has been affected. But it would, all the same, be possible to say also about what are called the impressions, that their character is quite different from what has been supposed,[1] and is like that which is also found in acts of thought; these, too, are activities which are able to know without being affected in any way; and in general our reasoned intention is not to subject the soul to changes and alterations of the same kind as heatings and coolings of bodies.[2] And we ought to survey the part of the soul which is said to be subject to affections, and consider whether we shall grant this, too, to be unchangeable,

[2] This again is an allusion to the Stoic view: cp. *Stoic. Vet. Fr.* I. 234 and III. 459.

τοῦτο ἄτρεπτον δώσομεν, ἢ τούτῳ μόνῳ τὸ πάσχειν συγχωρήσομεν. Ἀλλὰ τοῦτο μὲν ὕστερον, περὶ δὲ τῶν προτέρων τὰς ἀπορίας ἐπισκεπτέον. Πῶς γὰρ ἄτρεπτον καὶ τὸ πρὸ τοῦ παθητικοῦ καὶ τὸ πρὸ αἰσθήσεως καὶ ὅλως ψυχῆς ὁτιοῦν κακίας περὶ αὐτὴν ἐγγινομένης καὶ δοξῶν ψευδῶν καὶ ἀνοίας; Οἰκειώσεις δὲ καὶ ἀλλοτριώσεις ἡδομένης καὶ λυπουμένης, ὀργιζομένης, φθονούσης, ζηλούσης, ἐπιθυμούσης, ὅλως οὐδαμῇ ἡσυχίαν ἀγούσης, ἀλλ' ἐφ' ἑκάστῳ τῶν προσπιπτόντων κινουμένης καὶ μεταβαλλούσης. Ἀλλ' εἰ μὲν σῶμά ἐστιν ἡ ψυχὴ καὶ μέγεθος ἔχει, οὐ ῥᾴδιον, μᾶλλον δὲ ὅλως ἀδύνατον, ἀπαθῆ αὐτὴν καὶ ἄτρεπτον δεικνύναι ἐν ὁτῳοῦν τῶν λεγομένων γίγνεσθαι περὶ αὐτήν· εἰ δέ ἐστιν οὐσία ἀμεγέθης καὶ δεῖ καὶ τὸ ἄφθαρτον αὐτῇ παρεῖναι, εὐλαβητέον αὐτῇ πάθη διδόναι τοιαῦτα, μὴ καὶ λάθωμεν αὐτὴν φθαρτὴν εἶναι διδόντες. Καὶ δὴ εἴτε ἀριθμὸς εἴτε λόγος, ὥς φαμεν, ἡ οὐσία αὐτῆς, πῶς ἂν πάθος ἐγγένοιτο ἐν ἀριθμῷ ἢ λόγῳ; Ἀλλὰ μᾶλλον λόγους ἀλόγους καὶ ἀπαθῆ πάθη δεῖ ἐπιγίγνεσθαι αὐτῇ οἴεσθαι, καὶ ταῦτα τὰ ἀπὸ τῶν σωμάτων μετενηνεγμένα

---

[1] The view of Plotinus on the alleged "movements" and "changes" in the soul is very close to that of Aristotle, on whom he depends very much in this section of the treatise; cp. *De Anima* A.4. 408b1 ff. and B.5. 417b5 ff.

[2] That the soul is not a body, which would prevent it from being immortal and incorruptible, is argued at length in IV. 7 [2].

or whether we shall admit that this alone can be affected. But we will discuss this later; now we must consider the difficulties which arise about the higher parts of the soul. For how can the part which comes before that subject to affections, and the part before sense-perception, and in general any part of the soul, be unchangeable when vice and false opinions and stupidity occur in the soul? And the soul accepts things as its own or rejects them as alien when it feels pleasure and pain, anger, envy, jealousy, lust, and in general is never quiet but always moved and changed by every casual contact.[1] But if the soul is a body and has magnitude, it is not easy but rather altogether impossible, to show it as unaffected and unchangeable in any one of the occurrences which are said to take place in it. But if it is a substance without magnitude and must necessarily possess incorruptibility, we must be careful not to give it affections of this kind, so as to avoid making it corruptible without noticing that we have done so.[2] Then again, whether its substance is a number[3] or whether it is a rational formative principle, as we say it is, how can an affection occur in a number or a rational principle? But we must rather think that irrational reasons and unaffected affections come upon it; and it must be understood that these, which are transferred from bodies, are each and all of them there

[3] For the history of the doctrine that the soul is a number, which goes back to Xenocrates (Aristotle, *De Anima* I. 2. 404b27; cp. de Vogel, *Greek Philosophy* II. 759), see P. Merlan, *From Platonism to Neoplatonism* chs. I and II. It does not play an important part in the thought of Plotinus, but he recognises it as orthodox Platonism: cp. V. 1 [10] 5. 9; VI. 5 [23] 9. 13–14.

ἀντικειμένως ληπτέον ἕκαστα καὶ κατ᾽ ἀναλογίαν μετενηνεγμένα, καὶ ἔχουσαν οὐκ ἔχειν καὶ πάσχουσαν οὐ πάσχειν. Καὶ ὅστις ὁ τρόπος τῶν τοιούτων, ἐπισκεπτέον.

2. Πρῶτον δὲ περὶ κακίας καὶ ἀρετῆς λεκτέον, τί γίγνεται τότε, ὅταν κακία λέγηται παρεῖναι· καὶ γὰρ ἀφαιρεῖν δεῖν φαμεν ὥς τινος ὄντος ἐν αὐτῇ κακοῦ καὶ ἐνθεῖναι ἀρετὴν καὶ κοσμῆσαι καὶ κάλλος ἐμποιῆσαι ἀντὶ αἴσχους τοῦ πρόσθεν. Ἆρ᾽ οὖν λέγοντες ἀρετὴν ἁρμονίαν εἶναι, ἀναρμοστίαν δὲ τὴν κακίαν, λέγοιμεν ἂν δόξαν δοκοῦσαν τοῖς παλαιοῖς καί τι πρὸς τὸ ζητούμενον οὐ μικρὸν ὁ λόγος ἀνύσειεν; Εἰ γὰρ συναρμοσθέντα μὲν φύσιν τὰ μέρη τῆς ψυχῆς πρὸς ἄλληλα ἀρετή ἐστι, μὴ συναρμοσθέντα δὲ κακία, ἐπακτὸν οὐδὲν ἂν οὐδὲ ἑτέρωθεν γίγνοιτο, ἀλλ᾽ ἕκαστον ἥκοι ἂν οἷόν ἐστιν εἰς τὴν ἁρμογὴν καὶ οὐκ ἂν ἥκοι ἐν τῇ ἀναρμοστίᾳ τοιοῦτον ὄν, οἷον καὶ χορευταὶ χορεύοντες καὶ συνᾴδοντες ἀλλήλοις, εἰ καὶ μὴ οἱ αὐτοί εἰσι, καὶ μόνος τις ᾄδων τῶν ἄλλων μὴ ᾀδόντων, καὶ ἑκάστου καθ᾽ ἑαυτὸν ᾄδοντος· οὐ γὰρ μόνον δεῖ συνᾴδειν, ἀλλὰ καὶ ἕκαστον καλῶς τὸ αὐτοῦ ᾄδοντα οἰκείᾳ μουσικῇ· ὥστε κἀκεῖ ἐπὶ τῆς ψυχῆς ἁρμονίαν εἶναι ἑκάστου μέρους τὸ αὐτῷ προσῆκον ποιοῦντος. Δεῖ δὴ πρὸ τῆς ἁρμονίας

---

[1] The Pythagoreans; cp. Plato, *Phaedo* 93C.

in an opposed sense and are transferred in so far as something corresponds to them in the soul, and that in possessing them it does not possess and in being affected by them it is not affected. And we must consider how happenings of this sort come about.

2. First we must explain about virtue and vice, what happens at any time when vice is said to be present; for we assert that one must " take away," as if there was some evil in the soul, and " put in " virtue, and set the soul in order and produce beauty in it instead of the ugliness which was there before. Now if we say that " virtue is harmony " and vice lack of harmony, should we be expressing an opinion that accords with the views of the ancients,[1] and would the statement contribute something of no small value to our investigation? For if the natural harmony of the parts of the soul with each other is virtue, and their disharmony, vice, then there would be nothing brought in from outside, or from another source, but each part would enter into the harmony just as it is, or would not enter in, and remain in disharmony, because it was the sort of thing it was; just as dancers dance, and sing in accord with each other, even if it is not [always] the same ones who sing, and [sometimes] one sings when the others do not, and each sings in his own way, for they must not only sing together but each one, as they sing together, must also sing his own part beautifully by his own personal art of music;[2] so there, too, in the soul there is a harmony when each part does what is proper to it. It is certainly necessary that before

[2] The thought here is the same as in I. 6 [1] 1. 26–30. Contrast III. 2 [47] 17. 64 ff. (see notes *ad locc.*).

ταύτης ἄλλην ἑκάστου εἶναι ἀρετήν, καὶ κακίαν δὲ ἑκάστου πρὸ τῆς πρὸς ἄλληλα ἀναρμοστίας. Τίνος οὖν παρόντος ἕκαστον μέρος κακόν; Ἢ κακίας. Καὶ ἀγαθὸν αὖ; Ἢ ἀρετῆς. Τῷ μὲν οὖν λογιστικῷ τάχ' ἄν τις λέγων ἄνοιαν εἶναι τὴν κακίαν καὶ ἄνοιαν τὴν κατὰ ἀπόφασιν οὐ παρουσίαν τινὸς ἂν λέγοι. Ἀλλ' ὅταν καὶ ψευδεῖς δόξαι ἐνῶσιν, ὃ δὴ μάλιστα τὴν κακίαν ποιεῖ, πῶς οὐκ ἐγγίνεσθαι φήσει καὶ ἀλλοῖον ταύτῃ τοῦτο τὸ μόριον γίνεσθαι; Τὸ δὲ θυμοειδὲς οὐκ ἄλλως μὲν ἔχει δειλαῖνον, ἀνδρεῖον δὲ ὂν ἄλλως; Τὸ δ' ἐπιθυμοῦν ἀκόλαστον μὲν ὂν οὐκ ἄλλως, σωφρονοῦν δὲ ἄλλως; ᾗ πέπονθεν. Ἢ ὅταν μὲν ἐν ἀρετῇ ἕκαστον ᾖ, ἐνεργεῖν κατὰ τὴν οὐσίαν ᾗ[1] ἐστιν ἕκαστον ἐπαίον λόγου φήσομεν· καὶ τὸ μὲν λογιζόμενον παρὰ τοῦ νοῦ, τὰ δ' ἄλλα παρὰ τούτου. Ἢ τὸ ἐπαίειν λόγου ὥσπερ ὁρᾶν ἐστιν οὐ σχηματιζόμενον, ἀλλ' ὁρῶν καὶ ἐνεργείᾳ ὄν, ὅτε ὁρᾷ. Ὥσπερ γὰρ ἡ ὄψις καὶ δυνάμει οὖσα καὶ ἐνεργείᾳ ἡ αὐτὴ τῇ οὐσίᾳ, ἡ δὲ ἐνέργειά ἐστιν οὐκ ἀλλοίωσις, ἀλλ' ἅμα προσῆλθε πρὸς ὃ ἔχει [τὴν οὐσίαν][2] καὶ ἔστιν εἰδυῖα καὶ ἔγνω ἀπαθῶς, καὶ τὸ λογιζόμενον οὕτω πρὸς τὸν νοῦν ἔχει καὶ ὁρᾷ, καὶ ἡ δύναμις τοῦ νοεῖν τοῦτο, οὐ σφραγῖδος ἔνδον

[1] ᾗ Vitringa, H–S²: ἦν codd.
[2] τὴν οὐσίαν del. Theiler, H–S².

---

[1] Heraclitus may well be in Plotinus's mind here: cp. fragments, DK, B1 and 112.

this harmony there should be another virtue of each part, and a vice of each before their disharmony with each other. What is it then, by the presence of which each part is evil? Vice. And, again, by the presence of what is it good? Virtue. Now perhaps one might say that the vice of the reasoning part was unintelligence, and unintelligence in the negative sense, and would not be asserting the presence of anything. But when false opinions are there in the soul (and this is what most of all produces vice), how will one be able to assert that they have not come in and that this part of the soul has not in this way become different? And is not the spirited part in one state when it is cowardly and in another when it is brave? And is not the desiring part when it is unrestrainedly lustful in one state, and in another when it is under control? Well, then, it has been affected. Now we shall say in answer that when each part is in a state of virtue, it is active according to its real substantial being, by which each part listens to reason;[1] and the reasoning part receives its reason from Intellect and the other parts from the reasoning part. Now listening to reason is like seeing, not receiving a shape but seeing and existing actually when seeing takes place. For just as sight, which has both a potential and an actual existence, remains essentially the same [when it is potential and when it is actual], and its actuality is not an alteration but it simultaneously approaches what it has, and is it in knowing it and knows without being affected; in the same way, too, the reasoning part is related to Intellect and sees, and this is the power of intellection; there is no stamp impressed on it

γενομένης, ἀλλ' ἔχει ὃ εἶδε καὶ αὖ οὐκ ἔχει· ἔχει μὲν τῷ γινώσκειν, οὐκ ἔχει δὲ τῷ μὴ ἀποκεῖσθαί τι ἐκ τοῦ ὁράματος, ὥσπερ ἐν κηρῷ μορφήν. Μεμνῆσθαι δὲ δεῖ, ὅτι καὶ τὰς μνήμας οὐκ ἐναποκειμένων τινῶν ἐλέγετο εἶναι, ἀλλὰ τῆς ψυχῆς οὕτω τὴν δύναμιν ἐγειράσης, ὥστε καὶ ὃ μὴ ἔχει ἔχει. Τί οὖν; Οὐκ ἄλλη ἦν πρὶν οὕτω μνημονεύειν καὶ ὕστερον, ὅτε μνημονεύει; ἢ βούλει ἄλλην; οὔκουν ἀλλοιωθεῖσά γε, πλὴν εἰ μή τις τὸ ἐκ δυνάμεως εἰς ἐνέργειαν ἐλθεῖν ἀλλοίωσιν λέγοι, ἀλλ' ἔστιν οὐδὲν προσγενόμενον, ἀλλ' ἥπερ ἦν πεφυκυῖα τοῦτο ποιοῦσα. Ὅλως γὰρ αἱ ἐνέργειαι τῶν ἀύλων οὐ συναλλοιουμένων γίνονται· ἢ φθαρεῖεν ἄν· ἀλλὰ πολὺ μᾶλλον μενόντων, τὸ δὲ πάσχειν τὸ ἐνεργοῦν τοῦτο τῶν μεθ' ὕλης. Εἰ δὲ ἄυλον ὂν πείσεται, οὐκ ἔχει ᾧ μένει· ὥσπερ ἐπὶ τῆς ὄψεως τῆς ὁράσεως ἐνεργούσης τὸ πάσχον ὁ ὀφθαλμός ἐστιν, αἱ δὲ δόξαι ὥσπερ ὁράματα. Τὸ δὲ θυμοειδὲς πῶς δειλόν; πῶς δὲ καὶ ἀνδρεῖον; Ἢ δειλὸν μὲν τῷ ἢ μὴ ὁρᾶν πρὸς τὸν λόγον ἢ πρὸς φαῦλον ὄντα τὸν λόγον ὁρᾶν ἢ ὀργάνων ἐλλείψει, οἷον ἀπορίᾳ ἢ σαθρότητι ὅπλων σωματι-

[1] Plotinus seems to be thinking here of a famous Stoic dispute about "impressions." Chrysippus had corrected the too simple-minded view of Cleanthes that a mental image was a stamp like that made by a seal in wax, and had pointed out that this would make memory impossible: cp. *Stoic. Vet. Fragm.* II. 55–56.

internally, but it has what it sees and in another way does not have it; it has it by knowing it, but does not have it in that something is not put away in it from the seeing, like a shape in wax.[1] And we must remember that memories too, in our account of them, do not exist because things are put away in our minds but the soul awakes the power [of memory] in such a way as to have what it does not have.[2] Well, then, is not the soul different before it remembers in this way, and afterwards, when it remembers? Would you like to call it different? Very well, then, as long as you do not say that it is intrinsically altered, unless one is to call the passage from potentiality to actuality alteration, but nothing is added to it but it simply does what it is by nature.[3] For in general the actualisations of immaterial things take place without any accompanying alteration, otherwise they would perish; it is much truer to say that they remain unaltered when they become actual, and that being affected in actualisation belongs to things which have matter. But if a thing which is immaterial is going to be affected, it has no ground of permanence; just as in the case of sight, when the seeing faculty is active it is the eye which is affected, and opinions are like acts of seeing. But how is the spirited part cowardly and then again brave? It is cowardly either by not looking to the reason, or by looking to the reason when it is in a bad state, or else there will be a failure in its instruments, as when it is without its bodily weapons or they are decayed, or it is hindered from action,

[2] For Plotinus's doctrine of memory, see IV. 3 [27]. 26–31.
[3] Cp. Aristotle, *De Anima* B.5. 417b5–9.

κῶν, ἢ ἐνεργεῖν κωλυόμενον ἢ μὴ κινηθὲν οἷον ἐρεθισθέν· ἀνδρεῖον δέ, εἰ τὰ ἐναντία. Ἐν οἷς οὐδεμία ἀλλοίωσις οὐδὲ πάθος. Τὸ δὲ ἐπιθυμοῦν ἐνεργοῦν μὲν μόνον τὴν λεγομένην ἀκολασίαν παρέχεσθαι· πάντα γὰρ μόνον πράττει καὶ οὐ πάρεστι τὰ ἄλλα, οἷς ἂν ᾖ ἐν μέρει τὸ κρατεῖν παροῦσι καὶ δεικνύναι αὐτῷ. Τὸ δ' ὁρῶν ἦν ἂν ἄλλο, πράττον οὐ πάντα, ἀλλά που καὶ σχολάζον τῷ ὁρᾶν ὡς οἷόν τε τὰ ἄλλα. Τάχα δὲ τὸ πολὺ καὶ σώματος καχεξία ἡ τούτου λεγομένη κακία, ἀρετὴ δὲ τἀναντία· ὥστ' οὐδεμία ἐφ' ἑκάτερα προσθήκη τῇ ψυχῇ.

3. Τὰς δ' οἰκειώσεις καὶ ἀλλοτριώσεις πῶς; Καὶ λῦπαι καὶ ὀργαὶ καὶ ἡδοναὶ ἐπιθυμίαι τε καὶ φόβοι πῶς οὐ τροπαὶ καὶ πάθη ἐνόντα καὶ κινούμενα; Δεῖ δὴ καὶ περὶ τούτων ὧδε διαλαβεῖν. Ὅτι γὰρ ἐγγίγνονται ἀλλοιώσεις καὶ σφοδραὶ τούτων αἰσθήσεις μὴ οὐ λέγειν ἐναντία λέγοντός ἐστι τοῖς ἐναργέσιν. Ἀλλὰ χρὴ συγχωροῦντας ζητεῖν ὅ τι ἐστὶ τὸ τρεπόμενον. Κινδυνεύομεν γὰρ περὶ ψυχὴν ταῦτα λέγοντες ὅμοιόν τι ὑπολαμβάνειν, ὡς εἰ τὴν ψυχὴν λέγομεν ἐρυθριᾶν ἢ αὖ ἐν ὠχριάσει γίγνεσθαι, μὴ λογιζόμενοι, ὡς διὰ ψυχὴν μὲν ταῦτα τὰ πάθη, περὶ δὲ τὴν ἄλλην σύστασίν ἐστι γιγνό-

[1] The thought and language here and in what follows show some Stoic influence; cp. especially Posidonius quoted by Plutarch in *De Libidine et Aegritudine* 6 (p. 5; 14–23 Bernadakis). Posidonius here speaks of περὶ σῶμα ψυχικά of which he gives ὠχριάσεις as an example, and περὶ ψυχὴν σωματικά of which one example is διαχύσεις (cp. l. 17 below). Plotinus

or it is not really stirred to action, but as if it was only lightly touched; and it is brave when the opposite happens. In these circumstances there is no intrinsic alteration or affection. And the desiring part when it acts by itself produces what is called unrestrained lust, for it does everything by itself and the other parts of the soul are not present to it, whose function it would be, if they were present, to master and direct it. If it saw the other parts it would be different, and would not do everything but might perhaps take a rest by looking, as far as it could, at the other parts. But perhaps most often what we call the vice of this part is a bad state of the body, and virtue the opposite, so that in either case nothing is added to the soul.

3. But what about the soul's accepting things as its own or rejecting them as alien? And, surely, feelings of grief and anger, pleasures, desires and fears, are changes and affections present in the soul and moving there. About these, too, one must certainly make a distinction, in this way. To deny that alterations in the soul, and intense perceptions of them, do occur is to contradict the obvious facts. But when we accept this we ought to enquire what it is that is changed. For we run the risk, when we say this of the soul, of understanding it in the same sort of way as if we say that the soul blushes or turns pale again, not taking into account that these affections are brought about by the soul but occur in the other structure [the body].[1] But the shame is in

accepts the first, but will not admit that any feeling or affection can pass from body to soul; so he makes διάχυσις something entirely bodily.

μενα. Ἀλλ' ἡ μὲν αἰσχύνη ἐν ψυχῇ δόξης αἰσχροῦ γενομένης· τὸ δὲ σῶμα ἐκείνης τοῦτο οἷον σχούσης, ἵνα μὴ τοῖς ὀνόμασι πλανώμεθα, ὑπὸ τῇ ψυχῇ ὂν καὶ οὐ ταὐτὸν ἀψύχῳ ἐτράπη κατὰ τὸ αἷμα εὐκίνητον ὄν. Τά τε τοῦ λεγομένου φόβου ἐν μὲν τῇ ψυχῇ ἡ ἀρχή, τὸ δ' ὠχρὸν ἀναχωρήσαντος τοῦ αἵματος εἴσω. Καὶ τῆς ἡδονῆς δὲ τὸ τῆς διαχύσεως τοῦτο καὶ εἰς αἴσθησιν ἧκον περὶ τὸ σῶμα, τὸ δὲ περὶ τὴν ψυχὴν οὐκέτι πάθος. Καὶ τὸ τῆς λύπης ὡσαύτως. Ἐπεὶ καὶ τὸ τῆς ἐπιθυμίας ἐπὶ μὲν τῆς ψυχῆς τῆς ἀρχῆς οὔσης τοῦ ἐπιθυμεῖν λανθάνον ἐστίν, ἐκεῖθεν δὲ τὸ προελθὸν ἡ αἴσθησις ἔγνω. Καὶ γὰρ ὅταν λέγωμεν κινεῖσθαι αὐτὴν ἐν ἐπιθυμίαις, ἐν λογισμοῖς, ἐν δόξαις, οὐ σαλευομένην αὐτὴν λέγομεν ταῦτα ποιεῖν, ἀλλ' ἐξ αὐτῆς γίγνεσθαι τὰς κινήσεις. Ἐπεὶ καὶ τὸ ζῆν κίνησιν λέγοντες οὐκ ἀλλοίου μέν, ἑκάστου δὲ μορίου ἡ ἐνέργεια ἡ κατὰ φύσιν ζωὴ οὐκ ἐξιστᾶσα. Κεφάλαιον δὲ ἱκανόν· εἰ τὰς ἐνεργείας καὶ τὰς ζωὰς καὶ τὰς ὀρέξεις οὐκ ἀλλοιώσεις συγχωροῦμεν καὶ μνήμας οὐ τύπους ἐναποσφραγιζομένους οὐδὲ τὰς φαντασίας ὡς ἐν κηρῷ τυπώσεις, συγχωρητέον πανταχοῦ ἐν πᾶσι τοῖς λεγομένοις πάθεσι καὶ κινήσεσι τὴν ψυχὴν ὡσαύτως ἔχειν τῷ ὑποκειμένῳ καὶ τῇ οὐσίᾳ καὶ τὴν ἀρετὴν καὶ τὴν κακίαν μὴ ὡς τὸ μέλαν καὶ τὸ λευκὸν περὶ σῶμα γίγνεσθαι ἢ τὸ θερμὸν καὶ τὸ ψυχρόν, ἀλλ' ὃν εἴρηται τρόπον ἐπ' ἄμφω περὶ πάνθ' ὅλως τὰ ἐναντία γίγνεσθαι.

the soul, when the idea of something disgraceful arises in it; but the body, which the soul in a way possesses—not to be led astray by words—being subject to the soul and not the same thing as a lifeless body, is changed by way of the blood, which is easy to move. As for what is called fear, the beginning is in the soul, but the paleness comes from the blood withdrawing within. So with pleasure, the happy, relaxed feeling, which penetrates to sense-perception, belongs to the body, but the part of pleasure which belongs to the soul is no longer an affection. And the same is true of pain. For with lust, too, as long as its starting-point remains in the soul, it is unperceived; it is what comes out from there that sense-perception knows. In fact, when we say that the soul moves itself in lusts or reasonings or opinions, we are not saying that it does this because it is being shaken about by them, but that the movements originate from itself. For when we say that its life is movement, we do not mean that it is movement of something different, but the activity of each part is its natural life which does not go outside it. The sufficient conclusion is: if we agree that activities and lives and impulses are not alterations, and that memories are not stamps imprinted on the soul or mental pictures like impressions on wax, we must agree that everywhere, in all affections and movements, as they are called, the soul remains the same in substrate and essence, and that virtue and vice do not come into being like black and white or hot and cold in the body, but in the way which has been described, in both directions and in all respects, what happens in the soul is the opposite of what happens in the body.

4. Περὶ δὲ τοῦ λεγομένου παθητικοῦ τῆς ψυχῆς ἐπισκεπτέον. Ἤδη μὲν οὖν εἴρηται τρόπον τινὰ καὶ περὶ τούτου ἐν οἷς περὶ τῶν παθῶν ἁπάντων ἐλέγετο τῶν περὶ τὸ θυμοειδὲς καὶ τὸ ἐπιθυμοῦν γινομένων ὅπως ἕκαστα· οὐ μὴν ἀλλ᾽ ἔτι λεκτέον περὶ αὐτοῦ πρῶτον λαβόντας, ὅ τι ποτὲ τὸ παθητικὸν τῆς ψυχῆς λέγεται εἶναι. Λέγεται δὴ πάντως περὶ ὃ τὰ πάθη δοκεῖ συνίστασθαι· ταῦτα δ᾽ ἐστὶν οἷς ἕπεται ἡδονὴ καὶ λύπη. Τῶν δὲ παθῶν τὰ μὲν ἐπὶ δόξαις συνίσταται, ὡς ὅταν δοξάσας τις μέλλειν τελευτᾶν ἴσχῃ φόβον, ἢ οἰηθεὶς ἀγαθὸν αὐτῷ τι ἔσεσθαι ἡσθῇ, τῆς μὲν δόξης ἐν ἄλλῳ, τοῦ δὲ πάθους κινηθέντος ἐν ἄλλῳ· τὰ δέ ἐστιν ὡς ἡγησάμενα αὐτὰ ἀπροαιρέτως ἐμποιεῖν ἐν τῷ πεφυκότι δοξάζειν τὴν δόξαν. Ἡ μὲν δὴ δόξα ὅτι ἄτρεπτον ἐᾷ τὸ δοξάζειν εἴρηται· ὁ δ᾽ ἐκ τῆς δόξης φόβος ἐλθὼν ἄνωθεν αὖ ἀπὸ τῆς δόξης οἷον σύνεσίν τινα παρασχὼν τῷ λεγομένῳ τῆς ψυχῆς φοβεῖσθαι. Τί ποτε ποιεῖ τοῦτο τὸ φοβεῖσθαι; Ταραχὴν καὶ ἔκπληξίν, φασιν, ἐπὶ προσδοκωμένῳ κακῷ. Ὅτι μὲν οὖν ἡ φαντασία ἐν ψυχῇ, ἥ τε

---

1 At the end of ch. 2.

2 The Stoics; cp. *Stoic. Vet. Fragm.* III. 386. In this chapter Plotinus is critically revising Stoic doctrine in accordance with his own ideas about the nature of the soul which derive from Plato and Aristotle. He accepts the Stoic idea that emotions arise from opinions (cp. *Stoic Vet. Fragm.*

4. But we must now investigate that part of the soul which is said to be subject to affections. We have, of course, already discussed this, in a way, in what we have said about all the affections that occur in the spirited and desiring parts and how each of them arises:[1] but all the same there is something still to say about it, and we must first grasp whatever sort of thing it is that the part of the soul subject to affections is said to be. It is said in any case to be that about which affections appear to gather; the affections, that is, on which pleasure and pain follow. Some of the affections arise as the result of opinions, as when someone, being of the opinion that he will die, feels fear, or, thinking that some good is going to come to him, is pleased; the opinion is in one part, and the affection is stirred up in another; but some of them are of a sort to take the lead and, without any act of choice, to produce the opinion in the part of the soul whose natural function it is to have opinions. Now it has been said that the opinion leaves the opining [part] unmoved; but the fear which originates from the opinion, coming down from above, in its turn, from the opinion, in a way gives a kind of understanding to the part of the soul which is said to fear. What does this fear produce? Disturbance and shock, they say,[2] over the evil which is expected. It should, then, be obvious to anyone that the mental picture is in the soul, both the first

III. 385). But he insists on keeping the opinions and the emotions in watertight compartments; the disturbance and upset which accompanies certain opinions in the soul is strictly confined to the body; for the Stoic it was a diseased affection of the soul.

πρώτη, ἣν δὴ καλοῦμεν δόξαν, ἥ τε ἀπὸ ταύτης οὐκέτι δόξα, ἀλλὰ περὶ τὸ κάτω ἀμυδρὰ οἷον δόξα καὶ ἀνεπίκριτος φαντασία, οἵα τῇ λεγομένῃ φύσει ἐνυπάρχει ἐνέργεια καθ' ἃ ποιεῖ ἕκαστα, ὥς φασιν, ἀφαντάστως, δῆλον ἄν τῳ γένοιτο. Τὸ δ' ἀπὸ τούτων ἤδη αἰσθητὴ ἡ ταραχὴ περὶ τὸ σῶμα γινομένη ὅ τε τρόμος καὶ ὁ σεισμὸς τοῦ σώματος καὶ τὸ ὠχρὸν καὶ ἡ ἀδυναμία τοῦ λέγειν. Οὐ γὰρ δὴ ἐν τῷ ψυχικῷ μέρει ταῦτα· ἢ σωματικὸν φήσομεν αὐτὸ εἶναι, αὐτό τε εἴπερ ἦν παθὸν[1] ταῦτα, οὐδ' ἂν ἔτι εἰς τὸ σῶμα ταῦτα ἀφίκετο τοῦ πέμποντος οὐκέτι ἐνεργοῦντος τὸ πέμπειν διὰ τὸ κατέχεσθαι τῷ πάθει καὶ ἐξίστασθαι ἑαυτοῦ. Ἀλλ' ἔστι μὲν τοῦτο τὸ τῆς ψυχῆς μέρος τὸ παθητικὸν οὐ σῶμα μέν, εἶδος δέ τι. Ἐν ὕλῃ μέντοι καὶ τὸ ἐπιθυμοῦν καὶ τό γε θρεπτικόν τε καὶ αὐξητικὸν καὶ γεννητικόν, ὅ ἐστι ῥίζα καὶ ἀρχὴ τοῦ ἐπιθυμοῦντος καὶ παθητικοῦ εἴδους. Εἴδει δὲ οὐδενὶ δεῖ παρεῖναι ταραχὴν ἢ ὅλως πάθος, ἀλλ' ἑστηκέναι μὲν αὐτό, τὴν δὲ ὕλην αὐτοῦ ἐν τῷ πάθει γίγνεσθαι, ὅταν γίγνηται, ἐκείνου τῇ παρουσίᾳ κινοῦντος. Οὐ γὰρ δὴ τὸ φυτικόν, ὅταν φύῃ, φύεται, οὐδ', ὅταν αὔξῃ, αὔξεται, οὐδ' ὅλως, ὅταν κινῇ, κινεῖται ἐκείνην τὴν κίνησιν ἣν κινεῖ, ἀλλ' ἢ οὐδ' ὅλως, ἢ ἄλλος

[1] παθὸν Kirchhoff (*pateretur* Ficinus), H–S: παθόντα codd.

---

[1] The Stoics again. Plants are called ἀφάντασταa in *Stoic. Vet. Fragm.* II. 458 (p. 150, 12).

one, which we call opinion, and that which derives from it, which is no longer opinion, but an obscure quasi-opinion and an uncriticised mental picture, like the activity inherent in what is called nature in so far as it produces individual things, as they say,[1] without a mental image. That which results from these mental images is the disturbance in the body, which has already reached the level of perception, the trembling and shaking of the body and the pallor and inability to speak. These are certainly not in the part of soul [which we are discussing]; otherwise we shall say that it is corporeal, if it was really it which was affected in these ways; and these affections would not have reached the body if that which sent them no longer worked the sending because it was in the grip of the affection and beside itself. But this part of the soul which is subject to affections is not a body but a form. Certainly the desiring part is in matter, and so, too, is the part which governs nutrition, growth and generation,[2] which is the root and principle of the desiring and affective form. But it is not proper to any form to be disturbed or in any way affected, but it remains static itself, and its matter enters into the state of being affected, when it does so enter, and the form stirs up the affection by its presence. For, of course, the growth-principle does not grow when it causes growth, nor increase when it causes increase, nor in general, when it causes motion, is it moved by that particular kind of motion which it causes, but either it is not moved at all, or it is a

[2] Plotinus is here combining the Platonic desiring part of the soul and the Aristotelian growth-principle: cp. IV. 3 [27] 23. 40–42.

τρόπος κινήσεως ἢ ἐνεργείας. Αὐτὴν μὲν οὖν δεῖ τὴν τοῦ εἴδους φύσιν ἐνέργειαν εἶναι καὶ τῇ παρουσίᾳ ποιεῖν, οἷον εἰ ἡ ἁρμονία ἐξ αὑτῆς τὰς χορδὰς ἐκίνει. Ἔσται τοίνυν τὸ παθητικὸν πάθους μὲν αἴτιον ἢ παρ' αὐτοῦ γενομένου τοῦ κινήματος ἐκ τῆς φαντασίας τῆς αἰσθητικῆς ἢ καὶ ἄνευ φαντασίας· ἐπισκεπτέον δὲ τοῦτο, εἰ τῆς δόξης ἄνωθεν ἀρξάσης· αὐτὸ δὲ μένον ἐν ἁρμονίας εἴδει. Τὰ δὲ αἴτια τοῦ κινῆσαι ἀνάλογον τῷ μουσικῷ· τὰ δὲ πληγέντα διὰ πάθος πρὸς τὰς χορδὰς ἂν τὸν λόγον ἔχοι. Καὶ γὰρ κἀκεῖ οὐχ ἡ ἁρμονία πέπονθεν, ἀλλ' ἡ χορδή· οὐ μὴν ἐκινήθη ἂν ἡ χορδή, εἰ καὶ ὁ μουσικὸς ἐβούλετο, μὴ τῆς ἁρμονίας τοῦτο λεγούσης.

5. Τί οὖν χρὴ ζητεῖν ἀπαθῆ τὴν ψυχὴν ἐκ φιλοσοφίας ποιεῖν μηδὲ τὴν ἀρχὴν πάσχουσαν; Ἢ ἐπειδὴ καὶ τὸ εἰς αὐτὴν ἐπὶ τοῦ λεγομένου παθητικοῦ οἷον φάντασμα τὸ ἐφεξῆς πάθημα ποιεῖ, τὴν ταραχήν, καὶ συνέζευκται τῇ ταραχῇ ἡ τοῦ προσδοκωμένου κακοῦ εἰκών, πάθος τὸ τοιοῦτον λεγόμενον ἠξίου ὁ λόγος ὅλως ἀφαιρεῖν καὶ μὴ

---

[1] Plotinus is here using against the Stoics the Aristotelian doctrine that the soul is a form and as such causes bodily movement and changes while remaining itself unmoved. He does not advert to the fact that Aristotle worked out his own doctrine in conscious opposition to Plato's conception of soul as, not unmoved, but self-moved. Cp. the long discussion in *De Anima* A.3–4. 405b 31 ff.

[2] This sentence shows clearly how conscious Plotinus was of the central moral problem presented by his philosophical

different kind of motion and activity.[1] So, then, the actual nature of the form must be an activity, and produce by its presence, as if the melody proceeding from it plucked the strings. The part subject to affections, then, will be the cause of the affection, either because the movement starts from it, from the mental picture produced by sense-impressions, or even without a mental picture (we have to consider the question whether the affection is produced by the opinion starting from a higher level); but the part itself stays still in the manner of a melody. The causes of the movement are like the player, and the parts on which the affection makes its impact might correspond to the strings. For in the case of playing an instrument, too, it is not the tune which is affected, but the string; the string, however, would not be plucked [in tune] even if the player wished it, unless the tune said that it should be.

5. Why, then, ought we to seek to make the soul free from affections by means of philosophy when it is not affected to begin with?[2] Now, since the mental image (so to call it) which penetrates it at the part which is said to be subject to affections produces the consequent affection, disturbance, and the likeness of the expected evil is coupled with the disturbance, this kind of situation was called an affection and reason thought it right to do away with it altogether

anthropology. Why should we be obliged to strive to attain ἀπάθεια when the soul is ἀπαθής by nature already (a problem which did not arise for the Stoics, or for Plato himself)? His solution, sketched in this chapter, is that the attainment of ἀπάθεια involves no real change in the soul. It is simply a matter of " waking up " from illusion, turning one's attention from the lower and concentrating it on the higher.

ἐᾶν ἐγγίγνεσθαι ὡς γιγνομένου μὲν οὔπω τῆς ψυχῆς ἐχούσης εὖ, μὴ γιγνομένου δὲ ἀπαθῶς[1] ἰσχούσης τοῦ αἰτίου τοῦ πάθους τοῦ περὶ αὐτὴν ὁράματος οὐκέτι ἐγγιγνομένου, οἷον εἴ τις τὰς τῶν ὀνειράτων φαντασίας ἀναιρεῖν ἐθέλων ἐν ἐγρηγόρσει τὴν ψυχὴν τὴν φανταζομένην ποιοίη, εἰ[2] τὰ πάθη λέγοι πεποιηκέναι, τὰ ἔξωθεν οἷον ὁράματα παθήματα λέγων τῆς ψυχῆς εἶναι. Ἀλλὰ τίς ἡ κάθαρσις ἂν τῆς ψυχῆς εἴη μηδαμῇ μεμολυσμένης ἢ τί τὸ χωρίζειν αὐτὴν ἀπὸ τοῦ σώματος; Ἢ ἡ μὲν κάθαρσις ἂν εἴη καταλιπεῖν μόνην καὶ μὴ μετ' ἄλλων ἢ μὴ πρὸς ἄλλο βλέπουσαν μηδ' αὖ δόξας ἀλλοτρίας ἔχουσαν, ὅστις ὁ τρόπος τῶν δοξῶν, ἢ τῶν παθῶν, ὡς εἴρηται, μήτε ὁρᾶν τὰ εἴδωλα μήτε ἐξ αὐτῶν ἐργάζεσθαι πάθη. Εἰ δὲ ἐπὶ θάτερα τὰ ἄνω ἀπὸ τῶν κάτω, πῶς οὐ κάθαρσις καὶ χωρισμός γε πρὸς τῆς ψυχῆς τῆς μηκέτι ἐν σώματι γιγνομένης ὡς ἐκείνου εἶναι, καὶ τὸ ὥσπερ φῶς μὴ ἐν θολερῷ; Καίτοι ἀπαθὲς ὅμως ὃ καὶ ἐν θολερῷ. Τοῦ δὲ παθητικοῦ ἡ μὲν κάθαρσις ἡ ἔγερσις ἐκ τῶν ἀτόπων εἰδώλων καὶ μὴ ὅρασις, τὸ δὲ χωρίζεσθαι τῇ μὴ πολλῇ νεύσει καὶ τῇ περὶ τὰ κάτω μὴ φαντασίᾳ. Εἴη δ' ἂν καὶ τὸ χωρίζειν αὐτὸ τὸ ἐκεῖνα ἀφαιρεῖν ὧν τοῦτο χωρίζεται, ὅταν μὴ ἐπὶ πνεύματος θολεροῦ ἐκ γαστριμαργίας καὶ πλήθους οὐ καθαρῶν ᾖ σαρκῶν,

[1] ἀπαθῶς Kirchhoff, H–S: ἀπαθοῦς codd.

[2] ποιοίη εἰ H–S²: ποιοῖ ἢ εἰ xy: ποιεῖ ἢ εἰ w: ποιοῖ ἢ Q.

---

[1] Plato, *Phaedo* 67C, 5–6.

and not to allow it to occur in the soul, on the ground that if it does occur the soul is not yet in a good state, but if it does not the soul is in a state of freedom from affections since the cause of the affection, the seeing in the soul, is no longer present in it; it is as if someone who wanted to take away the mental pictures seen in dreams were to bring the soul which was picturing them to wakefulness, if he said that the soul had caused the affections, meaning that the visions as if from outside were the affections of the soul. But what could the " purification " of the soul be, if it had not been stained at all, or what its " separation " [1] from the body? The purification would be leaving it alone, and not with others, or not looking at something else or, again, having opinions which do not belong to it—whatever is the character of the opinions, or the affections, as has been said—and not seeing the images nor constructing affections out of them. But if there is turning in the other direction, to the things above, away from those below, it is surely (is it not?) purification, and separation too, when it is the act of a soul which is no longer in body as if it belonged to it, and is being like a light which is not in turbid obscurity. And yet even the light which is in obscurity remains unaffected. But the purification of the part subject to affections is the waking up from inappropriate images and not seeing them, and its separation is effected by not inclining much downwards and not having a mental picture of the things below. But separating it could also mean taking away the things from which it is separated when it is not standing over a vital breath turbid from gluttony and sated with impure meats,

ἀλλ' ᾖ ἰσχνὸν τὸ ἐν ᾧ, ὡς ἐπ' αὐτοῦ ὀχεῖσθαι ἡσυχῇ.

6. Τὴν μὲν δὴ οὐσίαν τὴν νοητὴν τὴν κατὰ τὸ εἶδος ἅπασαν τεταγμένην ὡς ἀπαθῆ δεῖ εἶναι δοκεῖν εἴρηται. Ἐπεὶ δὲ καὶ ἡ ὕλη ἕν τι τῶν ἀσωμάτων, εἰ καὶ ἄλλον τρόπον, σκεπτέον καὶ περὶ ταύτης τίνα τρόπον ἔχει, πότερα παθητή, ὡς λέγεται, καὶ κατὰ πάντα τρεπτή, ἢ καὶ ταύτην δεῖ ἀπαθῆ εἶναι οἴεσθαι, καὶ τίς ὁ τρόπος τῆς ἀπαθείας. Πρῶτον δὲ ληπτέον ἐπὶ τοῦτο στελλομένοις καὶ περὶ τῆς φύσεως αὐτῆς λέγουσιν ὁποία τις, ὡς ἡ τοῦ ὄντος φύσις καὶ ἡ οὐσία καὶ τὸ εἶναι οὐ ταύτῃ ἔχει, ὡς οἱ πολλοὶ νομίζουσιν. Ἔστι γὰρ τὸ ὄν, ὃ καὶ κατ' ἀλήθειαν ἄν τις εἴποι ὄν, ὄντως ὄν· τοῦτο δέ ἐστιν, ὃ πάντῃ ἐστὶν ὄν· τοῦτο δέ, ᾧ μηδὲν ἀποστατεῖ τοῦ εἶναι. Τελέως δὲ ὂν οὐδενὸς δεῖται ἵνα σῴζοιτο καὶ ᾖ, ἀλλὰ καὶ τοῖς ἄλλοις αἴτιον τοῖς δοκοῦσιν εἶναι τοῦ δοκεῖν εἶναι. Εἰ δὴ ταῦτα ὀρθῶς λέγεται, ἀνάγκη αὐτὸ ἐν ζωῇ

---

[1] This is one of the few passages in which Plotinus refers to the "pneumatic" or "astral" body, in the existence of which he believed, but which he found of little philosophical importance or interest: cp. IV. 3 [27] 15. 1–4; II. 2 [14] 2. 21–2. For the history of the belief in astral bodies before and after Plotinus, see E. R. Dodds, *Proclus, The Elements of Theology, Appendix II*.

[2] That matter is bodiless was contemporary Peripatetic doctrine, clearly stated by Alexander of Aphrodisias in the introductory section of his *De Anima* (cp. especially p. 5; 19–22 Bruns). Pre-Plotinian Platonists preferred the formula "neither body nor bodiless, but potentially body" (Albinus, *Eisagoge* VIII, p. 163, 6–7 Hermann; Apuleius,

but that in which it resides is so fine that it can ride on it in peace.[1]

6. It has already been said that the intelligible reality, which is all of the order of form, must be thought to be free from affections. But since matter, too, is one of the things without body,[2] even if it is so in a different sense, we must enquire about this too, and see what character it has, whether it is, as it is said to be, subject to affections and pliable in every way, or whether one must think that this, too, is free from affections, and what kind of freedom from affection it has. But first, as we address ourselves to this and state what sort of a nature it has, we must grasp that the nature of being and substance and existence are not as most people think they are. For being, what one could truly call being, is real being;[3] and this is that which has nothing lacking to its existence. Since it is completely it has no need of anything for its preservation and existence but is cause to the other things, which seem to exist, of their seeming existence. If this is a correct statement, it must necessarily be in life, and in perfect life; or,

De Platone I. V, p. 87, 11–15 Thomas). The Stoic doctrine is stated immediately below: matter for them was a body without qualities "subject to affections and pliable in every way"; cp. *Stoic Vet. Fragm.* II. 309, 482.

[3] The real being which Plotinus briefly describes here is of course his Second Hypostasis, Νοῦς. For the description of it as at once being, intelligence and life: cp. V. 1 [10] 4; V. 5 [32] 1. Brehier, perhaps rightly, sees this part of the chapter as a commentary on Plato, *Sophist* 248E, the famous passage, whose meaning is still much disputed, in which Plato insists that motion and life and soul and intelligence must be present to absolute being: the word ἀποστατεῖ occurs in Plato *Parmenides* 144B2, but the context is different.

καὶ ἐν τελείᾳ ζωῇ εἶναι· ἢ ἐλλεῖπον οὐ μᾶλλον ὂν ἢ μὴ ὂν ἔσται. Τοῦτο δὲ νοῦς καὶ πάντῃ φρόνησις. Καὶ ὡρισμένον ἄρα καὶ πεπερασμένον καὶ τῇ δυνάμει οὐδὲν ὅ τι μή, οὐδὲ τοσῇδε· ἐπιλείποι γὰρ ἄν. Διὸ καὶ τὸ ἀεὶ καὶ τὸ ὡσαύτως καὶ τὸ ἄδεκτον παντὸς καὶ οὐδὲν εἰς αὐτό· εἰ γάρ τι δέχοιτο, παρ᾽ αὐτὸ ἄν τι δέχοιτο· τοῦτο δὲ μὴ ὄν. Δεῖ δ᾽ αὐτὸ πάντῃ ὂν εἶναι· ἥκειν οὖν δεῖ παρ᾽ αὐτοῦ πάντα ἔχον εἰς τὸ εἶναι· καὶ ὁμοῦ πάντα καὶ ἓν πάντα. Εἰ δὴ τούτοις ὁρίζομεν τὸ ὄν—δεῖ δέ, ἢ οὐκ ἂν ἐκ τοῦ ὄντος ἥκοι νοῦς, καὶ ζωή, ἀλλὰ τῷ ὄντι ἐπακτὰ ταῦτα καὶ οὐκ (ἐξ οὐκ ὄντος) ἔσται, καὶ τὸ μὲν ὂν ἄζων καὶ ἄνουν ἔσται, ὃ δὲ μὴ ὄν ἐστιν ἀληθῶς ταῦτα ἕξει, ὡς ἐν τοῖς χείροσι δέον ταῦτα εἶναι καὶ τοῖς ὑστέροις τοῦ ὄντος· τὸ γὰρ πρὸ τοῦ ὄντος χορηγὸν μὲν τούτων εἰς τὸ ὄν, οὐ δεόμενον δὲ αὐτὸ τούτων·—εἰ οὖν τοιοῦτον τὸ ὄν, ἀνάγκη μήτε τι σῶμα αὐτὸ μήτε τὸ ὑποκείμενον τοῖς σώμασιν εἶναι, ἀλλ᾽ εἶναι τούτοις τὸ εἶναι τὸ μὴ οὖσιν εἶναι.

Καὶ πῶς ἡ τῶν σωμάτων φύσις μὴ οὖσα, πῶς δὲ ἡ ὕλη ἐφ᾽ ἧς ταῦτα, ὄρη καὶ πέτραι καὶ πᾶσα γῆ στερεά; Καὶ πάντα ἀντίτυπα καὶ ταῖς πληγαῖς

---

[1] Real Being or Intellect is limited for Plotinus in the sense that the number of Forms in it is finite, but unlimited in that it is eternal, its power is infinite and it has nothing outside to bound or measure it but is all-inclusive and so unincluded and is itself the absolute standard of measurement: cp. V. 7 [18] 1; VI. 5 [23] 12; VI. 6 [34] 18.

if it falls short of this, it will be no more existent than non-existent. But this means that it must be intellect, and wisdom in its fullness. And it must therefore be defined and limited, and there must be nothing to which its power does not extend, nor must its power be quantitatively limited; otherwise it would be defective.[1] And so, too, it must be eternal and always the same, and unreceptive of anything, and nothing must come into it, for if it received anything, it would have to receive something different from itself; but this would be non-existent. But real being must be being in every way; it must therefore come having everything for existence from itself: and it must be all things together, and all of them one. Now if we define being in these ways—and we must do so, or intellect and life would not come from being, but would be external additions to it and (as coming from the non-existent) will not exist, and being will be lifeless and devoid of intellect, and that which is not really being will have these [life and intellect] as if these ought to exist in inferior things and those posterior to being, for that which is prior to being conducts these into being but has no need of them itself; if then being is of this kind, it necessarily cannot be a body or what underlies bodies but the being of these is the being of things which do not exist.

And how can the nature of bodies, and the matter on which they are founded, be non-existent, mountains and rocks and all the earth in its solidity?[2] All things that offer resistance, and compel by their

[2] Plotinus may possibly be thinking here of Plato's materialists in *Sophist* 246A–B.

βιαζόμενα τὰ πληττόμενα ὁμολογεῖν αὐτῶν τὴν οὐσίαν. Εἰ οὖν τις λέγοι· πῶς δὲ τὰ μὴ θλίβοντα καὶ μὴ βιαζόμενα μηδὲ ἀντίτυπα μηδ᾽ ὅλως ὁρώμενα, ψυχὴ καὶ νοῦς, ὄντα καὶ ὄντως ὄντα; καὶ δὴ καὶ ἐπὶ τῶν σωμάτων μᾶλλον γῆς ἑστώσης τὸ μᾶλλον κινούμενον καὶ ἐμβριθὲς ἧττον, καὶ τούτου τὸ ἄνω; καὶ δὴ καὶ τὸ πῦρ φεῦγον ἤδη τὴν σώματος φύσιν; Ἀλλ᾽ οἶμαι, τὰ μὲν αὐταρκέστερα αὐτοῖς ἧττον ἐνοχλεῖ τὰ ἄλλα καὶ ἀλυπότερα τοῖς ἄλλοις, τὰ δὲ βαρύτερα καὶ γεωδέστερα, ὅσῳ ἐλλιπῆ καὶ πίπτοντα καὶ αἴρειν αὐτὰ οὐ δυνάμενα, ταῦτα πίπτοντα ὑπὸ ἀσθενείας τῇ καταφορᾷ καὶ νωθείᾳ πληγὰς ἔχει. Ἐπεὶ καὶ τὰ νεκρὰ τῶν σωμάτων ἀηδέστερα προσπεσεῖν, καὶ τὸ σφόδρα τῆς πληγῆς καὶ τὸ βλάπτειν ἔχει· τὰ δ᾽ ἔμψυχα μετέχοντα τοῦ ὄντος, ὅσῳ τούτου μέτεστιν αὐτοῖς, εὐχαριτώτερα τοῖς πέλας. Ἡ δὲ κίνησις ὥσπερ τις ζωὴ οὖσα ἐν τοῖς σώμασιν ἦν· καὶ μίμησιν ἔχουσα ταύτης μᾶλλόν ἐστι τοῖς ἧττον σώματος ἔχουσιν, ὡς τῆς ἀπολείψεως τοῦ ὄντος ὃ καταλείπει μᾶλλον τοῦτο σῶμα ποιούσης. Καὶ ἐκ τῶν δὲ λεγομένων παθημάτων μᾶλλον ἄν τις ἴδοι τὸ μᾶλλον σῶμα μᾶλλον παθητὸν ὄν, γῆν ἢ τὰ ἄλλα, καὶ τὰ ἄλλα κατὰ τὸν αὐτὸν λόγον· τὰ

---

[1] For the special status of fire among other bodies, see I. 6 [1] 3. 19–26, where it is said to "hold the rank of form in

impacts the things struck by them, attest their existence. Suppose someone were to say: "How can things which exercise no pressure or force and offer no resistance, and are not even visible, be existent, and really existent? And among bodies, how can the element which moves more and has less weight be more existent than the stable earth, and the element above be more real than this? And how can fire [be the most real of all the elements] which is now at the point of escaping from bodily nature?"[1] But, I think, the bodies which are more sufficient to themselves get less in the way of the other things and cause them less pain, but the heavier, more earthy bodies, in proportion as they are defective and fall and are unable to lift themselves up, when they fall because of their weakness, by their downward movement and heavy slowness cause collisions. Then, too, it is the dead ones among bodies which are more unpleasant to fall against, and are responsible for extremely hard blows and for hurting; but ensouled bodies, which have a share in being, are more agreeable to their neighbours the more of it they have. And movement is like a kind of life in bodies, and keeps an image of it, and there is more of it in the things which have less of body, as if it was the deficiency of being which made the thing which is deficient in it more a body. And one could see this more clearly from what are called the affections; the more a thing is a body the more it is affected, earth more than other things, and the other elements in the same proportion, for the other

relation to the other elements" (cp. Aristotle, *De Generatione et Corruptione* 8. 335a18–20) and to be "near to the bodiless."

μὲν γὰρ ἄλλα σύνεισι διαιρούμενα μὴ κωλύοντος μηδενὸς εἰς ἓν πάλιν, τμηθὲν δὲ γεηρὸν ἅπαν χωρὶς ἑκάτερον ἀεί· ὥσπερ τὰ ἀπαγορεύοντα τῇ φύσει, ἃ δὴ μικρᾶς πληγῆς γενομένης οὕτως ἔχει ὡς πέπληκται καὶ ἐφθάρη, οὕτω καὶ τὸ μάλιστα σῶμα γενόμενον ὡς μάλιστα εἰς τὸ μὴ ὂν ἧκον ἀναλαβεῖν αὐτὸ εἰς τὸ ἓν ἀσθενεῖ. Πτῶμα οὖν αἱ βαρεῖαι καὶ σφοδραὶ πληγαί, ἀλλὰ ποιεῖν εἰς ἄλληλα· ἀσθενὲς δὲ ἀσθενεῖ προσπῖπτον ἰσχυρόν ἐστι πρὸς ἐκεῖνο καὶ μὴ ὂν μὴ ὄντι.

Ταῦτα μὲν οὖν εἴρηται πρὸς τοὺς ἐν τοῖς σώμασι τιθεμένους τὰ ὄντα τῇ τῶν ὠθισμῶν μαρτυρίᾳ καὶ τοῖς διὰ τῆς αἰσθήσεως φαντάσμασι πίστιν τῆς ἀληθείας λαμβάνοντας, οἳ παραπλήσιον τοῖς ὀνειρώττουσι ποιοῦσι ταῦτα ἐνεργεῖν νομίζουσιν, ἃ ὁρῶσιν εἶναι ἐνύπνια ὄντα. Καὶ γὰρ τὸ τῆς αἰσθήσεως ψυχῆς ἐστιν εὐδούσης· ὅσον γὰρ ἐν σώματι ψυχῆς, τοῦτο εὕδει· ἡ δ' ἀληθινὴ ἐγρήγορσις ἀληθινὴ ἀπὸ σώματος, οὐ μετὰ σώματος, ἀνάστασις. Ἡ μὲν γὰρ μετὰ σώματος μετάστασίς ἐστιν ἐξ ἄλλου εἰς ἄλλον ὕπνον, οἷον ἐξ ἑτέρων δεμνίων· ἡ δ' ἀληθὴς ὅλως ἀπὸ τῶν σωμάτων, ἃ τῆς φύσεως ὄντα τῆς ἐναντίας ψυχῇ τὸ ἐναντίον εἰς οὐσίαν ἔχει. Μαρτυρεῖ δὲ καὶ ἡ γένεσις αὐτῶν καὶ ἡ ῥοὴ καὶ ἡ φθορὰ οὐ τῆς τοῦ ὄντος φύσεως οὖσα.

7. Ἀλλ' ἐπανιτέον ἐπί τε τὴν ὕλην τὴν ὑποκειμέ-

elements come together into one again when they are parted, if there is no obstacle in the way, but when every kind of earthy body is cut, each part stays separate for ever; just as with things of which the natural powers are failing, which if they receive a small blow stay in the state to which the blow has reduced them and perish, so the thing which has most completely become body, since it has approached most nearly to non-being, is too weak to collect itself again into a unity. So heavy and severe blows bring about the mutual ruin of bodies; a weak body falling against [another] weak one is strong against it, and a non-existent thing against [another] non-existent thing.

This, then, is our argument against those who place real beings in the class of bodies and find their guarantee of truth in the evidence of pushings and strikings and the apparitions which come by way of sense-perception; they act like people dreaming, who think that the things they see as real actually exist, when they are only dreams. For the activity of sense-perception is that of the soul asleep; for it is the part of the soul that is in the body that sleeps; but the true wakening is a true getting up from the body, not with the body. Getting up with the body is only getting out of one sleep into another, like getting out of one bed into another; but the true rising is a rising altogether away from bodies, which are of the opposite nature to soul and opposed in respect of reality. Their coming into being and flux and perishing, which does not belong to the nature of reality, are evidence of this.

7. But we must come back to matter, the underly-

νην ἢ τὰ[1] ἐπὶ τῇ ὕλῃ εἶναι λεγόμενα, ἐξ ὧν τό τε μὴ εἶναι αὐτὴν καὶ τὸ τῆς ὕλης ἀπαθὲς γνωσθήσεται. Ἔστι μὲν οὖν ἀσώματος, ἐπείπερ τὸ σῶμα ὕστερον καὶ σύνθετον καὶ αὐτὴ μετ' ἄλλου ποιεῖ σῶμα. Οὕτω γὰρ τοῦ ὀνόματος τετύχηκε τοῦ αὐτοῦ κατὰ τὸ ἀσώματον, ὅτι ἑκάτερον τό τε ὂν ἥ τε ὕλη ἕτερα τῶν σωμάτων. Οὔτε δὲ ψυχὴ οὖσα οὔτε νοῦς οὔτε ζωὴ οὔτε εἶδος οὔτε λόγος οὔτε πέρας—ἀπειρία γάρ—οὔτε δύναμις—τί γὰρ καὶ ποιεῖ;—ἀλλὰ ταῦτα ὑπερεκπεσοῦσα πάντα οὐδὲ τὴν τοῦ ὄντος προσηγορίαν ὀρθῶς ἂν δέχοιτο, μὴ ὂν δ' ἂν εἰκότως λέγοιτο, καὶ οὐχ ὥσπερ κίνησις μὴ ὂν ἢ στάσις μὴ ὄν, ἀλλ' ἀληθινῶς μὴ ὄν, εἴδωλον καὶ φάντασμα ὄγκου καὶ ὑποστάσεως ἔφεσις καὶ ἑστηκὸς οὐκ ἐν στάσει καὶ ἀόρατον καθ' αὑτὸ καὶ φεῦγον τὸ βουλόμενον ἰδεῖν, καὶ ὅταν τις μὴ ἴδῃ γιγνόμενον, ἀτενίσαντι δὲ οὐχ ὁρώμενον, καὶ τὰ ἐναντία ἀεὶ ἐφ' ἑαυτοῦ φανταζόμενον, μικρὸν καὶ μέγα καὶ ἧττον καὶ μᾶλλον, ἐλλεῖπόν τε καὶ ὑπερέχον, εἴδωλον οὐ μένον οὐδ' αὖ φεύγειν δυνάμενον· οὐδὲ γὰρ οὐδὲ τοῦτο ἰσχύει ἅτε μὴ ἰσχὺν παρὰ νοῦ λαβόν, ἀλλ' ἐν ἐλλείψει τοῦ ὄντος παντὸς γενόμενον. Διὸ πᾶν ὃ ἂν ἐπαγγέλληται ψεύδεται, κἂν μέγα φαντασθῇ, μικρόν

[1] ἢ τὰ J^{ypmg}: εἶτα codd.

---

[1] The εἶτα of most MSS will not do here, as a τὰ is required. Henry and Schwyzer think that the ἢ τὰ of a marginal note in J may represent a genuine tradition and "means practically

ing substrate and the things which are said to be based upon matter,[1] from which we shall acquire a knowledge of matter's non-existence and freedom from affections. Matter, then, is incorporeal, since body is posterior and a composite, and matter with something else produces body. In this way it has acquired the same name [as being] in respect of its incorporeality, because both being and matter are other than bodies. It is not soul or intellect or life or form or rational formative principle or limit—for it is unlimitedness[2]—or power—for what does it make?—but, falling outside all these, it could not properly receive the title of being but would appropriately be called non-being, not in the sense in which motion is not being or rest not being[3] but truly not-being; it is a ghostly image of bulk, a tendency towards substantial existence; it is static without being stable; it is invisible in itself and escapes any attempt to see it, and occurs when one is not looking, but even if you look closely you cannot see it. It always presents opposite appearances on its surface, small and great,[4] less and more, deficient and superabundant, a phantom which does not remain and cannot get away either, for it has no strength for this, since it has not received strength from intellect but is lacking in all being. Whatever announcement it makes, therefore, is a lie, and if it

the same" as Volkmann's *καὶ τὰ*. I translate, with some slight doubt, on this assumption.

[2] On matter as the unlimited, cp. II. 4 [12] 15.

[3] Cp. *Sophist* 256D–E.

[4] Cp. II. 4 [12] 11. 33 ff., for this Platonic way of describing matter.

ἐστι, κἂν μᾶλλον, ἧττόν ἐστι, καὶ τὸ ὂν αὐτοῦ ἐν φαντάσει οὐκ ὄν ἐστιν, οἷον παίγνιον φεῦγον· ὅθεν καὶ τὰ ἐν αὐτῷ ἐγγίγνεσθαι δοκοῦντα παίγνια, εἴδωλα ἐν εἰδώλῳ ἀτεχνῶς, ὡς ἐν κατόπτρῳ τὸ ἀλλαχοῦ ἱδρυμένον ἀλλαχοῦ φανταζόμενον· καὶ πιμπλάμενον, ὡς δοκεῖ, καὶ ἔχον οὐδὲν καὶ δοκοῦν τὰ πάντα. Τὰ δὲ εἰσιόντα καὶ ἐξιόντα τῶν ὄντων μιμήματα καὶ εἴδωλα εἰς εἴδωλον ἄμορφον καὶ διὰ τὸ ἄμορφον αὐτῆς ἐνορώμενα ποιεῖν μὲν δοκεῖ εἰς αὐτήν, ποιεῖ δὲ οὐδέν· ἀμενηνὰ γὰρ καὶ ἀσθενῆ καὶ ἀντερεῖδον οὐκ ἔχοντα· ἀλλ' οὐδὲ ἐκείνης ἐχούσης δίεισιν οὐ τέμνοντα οἷον δι' ὕδατος ἢ εἴ τις ἐν τῷ λεγομένῳ κενῷ μορφὰς οἷον εἰσπέμποι. Καὶ γὰρ αὖ, εἰ μὲν τοιαῦτα ἦν τὰ ἐνορώμενα, οἷα τὰ ἀφ' ὧν ἦλθεν εἰς αὐτήν, τάχ' ἄν τις διδοὺς αὐτοῖς δύναμίν τινα τῶν πεμψάντων τὴν εἰς αὐτὴν γενομένην πάσχειν ὑπ' αὐτῶν ἂν ὑπέλαβε· νῦν δ' ἄλλων μὲν ὄντων τῶν ἐμφανταζομένων, ἀλλοίων δὲ τῶν ἐνορωμένων, κἀκ τούτων μαθεῖν ἔστι τὸ τῆς πείσεως ψεῦδος ψευδοῦς ὄντος τοῦ ἐνορωμένου καὶ οὐδαμῇ ἔχοντος ὁμοιότητα πρὸς τὸ ποιῆσαν. Ἀσθενὲς δὴ καὶ ψεῦδος ὂν καὶ εἰς ψεῦδος ἐμπῖπτον, οἷα ἐν ὀνείρῳ ἢ ὕδατι ἢ κατόπτρῳ, ἀπαθῆ αὐτὴν εἴασεν ἐξ ἀνάγκης εἶναι· καίτοι ἔν γε τοῖς προειρημένοις ὁμοίωσις τοῖς ἐνορωμένοις ἐστὶ πρὸς τὰ ἐνορῶντα.

8. Ὅλως δὲ τὸ πάσχον δεῖ τοιοῦτον εἶναι οἷον ἐν ταῖς ἐναντίαις εἶναι δυνάμεσι καὶ ποιότησι τῶν

---

1 *Timaeus* 50C 4–5.

appears great, it is small, if more, it is less; its apparent being is not real, but a sort of fleeting frivolity; hence the things which seem to come to be in it are frivolities, nothing but phantoms in a phantom, like something in a mirror which really exists in one place but is reflected in another; it seems to be filled, and holds nothing; it is all seeming. "Imitations of real beings pass into and out of it,"[1] ghosts into a formless ghost, visible because of its formlessness. They seem to act on it, but do nothing, for they are wraith-like and feeble and have no thrust; nor does matter thrust against them, but they go through without making a cut, as if through water, or as if someone in a way projected shapes in the void people talk about. And again, if the things seen in matter were of the same kind as those from which they came to it, perhaps one might give them a power derived from those which sent them and, as this power reached matter, one might assume that it was affected by them; but, as it is, the producers of the appearances are different from the things seen in matter, and we can learn from this the falsity of the affection, since what is seen in matter is false and has no sort of likeness to what produced it. Certainly, then, since it is weak and false, and falling into falsity, like things in a dream or water or a mirror, it necessarily leaves matter unaffected; though in the examples just mentioned there is a likeness between the things seen [in water, etc.], and the things which are the causes of the appearances.

8. But in general that which is affected must be of such a kind that it is possessed of powers and qualities opposed to those of the things which come upon it

ἐπεισιόντων καὶ τὸ πάσχειν ἐμποιούντων. Τῷ γὰρ ἐνόντι θερμῷ ἡ ἀλλοίωσις ἡ παρὰ τοῦ ψύχοντος καὶ τῷ ἐνόντι ὑγρῷ ἡ ἀλλοίωσις ἡ παρὰ τοῦ ξηραίνοντος, καὶ ἠλλοιῶσθαι λέγομεν τὸ ὑποκείμενον, ὅταν ἐκ θερμοῦ ψυχρὸν ἢ ἐκ ξηροῦ ὑγρὸν γίγνηται. Μαρτυρεῖ δὲ καὶ ἡ λεγομένη πυρὸς φθορὰ μεταβολῆς γενομένης εἰς στοιχεῖον ἄλλο· τὸ γὰρ πῦρ ἐφθάρη, φαμέν, οὐχ ἡ ὕλη· ὥστε καὶ τὰ πάθη περὶ τοῦτο, περὶ ὃ καὶ ἡ φθορά· ὁδὸς γὰρ εἰς φθορὰν ἡ παραδοχὴ τοῦ πάθους· καὶ τούτῳ τὸ φθείρεσθαι, ᾧ καὶ τὸ πάσχειν. Τὴν δὲ ὕλην φθείρεσθαι οὐχ οἷόν τε· εἰς τί γὰρ καὶ πῶς; Πῶς οὖν λαβοῦσα ἐν αὐτῇ θερμότητας, ψυχρότητας, μυρίας καὶ ἀπείρους ὅλως ποιότητας καὶ ταύταις διαληφθεῖσα καὶ οἷον συμφύτους αὐτὰς ἔχουσα καὶ συγκεκραμένας ἀλλήλαις, οὐ γὰρ ἕκαστα χωρίς, αὐτὴ δὲ ἐν μέσῳ ἀποληφθεῖσα πασχουσῶν τῶν ποιοτήτων ἐν τῇ πρὸς ἀλλήλας ὑπ' ἀλλήλων μίξει οὐχὶ συμπάσχει καὶ αὐτή; Εἰ μὴ ἄρα ἔξω τις αὐτὴν θήσεται αὐτῶν παντάπασιν· ἐν ὑποκειμένῳ δὲ πᾶν οὕτω πάρεστι τῷ ὑποκειμένῳ, ὡς αὐτῷ τι παρ' αὐτοῦ διδόναι.

9. Ληπτέον δὴ τὸ παρεῖναι ἕτερον ἑτέρῳ καὶ τὸ εἶναι ἄλλο ἐν ἄλλῳ πρῶτον ὡς οὐ καθ' ἕνα τρόπον ὑπάρχει, ἀλλὰ τὸ μέν ἐστιν οἷον μετὰ τοῦ παρεῖναι ἢ χεῖρον ἢ βέλτιον ποιεῖν ἐκεῖνο μετὰ τοῦ τρέπειν,

---

[1] This is Aristotelian doctrine: cp. *De Generatione et Corruptione* A.7. 323b6 ff.

and produce affections in it.[1] For it is from that which cools it that the change comes to the heat in a thing, and from that which dries it that the change comes to the moistness in it, and we say that the substrate is changed when it becomes cold instead of hot or moist instead of dry. And what is called the destruction of fire is evidence of this; there is a change into another element, for, we assert, the fire is destroyed, not the matter; so that the affections belong to that which it belongs to be destroyed, for receiving affections is the way to destruction; and being destroyed is brought about by that which is also the cause of being affected. But it is impossible for matter to be destroyed, for into what could it [be changed when it is] destroyed, and how? How then, when matter receives in itself heats and coldnesses, and thousands, in fact, an infinite number, of qualities, and is divided by them and holds them, so to speak, grown together and mixed up with each other (for individual qualities are not separate in it), can it, set apart in the middle of them, not be itself affected along with them when the qualities are affected by their interaction on each other in their mixture with each other? Unless, of course, one is to put it quite outside the qualities; but everything which is present in a substrate is present in such a way as to give something from itself to the substrate.

9. One must, of course, understand first of all that there is not only one way in which one thing is present to another or in another; but there is one way in which the presence of the thing goes with an improvement or deterioration in the other which

οἷον ἐπὶ τῶν σωμάτων ὁρᾶται ἐπί γε τῶν ζῴων, τὸ δ' οἷον ποιεῖν βέλτιον ἢ χεῖρον ἄνευ τοῦ πάσχειν ἐκεῖνο, ὥσπερ ἐπὶ τῆς ψυχῆς ἐλέγετο, τὸ δ' οἷον ὅταν τις σχῆμα κηρῷ προσαγάγῃ, ἔνθα οὔτε τι πάθος, ὡς ἄλλο τι ποιῆσαι τὸν κηρὸν εἶναι, ὅταν παρῇ τὸ σχῆμα, οὔτε ἐλλείψεις [ἐκεῖνο][1] ἀπεληλυθότος ἐκείνου. Τὸ δὲ δὴ φῶς οὐδὲ σχήματος ἀλλοίωσιν περὶ τὸ φωτιζόμενον ποιεῖ. Ὁ δὲ δὴ λίθος ψυχρὸς γενόμενος τί παρὰ τῆς ψυχρότητος μένων λίθος ἔχει; Τί δ' ἂν γραμμὴ πάθοι ὑπὸ χρώματος; Οὐδὲ δὴ τὸ ἐπίπεδον, οἶμαι. Ἀλλὰ τὸ ὑποκείμενον ἴσως σῶμα; Καίτοι ὑπὸ χρώματος τί ἂν πάθοι; Οὐ γὰρ δεῖ τὸ παθεῖν λέγειν τὸ παρεῖναι οὐδὲ τὸ μορφὴν περιθεῖναι. Εἰ δέ τις καὶ τὰ κάτοπτρα λέγοι καὶ ὅλως τὰ διαφανῆ ὑπὸ τῶν ἐνορωμένων εἰδώλων μηδὲν πάσχειν, οὐκ ἀνόμοιον ἂν τὸ παράδειγμα φέροι. Εἴδωλα γὰρ καὶ τὰ ἐν τῇ ὕλῃ, καὶ αὕτη ἔτι μᾶλλον ἀπαθέστερον ἢ τὰ κάτοπτρα. Ἐγγίγνονται μὲν δὴ ἐν αὐτῇ θερμότητες καὶ ψυχρότητες, ἀλλ' οὐκ αὐτὴν θερμαίνουσαι· τὸ γὰρ θερμαίνεσθαί ἐστι καὶ τὸ ψύχεσθαι ποιότητος ἐξ ἄλλης εἰς ἄλλην τὸ ὑποκείμενον ἀγούσης. Ἐπισκεπτέον δὲ περὶ τῆς ψυχρότητος μήποτε ἀπουσία καὶ στέρησις. Συνελθοῦσαι δὲ εἰς αὐτὴν αἱ ποιότητες εἰς ἀλλήλας μὲν αἱ πολλαὶ αὐτῶν ποιήσουσι, μᾶλλον δὲ αἱ ἐναντίως

[1] ἐλλείψεις H–S[2]: ἔλλειψιν εἰς ἐκεῖνο ExC, H–S[1]: ἔλλειψιν ἐκεῖνο US: εἰς ἔλλειψιν εἰς ἐκεῖνο A: ἀλείψειν εἰς ἐκεῖνο Q.

involves change; this is the kind of presence which is observed in bodies, living ones at any rate; and there is another which brings about improvement or deterioration without the other being affected; this is what we have said happens in the case of the soul. There is another way, too, which is like what happens when someone impresses a shape on wax, where there is no affection, so as to make the wax into something else when the shape is there, and there are no deficiencies when the shape is gone. And light, certainly, does not even produce an alteration of shape in the thing illuminated. And when a stone becomes cold, what does it get from the coldness, since it remains a stone? And in what way could a line be affected by colour?[1] I do not think that even a surface could be. But, perhaps, the body underlying it could? Yet how could it be affected by colour? For one must not call presence or putting on a shape "being affected." If one said that mirrors and transparent things generally were in no way affected by the images seen in them, he would be giving a not inappropriate example. For the things in matter are images too, and matter is still less liable to affections than are mirrors. For certainly heats and coldnesses occur in it, but they do not heat it; for heating and cooling belong to quality, which brings the substrate from one state to another. (But we should consider whether coldness is not an absence and a privation.) But when the qualities come together in matter most of them will act upon each other, or, rather, those will which are opposed to

[1] Cp. Aristotle, *De Gen. et Corr.* A.7. 323b25–6.

ἔχουσαι. Τί γὰρ ἂν εὐωδία γλυκύτητα ἐργάσαιτο ἢ χρῶμα σχῆμα ἢ τὸ ἐξ ἄλλου γένους ἄλλο; Ὅθεν ἄν τις καὶ μάλιστα πιστεύσειεν ὡς ἔστιν ἐν τῷ αὐτῷ εἶναι ἄλλο ἄλλῳ ἢ ἕτερον ἐν ἑτέρῳ ἄλυπον ὂν τῇ αὐτοῦ παρουσίᾳ ᾧ ἢ ἐν ᾧ πάρεστιν. Ὥσπερ οὖν καὶ τὸ βλαπτόμενον οὐχ ὑπὸ τοῦ τυχόντος, οὕτως οὐδὲ τὸ τρεπόμενον καὶ πάσχον ὑφ᾽ ὁτουοῦν ἂν πάθοι, ἀλλὰ τοῖς ἐναντίοις ὑπὸ τῶν ἐναντίων ἡ πεῖσις, τὰ δ᾽ ἄλλα ὑπ᾽ ἄλλων ἄτρεπτα. Οἷς δὴ μηδεμία ἐναντιότης ὑπάρχει, ταῦτα ὑπ᾽ οὐδενὸς ἂν ἐναντίου πάθοι. Ἀνάγκη τοίνυν, εἴ τι πάσχοι, μὴ ὕλην, ἀλλά τι συναμφότερον ἢ ὅλως πολλὰ ὁμοῦ εἶναι. Τὸ δὲ μόνον καὶ ἔρημον τῶν ἄλλων καὶ παντάπασιν ἁπλοῦν ἀπαθὲς ἂν εἴη πάντων καὶ ἐν μέσοις ἅπασιν ἀπειλημμένον [ἢ] [1] τοῖς εἰς ἄλληλα ποιοῦσιν· οἷον ἐν οἴκῳ τῷ αὐτῷ ἀλλήλους παιόντων ὁ οἶκος ἀπαθὴς καὶ ὁ ἐν αὐτῷ ἀήρ. Συνιόντα δὲ τὰ ἐπὶ τῆς ὕλης ἄλληλα ποιείτω, ὅσα ποιεῖν πέφυκεν, αὐτὴ δ᾽ ἀπαθὴς ἔστω πολὺ μᾶλλον, ἢ ὅσαι ποιότητες ἐν αὐτῇ τῷ μὴ ἐναντίαι εἶναι ἀπαθεῖς ὑπ᾽ ἀλλήλων εἰσίν.

10. Ἔπειτα, εἰ πάσχει ἡ ὕλη, δεῖ τι ἔχειν αὐτὴν ἐκ τοῦ πάθους ἢ αὐτὸ τὸ πάθος ἢ ἑτέρως διακεῖσθαι ἢ πρὶν εἰσελθεῖν εἰς αὐτὴν τὸ πάθος. Ἐπιούσης τοίνυν ἄλλης μετ᾽ ἐκείνην ποιότητος οὐκέτι ὕλη ἔσται τὸ δεχόμενον, ἀλλὰ ποιὰ ὕλη. Εἰ δὲ καὶ

1 ἢ del. Kirchhoff.

1 The phrase comes from Plato, *Philebus* 63B6–7, but the context there is quite different.

each other. For what could fragrance do to sweetness or colour to shape, or a thing which belongs to one kind to a thing of another kind? This would very much confirm one's belief that it is possible for one thing to be in the same place as another, or in another, without troubling by its presence that with which or in which it is. So then, just as a thing does not suffer injury from any and every chance encounter, so that which is changed and affected is not affected by anything and everything, but it is opposites which affect opposites, and other things remain unchanged by each other. Those, then, in which there is no opposition could not be affected by any opposite. So that, if anything is affected, it cannot be matter but must be a composite or in general a multiplicity of things all together. But that which is "single and set apart"[1] from all other things and in every way simple would be unaffected by everything and set apart in the midst of all the things which act on each other; just as when people are hitting each other in the same house the house is unaffected, and so is the air in it. So let the things which have matter as their substrate act on each other as it is their nature to do, but let matter itself be unaffected, much more so than those qualities in it which are unaffected by each other because they are not opposed.

10. Then further, if matter is affected, it must retain something from the affection, either the affection itself, or the being in a different state from that in which it was before the affection came to it. Now, if another quality comes to it after that [first one which affected it], what receives it will no longer be matter but qualified matter. But if this quality,

αὕτη[1] ἡ ποιότης ἀποσταίη καταλιποῦσά τι αὐτῆς τῷ ποιῆσαι, ἄλλο ἂν ἔτι μᾶλλον γίγνοιτο τὸ ὑποκείμενον. Καὶ προιοῦσα τοῦτον τὸν τρόπον ἄλλο τι ἢ ὕλη ἔσται τὸ ὑποκείμενον, πολύτροπον δὲ καὶ πολυειδές· ὥστε οὐδ' ἂν ἔτι πανδεχὲς γένοιτο ἐμπόδιον πολλοῖς τοῖς ἐπεισιοῦσι γιγνόμενον, ἥ τε ὕλη οὐκέτι μένει· οὐδὲ ἄφθαρτος τοίνυν· ὥστε, εἰ δεῖ ὕλην εἶναι, ὥσπερ ἐξ ἀρχῆς ἦν, οὕτως ἀεὶ δεῖ αὐτὴν εἶναι τὴν αὐτήν· ὡς τό γε ἀλλοιοῦσθαι λέγειν οὐκ ἔστιν αὐτὴν ὕλην τηρούντων. Ἔπειτα δέ, εἰ ὅλως τὸ ἀλλοιούμενον πᾶν δεῖ μένον ἐπὶ τοῦ αὐτοῦ εἴδους ἀλλοιοῦσθαι, καὶ κατὰ συμβεβηκότα ἀλλ' οὐ καθ' αὑτά· εἰ δεῖ μένειν τὸ ἀλλοιούμενον καὶ οὐ τὸ μένον ἐστὶν αὐτοῦ τὸ πάσχον, δυοῖν θάτερον ἀνάγκη, ἢ ἀλλοιουμένην τὴν ὕλην αὑτῆς ἐξίστασθαι, ἢ μὴ ἐξισταμένην αὑτῆς μὴ ἀλλοιοῦσθαι. Εἰ δέ τις λέγοι μὴ καθ' ὅσον ὕλη ἀλλοιοῦσθαι, πρῶτον μὲν κατὰ τί ἀλλοιώσεται οὐχ ἕξει λέγειν, ἔπειτα ὁμολογήσει καὶ οὕτω τὴν ὕλην αὐτὴν μὴ ἀλλοιοῦσθαι. Ὥσπερ γὰρ τοῖς ἄλλοις εἴδεσιν οὖσιν οὐκ ἔστιν ἀλλοιοῦσθαι κατὰ τὴν οὐσίαν τῆς οὐσίας αὐτοῖς ἐν τούτῳ οὔσης, οὕτως, ἐπειδὴ τὸ εἶναι τῇ ὕλῃ ἐστὶ τὸ εἶναι ᾗ ὕλη, οὐκ ἔστιν αὐτὴν ἀλλοιοῦσθαι καθ' ὅ τι ὕλη ἐστίν, ἀλλὰ μένειν, καὶ ὥσπερ ἐκεῖ ἀναλλοίωτον αὐτὸ τὸ εἶδος, οὕτω καὶ ἐνταῦθα ἀναλλοίωτον αὐτὴν τὴν ὕλην.

[1] αὕτη Kirchhoff, H–S²: αὐτὴ codd.

---

[1] Cp. *Timaeus* 50B7–8.

too, goes away leaving something of itself behind as the result of its action, the substrate will become still more different. And if it went on in this way the substrate would become something other than matter, something existing in many modes and many shapes; so that it would not be able to receive everything but would obstruct the entry of many of the things which came to it—and then there is no more matter, so it is not indestructible; so, if there must be matter, as there was from the beginning, it must consequently always be the same, so that it is not possible to keep matter and speak of it as being altered. Then again, if, speaking generally, everything which is altered must retain the same essential form in the alteration, and be altered only accidentally, not intrinsically; if that which is altered must really remain, and it is not that of it which remains which is affected, then one of two consequences must necessarily follow; either matter will be altered and pass out of its own nature, or it will not pass out of its own nature and will not be altered.[1] But if anyone should say that it is not altered in so far as it is matter, first of all he will not be able to say in what respect it is going to be altered, and then he will admit, this way too, that matter itself is not altered. For, just as other things, which are forms, cannot be altered in their essential being, since their essential being consists in this, since existing, for matter, is existing precisely as matter, it is not possible for it to be altered in so far as it is matter, but it must stay as it is, and, just as in the case of things which are forms the form itself must remain unaltered, so here too matter itself must remain unaltered.

11. Ὅθεν δὴ καὶ τὸν Πλάτωνα οὕτω διανοούμενον ὀρθῶς εἰρηκέναι νομίζω, τὰ δ' εἰσιόντα καὶ ἐξιόντα τῶν ὄντων μιμήματα μὴ μάτην εἰσιέναι καὶ ἐξιέναι εἰρηκέναι, ἀλλὰ βουλόμενον ἡμᾶς συνεῖναι ἐπιστήσαντας τῷ τρόπῳ τῆς μεταλήψεως, καὶ κινδυνεύει τὸ ἄπορον ἐκεῖνο τὸ ὅπως ἡ ὕλη τῶν εἰδῶν μεταλαμβάνει μὴ ἐκεῖνο εἶναι ὃ οἱ πολλοὶ ᾠήθησαν τῶν πρὸ ἡμῶν, τὸ πῶς ἔρχεται εἰς αὐτήν, ἀλλὰ μᾶλλον πῶς ἔστιν ἐν αὐτῇ. Ὄντως γὰρ θαυμαστὸν εἶναι δοκεῖ, πῶς τούτων τῶν εἰδῶν παρόντων αὐτῇ μένει ἡ αὐτὴ ἀπαθὴς αὐτῶν οὖσα καὶ προσέτι αὐτῶν τῶν εἰσιόντων πασχόντων ὑπ' ἀλλήλων. Ἀλλὰ καὶ αὐτὰ τὰ εἰσιόντα ἐξωθεῖν τὰ πρότερα ἕκαστα, καὶ εἶναι τὸ παθεῖν ἐν τῷ συνθέτῳ καὶ οὐδὲ ἐν παντὶ συνθέτῳ, ἀλλ' ᾧ χρεία τοῦ προσελθόντος ἢ ἀπελθόντος καὶ ὃ ἐλλιπὲς μὲν τῇ συστάσει ἀπουσίᾳ τινός, τέλειον δὲ τῇ παρουσίᾳ. Τῇ δὲ ὕλῃ οὔτε τι πλέον εἰς τὴν αὐτῆς σύστασιν προσελθόντος ὁτουοῦν· οὐ γὰρ γίγνεται τότε ὅ ἐστι προσελθόντος, οὔτε ἔλαττον ἀπελθόντος· μένει γὰρ ὃ ἐξ ἀρχῆς ἦν. Τοῦ δὲ κεκοσμῆσθαι τοῖς μὲν κόσμου καὶ τάξεως δεομένοις εἴη ἂν χρεία, καὶ ὁ κόσμος δὲ γένοιτο ἂν ἄνευ μεταλλοιώσεως, οἷον οἷς περιτίθεμεν· εἰ δὲ οὕτω τις κοσμηθείη ὡς σύμφυτον εἶναι, δεήσει ἀλλοιωθὲν ὃ πρότερον αἰσχρὸν ἦν καὶ ἕτερον

---

[1] *Timaeus* 50C4–5: cp. ch. 7.

11. This I think was Plato's opinion, which led him to say, correctly, " The things that enter and leave it are copies of the real things ";[1] he spoke of entering and leaving with deliberate purpose, wishing us to understand and apply our minds to the manner of the participation; and it seems that the well-known difficulty about how matter participates in forms is not what most of our predecessors thought it was, how the forms come into matter, but rather how they are in matter. For it really does appear remarkable how, when these forms are present to it, matter remains the same and is unaffected by them, and still more so since the very forms which enter it are affected by each other. But it is remarkable, too, that the things which enter push out on each occasion the things which were there before them, and that being affected occurs in the composite thing, and not in every composite but only in that which has a need for something to come to it or go away from it, and which has a defect in its composition if something is not there, but is complete if it is present. But matter gains nothing towards its composition if anything whatever comes to it, for it does not become what it is at the time when something comes, or become less when it goes away; for it remains what it was from the beginning. But as for being beautified and set in order, there could be a need for it in those things which need decoration and ordering, and the beautifying and ordering could take place without alteration, as when we dress people up; but if someone is to be so beautified and set in order that the beauty and order are a part of his nature, there will be need of an alteration in what

γενόμενον ἐκεῖνο τὸ κεκοσμημένον οὕτω καλὸν ἐξ αἰσχροῦ εἶναι. Εἰ τοίνυν αἰσχρὰ οὖσα ἡ ὕλη καλὴ ἐγένετο, ὃ ἦν πρότερον τῷ[1] αἰσχρὰ εἶναι οὐκέτ' ἐστίν· ὥστε ἐν τῷ οὕτω κεκοσμῆσθαι ἀπολεῖ τὸ ὕλην εἶναι καὶ μάλιστα, εἰ μὴ κατὰ συμβεβηκὸς αἰσχρά· εἰ δ' οὕτως αἰσχρὰ ὡς αἶσχος εἶναι, οὐδ' ἂν μεταλάβοι κόσμου, καὶ εἰ οὕτω κακὴ ὡς κακὸν εἶναι, οὐδ' ἂν μεταλάβοι ἀγαθοῦ· ὥστε οὐχ οὕτως ἡ μετάληψις ὡς οἴονται[2] παθούσης, ἀλλ' ἕτερος τρόπος οἷον δοκεῖν. Ἴσως δὲ καὶ τοῦτον τὸν τρόπον λύοιτο ἂν τὸ ἄπορον, πῶς οὖσα κακὴ ἐφίοιτο ἂν τοῦ ἀγαθοῦ, ὡς μὴ μεταλήψει ἀπολλυμένης ὃ ἦν· εἰ γὰρ τοῦτον τὸν τρόπον ἡ λεγομένη μετάληψις, ὡς τὴν αὐτὴν μένειν μὴ ἀλλοιουμένην, ὡς λέγομεν, ἀλλ' εἶναι ἀεὶ ὅ ἐστιν, οὐκέτι θαυμαστὸν γίνεται τὸ πῶς οὖσα κακὴ μεταλαμβάνει. Οὐ γὰρ ἐξίσταται ἑαυτῆς, ἀλλ' ὅτι μὲν ἀναγκαῖόν ἐστι μεταλαμβάνειν ἀμηγέπῃ μεταλαμβάνει ἕως ἂν ᾖ, τῷ δ' εἶναι ὅ ἐστι τρόπῳ μεταλήψεως τηροῦντι αὐτὴν οὐ βλάπτεται εἰς τὸ εἶναι παρὰ τοῦ οὕτω διδόντος, καὶ κινδυνεύει διὰ τοῦτο οὐχ ἧττον εἶναι κακή, ὅτι ἀεὶ μένει τοῦτο ὅ ἐστι. Μεταλαμβάνουσα γὰρ ὄντως καὶ ἀλλοιουμένη ὄντως ὑπὸ τοῦ ἀγαθοῦ οὐκ ἂν ἦν τὴν φύσιν κακή. Ὥστε εἴ τις τὴν ὕλην λέγει κακήν, οὕτως ἂν ἀληθεύοι, εἰ

[1] τῷ Kirchhoff; τὸ codd. H–S.

[2] οἴονται Cizensis e corr: οἷόν τε codd.

---

[1] Henry-Schwyzer retain the MSS τὸ here and explain that τὸ αἰσχρὰ εἶναι is in apposition to ὃ ἦν πρότερον. But what matter was before was αἰσχρά, not τὸ αἰσχρὰ εἶναι (this does

was ugly before, and what is beautified and ordered must become different and so be beautiful instead of ugly. Now, if matter was ugly and became beautiful, it is no longer what it was before by the fact of being ugly; [1] so that by being beautified and set in order in this way it will stop being matter, particularly if it is not only accidentally ugly; but if it is ugly in such a way that it is ugliness, it could have no part in beauty and order, and if it is bad in such a way that it is badness, it could have no part in good; so that its participation would not be, as people think, by being affected, but of another kind, so that it only seems to be affected. Perhaps in this way the difficulty can be resolved how, though it is evil, it can reach towards the good, in that it does not by its participation lose what it was before, for if, as we say, its so-called participation is of this kind, so that it remains the same and is not altered but is always what it is, it becomes no longer remarkable how it participates [in the good] though it is evil. For it does not abandon itself but, since it must participate, it participates in a kind of way as long as it is there; but, as the manner of participation keeps it what it is, it receives no damage which extends to its being from that which gives it [form] in this way, and because of this it is, so it seems, no less evil, because it always remains what it is. For if it really participated and was really altered by the good it would not be evil by nature. So that if someone calls matter evil, he would speak the truth if he meant that it was

not mean the same as *αἶσχος εἶναι* below, which in any case should not be anticipated here). I therefore print and translate Kirchhoff's correction *τῷ*.

τοῦ ἀγαθοῦ ἀπαθῆ λέγοι· τοῦτο δὲ ταὐτόν ἐστι τῷ ὅλως ἀπαθῆ εἶναι.

12. Ὁ δέ γε Πλάτων τοῦτο νοῶν περὶ αὐτῆς καὶ τὴν μετάληψιν οὐχ ὡς ἐν ὑποκειμένῳ εἴδους γενομένου καὶ μορφὴν διδόντος ὥστε ἓν σύνθετον γενέσθαι συντραπέντων καὶ οἷον συγκραθέντων καὶ συμπαθόντων τιθέμενος, ὅτι μὴ οὕτω λέγει παραστῆσαι βουλόμενος, καὶ πῶς ἂν αὐτὴ ἀπαθὴς μένουσα ἔχοι τὰ εἴδη ἀπαθοῦς μεταλήψεως ζητῶν[1] παράδειγμα—ἄλλον τρόπον οὐ ῥᾴδιον διδάξαι ἃ μάλιστα παρόντα σῴζει τὸ ὑποκείμενον ταὐτὸν εἶναι—ὑπέστη πολλὰς ἀπορίας σπεύδων ἐφ᾽ ὃ βούλεται καὶ προσέτι παραστῆσαι θέλων τὸ ἐν τοῖς αἰσθητοῖς κενὸν τῆς ὑποστάσεως καὶ τὴν χώραν τοῦ εἰκότος οὖσαν πολλήν. Τὴν οὖν ὕλην σχήμασιν ὑποθέμενος τὰ πάθη ποιεῖν τοῖς ἐμψύχοις σώμασιν οὐδὲν αὐτὴν ἔχουσαν τούτων τῶν παθημάτων τὸ μένον ταύτης [ταύτην][2] ἐνδείκνυται διδοὺς συλλογίζεσθαι, ὡς οὐδὲ παρὰ τῶν σχημάτων ἔχει τὸ πάσχειν αὐτὴ καὶ ἀλλοιοῦσθαι. Τοῖς μὲν γὰρ σώμασι τούτοις ἐξ ἑτέρου σχήματος ἕτερον σχῆμα δεχομένοις τάχα ἄν τις ἀλλοίωσιν λέγοι γίγνεσθαι τὴν τοῦ σχήματος μεταβολὴν ὁμώνυμον

[1] ζητῶν Cizensis e corr., Kirchhoff: ζητοῦσα codd., H.–S.
[2] ταύτην del. H–S.

---

[1] Plotinus seems to be considering here the whole passage dealing with the "third kind" in the *Timaeus* (47E–53C) rather than any particular part of it.

unaffected by the good; but this is the same as being totally incapable of being affected.

12. This is Plato's thought about matter;[1] he does not suppose that its participation was like that in which a form becomes present in a substrate and gives it shape so that one composite thing comes into existence, with form and substrate combined, and so to speak mixed up and mutually affected; he wants to show that he does not mean this, and how matter could remain unaffected and receive the forms, looking for an example of participation without affection[2]—in any other way it would not be easy to explain what things precisely, when they are present, keep the substrate unaltered, so he raised many difficulties in hurrying on to express what he wants, and, further, wishing to show the emptiness of substantial being in the things of sense and the great area which there is of mere appearance. So when he makes it his initial supposition that matter by its shapes produces the affections in ensouled bodies, he demonstrates its persistence, and enables us to conclude that it does not itself experience any affection or alteration even from the shapes. For one might perhaps say that alteration occurs in these bodies which receive one shape after another, meaning that the equivocal term "alteration"

[2] Henry-Schwyzer here keep the MSS ζητοῦσα. But it does not seem to make any sort of reasonable sense to say that *matter* looks for an example of unaffected participation, whereas it makes excellent sense to say that *Plato* does; and it is easy to see how a scribe could have written ζητοῦσα for ζητῶν under the influence of the immediately preceding μένουσα. I therefore, with Kirchhoff and other editors (including Beutler-Theiler), print and translate ζητῶν. (Dr. Schwyzer now agrees.)

τὴν ἀλλοίωσιν εἶναι λέγων· τῆς δὲ ὕλης οὐδὲν σχῆμα ἐχούσης οὐδὲ μέγεθος πῶς ἄν τις τὴν τοῦ σχήματος ὁπωσοῦν παρουσίαν ἀλλοίωσιν εἶναι κἂν ὁμωνύμως λέγοι; Εἴ τις οὖν ἐνταῦθα τὸ νόμῳ χροιὴ καὶ τὰ ἄλλα νόμῳ λέγοι τῷ τὴν φύσιν τὴν ὑποκειμένην μηδὲν οὕτως ἔχειν, ὡς νομίζεται, οὐκ ἂν ἄτοπος εἴη τοῦ λόγου. Ἀλλὰ πῶς ἔχει, εἰ μηδὲ τὸ ὡς σχήματα ἀρέσκει; Ἀλλ᾽ ἔχει ἔνδειξιν ἡ ὑπόθεσις ὡς οἷόν τε τῆς ἀπαθείας καὶ τῆς οἷον εἰδώλων οὐ παρόντων δοκούσης παρουσίας.

Ἢ πρότερον ἔτι περὶ τῆς ἀπαθείας αὐτῆς λεκτέον διδάσκοντας ὡς χρὴ ταῖς συνηθείαις τῶν ὀνομάτων ἐπὶ τὸ πάσχειν αὐτὴν φέρεσθαι, οἷον ὅταν [ξηραινομένην] [1] τὴν αὐτὴν πυρουμένην καὶ ὑγραινομένην ἐνθυμουμένους καὶ τὰ ἑξῆς «καὶ τὰς ἀέρος καὶ ὕδατος μορφὰς δεχομένην». Τὸ γὰρ «καὶ τὰς ἀέρος καὶ ὕδατος μορφὰς δεχομένην» ἀπαμβλύνει μὲν τὸ «πυρουμένην καὶ ὑγραινομένην», δηλοῖ τε ἐν τῷ «μορφὰς δεχομένην» οὐ τὸ μεμορφῶσθαι αὐτήν, ἀλλ᾽ εἶναι τὰς μορφὰς ὡς εἰσῆλθον, τό τε «πυρουμένην» οὐ κυρίως εἰρῆσθαι, ἀλλὰ μᾶλλον πῦρ γινομένην· οὐ γὰρ τὸ αὐτὸ πῦρ γίνεσθαι καὶ πυροῦσθαι· ὑπ᾽ ἄλλου μὲν γὰρ τὸ πυροῦσθαι, ἐν ᾧ καὶ τὸ πάσχειν· ὃ δ᾽ αὐτὸ μέρος ἐστὶ πυρὸς

[1] ξηραινομένην del. Page, H–S[2].

---

[1] Democritus, fr. DK, B9.

[2] *Timaeus* 52D5–6. [ξηραινομένην] "drying up" is a gloss on πυρουμένην.

includes the sense of " change of shape "; but, since matter has not shape or size, how could one say that any sort of presence of shape in it was alteration, even using the word in this equivocal sense? If, then, anyone at this point should quote " colour by convention and other things by convention," [1] because the underlying nature has nothing in the way in which it is conventionally supposed to, his quotation would not be out of place. But how does it have the forms, if not even the statement that it has them as shapes satisfies us? But Plato's supposition does at least indicate as clearly as possible the impassibility of matter and the seeming presence in it of a kind of phantasms which are not really present.

We must still make another preliminary point about its impassibility, that it is inevitable that we should be led by our customary way of speaking to suppose that it is affected, as, for instance, when we think of the same matter as being [as Plato says] set on fire and moistened, and, what follows this " receiving the shapes of air and water." [2] This phrase too, " receiving the shapes of air and water," takes away the force of the " being set on fire " and " moistened," and makes clear that in the phrase " receiving shapes " Plato is not speaking of matter itself having been shaped but that the shapes are there in the way in which they entered it, and that " being set on fire " is not used in its proper sense, but means that matter has become fire, for it is not the same thing to become fire and to be set on fire; being set on fire is due to the agency of another thing, and this also implies being affected; but how could that which is itself a part of fire be set on fire? It

πῶς ἂν πυροῖτο; Τοιοῦτον γὰρ ἂν εἴη, οἷον εἴ τις διὰ τοῦ χαλκοῦ τὸν ἀνδριάντα λέγοι πεφοιτηκέναι, εἰ τὸ πῦρ διὰ τῆς ὕλης λέγοι κεχωρηκέναι καὶ προσέτι πυρῶσαι. Ἔτι, εἰ λόγος ὁ προσιών, πῶς ἂν πυρώσειεν; Ἢ εἰ σχῆμα; Ἀλλὰ τὸ πυρούμενον ὑπ' ἀμφοῖν ἤδη. Πῶς οὖν ὑπ' ἀμφοῖν μὴ ἑνὸς ἐξ ἀμφοῖν γενομένου; Ἤ, κἂν ἓν ᾖ γενόμενον, οὐκ ἐν ἀλλήλοις τὰ πάθη ἐχόντων, ἀλλὰ πρὸς ἄλλα ποιούντων. Ἆρ' οὖν ἀμφοτέρων ποιούντων; Ἢ θατέρου θάτερον παρέχοντος μὴ φυγεῖν. Ἀλλ' ὅταν διαιρεθῇ τι σῶμα, πῶς οὐ καὶ αὐτὴ διῄρηται; Καὶ πεπονθότος ἐκείνου τῷ διῃρῆσθαι πῶς οὐ καὶ αὐτὴ τῷ αὐτῷ τούτῳ παθήματι πέπονθεν; Ἢ τί κωλύει τῷ αὐτῷ λόγῳ τούτῳ καὶ φθεῖραι λέγοντας πῶς φθαρέντος τοῦ σώματος οὐκ ἔφθαρται; Ἔτι λεκτέον τοσόνδε γὰρ εἶναι καὶ μέγεθος εἶναι, τῷ δὲ μὴ μεγέθει οὐδὲ τὰ μεγέθους πάθη ἐγγίγνεσθαι καὶ ὅλως δὴ τῷ μὴ σώματι μηδὲ τὰ σώματος πάθη γίγνεσθαι· ὥστε ὅσοι παθητὴν ποιοῦσι καὶ σῶμα συγχωρείτωσαν αὐτὴν εἶναι.

13. Ἔτι δὲ κἀκεῖνο ἐπιστῆσαι αὐτοὺς προσήκει, πῶς λέγουσι φεύγειν αὐτὴν τὸ εἶδος· πῶς γὰρ ἂν λίθους—τὰ περιλαβόντα αὐτήν—καὶ πέτρας φύγοι;

---

[1] The bronze and the statue provide an example which Aristotle frequently uses in his discussions of matter and its formation: cp., e.g., *Physics* B.3 194b2 ff. The point which Plotinus is making here is the absurdity of thinking of the relationship of form and matter in terms of one body entering and acting on another.

[2] Plotinus is clearly arguing here and in the next chapter against Platonists who quote the *Timaeus* as an authority for

would be the same sort of thing as saying that the statue took regular walks through the bronze,[1] if one said that the fire passed through the matter and, besides that, set it on fire! Besides, if what comes to matter is a rational forming principle, how could it set it on fire? Or if it is a shape? But that which is set on fire is kindled by what is already a composite of both [matter and form]. How, then, is it kindled by both if one thing has not come into existence from both? Even if one thing has come into existence, its two components do not have reciprocal affections but a common action on other things. Do they then both act? Rather, one prevents the other from getting away. But when a body is divided, how is the matter not divided too? And when the body is affected by being divided, how is the matter, too, not affected with the very same affection? Now, what prevents us by this very same line of argument from asserting its destruction, asking how when the body is destroyed the matter is not destroyed too? Besides, it must be pointed out that body is quantitatively determined and is size, but that which is not size is not subject to the affections of size, and in general what is not body is not subject to the affections of body, so that all those who make matter subject to affections must admit also that it is a body.[2]

13. But there is this further question which they ought to give their minds to, what they mean by saying that it tries to escape from form, for how could it escape from stones and rocks—things which

their view that matter is subject to affections, not against Stoics, who were quite certain that matter was a body (cp. note to ch. 6 above).

Οὐ γὰρ δὴ ποτὲ μὲν φεύγειν, ποτὲ δὲ μὴ φεύγειν φήσουσιν. Εἰ γὰρ βουλήσει αὐτῆς φεύγει, διὰ τί οὐκ ἀεί; Εἰ δὲ ἀνάγκῃ μένει, οὐκ ἔστιν ὅτε οὐκ ἐν εἴδει τινί ἐστιν. Ἀλλὰ τοῦ μὴ τὸ αὐτὸ εἶδος ἀεὶ ἴσχειν ἑκάστην ὕλην ζητητέον τὴν αἰτίαν, καὶ ἐν τοῖς εἰσιοῦσι μᾶλλον. Πῶς οὖν λέγεται φεύγειν; ἢ τῇ αὐτῆς φύσει καὶ ἀεί· τοῦτο δὲ τί ἂν εἴη ἢ μηδέποτε αὐτῆς ἐξισταμένην οὕτως ἔχειν τὸ εἶδος ὡς μηδέποτε ἔχειν; ἢ ὅ τι χρήσονται τῷ ὑφ' αὐτῶν λεγομένῳ οὐχ ἕξουσιν ἡ δὲ ὑποδοχὴ καὶ τιθήνη γενέσεως ἁπάσης· εἰ γὰρ ὑποδοχὴ καὶ τιθήνη, ἡ δὲ γένεσις ἄλλο αὐτῆς, τὸ δὲ ἀλλοιούμενον ἐν τῇ γενέσει, πρὸ γενέσεως οὖσα εἴη ἂν καὶ πρὸ ἀλλοιώσεως· ἥ τε «ὑποδοχὴ» καὶ ἔτι «ἡ τιθήνη» τηρεῖν ἐν ᾧ ἐστιν ἀπαθῆ οὖσαν, καὶ τὸ ἐν ᾧ ἐγγινόμενον ἕκαστον φαντάζεται καὶ πάλιν ἐκεῖθεν ἔξεισι καὶ χώραν εἶναι καὶ ἕδραν. Καὶ τὸ λεγόμενον δὲ καὶ εὐθυνόμενον ὡς τόπον εἰδῶν λέγοντος οὐ πάθος λέγει περὶ ἐκεῖνο, ἀλλὰ τρόπον ἕτερον ζητεῖ. Τίς οὖν οὗτος; Ἐπειδὴ τὴν λεγομένην ταύτην φύσιν οὐδὲν δεῖ εἶναι τῶν ὄντων, ἀλλ' ἅπασαν ἐκπεφευγέναι τὴν τῶν ὄντων

---

[1] Cp. *Timaeus* 49E2.

[2] Cp. *Timaeus* 49A5–6. I punctuate here as Beutler-Theiler, not as Henry-Schwyzer.

[3] *Timaeus* 49E7–8; but the last word in Plato is ἀπόλλυται, not ἔξεισι.

encompass and contain it? They will not, certainly, assert that it tries to escape at some times and not at others. For if it tries to escape by its own wish, why does it not always do it? But if it remains by necessity, there is never a time when it is not in some form. But, then, we must try to find the reason why each matter does not always have the same form but is rather in the [always different] forms which enter into it. In what way, then, is it said to "try to escape"?[1] By its own nature, and always. But what can this mean except that it never departs from itself and has the form in such a way that it never has it? On any other interpretation they will be able to do nothing with the phrase which they themselves use, "The receptacle and nurse of all becoming."[2] For if it is receptacle and nurse, becoming is other than it, but that which is altered is in becoming, so matter would be existent before becoming, and before alteration; and the words "receptacle" and also "nurse" imply its maintenance in the state in which it is free from affections; and so does "that in which each thing appears on its entrance, and again goes out from it"[3] and the statements that it is "space" and "seat."[4] And the statement which has been criticised as speaking of a "place of the forms"[5] does not mean an affection of the substrate, but is trying to find another way [of participation]. What is this way, then? Since this nature of which we are speaking must not be any real thing, but must have escaped altogether from the reality of real beings, and be altogether

[4] Cp. *Timaeus* 52A8–B1.
[5] Cp. *Timaeus* 52B4–5.

οὐσίαν καὶ πάντη ἑτέραν—λόγοι γὰρ ἐκεῖνα καὶ ὄντως ὄντες—, ἀνάγκη δὴ αὐτὴν τῷ ἑτέρῳ τούτῳ φυλάττουσαν αὑτῆς ἣν εἴληχε σωτηρίαν—ἀνάγκη αὐτὴν μὴ μόνον τῶν ὄντων ἄδεκτον εἶναι, ἀλλὰ καί, εἴ τι μίμημα αὐτῶν, καὶ τούτου ἄμοιρον εἰς οἰκείωσιν εἶναι. Οὕτω γὰρ ἂν ἑτέρα πάντη· ἢ εἶδός τι εἰσοικισαμένη μετ' ἐκείνου ἄλλο γενομένη ἀπώλεσε τὸ ἑτέρα εἶναι καὶ χώρα πάντων, καὶ οὐδενὸς ὅτου οὐχ[1] ὑποδοχή. Ἀλλὰ δεῖ καὶ εἰσιόντων τὴν αὐτὴν μένειν καὶ ἐξιόντων ἀπαθῆ, ἵνα καὶ εἰσίῃ τι ἀεὶ εἰς αὐτὴν καὶ ἐξίῃ. Εἴσεισι δὴ τὸ εἰσιὸν εἴδωλον ὂν καὶ εἰς οὐκ ἀληθινὸν οὐκ ἀληθές. Ἆρ' οὖν ἀληθῶς; Καὶ πῶς, ᾧ μηδαμῶς θέμις ἀληθείας μετέχειν διὰ τὸ ψεῦδος εἶναι; Ἆρα οὖν ψευδῶς εἰς ψεῦδος ἔρχεται καὶ παραπλήσιον γίνεται οἷον καὶ εἰς τὸ κάτοπτρον, εἰ ὁρῷτο[2] τὰ εἴδωλα τῶν ἐνορωμένων καὶ ἕως ἐνορᾷ ἐκεῖνα; Καὶ γὰρ εἰ ἐνταῦθα ἀνέλοις τὰ ὄντα, οὐδὲν ἂν οὐδένα χρόνον φανείη τῶν νῦν ἐν αἰσθητῷ ὁρωμένων. Τὸ μὲν οὖν κάτοπτρον ἐνταῦθα καὶ αὐτὸ [ἐν][3] ὁρᾶται· ἔστι γὰρ καὶ αὐτὸ εἶδός τι· ἐκεῖ δὲ οὐδὲν εἶδος ὂν αὐτὸ μὲν οὐχ ὁρᾶται· ἔδει γὰρ αὐτὸ πρότερον καθ' αὑτὸ ὁρᾶσθαι· ἀλλὰ τοιοῦτόν

[1] ὅτου οὐχ Kirchhoff, H–S²: ὁτουοῦν codd.
[2] εἰ ὁρῷτο H–S: ἐνορῷτο codd.
[3] ὁρᾶται Vitringa, H–S: ἐνορᾶται codd.

---

[1] The English here is intended to represent the probable general sense: the text is obscure and uncertain. Theiler wishes to delete the MSS ἐνορῷτο (H–S εἰ ὁρῷτο) and, (following E. R. Dodds, *Select Passages Illustrating Neoplatonism* 39)

different—for those real beings are rational principles and really real—it is necessary for it by this difference to guard its own proper self-preservation; it is necessary for it not only to be irreceptive of real beings but as well, if there is [in it] some imitation of them, to have no share in it which will really make it its own. In this way it would be altogether different; otherwise, if it took any form to itself it would in conjunction with it become something else and would cease to be different and space for all things, and the receptacle of absolutely everything. But it must remain the same when the forms come into it and stay unaffected when they leave it, so that something may always be coming into it and leaving it. So certainly what comes into it comes as a phantasm, untrue into the untrue. Does it, then, truly come? How could it, to that which is utterly forbidden to have any part in truth because it is falsehood? Does it, then, come falsely into falsehood, and is what happens very much like the way in which the images of the faces seen in a mirror are perceived there as long as people look into it? [1] For if here below you took away the real beings, none of the things which we now see in the world perceived by the senses would ever at any time appear. Here, certainly, the mirror itself is seen, for it, too, is a form; but in the case of matter, since it is in no way a form, it is not itself seen, for [if it was] it would have to be seen by itself, before the forms come to it; but what happens to it is like the way in which

to read ἐνορώντων for ἐνορωμένων; these corrections would make the text rather easier to understand, but cannot be regarded as certain.

τι πάσχει, οἷον καὶ ὁ ἀὴρ φωτισθεὶς ἀφανής ἐστι καὶ τότε, ὅτι καὶ ἄνευ τοῦ φωτισθῆναι οὐχ ἑωρᾶτο. Ταύτῃ οὖν τὰ μὲν ἐν τοῖς κατόπτροις οὐ πιστεύεται εἶναι ἢ ἧττον, ὅτι ὁρᾶται τὸ ἐν ᾧ ἐστι καὶ μένει μὲν αὐτό, τὰ δὲ ἀπέρχεται· ἐν δὲ τῇ ὕλῃ οὐχ ὁρᾶται αὐτὴ οὔτε ἔχουσα οὔτε ἄνευ ἐκείνων. Εἰ δέ γε ἦν μένειν τὰ ἀφ᾽ ὧν πληροῦται τὰ κάτοπτρα καὶ αὐτὰ μὴ ἑωρᾶτο, οὐκ ἂν μὴ εἶναι ἀληθινὰ ἠπιστήθη τὰ ἐνορώμενα. Εἰ μὲν οὖν ἔστι τι ἐν τοῖς κατόπτροις, καὶ ἐν τῇ ὕλῃ οὕτω τὰ αἰσθητὰ ἔστω· εἰ δὲ μὴ ἔστι, φαίνεται δὲ εἶναι, κἀκεῖ φατέον φαίνεσθαι ἐπὶ τῆς ὕλης αἰτιωμένους τῆς φαντάσεως τὴν τῶν ὄντων ὑπόστασιν, ἧς τὰ μὲν ὄντα ὄντως ἀεὶ μεταλαμβάνει, τὰ δὲ μὴ ὄντα μὴ ὄντως, ἐπείπερ οὐ δεῖ οὕτως ἔχειν αὐτὰ ὡς εἶχεν ἂν τοῦ ὄντως μὴ ὄντος, εἰ ἦν αὐτά.

14. Τί οὖν; Μὴ οὔσης οὐδὲν ὑπέστη ἄν; Ἢ οὐδὲ εἴδωλον κατόπτρου μὴ ὄντος ἤ τινος τοιούτου. Τὸ γὰρ ἐν ἑτέρῳ πεφυκὸς γίνεσθαι ἐκείνου μὴ ὄντος οὐκ ἂν γένοιτο· τοῦτο γὰρ φύσις εἰκόνος τὸ ἐν ἑτέρῳ. Εἰ μὲν γάρ τι ἀπῄει ἀπὸ τῶν ποιούντων, καὶ ἄνευ τοῦ ἐν ἑτέρῳ ἦν ἄν. Ἐπεὶ δὲ μένει ἐκεῖνα, εἰ ἐμφαντασθήσεται ἐν ἄλλῳ, δεῖ τὸ ἄλλο

the air is invisible even when it is illuminated, because it was unseen without the illumination. So in this way the images in mirrors are not believed or are less believed to be real, because that in which they are is seen, and it remains but they go away; but in matter, it itself is not seen either when it has the images or without them. But if it was possible for the images with which the mirrors are filled to remain, and the mirrors themselves were not seen, we should not disbelieve that the reflections seen in mirrors were real. If, then, there really is something in mirrors, let there really be objects of sense in matter in the same way; but if there is not, but only appears to be something, then we must admit, too, that things only appear on matter, and make the reason for their appearance the existence of the real beings, an existence in which the real beings always really participate, but the beings which are not real, not really; since they cannot be in the same state as they would be if real beings did not really exist and they did.

14. Well, then, if matter did not exist, would nothing come into existence? No, and there would be no image, either, if a mirror or something of the sort did not exist. For that whose nature is to come into existence in something else would not come into existence if that something else did not exist, for this is the nature of an image, being in something else. If, of course, something came away from the productive powers, it would exist without being in something else. But since these remain unmoved, if an image of them is going to appear in another thing, the other thing must exist, offering a base to

εἶναι ἕδραν παρέχον τῷ οὐκ ἐλθόντι, τῇ δ᾽ αὐτοῦ παρουσίᾳ καὶ τῇ τόλμῃ καὶ οἷον προσαιτήσει καὶ πενίᾳ οἷον βιασάμενον λαβεῖν καὶ ἀπατηθὲν τῇ οὐ λήψει, ἵνα μένῃ ἡ πενία καὶ ἀεὶ προσαιτῇ. Ἐπεὶ γὰρ ἅρπαξ[1] ὑπέστη, ὁ μὲν μῦθος αὐτὴν ποιεῖ προσαιτοῦσαν ἐνδεικνύμενος αὐτῆς τὴν φύσιν, ὅτι ἀγαθοῦ ἔρημος. Αἰτεῖ τε ὁ προσαιτῶν οὐχ ἃ ἔχει ὁ διδούς, ἀλλ᾽ ἀγαπᾷ ὅ τι ἂν λάβῃ· ὥστε καὶ τοῦτο ἐνδείκνυσθαι, ὡς ἕτερον τὸ ἐν αὐτῇ φανταζόμενον. Τό τε ὄνομα ὡς οὐ πληρουμένης. Τὸ δὲ τῷ Πόρῳ συγγίνεσθαι οὐ τῷ ὄντι δηλοῦντός ἐστι συγγίνεσθαι οὐδὲ τῷ κόρῳ, ἀλλά τινι πράγματι εὐμηχάνῳ· τοῦτο δέ ἐστι τῇ σοφίᾳ τοῦ φαντάσματος. Ἐπεὶ γὰρ οὐχ οἷόν τε τοῦ ὄντος πάντῃ μὴ μετέχειν ὅ τι περ ὁπωσοῦν ἔξω ὂν αὐτοῦ ἐστιν —αὕτη γὰρ ὄντος φύσις ⟨εἰς⟩[2] τὰ ὄντα ποιεῖν—τὸ δὲ πάντῃ μὴ ὂν ἄμικτον τῷ ὄντι, θαῦμα τὸ χρῆμα γίγνεται, πῶς μὴ μετέχον μετέχει, καὶ πῶς οἷον παρὰ τῆς γειτνιάσεως ἔχει τι καίπερ τῇ αὐτοῦ φύσει μὲν οἷον κολλᾶσθαι ἀδυνατοῦν. Ἀπολισθάνει οὖν ὡς ἂν ἀπὸ φύσεως ἀλλοτρίας ὃ ἔλαβεν ἄν, οἷον ἠχὼ ἀπὸ τόπων λείων καὶ ὁμαλῶν· ὅτι μὴ μένει ἐκεῖ, τούτῳ καὶ ἐφαντάσθη ἐκεῖ κἀκεῖθεν

[1] ἅρπαξ Harder, H–S: ἅπαξ codd.
[2] ⟨εἰς⟩ Harder, H–S².

---

[1] The interpretation of the beggar-woman Poverty in Plato's myth of the birth of Love (*Symposium* 203B ff.) as matter is pre-Plotinian (see note to ch. 5 of III. 5 [50]). Plotinus uses it differently in different places to suit his philosophical purposes. In his full-length interpretation of the

that which does not come to it; this other thing by its presence and its self-assertion and a kind of begging and its poverty makes a sort of violent attempt to grasp, and is cheated by not grasping, so that its poverty may remain and it may be always begging. For since it is a rapacious thing, the myth makes it a beggar woman to show its nature, that it is destitute of the good. And the beggar does not ask for what the giver has but is satisfied with what he gets, so that this, too, shows that what is imaged in matter is other [than real being]. And the name [Poverty] shows that matter is not satisfied. And by its union with " Resource " Plato makes clear that it is not united with real being or with plenitude but with a resourceful thing, that is, with the cleverness of the apparition.[1] For, since it is impossible for anything whatever, which in any sort of way exists outside it, to have altogether no share in being—for this is the nature of being, to work on beings—and since, on the other hand, the altogether non-existent cannot combine with being, what happens is a wonder; how does the non-participant participate, and how does it have something as if from being next door, although by its own nature it is incapable of being, so to speak, stuck on to it? What it might have grasped, then, slips away from it as if from an alien nature, like an echo from smooth flat surfaces; because it does not stay there, by this very fact the illusion is created that

myth in III. 5. 6–9, Poverty is intelligible matter. Here, and in the verbal allusion (προσαιτεῖ) to the myth at I. 8 [51] 14. 35, she is the matter of the sense-world. The idea that the name Πόρος (Resource) indicates something tricky, illusory, phantasmal, occurs only here.

εἶναι. Εἰ δ' ἦν μετασχοῦσα καὶ οὕτω δεξαμένη, ὥσπερ τις ἀξιοῖ, καταποθὲν ἂν εἰς αὐτὴν τὸ προσελθὸν ἔδυ. Νῦν δὲ φαίνεται, ὅτι μὴ κατεπόθη, ἀλλ' ἔμεινεν ἡ αὐτὴ οὐδὲν δεξαμένη, ἀλλ' ἐπισχοῦσα τὴν πρόσοδον[1] ὡς ἕδρα ἀπωθουμένη καὶ εἰς τὸ αὐτὸ τῶν προσιόντων κἀκεῖ μιγνυμένων ὑποδοχή, οἷον ὅσα πρὸς ἥλιον πῦρ ζητοῦντες λαβεῖν ἱστᾶσι λεῖα, τὰ δὲ καὶ πληροῦντες ὕδατος, ἵνα μὴ διέλθῃ κωλυομένη ὑπὸ τοῦ ἔνδον ἐναντίου ἡ φλόξ, ἔξω δὲ συνίσταιτο. Γίνεται οὖν αἰτία τῆς γενέσεως οὕτω καὶ τὰ ἐν αὐτῇ συνιστάμενα τοιοῦτον συνίσταται τρόπον.

15. Ἐπὶ μὲν οὖν τῶν τὸ πῦρ ἐξ ἡλίου περὶ αὐτὰ συναγόντων ἅτε παρὰ αἰσθητοῦ πυρὸς λαμβανόντων τὴν περὶ αὐτὰ γινομένην ἔξαψιν τὸ αἰσθητοῖς εἶναι καὶ αὐτοῖς ὑπάρχει· διὸ καὶ φαίνεται, ὅτι ἔξω τὰ συνιστάμενα καὶ ἐφεξῆς καὶ πλησίον καὶ ἅπτεται καὶ πέρατα δύο· ὁ δ' ἐπὶ τῆς ὕλης λόγος ἄλλον ἔχει τρόπον τὸ ἔξω. Ἡ γὰρ ἑτερότης τῆς φύσεως ἀρκεῖ οὐδὲν πέρατος διπλοῦ δεομένη, ἀλλὰ πολὺ μᾶλλον παντὸς πέρατος ἀλλοτρία[2] τῇ ἑτερότητι τῆς οὐσίας καὶ οὐδαμῇ συγγενείᾳ τὸ ἀμιγὲς ἔχουσα· καὶ τὸ αἴτιον τοῦ μένειν ἐπ' αὐτῆς τοῦτο, ὅτι μή τι τὸ εἰσιὸν

[1] πρόσοδον Creuzer, H–S²: πρόοδον codd.
[2] ἀλλοτρία Kirchhoff, H–S: ἀλλοτρίου wxy: ἀλλοτριουμένη Q.

---

[1] This is a striking example of the way in which Plotinus suggests the true nature and relationship of immaterial realities

it is there and comes from there. But if matter really was participant and received being in the way one thinks it does, what came to it would be swallowed and sink into it. But as things are, it is apparent that it is not swallowed but matter remains the same and receives nothing, but checks the approach as a repellent base and a receptacle for the things which come to the same point and there mingle; it is like the polished objects which people set against the sun when they want to get fire (and they fill some of them with water), so that the ray, being hindered by the resistance within, may not pass through, but be concentrated on the outside. So matter becomes in this way the cause of coming into being, and the things that are constructed in it are constructed in this way.

15. In the case of the things which collect around them the fire from the sun, since they receive the lighting up which occurs around them from a perceptible fire, they themselves have the property of being perceptible; therefore it is clear, too, that the rays which come together on them are outside them and next and close to them, and touch them, and there are two edges; but the formative principle on matter is outside in a different way. The difference of its nature is enough, with no need of a pair of edges; but it is, rather, completely incompatible with any sort of edge,[1] and owes its freedom from mixture with matter to the difference of its being and its having no sort of kinship with it; and this is the reason why matter remains by itself, that neither does that which

by taking an analogy from the material world and "dematerialising" it; cp. the remarkable use of this method to describe spiritual omnipresence in VI. 4 [22] 7.

ἀπολαύει αὐτῆς, οὐδ' αὐτὴ τοῦ εἰσιόντος· ἀλλ' ὥσπερ αἱ δόξαι καὶ αἱ φαντασίαι ἐν ψυχῇ οὐ κέκρανται, ἀλλ' ἄπεισι πάλιν ἑκάστη ὡς οὖσα ὅ ἐστι μόνη οὐδὲν ἐφέλκουσα οὐδὲ καταλείπουσα, ὅτι μὴ ἐμέμικτο· καὶ τὸ ἔξω, οὐχ ὅτι ἐπέκειτο, καὶ ἐφ' ᾧ ἐστιν οὐχ ὁράσει ἕτερον, ἀλλ' ὁ λόγος φησίν. Ἐνταῦθα μὲν οὖν εἴδωλον ὂν ἡ φαντασία οὐκ εἰδώλου τὴν φύσιν οὔσης τῆς ψυχῆς, καίπερ πολλὰ δοκοῦσα ἄγειν καὶ ὅπῃ θέλει ἄγειν, χρῆται μὲν αὐτῇ οὐδὲν ἧττον ὡς ὕλῃ ἢ ἀνάλογον, οὐ μέντοι ἔκρυψε ταῖς παρ' αὐτῆς ἐνεργείαις πολλάκις ἐξωθουμένη οὐδὲ ἐποίησεν αὐτήν, οὐδ' εἰ μετὰ πάσης ἔλθοι, κεκρύφθαι καί τι αὐτὴν φαντάζεσθαι· ἔχει γὰρ ἐν αὐτῇ ἐνεργείας καὶ λόγους ἐναντίους, οἷς ἀπωθεῖται τὰ προσιόντα. Ἡ δὲ—ἀσθενεστέρα γάρ ἐστιν [ἢ] [1] ὡς πρὸς δύναμιν πολλῷ ψυχῆς καὶ ἔχει οὐδὲν τῶν ὄντων οὔτ' ἀληθὲς οὔτ' αὖ οἰκεῖον ψεῦδος—οὐκ ἔχει δὲ δι' ὅτου φανῇ ἐρημία πάντων οὖσα, ἀλλὰ γίνεται μὲν αἰτία ἄλλοις τοῦ φαίνεσθαι, οὐ δύναται δὲ εἰπεῖν οὐδὲ τοῦτο, ὡς « ἐγὼ ἐνταῦθα », ἀλλ' εἴ ποτε ἐξεύροι αὐτὴν λόγος βαθύς τις ἐξ ἄλλων ὄντων, ὡς ἄρα ἐστί τι ἀπολελειμμένον πάντων τῶν ὄντων καὶ τῶν ὕστερον δοξάντων

[1] ἢ del. Kirchhoff, H–S².

enters it get anything from it, nor does it get anything from what comes into it; but it is like what happens with opinions and mental pictures in the soul, which are not blended with it, but each one goes away again, as being what it is alone, carrying nothing off with it and leaving nothing behind, because it was not mixed with soul; and being outside does not mean that the form rests upon the matter, and that upon which it is, is not visibly other, but reason declares that it is. Now in the soul the mental picture is a phantasm, while the nature of the soul is not phantasmal; and although the mental picture in many ways seems to lead the soul and take it wherever it wants to, the soul none the less uses it as if it was matter or something like it, and certainly the mental picture does not conceal it, since it is often expelled by the activities springing from it, and it does not, even if it comes with all its pictorial power, make the soul to be completely concealed and to appear in any way to be the picture itself, for the soul has in it activities and rational principles which are in opposition, with which it repels the things which attack it. But matter—for it is much weaker, as far as any exercise of power goes, than soul, and has none of the things that exist, neither a true one nor a falsity which is really its own—has nothing by means of which it can appear since it is destitution of everything, but it becomes the cause for other things of their appearing but is not even able to say " Here I am "; but if some deep research should discover it and distinguish it from other existing things [it would appear] that it is something abandoned by all existing things and by the things which come after

εἶναι, ἑλκόμενον εἰς πάντα καὶ ἀκολουθοῦν ὡς δόξαι καὶ αὖ οὐκ ἀκολουθοῦν.

16. Καὶ μέν τις ἐλθὼν λόγος ἀγαγὼν εἰς ὅσον αὐτὸς ἤθελεν ἐποίησεν αὐτὴν μέγα παρ' αὐτοῦ τὸ μέγα περιθεὶς αὐτῇ οὐκ οὔσῃ, τοῦτο δὲ οὐδὲ γενομένῃ· τὸ γὰρ ἐπ' αὐτῇ μέγα μέγεθος ἦν. Ἐὰν οὖν τις τοῦτο ἀφέλῃ τὸ εἶδος, οὐκέτ' ἐστὶν οὐδὲ φαίνεται τὸ ὑποκείμενον μέγα, ἀλλ' εἰ ἦν τὸ γενόμενον μέγα ἄνθρωπος καὶ ἵππος καὶ μετὰ τοῦ ἵππου τὸ μέγα τοῦ ἵππου ἐπελθόν, ἀπελθόντος τοῦ ἵππου καὶ τὸ μέγα αὐτοῦ ἀπέρχεται. Εἰ δέ τις λέγοι ὡς ὁ ἵππος ἐπὶ μεγάλου τινὸς ὄγκου καὶ τοσοῦδε γίνεται καὶ μένει τὸ μέγα, φήσομεν μὴ τὸ τοῦ ἵππου μέγα, ἀλλὰ τὸ τοῦ ὄγκου μέγα μένειν ἐκεῖ. Εἰ μέντοι ὁ ὄγκος οὗτος πῦρ ἐστιν ἢ γῆ, ἀπελθόντος τοῦ πυρὸς τὸ τοῦ πυρὸς ἀπέρχεται ἢ τὸ τῆς γῆς μέγα. Οὐ τοίνυν οὐδὲ τοῦ σχήματος οὐδὲ τοῦ μεγέθους ἀπολαύσειεν ἄν· ἢ οὐκ ἐκ πυρὸς ἄλλο τι ἔσται, ἀλλὰ μένουσα πῦρ οὐ πῦρ γενήσεται. Ἐπεὶ καὶ νῦν τοσαύτη γενομένη, ὡς δοκεῖ, ὅσον τόδε τὸ πᾶν, εἰ παύσαιτο ὁ οὐρανὸς καὶ τὰ ἐντὸς πάντα, σὺν πᾶσι [1] τούτοις καὶ τὸ μέγεθος πᾶν οἰχήσεται ἀπ' αὐτῆς καὶ αἱ ἄλλαι δηλονότι ὁμοῦ ποιότητες, καὶ καταλειφθήσεται ὅπερ ἦν σῴζουσα οὐδὲν τῶν πρότερον περὶ αὐτὴν οὕτως ὄντων. Καίτοι ἐν οἷς ὑπάρχει τὸ πεπονθέναι

[1] σὺν πᾶσι Creuzer: σύμπασι codd.

them that seem to exist, dragged into all things and corresponding to them as far as seeming goes, and again not [really] corresponding.

16. And further, when some rational formative principle comes upon it and brings it to the size which the principle itself wishes, it makes it a size by imposing the size from itself on matter, which is not the size and does not in this way become it; for [if it did] the size imposed on it would be [real] magnitude. If, then, one were to take away this form, what underlies it neither is any longer nor appears a thing of size, but if the thing of size which came to be was a man or a horse, and with the horse the size of the horse came upon the matter, when the horse goes away its size goes too. But if someone were to say that the basis of the horse is a mass of a certain size, and the size remains, our answer is that what remains in the matter is not the size of the horse but the size of the mass. If, then, this mass is fire or earth, when the fire goes away the size of fire (or of earth) goes away too. So, then, matter will not profit by either shape or size; otherwise it will not be something else after being fire, but will remain fire while becoming something which is not fire. Since, even now, when matter, as it seems, has become so great that it is the size of this universe, if the heaven and all within it had a stop, with all these the magnitude, all of it, would go away from matter and, obviously, all the other qualities as well, and matter would be left what it was and keep none of the qualifications which previously existed in it. Certainly, in the things which have the property of being affected by the presence of certain other things, even when those

παρουσίᾳ τινῶν, καὶ ἀπελθόντων ἔστι τι ἔτι ἐν τοῖς λαβοῦσιν· ἐν δὲ τοῖς μὴ παθοῦσιν οὐκέτι, ὥσπερ ἐπὶ τοῦ ἀέρος φωτὸς περὶ αὐτὸν ὄντος καὶ ἀπελθόντος τούτου. Ἐὰν δέ τις θαυμάζῃ, πῶς οὐκ ἔχον μέγεθος μέγα ἔσται, πῶς δ' οὐκ ἔχον θερμότητα θερμὸν ἔσται; οὐ γὰρ δὴ τὸ αὐτὸ τὸ εἶναι αὐτῇ καὶ μεγέθει εἶναι, εἴπερ καὶ ἄυλον μέγεθός ἐστιν, ὥσπερ καὶ ἄυλον σχῆμα. Καὶ εἰ τηροῦμεν τὴν ὕλην, μεταλήψει πάντα· ἓν δὲ τῶν πάντων καὶ τὸ μέγεθος. Ἐν μὲν οὖν τοῖς σώμασι συνθέτοις οὖσιν ἔστι καὶ μέγεθος μετὰ τῶν ἄλλων, οὐ μὴν ἀφωρισμένον, ἐπειδὴ ἐν σώματος λόγῳ ἔγκειται καὶ μέγεθος· ἐν δὲ τῇ ὕλῃ οὐδὲ τὸ οὐκ ἀφωρισμένον· οὐ γὰρ σῶμα.

17. Οὐδ' αὖ μέγεθος αὐτὸ ἔσται. Εἶδος γὰρ τὸ μέγεθος, ἀλλ' οὐ δεκτικόν· καὶ καθ' αὑτὸ δὲ τὸ μέγεθος [ἀλλὰ καὶ εἴ τι μίμημα αὐτῶν καὶ τούτου ἄμοιρον εἰς οἰκείωσιν εἶναι],[1] οὐχ οὕτω μέγεθος. Ἀλλ' ἐπεὶ βούλεται ἐν νῷ ἢ ἐν ψυχῇ κείμενον μέγα εἶναι, ἔδωκε τοῖς οἷον ἐθέλουσι μιμεῖσθαι ἐφέσει αὐτοῦ ἢ κινήσει τῇ πρὸς αὐτὸ τὸ αὑτῶν πάθος ἐνσείσασθαι εἰς ἄλλο. Τὸ οὖν μέγα ἐν προόδῳ φαντάσεως θέον εἰς αὐτὸ δὴ τοῦτο τὸ μέγα συνθεῖν ποιῆσαν τὸ μικρὸν τῆς ὕλης, πεποίη-

[1] ἀλλὰ . . . εἶναι del. Kirchhoff, H–S.

---

[1] The words bracketed here in the Greek text are a repetition of ch. 13. 26–27: they do not fit here, and are omitted in the translation.

other things have gone away there is something still remaining in the things which have received them; but in things which are not affected there is nothing any more, in the air, for instance, when light has been in it and gone away. But suppose someone wondered how, without having magnitude, matter could be a size—well, how, without having heat, will it be hot? For certainly it is not the same thing for it to exist and to exist in magnitude, granted that magnitude is immaterial, just as shape is immaterial. And if we are to keep matter as matter, it will be all things [only] by participation; but magnitude, too, is one of all the things it will be. So, then, in composite bodies magnitude is present along with their other determinations (certainly not separated from them), since magnitude, too, is included in the definition of body; but in matter not even this non-separated magnitude is present, for it is not a body.

17. Nor, again, will it be absolute magnitude. For magnitude is a form but not something receptive; and magnitude is something which is by itself,[1] and not magnitude in this particular relation. But since, while it is at rest in intellect or in soul, it wants to be large,[2] it gives to the things which, in a way, want to imitate it by an aspiration for it or a movement towards it the ability to insert their affection into something else. So, then, size, running on in its image-making progression, and making the littleness of matter run with it towards this very size, has made

[2] Cp. the account of the origin of time in III. 7 [45] 11. 20 ff. These two chapters show very well Plotinus's dynamic conception of form. Even so abstract (to our way of thinking) a form as that of size is for him a living active reality.

κεν αὐτὸ τῇ παρατάσει οὐ πληρούμενον δοκεῖν εἶναι μέγα. Τὸ γὰρ ψευδῶς μέγα τοῦτό ἐστιν, ὅταν τῷ μὴ ἔχειν τὸ μέγα εἶναι ἐκτεινόμενον πρὸς ἐκεῖνο παραταθῇ τῇ ἐκτάσει. Ποιούντων γὰρ πάντων ὄντων εἰς τὰ ἄλλα ἢ τὸ ἄλλο τὴν αὐτῶν ἐνόπτρισιν ἕκαστόν τε τῶν ποιούντων ὡς αὐτὸ ἦν μέγα, τό τε πᾶν ἦν ἐκείνως μέγα. Συνῄει οὖν τὸ ἑκάστου λόγου μετὰ τό τι μέγα, οἷον ἵππου καὶ ὁτουοῦν ἄλλου, καὶ τὸ μέγα[1] αὐτό· καὶ ἐγίγνετο πᾶσα μὲν μέγα πρὸς αὐτόμεγα ἐλλαμπομένη, καὶ ἑκάστη δὲ μοῖρα μέγα τι· καὶ ὁμοῦ πάντα ἐφαίνετο ἐκ παντὸς τοῦ εἴδους, οὗ τὸ μέγα, καὶ ἐξ ἑκάστου· καὶ οἷον παρετέτατο καὶ πρὸς πᾶν καὶ πάντα, καὶ ἐν εἴδει τοῦτο ἀναγκασθεῖσα εἶναι καὶ ἐν ὄγκῳ, ὅσον ἡ δύναμις πεποίηκε τὸ μηδὲν ὂν αὐτὸ πάντα εἶναι· οἷον αὐτῷ τῷ φαίνεσθαι καὶ τὸ χρῶμα τὸ ἐξ οὐ χρώματος καὶ ἡ ποιότης ἡ ἐνταῦθα ἡ ἐξ οὐ ποιότητος ἔσχε τὴν ὁμωνυμίαν τὴν ἀπ' ἐκείνων, καὶ τὸ μέγεθος ἐξ οὐ μεγέθους ἢ ὁμωνύμου μεταξὺ θεωρουμένων ἐκείνων καὶ αὐτῆς τῆς ὕλης καὶ τοῦ εἴδους αὐτοῦ. Καὶ φαίνεται μέν, ὅτι ἐκεῖθεν, ψεύδεται δέ, ὅτι οὐκ ἔστι τὸ ἐν ᾧ φαίνεται. Μεγεθύνεται δὲ ἕκαστα ἑλκόμενα τῇ δυνάμει τῶν

[1] μέγα Vitringa, H–S²: μὲν codd.

it by extension, though it is not filled, appear to be large. For this is what false size is, when, because it does not possess real size, being stretched out towards it, it is extended by the stretching out. For, since all real beings produce upon other things, or the other thing, a mirroring of themselves, as each one of the beings that act had size, in that way the totality of them had size. So the size of each individual forming principle which is the consequence of its distinctive character, of a horse, for instance, or anything else, came together, and also absolute size; and matter as a whole became a size, illumined by absolute size, and each part of it became a particular size; and all the sizes appeared together, from the whole form, to which the size belonged, and from each individual [partial] form; and it was as if extended to the whole form and all the forms, and was compelled to be this size in form and in bulk, in so far as the power [of form] made what was nothing in itself to be everything, as, then, by the very fact of appearing the colour which comes from that which is not colour, and the quality here which comes from that which is not quality, have a name which is the same as and derives from their intelligible principles, so also magnitude comes from that which is not magnitude, or [only] has the same name, since those [form-appearances in matter] present themselves to our contemplation in the middle between matter itself and form itself. They appear because they come from the higher world, but their appearance is false because that in which they appear does not exist. Individual things acquire magnitude by being drawn out by the power of the

ἐνορωμένων καὶ χώραν ἑαυτοῖς ποιούντων, ἕλκεται δὲ ἐπὶ πάντα οὐ βίᾳ τῷ ὕλῃ τὸ πᾶν εἶναι. Ἕλκει δὲ ἕκαστον κατὰ τὴν αὐτοῦ δύναμιν ἣν ἔχει· ἔχει δὲ ἐκεῖθεν. Καὶ τὸ μὲν ποιοῦν μέγα τὴν ὕλην, ὡς δοκεῖ, ἀπὸ τῆς ἐμφαντάσεως τοῦ μέγα καὶ τοῦτό ἐστι τὸ ἐμφαντασθέν, τὸ ἐνταῦθα μέγα· ἡ δὲ ὕλη, ἐφ' ἧς ἀναγκάζεται συνθεῖν, ὁμοῦ πᾶσα καὶ πανταχοῦ παρέχει ἑαυτήν· ὕλη γάρ ἐστι καὶ τούτου καὶ οὐ τουτί· ὃ δὲ μή ἐστί τι παρ' αὐτοῦ, δύναται γενέσθαι καὶ τὸ ἐναντίον δι' ἄλλο καὶ γενόμενον τὸ ἐναντίον οὐδὲ ἐκεῖνό ἐστιν· ἔστη γὰρ ἄν.

18. Ὁ τοίνυν νόησιν μεγάλου ἔχων, εἰ αὐτοῦ ἡ νόησις δύναμιν ἔχοι μὴ μόνον ἐν αὐτῇ εἶναι, ἀλλὰ καὶ οἷον πρὸς τὸ ἔξω ὑπὸ δυνάμεως φέροιτο, λάβοι ἂν φύσιν οὐκ οὖσαν ἐν τῷ νοοῦντι, οὐδέ τι ἔχουσαν εἶδος οὐδέ τι ἴχνος τοῦ μεγάλου, ἀλλ' οὐδὲ οὐδενός του [1] ἄλλου. Τί ἂν ποιήσειε ταύτῃ τῇ δυνάμει; Οὐχ ἵππον, οὐ βοῦν· ταῦτα γὰρ ἄλλοι ποιήσουσιν. Ἤ, ἐπειδὴ παρὰ μεγάλου πατρὸς ἔρχεται, οὐ δύναται τὸ ἄλλο χωρῆσαι μέγα, τοῦτο δ' ἕξει ἐμφανταζόμενον. Τῷ δὴ μὴ οὕτως εὐτυχήσαντι τοῦ μεγάλου ὡς αὐτὸ μέγα εἶναι ἐν τοῖς αὐτοῦ καθ' ὅσον οἷόν τε μεγάλῳ φαίνεσθαι λοιπόν ἐστι. Τοῦτο δ' ἐστὶ μὴ ἐλλείπειν καὶ τὸ μὴ ἐπὶ πολλὰ πολλαχοῦ καὶ ἐν αὐτῷ τὰ συγγενῆ ἔχειν μέρη καὶ ἀπολείπεσθαι μηδενός. Οὐδὲ γὰρ ἠνείχετο ἐν σμικρῷ ὄγκῳ [τὸ] [2] ἴσον ἔτι τὸ τοῦ μεγάλου εἴδωλον εἶναι μεγάλου ὄν, ἀλλ' ὅσῳ ἐφίετο τῆς ἐλπίδος

[1] του Kirchhoff, H–S: τε codd.
[2] τὸ del. Müller, H–S².

forms which are visible in matter and make a place for themselves, and they are drawn out to everything without violence because the universe exists by matter. Each form draws out by its own power which it has; and it has it from the higher world. And that which makes matter large (as it seems) comes from the imaging in it of size, and that which is imaged in it is size in this world; and the matter on which it is imaged is compelled to keep pace with it, and submits itself to it all together and everywhere, for it is matter and belongs to this size and is not this size; but what is nothing of itself can become the opposite, too, by means of something else, and when it has become the opposite is not that either, for if it was it would be static.

18. Suppose that someone had a thought of size, if his thought had power not only to exist in itself but was taken outside, so to speak, by its power, it would take hold of a nature which did not exist in the thinker, and had no form and no trace of size, or of anything else either. What, then, would it make with this power? Not a horse or an ox; others will make these. Since it comes from a father of size, the other thing cannot attain to size but will have it imaged in it. Certainly, for a thing which has not the good fortune to be so well endowed with size as to be a size itself, what is left is to appear to have size in its parts as much as is possible for it. But this means not being deficient, and not being scattered all over the place, and having related parts in itself, and not falling short in anything. For the image of size, since it is an image of size, cannot endure to be equal still in a small mass, but in proportion as it

ἐκείνου προσῆλθέ τε ὅσον οἷόν τε ἦν αὐτῷ μετὰ τοῦ συνθέοντος αὐτῷ ἀπολειφθῆναι οὐ δυναμένου, καὶ πεποίηκε μέγα τε ἐκεῖνο τὸ μὴ μέγα μηδ' οὕτω δόξαι καὶ τὸ ὁρώμενον ἐν ὄγκῳ μέγα. Ἡ δ' ὅμως φυλάττει τὴν αὑτῆς φύσιν ἀποχρωμένη τούτῳ τῷ μεγάλῳ οἷον ἀμφιέσματι, ὃ συνδραμοῦσα αὐτῷ ὅτε θέον αὐτὴν ἦγεν ἀμπέσχετο· ὃ εἰ ὁ ἀμφιέσας ἀφέλοιτο, μενεῖ πάλιν ἡ αὐτή, οἵαπερ παρ' αὐτῆς ἦν ἢ [1] τοσαύτη, ὅσον ἂν τὸ παρὸν εἶδος αὐτὴν ποιῇ. Ἡ μέν γε ψυχὴ τὰ τῶν ὄντων εἴδη ἔχουσα εἶδος οὖσα καὶ αὐτὴ ὁμοῦ πάντα ἔχει καὶ τοῦ εἴδους ἑκάστου ὁμοῦ ὄντος αὐτῷ, τά τε τῶν αἰσθητῶν εἴδη οἷον ἀναστρέφοντα πρὸς αὐτὴν καὶ προσιόντα ὁρῶσα οὐκ ἀνέχεται μετὰ πλήθους δέχεσθαι, ἀλλ' ἀποθέμενα τὸν ὄγκον ὁρᾷ· οὐ γὰρ δύναται ἄλλο τι ἢ ὅ ἐστι γενέσθαι. Ἡ δὲ ὕλη οὐδὲν ἔχουσα τὸ ἀντικόπτον, οὐ γὰρ ἔχει ἐνέργειαν, οὖσα δὲ σκιά, ἀναμένει παθεῖν ὅ τι ἂν ἐθέλῃ τὸ ποιῆσον. Τό τε οὖν προιὸν ἐκ τοῦ ἐκεῖ λόγου ἤδη ἴχνος ἔχει τοῦ μέλλοντος γενήσεσθαι· οἷον γὰρ ἐν φαντασίᾳ εἰκονικῇ κινούμενος ὁ λόγος ἢ ἡ κίνησις ἡ ἀπὸ τούτου μερισμός ἐστιν· ἤ, εἰ ταὐτὸν εἴη ἕν, οὐδὲ ἐκινήθη, ἀλλὰ μένει· ἥ τε ὕλη πάντα ὁμοῦ ὥσπερ

[1] ἢ CQ; ἡ wxUS, H–S.

aspires to the hope of reaching [real] size, it advances as far as it can with that which runs along with it and cannot be left behind, and gives size to that which has not got it and does not appear to have it, and to the size which appears in mass. But matter, all the same, keeps its own nature and makes use of this size as a kind of garment, which it put on when it ran with it as the size in its course led it along; but if what put this garment on takes it off, matter remains again the same as it is of itself, or the size which the form present to it makes it.[1] Now the soul which holds the forms of real beings, and is itself, too, a form, holds them all gathered together, and each individual form is gathered together in itself; and when it sees the forms of things perceived by the senses as it were turning back towards it and approaching it, it does not endure to receive them with their multiplicity, but sees them stripped of their mass; for it cannot become anything else than what it is. But matter, which has no resistance, for it has no activity, but is a shadow, waits passively to endure whatever that which acts upon it wishes. So therefore, both that which proceeds from the rational principle in the higher world has already a trace of what is going to come into being, for when the rational principle is moved in a sort of picture-making imagination, either the movement which comes from it is a division, or, if it did remain one and the same, it would not be moved, but stay as it was; and matter, too, is not able to harbour all things gathered

[1] I adopt here with Beutler-Theiler and other editors the reading ἦ, which seems to me to give a better sense: Henry-Schwyzer prefer ἥ.

ἡ ψυχὴ οὐ δύναται εἰσοικίσασθαι· ἢ ἦν ἄν τι ἐκείνων· αὐτήν τε αὖ δεῖ τὰ πάντα δέξασθαι, μὴ ἀμερῶς δὲ δέξασθαι. Δεῖ τοίνυν πᾶσι τόπον οὖσαν ἐπὶ πάντα αὐτὴν ἐλθεῖν καὶ πᾶσιν ἀπαντῆσαι καὶ πρὸς πᾶν διάστημα ἀρκέσαι, ὅτι μὴ κατείληπται διαστήματι αὐτή, ἀλλ' ἦν ἐκκειμένη τῷ μέλλοντι. Πῶς οὖν οὐκ εἰσελθὸν ἕν τι ἐκώλυσε τὰ ἄλλα, ἃ οὐχ οἷόν τε ἦν ἐπ' ἀλλήλοις εἶναι; Ἢ οὐκ ἦν οὐδὲν πρῶτον· εἰ δ' ἄρα, τὸ τοῦ παντὸς εἶδος· ὥστε πάντα μὲν ἅμα, ἐν μέρει δὲ ἕκαστον· ζῴου γὰρ ὕλη μερισθεῖσα σὺν τῷ τοῦ ζῴου μερισμῷ· εἰ δὲ μή, οὐκ ἂν ἐγένετό τι παρὰ τὸν λόγον.

19. Τὰ μὲν δὴ εἰσελθόντα εἰς τὴν ὕλην ὥσπερ μητέρα ἀδικεῖ οὐδὲν οὐδ' αὖ ὠφελεῖ. Οὐδέ γε αἱ πληγαὶ αἱ τούτων πρὸς αὐτήν, πρὸς ἄλληλα δέ, ὅτι αἱ δυνάμεις πρὸς τὰ ἐναντία, οὐ πρὸς τὰ ὑποκείμενα, εἰ μή τις συνειλημμένα θεωρεῖ τοῖς ἐπεισιοῦσι· θερμὸν γὰρ ἔπαυσε τὸ ψυχρὸν καὶ μέλαν τὸ λευκὸν ἢ συγκραθέντα ἄλλην ποιότητα ἐξ αὐτῶν ἐποίησε. Τὰ παθόντα οὖν τὰ κρατηθέντα,[1] τὸ δὲ παθεῖν αὐτοῖς τὸ μὴ εἶναι ὅπερ ἦσαν. Καὶ

[1] κρατηθέντα Harder, H–S²: κραθέντα codd.

---

[1] For the contrast here between soul which contains all forms non-spatially and so undivided and matter, which must necessarily receive them as dimensional and divided, cp. II. 4 [12] 11. 15 ff.

[2] Cp. *Timaeus* 52B4.

together, as soul is; if it could, it would belong to the higher world; it must certainly receive all things, but not receive them undivided.[1] It must then, since it is a place for all things,[2] come to all of them itself and meet them and be sufficient for every dimension, because it is not itself captured by dimension but lies open to that which is going to come to it. How, then, when one particular form enters it, does it not hinder the others, which cannot be [present in it] one upon another? The answer is that there is no first form, unless perhaps it is the form of the universe, so that all forms will be present together, and each individual one in its own part, for the matter of a living thing is divided along with the division of the living thing;[3] otherwise, there would be nothing besides the forming principle.

19. The forms which enter into matter as their "mother"[4] do it no wrong, nor again do they do it any good. Their blows are not for it, but for each other, because their powers are directed towards their opposites, not their substrates (unless one considers these as included with the entering forms), for cold puts a stop to heat and white to black, or they are mixed together and make another quality out of themselves. The things which are affected, then, are the things which are overcome, and their being affected consists in their not being what they

[3] The universe is, of course, for Plotinus a single living organism, so this is not a mere analogy.

[4] Cp. *Timaeus* 50D3 and 51A4–5. Plotinus has to accept the name "mother" on the authority of Plato, but finds it an embarrassing one, as it conflicts with his conviction of the essential barrenness of matter, and does his best to explain it away; see below.

ἐν τοῖς ἐμψύχοις δὲ αἱ μὲν πείσεις περὶ τὰ σώματα κατὰ τὰς ποιότητας καὶ τὰς δυνάμεις τὰς ἐνυπαρχούσας τῆς ἀλλοιώσεως γινομένης, λυομένων δὲ τῶν συστάσεων ἢ συνιουσῶν ἢ μετατιθεμένων παρὰ τὴν κατὰ φύσιν σύστασιν τὰ μὲν πάθη ἐν τοῖς σώμασι, ταῖς δὲ ψυχαῖς αἱ γνώσεις συνημμέναις τῶν σφοδροτέρων· εἰ δὲ μή, οὐ γινώσκουσιν. Ἡ δὲ ὕλη μένει· οὐδὲν γὰρ ἀπελθόντος μὲν πέπονθε τοῦ ψυχροῦ, τοῦ δὲ θερμοῦ ἐπελθόντος· οὐ γὰρ ἦν οὔτε φίλον αὐτῇ οὔτε ἀλλότριον ὁποτερονοῦν. Ὥστε οἰκειότερον αὐτῇ ἡ ὑποδοχὴ καὶ τιθήνη· ἡ δὲ μήτηρ οἷον εἴρηται· οὐδὲν γὰρ αὕτη γεννᾷ. Ἀλλ' ἐοίκασι μητέρα αὐτὴν λέγειν ὅσοι καὶ τὴν μητέρα τάξιν ὕλης πρὸς τὰ γεννώμενα ἀξιοῦσιν ἔχειν, ὡς ὑποδεχομένης μόνον, οὐδὲν δὲ εἰς τὰ γεννώμενα διδούσης· ἐπεὶ καὶ ὅσον σῶμα τοῦ γινομένου ἐκ τῆς τροφῆς. Εἰ δὲ δίδωσιν ἡ μήτηρ τι τῷ γεννωμένῳ, οὐ καθ' ὅσον ὕλη, ἀλλ' ὅτι καὶ εἶδος· μόνον γὰρ τὸ εἶδος γόνιμον, ἡ δ' ἑτέρα φύσις ἄγονος. Ὅθεν, οἶμαι, καὶ οἱ πάλαι σοφοὶ μυστικῶς καὶ ἐν τελεταῖς αἰνιττόμενοι Ἑρμῆν μὲν ποιοῦσι τὸν ἀρχαῖον τὸ τῆς γενέσεως ὄργανον ἀεὶ ἔχοντα πρὸς ἐργασίαν τὸν γεννῶντα τὰ ἐν αἰσθήσει δηλοῦντες εἶναι τὸν νοητὸν λόγον,

---

[1] This view was current in Greece in the 5th century B.C.: it was held by Anaxagoras and others (Aristotle *De Gen. An.* Δ 1. 763b32–34). Aeschylus makes Apollo bring it forward in defence of Orestes (*Eumenides* 658–661). Aristotle himself accepted it with some refinements and modifications (perhaps

were. And in beings endowed with soul the affections are in their bodies, when alteration takes place according to their qualities and immanent powers; and when the unions of their constituent parts are dissolved, or when they come together, or are changed against their natural constitution, it is only knowledge of the more extreme changes which reaches their associated souls; if the changes are not extreme, they know nothing of them. But matter abides, for it was affected in no way when the cold went away and the heat came to it; for neither of them was in friendly association with it or alien to it. So that " receptacle " and " nurse " are more proper terms for it; but " mother " is only used in a manner of speaking, for matter itself brings forth nothing. But those people seem to call it " mother " who claim that the mother holds the position of matter in respect to her children, in that she only receives [the seed] and contributes nothing to the children,[1] since all the body of the child which is born, too, comes from the food. But if the mother does contribute something to the child, it is not in so far as she is matter, but because she is also form, for only form can produce offspring, but the other nature is sterile. It was for this reason, I think, that the ancient sages, speaking in riddles secretly and in the mystery rites, make the ancient Hermes always have the organ of generation ready for its work, revealing that the intelligible formative principle is the generator of the things in the sense-world, but revealing, too, the

alluded to by Plotinus in the next sentence): cp. *De Gen. An.* A.20 729a10 ff., with A. L. Peck's comments in the introduction to his Loeb edition, p. xi ff.

τὸ δὲ ἄγονον τῆς ὕλης μενούσης τὸ αὐτὸ ἀεὶ διὰ τῶν περὶ αὐτὴν ἀγόνων δηλοῦντες. Μητέρα γὰρ πάντων ποιήσαντες, ἣν δὴ οὕτως ἐπιφημίζουσι τὴν κατὰ τὸ ὑποκείμενον ἀρχὴν λαβόντες καὶ ὄνομα τοῦτο θέμενοι, ἵνα δηλοῖεν ὃ βούλονται, τὸ πρὸς τὴν μητέρα οὐχ ὅμοιον πάντη ἐνδείκνυσθαι θέλοντες, τοῖς ὅστις ὁ τρόπος βουλομένοις ἀκριβέστερον λαβεῖν καὶ μὴ ἐπιπολῆς ζητοῦσι πόρρωθεν μέν, ὅμως δὲ ὡς ἐδύναντο, ἐνεδείξαντο ὡς ἄγονός τε καὶ οὐδὲ πάντη θῆλυς, ἀλλὰ τοσοῦτον μὲν θῆλυς, ὅσον ὑποδέξασθαι, ὅσον δὲ γεννᾶν οὐκέτι, τῷ τὸ πρὸς αὐτὴν κεχωρηκὸς πρὸς αὐτὴν μήτε θῆλυ εἶναι, μήτε γεννᾶν δύνασθαι, ἀποτετμημένον δὲ πάσης τῆς τοῦ γεννᾶν δυνάμεως, ἣ μόνῳ ὑπάρχει τῷ μένοντι ἄρρενι.

---

[1] This allegorical interpretation of the ithyphallic Hermes is Stoic in origin, though, as always, Plotinus adapts it to his own philosophical system: for the original Stoic form, cp. Cornutus, *Theologiae Graecae Compendium*, p. 23, 16–22 Lang. The allegorical interpretation of the eunuchs who sur-

sterility of matter which always remains the same through the eunuchs who accompany her [the Great Mother].[1] For when they make matter the mother of all things, they apply this title to it taking it in the sense of the principle which has the function of substrate; they give it this name in order to declare what they wish, not wishing to make matter in every way exactly like the mother; to those who want to know more accurately in what way [it is a mother] and do not make a merely superficial investigation, they show, by a far-fetched analogy, but all the same as best they could, that matter is sterile and not in every way female but only female as far as receiving goes, but no longer when it comes to generation; they show this by making that which approaches it neither female nor able to generate, but cut off from all power of generation, which only that which remains male has.

round the Great Mother given here seems to have no parallel (Cp. Lucretius II. 614–617 and Augustine *De Civitate Dei* VII. chs. 24–25 for other interpretations). It is so far-fetched (as Plotinus admits, cp. l. 36 below) and so exactly adapted to Plotinus's own distinctive doctrine of the absolute sterility of matter that it may well be his own invention.

ENNEAD III. 7

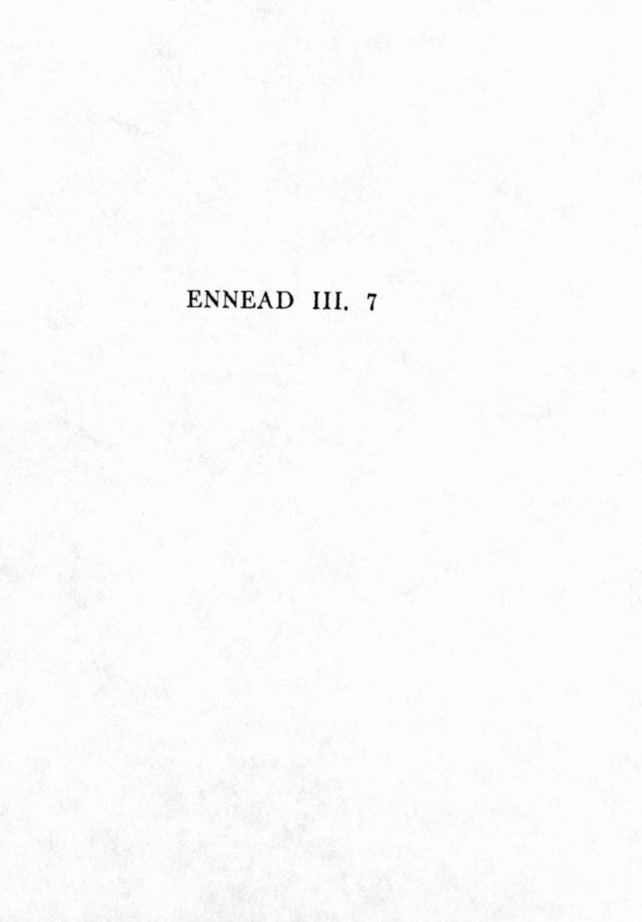

III. 7. ON ETERNITY AND TIME

Introductory Note

This treatise is No. 45 in Porphyry's chronological order. It is one of the two major discussions of time in the surviving works of ancient philosophers, the other being that by Aristotle (*Physics* IV. 10–14. 217b–224a) which Plotinus criticises in chs. 9 and 12–13. There do not seem to have been any changes or developments of great importance in philosophical thought about time between Aristotle and Plotinus. Though Stoic and Epicurean views are dealt with in the critical part of the treatise (chs. 7–10), Plotinus is mainly concerned with ways of thinking about time which were already current in the early Academy, which linked time very closely with the movement of the heavens, and with Aristotle's view of time as the number or measure of motion.

As a Platonist, Plotinus bases his discussion of eternity and time on the passage of the *Timaeus* (37D–38B) where Plato speaks of the making of time as a " moving image of eternity." It is this conception of time as the image of eternity which is the starting-point of his own thought about both. They are for him essentially two kinds of life, the life of the divine Intellect and the life of Soul. In the first part of the treatise (chs. 1–6) he develops his profound conception of eternity as " the life which belongs to that which exists and is in being, all together and full, completely without extension or interval " (ch. 3. 36–38), which deeply influenced Christian patristic and medieval thought: cp. the classical definition of Boethius, *interminabilis vitae tota simul et perfecta possessio* (*De Consolatione Philosophiae* V. Prosa 6). And in ch. 11, one of his

liveliest and most original passages of philosophical exposition, after criticising the views of his predecessors on time in the preceding chapters, he explains his own idea of it as the life of the soul in movement. This certainly influenced the thought of St. Augustine on time (cp. especially *Confessions* XI. 14–28), though the two differ in accordance with their different conceptions of soul. The later Neoplatonists are further removed from Plotinus than the Christians are in their conceptions of eternity and time, because of their insistence on making both into substantive principles, divine beings with their own proper places in the hierarchy of reality (cp. Proclus, *Elements of Theology* Prop. 53, with the commentary of E. R. Dodds).

Synopsis

The starting-point of our thought about eternity and time is our own experience of both; but when we concentrate on this and try to arrive at full understanding of it we meet difficulties which can be cleared up by a close and discriminating study of the opinions of the ancient philosophers. We will begin with eternity of which time is the image, though it would be possible also to go the other way, from image to archetype (ch. 1). What is eternity? Not the intelligible universe itself, nor the rest in it (ch. 2). It is the life of that which exists completely and simultaneously, without before and after (ch. 3). Eternity and the wholeness of real being; duration and movement in time are essential to the existence of things which come into being (ch. 4). We contemplate eternity by the eternal in ourselves; it is the self-manifestation of divinity, a total life (ch. 5). Eternity and unity; it is the life of real being around the One; "always existing" really means "truly existing"; that which exists in time is deficient in existence (ch. 6). We are in some way both in eternity and in time. What is time? Classification of the accounts of earlier philosophers:

(i) time is movement, (ii) it is what is moved, (iii) it is something belonging to movement (ch. 7). Refutation of (i) and (ii); time cannot be either all movement, or ordered movement or the particular ordered movement of the sphere of heaven, nor can it be the sphere itself. Refutation of the Stoic form of (iii); time cannot be the distance covered by any movement, the movement of the universe included (ch. 8). Refutation of the Aristotelian form of (iii); time cannot be the number or measure of movement (ch. 9). Brief refutation of the Epicurean form of (iii); time cannot be an accompaniment of movement (ch. 10). Plotinus's own view of the origin and nature of time; it is the life of the soul in the restless movement from one thing to another which characterises it when it separates itself from the quiet unity of Intellect; the universe is in time because soul has put itself into time (ch. 11). If soul turned back altogether to the intelligible world and its eternity, time would have a stop. How we measure time by regular recurrences in the movements of the universe. How time and the movement of the universe in different ways measure each other (ch. 12). The universe is in time and shows time; the Aristotelians have got the relationship the wrong way round. Superiority of Plato's account, understood as meaning that time is the life of soul (ch. 13).

III. 7. (45) ΠΕΡΙ ΑΙΩΝΟΣ ΚΑΙ ΧΡΟΝΟΥ

1. Τὸν αἰῶνα καὶ τὸν χρόνον ἕτερον λέγοντες ἑκάτερον εἶναι καὶ τὸν μὲν περὶ τὴν ἀίδιον εἶναι φύσιν, τὸν δὲ χρόνον περὶ τὸ γινόμενον καὶ τόδε τὸ πᾶν, αὐτόθεν μὲν καὶ ὥσπερ ταῖς τῆς ἐννοίας ἀθροωτέραις ἐπιβολαῖς ἐναργές τι παρ᾽ αὐτοῖς περὶ αὐτῶν ἐν ταῖς ψυχαῖς ἔχειν πάθος νομίζομεν λέγοντές τε ἀεὶ καὶ παρ᾽ ἅπαντα ὀνομάζοντες. Πειρώμενοι μὴν εἰς ἐπίστασιν αὐτῶν ἰέναι καὶ οἷον ἐγγὺς προσελθεῖν πάλιν αὖ ταῖς γνώμαις ἀποροῦντες τὰς τῶν παλαιῶν ἀποφάσεις περὶ αὐτῶν ἄλλος ἄλλας, τάχα δὲ καὶ ἄλλως τὰς αὐτὰς λαβόντες ἐπὶ τούτων ἀναπαυσάμενοι καὶ αὔταρκες νομίσαντες, εἰ ἔχοιμεν ἐρωτηθέντες τὸ δοκοῦν ἐκείνοις λέγειν, ἀγαπήσαντες ἀπαλλαττόμεθα τοῦ ζητεῖν ἔτι περὶ αὐτῶν. Εὑρηκέναι μὲν οὖν τινας τῶν ἀρχαίων καὶ μακαρίων φιλοσόφων τὸ ἀληθὲς δεῖ νομίζειν· τίνες δ᾽ οἱ τυχόντες μάλιστα, καὶ πῶς ἂν καὶ ἡμῖν σύνεσις περὶ τούτων γένοιτο, ἐπισκέψασθαι προσήκει. Καὶ πρότερον περὶ τοῦ αἰῶνος

[1] This passage gives a clearer idea of Plotinus's way of philosophising than any other in the *Enneads*. He starts by reflecting on his own experience and trying to clarify it. In doing this his respect for tradition leads him naturally to seek help from the ancient philosophers, but he is never satisfied simply to repeat their statements; they are for him helps to

III. 7. ON ETERNITY AND TIME

1. Eternity and time, we say, are two different things, the one belonging to the sphere of the nature which lasts for ever, the other to that of becoming and of this universe; and at once, and as if by a fairly continuous application of our concept of them, we think that we have a clear and distinct experience of them in our own souls, as we are always speaking of them and using their names on every occasion. Of course, when we try to concentrate on them and, so to speak, to get close to them, we find again that our thought runs into difficulties; we consider the statements of the ancient philosophers about them, who differ one from the other, and perhaps also different interpretations of the same statements, and we set our minds at rest about them and think it sufficient if we are able, when we are asked, to state the opinion of the ancients, and so we are satisfied to be freed from the need of further research about them. Now we must consider that some of the blessed philosophers of ancient times have found out the truth; but it is proper to investigate which of them have attained it most completely, and how we too could reach an understanding about these things.[1] And first we should enquire about eternity, what sort of

further reflection leading to clearer understanding. It is, of course, Plato, here and elsewhere, who has "attained the truth most completely" (l. 15).

ζητεῖν, τί ποτε νομίζουσιν εἶναι αὐτὸν οἱ ἕτερον τοῦ χρόνου τιθέντες εἶναι· γνωσθέντος γὰρ τοῦ κατὰ τὸ παράδειγμα ἑστῶτος καὶ τὸ τῆς εἰκόνος αὐτοῦ, ὃν δὴ χρόνον λέγουσιν εἶναι, τάχ' ἂν σαφὲς γένοιτο. Εἰ δέ τις πρὸ τοῦ τὸν αἰῶνα θεάσασθαι τὸν χρόνον ὅς ἐστι φαντασθείη, γένοιτ' ἂν καὶ τούτῳ ἐντεῦθεν ἐκεῖ κατὰ ἀνάμνησιν ἐλθόντι ᾧ ἄρα ὡμοίωτο ὁ χρόνος θεάσασθαι, εἴπερ ὁμοιότητα οὗτος πρὸς ἐκεῖνον ἔχοι.

2. Τίνα οὖν ποτε χρὴ φάναι τὸν αἰῶνα εἶναι; Ἆρά γε τὴν νοητὴν αὐτὴν οὐσίαν, ὥσπερ ἂν εἴ τις λέγοι τὸν χρόνον τὸν σύμπαντα οὐρανὸν καὶ κόσμον εἶναι; Καὶ γὰρ αὖ καὶ ταύτην τὴν δόξαν ἔσχον τινές, φασι, περὶ τοῦ χρόνου. Ἐπεὶ γὰρ σεμνότατόν τι τὸν αἰῶνα εἶναι φανταζόμεθα καὶ νοοῦμεν, σεμνότατον δὲ τὸ τῆς νοητῆς φύσεως, καὶ οὐκ ἔστιν εἰπεῖν ὅ τι σεμνότερον ὁποτερονοῦν—τοῦ δ' ἐπέκεινα οὐδὲ τοῦτο κατηγορητέον—εἰς ταὐτὸν ἄν τις οὕτω συνάγοι. Καὶ γὰρ αὖ ὅ τε κόσμος ὁ νοητὸς ὅ τε αἰὼν περιεκτικὰ ἄμφω καὶ τῶν αὐτῶν. Ἀλλ' ὅταν τὰ ἕτερα ἐν θατέρῳ λέγωμεν—ἐν τῷ αἰῶνι—κεῖσθαι, καὶ ὅταν τὸ αἰώνιον κατηγορῶμεν αὐτῶν—ἡ μὲν γάρ, φησι, τοῦ παραδείγματος φύσις ἐτύγχανεν οὖσα αἰώνιος, —ἄλλο τὸν αἰῶνα πάλιν αὖ λέγομεν, εἶναι μέντοι

---

1 Cp. Plato, *Timaeus* 37D7.

2 The Pythagoreans: cp. Aristotle, *Physics* Δ 10. 218b1–2,

thing those who make it different from time consider it to be, for when we know that which holds the position of archetype, it will perhaps become clear how it is with its image, which the philosophers say time is.[1] But if someone, before contemplating eternity, should form a picture in his mind of what time is, it would be possible for him, too, to go from this world to the other by recollection and contemplate that of which time is a likeness, if time really has a likeness to eternity.

2. What sort of thing, then, ought we to say that eternity is? Should we say that it is the intelligible substance itself, as if one were to say that time is the whole heaven and universal order? For, so people say, some philosophers have held just this opinion about time.[2] For, since we picture and think of eternity as something most majestic, and the highest degree of majesty belongs to the intelligible nature, and it is impossible to mention anything at all which is more majestic—not even majesty can be predicated of that which lies beyond it—one could in this way come to the conclusion that eternity and the intelligible nature are one and the same. Then, again, the intelligible universe and eternity are both inclusive, and include the same things. But when we say that one set of things [the intelligible realities] lies in the other—in eternity—and when we predicate eternal existence of the intelligible realities—for, Plato says, the nature of the archetype was eternal[3]—we are again making eternity something

with the comment of Simplicius (*In Phys.* IV. 10, p. 700, 19–20.)

[3] *Timaeus* 37D3.

περὶ ἐκείνην ἢ ἐν ἐκείνῃ ἢ παρεῖναι ἐκείνῃ φαμέν. Τὸ δὲ σεμνὸν ἑκάτερον εἶναι ταὐτότητα οὐ δηλοῖ· ἴσως γὰρ ἂν καὶ τῷ ἑτέρῳ αὐτῶν παρὰ τοῦ ἑτέρου τὸ σεμνὸν γίνοιτο. Ἥ τε περιοχὴ τῷ μὲν ὡς μερῶν ἔσται, τῷ δὲ αἰῶνι ὁμοῦ τὸ ὅλον οὐχ ὡς μέρος, ἀλλ' ὅτι πάντα τὰ τοιαῦτα οἷα αἰώνια κατ' αὐτόν.

Ἀλλ' ἆρα κατὰ τὴν στάσιν φατέον τὴν ἐκεῖ τὸν αἰῶνα εἶναι, ὥσπερ ἐνταῦθα τὸν χρόνον κατὰ τὴν κίνησίν φασιν; Ἀλλ' εἰκότως ἄν τις τὸν αἰῶνα[1] ζητήσειε πότερα ταὐτὸν τῇ στάσει λέγοντες ἢ οὐχ ἁπλῶς, ἀλλὰ τῇ στάσει τῇ περὶ τὴν οὐσίαν. Εἰ μὲν γὰρ τῇ στάσει ταὐτόν, πρῶτον μὲν οὐκ ἐροῦμεν αἰώνιον τὴν στάσιν, ὥσπερ οὐδὲ τὸν αἰῶνα αἰώνιον· τὸ γὰρ αἰώνιον τὸ μετέχον αἰῶνος. Ἔπειτα ἡ κίνησις πῶς αἰώνιον; Οὕτω γὰρ ἂν καὶ στάσιμον εἴη. Εἶτα πῶς ἔχει ἡ τῆς στάσεως ἔννοια ἐν αὑτῇ τὸ ἀεί; Λέγω δὲ οὐ τὸ ἐν χρόνῳ, ἀλλὰ οἷον νοοῦμεν, ὅταν τὸ ἀίδιον λέγωμεν. Εἰ δὲ τῇ τῆς οὐσίας στάσει, ἔξω πάλιν αὖ τὰ ἄλλα γένη τοῦ αἰῶνος ποιήσομεν. Εἶτα τὸν αἰῶνα οὐ μόνον ἐν στάσει δεῖ νοεῖν, ἀλλὰ καὶ ἐν ἑνί· εἶτα καὶ ἀδιάστατον, ἵνα μὴ ταὐτὸν ᾖ χρόνῳ· ἡ δὲ στάσις οὔτε τὴν τοῦ ἓν οὔτε τὴν τοῦ ἀδιαστάτου ἔχει ἔννοιαν ἐν αὑτῇ ᾗ στάσις. Εἶτα τοῦ μὲν

[1] *αἰῶνα* A^pc Creuzer, H–S: *χρόνον* A^ac ExyQL.

---

[1] Rest and motion here are the Platonic "categories of the intelligible world": cp. V. 1 [10] 4; VI. 2 [43] 8.

different, but are saying that it has something to do with the intelligible nature, or is in it, or is present to it. That both are majestic does not make their identity clear, for perhaps majesty might come to one of them from the other. And as for inclusiveness, the intelligible world has it in the way in which a whole includes its parts, but eternity includes the whole all at once, not as a part, but in the sense that all things which are of such a kind as to be eternal are so by conforming to it.

But should eternity, perhaps, be said to correspond to the rest there as people say that time corresponds to motion?[1] But one might reasonably enquire whether, when people say this, they mean that eternity is the same as rest or, not simply as rest, but as the rest which belongs to substance. Now if it is the same as rest, first of all we shall not call rest eternal, just as we do not call eternity eternal, for the eternal is that which participates in eternity. Then, how is motion to be something eternal? For, on this assumption, it would also be at rest. Then again, how does the idea of rest contain in itself the " always "? I mean, not the " always " in time, but the kind of " always " we have in mind when we are speaking of what is eternal. But if eternity is the same as the rest which belongs to substance, then again, we shall put the other kinds of substance outside eternity. Then again, we must think of eternity not only in terms of rest but of unity; then, too, it must be thought of as without extension or interval, that it may not be the same as time; but rest in so far as it is rest, does not include in itself the idea of one nor of the unextended. Then

αἰῶνος κατηγοροῦμεν τὸ μένειν ἐν ἑνί· μετέχοι ἂν οὖν στάσεως, ἀλλ' οὐκ αὐτοστάσις εἴη.

3. Τί ἂν οὖν εἴη τοῦτο, καθ' ὃ τὸν κόσμον πάντα τὸν ἐκεῖ αἰώνιον λέγομεν καὶ ἀίδιον εἶναι, καὶ τί ἡ ἀιδιότης, εἴτε ταὐτὸν καὶ ἡ αὐτὴ τῷ αἰῶνι, εἴτε κατ' αὐτὴν ὁ αἰών; Ἆρά γε[1] καθ' ἕν τι δεῖ, ἀλλὰ ἐκ πολλῶν συνηθροισμένην τινὰ νόησιν, ἢ καὶ φύσιν εἴτ' ἐπακολουθοῦσαν τοῖς ἐκεῖ εἴτε συνοῦσαν εἴτ' ἐνορωμένην, πάντα δὲ ταῦτα ἐκείνην μίαν μὲν οὖσαν, πολλὰ δὲ δυναμένην καὶ πολλὰ οὖσαν; Καὶ ὅ γε τὴν πολλὴν δύναμιν εἰσαθρήσας κατὰ μὲν τοδὶ τὸ οἷον ὑποκείμενον λέγει οὐσίαν, εἶτα κίνησιν τοῦτο, καθ' ὃ ζωὴν ὁρᾷ, εἶτα στάσιν τὸ πάντη ὡσαύτως, θάτερον δὲ καὶ ταὐτόν, ᾗ ταῦτα ὁμοῦ ἕν. Οὕτω δὴ καὶ συνθεὶς πάλιν αὖ εἰς ἓν ὁμοῦ ⟨ὥστε⟩[2] εἶναι ζωὴν μόνην, ἐν τούτοις τὴν ἑτερότητα συστείλας, καὶ τῆς ἐνεργείας τὸ ἄπαυστον καὶ τὸ ταὐτὸν καὶ οὐδέποτε ἄλλο καὶ οὐκ ἐξ ἄλλου εἰς ἄλλο νόησιν ἢ ζωήν, ἀλλὰ τὸ ὡσαύτως καὶ ἀεὶ ἀδιαστάτως, ταῦτα πάντα ἰδὼν αἰῶνα εἶδεν ἰδὼν ζωὴν μένουσαν ἐν τῷ αὐτῷ ἀεὶ παρὸν τὸ πᾶν ἔχουσαν, ἀλλ' οὐ νῦν μὲν τόδε, αὖθις δ' ἕτερον, ἀλλ' ἅμα τὰ πάντα, καὶ οὐ νῦν

[1] ἆρά γε Kirchhoff, H–S²: ἄρα γὰρ codd.
[2] ⟨ὥστε⟩ Theiler.

---

[1] *Timaeus* 37D6.

[2] The complete list of the "Platonic categories," taken from *Sophist* 254D–E. For passages in which Plotinus ex-

again we predicate " abiding in one " of eternity;[1] so, then, it would participate in rest, but not be absolute rest.

3. What, then, would this be by reason of which we call the whole universe There eternal and everlasting, and what is everlastingness? Is it the same thing as, and identical with eternity, or is eternity in conformity with it? Should we then think of it as an idea corresponding to some one thing, but gathered together into a unity from many sources, or even a nature either consequent upon the beings of that other world or existing along with them or perceived in them? Are all these beings that nature, which is one, but has many powers and is many things? And when one looks closely into this manifold power, then according as one sees it as a subject, a kind of substrate, one calls it " substance "; then one calls it " motion," according as one sees it as life; then " rest " in so far as it is always in every way unchangingly itself; " the other " and " the same " in that these [different] realities are all together one.[2] So, too, one puts it all together again into one, so as to be only life, compressing the otherness in these intelligible realities, and seeing the unceasingness and self-identity of their activity, and that it is never other and is not a thinking or life that goes from one thing to another but is always the selfsame without extension or interval; seeing all this one sees eternity in seeing a life that abides in the same, and always has the all present to it, not now this, and then again that, but all things at once, and not

plains his application of them to the intelligible world more fully, see note on previous chapter.

μὲν ἕτερα, αὖθις δ᾽ ἕτερα, ἀλλὰ τέλος ἀμερές, οἷον ἐν σημείῳ ὁμοῦ πάντων ὄντων καὶ οὔποτε εἰς ῥύσιν προϊόντων, ἀλλὰ μένοντος ἐν τῷ αὐτῷ ἐν αὐτῷ καὶ οὐ μὴ μεταβάλλοντος, ὄντος δ᾽ ἐν τῷ παρόντι ἀεί, ὅτι οὐδὲν αὐτοῦ παρῆλθεν οὐδ᾽ αὖ γενήσεται, ἀλλὰ τοῦτο ὅπερ ἔστι, τοῦτο καὶ ὄντος· ὥστε εἶναι τὸν αἰῶνα οὐ τὸ ὑποκείμενον, ἀλλὰ τὸ ἐξ αὐτοῦ τοῦ ὑποκειμένου οἷον ἐκλάμπον κατὰ τὴν [τοῦ] [1] ἣν ἐπαγγέλλεται περὶ τοῦ μὴ μέλλοντος, ἀλλὰ ἤδη ὄντος, ταυτότητα, ὡς ἄρα οὕτως καὶ οὐκ ἄλλως· τί γὰρ ἂν καὶ ὕστερον αὐτῷ γένοιτο, ὃ μὴ νῦν ἐστι; Μηδ᾽ αὖ ὕστερον ἐσομένου, ὃ μὴ ἔστιν ἤδη· οὔτε γὰρ ἔστιν, ἀφ᾽ οὗ εἰς τὸ νῦν ἥξει· ἐκεῖνο γὰρ ἦν οὐκ ἄλλο, ἀλλὰ τοῦτο. Οὔτε μέλλοντος ἔσεσθαι, ὃ μὴ νῦν ἔχει. Ἐξ ἀνάγκης οὔτε τὸ ἦν ἕξει περὶ αὐτό· τί γὰρ ἔστιν, ὃ ἦν αὐτῷ καὶ παρελήλυθεν; οὔτε τὸ ἔσται· τί γὰρ ἔσται αὐτῷ; Λείπεται δὴ ἐν τῷ εἶναι τοῦτο ὅπερ ἔστιν εἶναι. Ὃ οὖν μήτε ἦν, μήτε ἔσται, ἀλλ᾽ ἔστι μόνον, τοῦτο ἑστὼς ἔχον τὸ εἶναι τῷ μὴ μεταβάλλειν εἰς τὸ ἔσται μηδ᾽ αὖ μεταβεβληκέναι ἐστὶν ὁ αἰών. Γίνεται τοίνυν ἡ περὶ τὸ ὂν ἐν τῷ εἶναι ζωὴ ὁμοῦ πᾶσα καὶ πλήρης ἀδιάστατος πανταχῇ τοῦτο, ὃ δὴ ζητοῦμεν, αἰών.

4. Οὐκ ἔξωθεν δὲ δεῖ συμβεβηκέναι νομίζειν τοῦτον ἐκείνῃ τῇ φύσει, ἀλλ᾽ ἐκείνη καὶ ἐξ ἐκείνης καὶ σὺν ἐκείνῃ. Ἐνορᾶται γὰρ ἐνοῦσα παρ᾽

[1] τὴν A^{pc} Kirchhoff, H–S: τὴν τοῦ A^{ac}ExyQL.

---

[1] Cp. *Timaeus* 37E6–38A2.

now some things, and then again others, but a partless completion, as if they were all together in a point, and had not yet begun to go out and flow into lines; it is something which abides in the same in itself and does not change at all but is always in the present, because nothing of it has passed away, nor again is there anything to come into being, but that which it is, it *is*; so that eternity is not the substrate but something which, as it were, shines out from the substrate itself in respect of what is called its sameness, in speaking about the fact that it is not going to be but is already, that it is as it is and not otherwise, for what could come to be for it afterwards, which it is not already? Nor again will it be afterwards what it is not already. For there is nothing starting from which it will arrive at the present moment, for that could be nothing else but what is [now]. Nor is it going to be what it does not now contain in itself. Necessarily there will be no " was " about it, for what is there that was for it and has passed away? Nor any " will be," for what will be for it? So there remains for it only to be in its being just what it is. That, then, which was not, and will not be, but *is* only,[1] which has being which is static by not changing to the " will be," nor ever having changed, this is eternity. The life, then, which belongs to that which exists and is in being, all together and full, completely without extension or interval, is that which we are looking for, eternity.

4. But one must not think that eternity has come to that [intelligible] nature accidentally, from outside, but it is that nature, and from it and with it. For the nature of eternity is contemplated in the

αὐτῆς, ὅτι καὶ τὰ ἄλλα πάντα ὅσα λέγομεν ἐκεῖ εἶναι ἐνυπάρχοντα ὁρῶντες λέγομεν ἐκ τῆς οὐσίας ἅπαντα καὶ σὺν τῇ οὐσίᾳ. Τὰ γὰρ πρώτως ὄντα συνόντα δεῖ τοῖς πρώτοις καὶ ἐν τοῖς πρώτοις εἶναι· ἐπεὶ καὶ τὸ καλὸν ἐν αὐτοῖς καὶ ἐξ αὐτῶν καὶ ἡ ἀλήθεια ἐν αὐτοῖς. Καὶ τὰ μὲν ὥσπερ ἐν μέρει τοῦ παντὸς ὄντος, τὰ δ' ἐν παντί, ὥσπερ καὶ τὸ ἀληθῶς τοῦτο πᾶν οὐκ ἐκ τῶν μερῶν ἠθροισμένον, ἀλλὰ τὰ μέρη γεννῆσαν αὐτό, ἵνα καὶ ταύτῃ ὡς ἀληθῶς πᾶν ᾖ. Καὶ ἡ ἀλήθεια δὲ οὐ συμφωνία πρὸς ἄλλο ἐκεῖ, ἀλλ' αὐτοῦ ἑκάστου οὗπερ ἀλήθεια. Δεῖ δὴ τὸ πᾶν τοῦτο τὸ ἀληθινόν, εἴπερ ἔσται πᾶν ὄντως, μὴ μόνον εἶναι πᾶν ᾗ ἐστι τὰ πάντα, ἀλλὰ καὶ τὸ πᾶν ἔχειν οὕτως ὡς μηδενὶ ἐλλείπειν. Εἰ τοῦτο, οὐδ' ἔσται τι αὐτῷ· εἰ γὰρ ἔσται, ἐλλεῖπον ἦν τούτῳ· οὐκ ἄρα ἦν πᾶν. Παρὰ φύσιν δὲ τί ἂν αὐτῷ γένοιτο; Πάσχει γὰρ οὐδέν. Εἰ οὖν μηδὲν αὐτῷ γένοιτο, οὐδὲ μέλλει οὐδὲ ἔσται οὐδ' ἐγένετο. Τοῖς μὲν οὖν γενητοῖς, εἰ ἀφέλοις τὸ ἔσται, ἅτε ἐπικτωμένοις ἀεὶ εὐθὺς ὑπάρχει μὴ εἶναι· τοῖς δὲ μὴ τοιούτοις, εἰ προσθείης τὸ ἔσται, ὑπάρχει τὸ ἔρρειν ἐκ τῆς τοῦ εἶναι ἕδρας· δῆλον γὰρ ὅτι ἦν αὐτοῖς τὸ εἶναι οὐ σύμφυτον, εἰ γίγνοιτο ἐν τῷ

---

[1] There is a verbal reminiscence here of Plato, *Philebus* 24D2, but no real connection of thought.

intelligible nature, existing in it as originated from it, because we see all the other things, too, which we say are There existing in it, and say that they all come from its substance and are with its substance. For the things which have primary existence must have a common existence with the primaries and be among them; since beauty, too, is among them and originates from them, and truth is among them. And some of these are as if in a part of the existent whole, others in the whole, just as this which is really a whole has not been put together out of its parts, but has produced its parts itself, in order that it may truly be a whole in this way too. And There the truth is not correspondence with something else, but really belongs to each individual thing of which it is the truth. Now this true whole, if it really is a whole, must not only be whole in the sense that it is all things, but it must have its wholeness in such a way that it is deficient in nothing. If this is so, there is nothing that is going to be for it, for if something is going to be, it was lacking to it before; so it was not whole. But what could happen to it contrary to its nature? For it is not affected in any way. If, then, nothing could happen to it, there is no postponement of being, and it is not going to be, nor did it come to be. Now with things which have come to be, if you take away the " will be " what happens is that they immediately cease to exist, as they are continually acquiring being; but with things which are not of this kind, if you add to them the " will be," what happens is that they fall from the seat of being,[1] for it is clear that their being was not connatural to them, if they came to be in a state of putting off

μέλλειν καὶ γενέσθαι καὶ ἔσεσθαι εἰς ὕστερον. Κινδυνεύει γὰρ τοῖς μὲν γενητοῖς ἡ οὐσία εἶναι τὸ ἐκ τοῦ ἐξ ἀρχῆς εἶναι τῆς γενέσεως, μέχριπερ ἂν εἰς ἔσχατον ἥκῃ τοῦ χρόνου, ἐν ᾧ μηκέτ' ἐστί· τοῦτο δὴ τὸ ἔστιν εἶναι, καί, εἴ τις τοῦτο παρέλοιτο, ἠλαττῶσθαι ὁ βίος· ὥστε καὶ τὸ εἶναι. Καὶ τῷ παντὶ δεῖ, εἰς ὅπερ οὕτως ἔσται. Διὸ καὶ σπεύδει πρὸς τὸ μέλλον εἶναι καὶ στῆναι οὐ θέλει ἕλκον τὸ εἶναι αὐτῷ ἐν τῷ τι ἄλλο καὶ ἄλλο ποιεῖν καὶ κινεῖσθαι κύκλῳ ἐφέσει τινὶ οὐσίας· ὥστε εἶναι ἡμῖν εὑρημένον καὶ τὸ αἴτιον τῆς κινήσεως τῆς οὕτω σπευδούσης ἐπὶ τὸ ἀεὶ εἶναι τῷ μέλλοντι. Τοῖς δὲ πρώτοις καὶ μακαρίοις οὐδὲ ἔφεσίς ἐστι τοῦ μέλλοντος· ἤδη γάρ εἰσι τὸ ὅλον, καὶ ὅπερ αὐτοῖς οἷον ὀφείλεται ζῆν ἔχουσι πᾶν· ὥστε οὐδὲν ζητοῦσι, διότι τὸ μέλλον αὐτοῖς οὐδέν ἐστιν οὐδ' ἄρα ἐκεῖνο, ἐν ᾧ τὸ μέλλον. Ἡ οὖν τοῦ ὄντος παντελὴς οὐσία καὶ ὅλη, οὐχ ἡ ἐν τοῖς μέρεσι μόνον, ἀλλὰ καὶ ἡ ἐν τῷ μηδ' ἂν ἔτι ἐλλείψειν καὶ τὸ μηδὲν ἂν μὴ ὂν αὐτῇ προσγενέσθαι —οὐ γὰρ μόνα τὰ ὄντα πάντα δεῖ παρεῖναι τῷ παντὶ καὶ ὅλῳ, ἀλλὰ καὶ μηδὲν τοῦ ποτε μὴ ὄντος—αὕτη ἡ διάθεσις αὐτοῦ καὶ φύσις εἴη ἂν αἰών· αἰὼν γὰρ ἀπὸ τοῦ ἀεὶ ὄντος.

[1] For a fuller discussion of the circular motion of the universe and its cause, cp. II. 2 [14].

being and having come to be and going to be afterwards. For the substantial existence of things that have come into being seems to be their existing from their point of origin, their coming to be, until they reach the end of their time, in which they cease to exist; this is their " is," and if anyone takes this away, their life-span is lessened, and so also their being. And the universe, too, must have a future, in moving towards which it " will be " in this way. This is why it, too, hastens towards what is going to be, and does not want to stand still, as it draws being to itself in doing one thing after another and moving in a circle in a sort of aspiration to substance. So we have found, incidentally, the cause of the movement of the universe, which hastens in this way to everlasting existence by means of what is going to be.[1] But the primal, blessed beings have not even an aspiration to what is going to be, for they are already the whole, and they have all the life which is, so to speak, owed to them; so they seek nothing, because there is nothing which is going to be for them, nor, indeed, that in which what is going to be can develop. So, then, the complete and whole substance of reality, not that in the parts only but that which consists in the impossibility of any future diminution and the fact that nothing non-existent could be added to it—for the all and whole must not only have all real beings present in it, but must not have anything that is at any time non-existent—this state and nature of complete reality would be eternity: for " eternity " [*aion*] is derived from " always existing " [*aei on*].[2]

[2] For this derivation of αἰών, cp. Aristotle, *De Caelo* A.9. 279a25–28.

5. Τοῦτο δέ, ὅταν τινὶ προσβαλὼν τῇ ψυχῇ ἔχω λέγειν περὶ αὐτοῦ, μᾶλλον δὲ ὁρᾶν αὐτὸ τοιοῦτον οἷον μηδὲν περὶ αὐτὸ ὅλως γεγονέναι—εἰ γὰρ τοῦτο, οὐκ ἀεὶ ὄν, ἢ οὐκ ἀεί τι ὅλον ὄν—ἆρ' οὖν ἤδη ἀίδιον, εἰ μὴ καὶ ἐνυπάρχοι αὐτῷ τοιαύτη φύσις, ὡς πίστιν ἔχειν περὶ αὐτοῦ, ὡς οὕτω καὶ μὴ ἄλλως ἔτι, ὡς, εἰ πάλιν προσβάλοις, εὑρεῖν τοιοῦτον; Τί οὖν, εἰ μηδὲ ἀφίσταιτό τις αὐτοῦ τῆς θέας, ἀλλὰ συνὼν εἴη τῆς φύσεως ἀγασθεὶς καὶ δυνατὸς τοῦτο πράττειν ἀτρύτῳ φύσει; Ἢ δραμὼν καὶ αὐτὸς εἰς αἰῶνα ἔσται καὶ οὐκ ἀποκλίνων οὐδαμῇ, ἵν' ᾖ ὅμοιος καὶ αἰώνιος, τῷ ἐν αὐτῷ αἰωνίῳ τὸν αἰῶνα καὶ τὸ αἰώνιον θεώμενος. Εἰ οὖν τὸ οὕτως ἔχον αἰώνιον καὶ ἀεὶ ὄν, τὸ μὴ ἀποκλῖνον εἰς ἑτέραν φύσιν κατὰ μηδέν, ζωὴν ἔχον, ἣν ἔχει πᾶσαν ἤδη, οὐ προσλαβὸν οὐδὲ προσλαμβάνον ἢ προσληψόμενον, εἴη ἂν ἀίδιον μὲν τὸ οὕτως ἔχον, ἀιδιότης δὲ ἡ τοιαύτη κατάστασις τοῦ ὑποκειμένου ἐξ αὐτοῦ οὖσα καὶ ἐν αὐτῷ, αἰὼν δὲ τὸ ὑποκείμενον μετὰ τῆς τοιαύτης καταστάσεως ἐμφαινομένης. Ὅθεν σεμνὸν ὁ αἰών, καὶ ταὐτὸν τῷ θεῷ ἡ ἔννοια λέγει· λέγει δὲ τούτῳ τῷ θεῷ. Καὶ καλῶς ἂν λέγοιτο ὁ αἰὼν θεὸς ἐμφαίνων καὶ προφαίνων ἑαυτὸν οἷός ἐστι, τὸ εἶναι ὡς ἀτρεμὲς καὶ ταὐτὸν καὶ οὕτως καὶ τὸ

[1] The god is Intellect or Real Being, the Second Hypostasis.

5. But now, whenever, concentrating the attention of my soul on something, I am able to say this about it, or rather to see it as a thing of such a kind that nothing at all about it has ever come into being—for if it has, it is not always existing, or not always existing as a whole—is it, therefore, already eternal, if there is not also in it a nature of such a kind as to give an assurance about it that it will stay as it is and never become different, so that, if you look attentively at it again, you will find it as it was? What then, if one does not depart at all from one's contemplation of it but stays in its company, wondering at its nature, and able to do so by a natural power which never fails? Surely one would be (would one not?), oneself on the move towards eternity and never falling away from it at all, that one might be like it and eternal, contemplating eternity and the eternal by the eternal in oneself. If, then, what is in this state is eternal and always existing, that which does not fall away in any respect into another nature, which has life which it possesses already as a whole, which has not received any addition and is not now receiving any and will not receive any, then that which is in this state would be eternal, and everlastingness would be the corresponding condition of the substrate, existing from it and in it, and eternity the substrate with the corresponding condition appearing in it. Hence eternity is a majestic thing, and thought declares it identical with the god;[1] it declares it identical with this god [whom we have been describing]. And eternity could be well described as a god proclaiming and manifesting himself as he is, that is, as being which is unshakeable and self-identical, and

βεβαίως ἐν ζωῇ. Εἰ δ᾽ ἐκ πολλῶν λέγομεν αὐτόν, οὐ δεῖ θαυμάζειν· πολλὰ γὰρ ἕκαστον τῶν ἐκεῖ διὰ δύναμιν ἄπειρον· ἐπεὶ καὶ τὸ ἄπειρον τὸ μὴ ἂν ἐπιλείπειν, καὶ τοῦτο κυρίως, ὅτι μηδὲν αὐτοῦ ἀναλίσκει. Καὶ εἴ τις οὕτω τὸν αἰῶνα λέγοι ζωὴν ἄπειρον ἤδη τῷ πᾶσαν εἶναι καὶ μηδὲν ἀναλίσκειν αὐτῆς τῷ μὴ παρεληλυθέναι μηδ᾽ αὖ μέλλειν—ἤδη γὰρ οὐκ ἂν εἴη πᾶσα—ἐγγὺς ἂν εἴη τοῦ ὁρίζεσθαι. [Τὸ γὰρ ἑξῆς « τῷ πᾶσαν εἶναι καὶ μηδὲν ἀναλίσκειν » ἐξήγησις ἂν εἴη τοῦ « ἄπειρον ἤδη εἶναι.»] [1]

6. Ἐπειδὴ δὲ ἡ τοιαύτη φύσις οὕτω παγκάλη καὶ ἀίδιος περὶ τὸ ἓν καὶ ἀπ᾽ ἐκείνου καὶ πρὸς ἐκεῖνο, οὐδὲν ἐκβαίνουσα ἀπ᾽ αὐτοῦ, μένουσα δὲ ἀεί περὶ ἐκεῖνο καὶ ἐν ἐκείνῳ καὶ ζῶσα κατ᾽ ἐκεῖνο, εἴρηταί τε, ὡς ἐγὼ οἶμαι, τοῦτο τῷ Πλάτωνι καλῶς καὶ βαθείᾳ τῇ γνώμῃ καὶ οὐκ ἄλλως, τοῦτο δὴ τὸ μένοντος αἰῶνος ἐν ἑνί, ἵνα μὴ μόνον ᾖ αὐτὸς αὐτὸν εἰς ἓν πρὸς ἑαυτὸν ἄγων, ἀλλ᾽ ἡ περὶ τὸ ἓν τοῦ ὄντος ζωὴ ὡσαύτως, τοῦτο ὃ δὴ ζητοῦμεν· καὶ τὸ οὕτω μένειν [2] αἰὼν εἶναι. Τὸ γὰρ τοῦτο καὶ οὕτω μένον καὶ αὐτὸ τὸ μένον ὅ ἐστιν ἐνέργεια ζωῆς μενούσης παρ᾽ αὐτῆς πρὸς ἐκεῖνο καὶ ἐν ἐκείνῳ καὶ οὔτε τὸ εἶναι οὔτε τὸ ζῆν ψευδομένη ἔχοι ἂν τὸ αἰὼν εἶναι. Τὸ γὰρ ἀληθῶς εἶναί ἐστι τὸ οὐδέποτε μὴ εἶναι οὐδ᾽ ἄλλως εἶναι·

[1] τὸ . . . εἶναι del. Heinemann, Dodds.
[2] μένειν Dodds: μένον codd., H–S: καὶ . . . εἶναι del. Theiler.

---

[1] The sentence bracketed here is clearly a rather unintelligent gloss on the one before it.
[2] *Timaeus* 376D.

[always] as it is, and firmly grounded in life. But if we say that it is made up of many parts, there is no need to be surprised, for each of the beings There is many through its unending power, since endlessness, too, is not having any possibility of failing, and eternity is endless in the strict and proper sense, because it never expends anything of itself. And if someone were in this way to speak of eternity as a life which is here and now endless because it is total and expends nothing of itself, since it has no past or future—for if it had, it would not now be a total life—he would be near to defining it. [For that which comes next " because it is total and expends nothing " would be an explanation of the phrase " here and now endless."] [1]

6. Now since the nature which is of this kind, altogether beautiful and everlasting in this way, is around the One and comes from it and is directed towards it, in no way going out from it but always abiding around it and in it, and living according to it; and since this was stated by Plato, as I think finely and with deep meaning and not to no purpose, in these words of his " as eternity remains in one," [2] the intention of which is not merely that eternity brings itself into unity with relation to itself, but that it is the life, always the same, of real being around the One; this, then, is what we are seeking; and abiding like this is being eternity. For that which is this and abides like this and abides what it is, an activity of life abiding of itself directed to the One and in the One, with no falsehood in its being or its life, this would possess the reality of eternity. For true being is never not being, or being otherwise; and this is being

τοῦτο δὲ ὡσαύτως εἶναι· τοῦτο δὲ ἀδιαφόρως εἶναι. Οὐκ ἔχει οὖν ὁτιοῦν [τὸ][1] ἄλλο καὶ ἄλλο, οὐδ' ἄρα διαστήσεις, οὐδ' ἐξελίξεις, οὐδὲ προάξεις, οὐδὲ παρατενεῖς, οὐδ' ἄρα οὐδὲ πρότερον αὐτοῦ οὐδέ τι ὕστερον λαβεῖν ἔχεις. Εἰ οὖν μήτε πρότερον μήτε ὕστερον περὶ αὐτό, τὸ δ' « ἔστιν » ἀληθέστατον τῶν περὶ αὐτὸ καὶ αὐτό, καὶ οὕτω δέ, ὅτι ἐστὶν ὡς οὐσίᾳ ἢ τῷ ζῆν, πάλιν αὖ ἥκει ἡμῖν τοῦτο, ὃ δὴ λέγομεν, ὁ αἰών. Ὅταν δὲ τὸ ἀεὶ λέγωμεν καὶ τὸ οὐ ποτὲ μὲν ὄν, ποτὲ δὲ μὴ ὄν, ἡμῶν ἕνεκα [τῆς σαφηνείας][2] δεῖ νομίζειν λέγεσθαι· ἐπεὶ τό γε ἀεὶ τάχ' ἂν οὐ κυρίως λέγοιτο, ἀλλὰ ληφθὲν εἰς δήλωσιν τοῦ ἀφθάρτου πλανῷ ἂν τὴν ψυχὴν εἰς ἔκτασιν[3] τοῦ πλείονος καὶ ἔτι ὡς μὴ ἐπιλείψοντός ποτε. Τὸ δὲ ἴσως βέλτιον ἦν μόνον τὸ « ὢν » λέγειν. Ἀλλὰ ὥσπερ τὸ ὂν ἀρκοῦν ὄνομα τῇ οὐσίᾳ, ἐπειδὴ καὶ τὴν γένεσιν οὐσίαν ἐνόμιζον, ἐδεήθησαν πρὸς τὸ μαθεῖν καὶ προσθήκης τοῦ ἀεί. Οὐ γὰρ ἄλλο μέν ἐστιν ὄν, ἄλλο δὲ τὸ ἀεὶ ὄν, ὥσπερ οὐδ' ἄλλο μὲν φιλόσοφος, ἄλλο δὲ ὁ ἀληθινός· ἀλλ' ὅτι τὸ ὑποδυόμενον ἦν φιλοσοφίαν, ἡ προσθήκη τοῦ ἀληθινοῦ ἐγένετο. Οὕτω καὶ τῷ ὄντι τὸ ἀεὶ καὶ τῷ « ὢν » τὸ ἀεί, ὥστε λέγεσθαι « ἀεὶ ὤν »· διὸ ληπτέον τὸ ἀεὶ οἷον « ἀληθῶς ὢν » λέγεσθαι καὶ συναιρετέον τὸ ἀεὶ εἰς ἀδιάστατον δύναμιν τὴν οὐδὲν δεομένην οὐδενὸς μεθ' ὃ ἤδη ἔχει· ἔχει δὲ τὸ πᾶν.

[1] τὸ del. Volkmann.
[2] τῆς σαφηνείας ut glossam ad ἡμῶν del. Dodds.
[3] ἔκτασιν Bury: ἔκβασιν codd.

always the same; and this is being without any difference. So it does not have any " this and that "; nor, therefore, will you be able to separate it out or unroll it or prolong it or stretch it; nor, then, can you apprehend anything of it as before or after. If, then, there is no before or after about it, but its " is " is the truest thing about it, and itself, and this in the sense that it is by its essence or its life, then again there has come to us what we are talking about, eternity. But when we use the word " always " and say that it does not exist at one time but not at another, we must be thought to be putting it this way for our own sake; for the " always " was perhaps not being used in its strict sense, but, taken as explaining the incorruptible, might mislead the soul into imagining an expansion of something becoming more, and again, of something which is never going to fail. It would perhaps have been better only to use the word " existing." But, as " existing " is an adequate word for substance, since, however, people thought becoming was substance, they required the addition of " always " in order to understand [what " existing " really meant]. For existing is not one thing and always existing another, just as a philosopher is not one thing and the true philosopher another, but because there was such a thing as putting on a pretence of philosophy, the addition of " true " was made. So, too, " always " is applied to " existing," that is " *aei* " to " *on*," so that we say " *aei on* [*aion*]," so the " always " must be taken as saying " truly existing "; it must be included in the undivided power which in no way needs anything beyond what it already possesses; but it possesses the whole.

Πᾶν οὖν καὶ ὂν καὶ κατὰ πᾶν οὐκ ἐνδεὲς καὶ οὐ ταύτῃ μὲν πλῆρες, ἄλλῃ δὲ ἐλλεῖπον ἡ τοιαύτη φύσις. Τὸ γὰρ ἐν χρόνῳ, κἂν τέλειον ᾖ, ὡς δοκεῖ, οἷον σῶμά τι ἱκανὸν ψυχῇ τέλειον, δεόμενον καὶ τοῦ ἔπειτα, ἐλλεῖπον τῷ χρόνῳ, οὗ δεῖται, ἅτε σὺν ἐκείνῳ, εἰ παρείη αὐτῷ καὶ συνθέοι, ὂν ἀτελές· ταύτῃ ὂν ὁμωνύμως ἂν τέλειον λέγοιτο. Ὅτῳ δὲ ὑπάρχει μηδὲ τοῦ ἔπειτα δεῖσθαι μήτε εἰς χρόνον ἄλλον μεμετρημένον μήτε τὸν ἄπειρον καὶ ἀπείρως ἐσόμενον, ἀλλ' ὅπερ δεῖ εἶναι, τοῦτο ἔχει, τοῦτό ἐστιν οὗ ἡ ἔννοια ἐπορέγεται, ᾧ τὸ εἶναι οὐκ ἐκ τοῦ τοσοῦδε, ἀλλὰ πρὸ τοῦ τοσοῦδε. Ἔπρεπε γὰρ αὐτῷ μηδὲ τοσῷδε ὄντι πάντῃ μηδενὸς ἐφάπτεσθαι τοσοῦδε, ἵνα μὴ ἡ ζωὴ αὐτοῦ μερισθεῖσα τὸ καθαρῶς ἀμερὲς αὐτοῦ ἀνέλῃ, ἀλλ' ᾖ καὶ τῇ ζωῇ ἀμερὲς καὶ τῇ οὐσίᾳ. Τὸ δ' « ἀγαθὸς ἦν » ἀναφέρει εἰς ἔννοιαν τοῦ παντὸς σημαίνων τῷ ἐπέκεινα παντὶ τὸ μὴ ἀπὸ χρόνου τινός· ὥστε μηδὲ τὸν κόσμον ἀρχήν τινα χρονικὴν εἰληφέναι τῆς αἰτίας τοῦ εἶναι αὐτῷ τὸ πρότερον παρεχούσης. Ἀλλ' ὅμως δηλώσεως χάριν τοῦτο εἰπὼν μέμφεται ὕστερον καὶ τούτῳ τῷ ὀνόματι ὡς οὐδ' αὐτοῦ ὀρθῶς πάντῃ λεγομένου ἐπὶ τῶν τὸν λεγόμενον καὶ νοούμενον αἰῶνα εἰληχότων.

---

[1] *Timaeus* 29E1.

[2] "The point is that the cosmos has indeed a prior (as it must have), but only in the sense of having a cause" (E. R. Dodds in a letter to H.-R. Schwyzer).

[3] Plotinus goes back here, rather abruptly, to the description of eternal being as "always" existing, and points out

The nature which is of this kind, then, is all, and existent, and not deficient in its wholeness, and not full at one point and deficient at another. For that which is in time, even if it is perfect, as it seems, in the way in which a body which is adequate for a soul is perfect, needs also time to come, being deficient in time, which it needs because it is with it, if time is present to and runs along with it, and so it is incomplete; and, existing in this way, it could only be called perfect by a mere coincidence of name. But that which has no need of time to come, which is not measured by another time or by an unlimited time which will be without end, but possesses what it ought to be, this is what our thought stretches out to, that whose being does not come from a certain extent [of time], but exists before extent [of time]. For, since it is not of any temporal extent itself, it was not right for it to have contact in any way with anything temporally extended, so that its life might not be divided into parts and destroy its pure partlessness, but it might be partless in life and substance. But Plato's " He was good " [1] takes us back to the thought of the All [the physical universe]; he indicates that by virtue of the transcendent All it has no beginning in time; so that the universe, too, did not have a temporal beginning because the cause of its being provides what is prior to it.[2] But all the same, after saying this for the sake of explanation, he objects to this expression, too, afterwards, as not being entirely correctly used about things which have a part in what we speak and think of as eternity.[3]

that Plato, too, objected to the use of expressions implying duration in time when referring to it (cp. *Timaeus* 37E).

7. Ταῦτα οὖν λέγομεν ἆρά γε μαρτυροῦντες ἑτέροις καὶ ὡς περὶ ἀλλοτρίων τοὺς λόγους ποιούμεθα; Καὶ πῶς; Τίς γὰρ ἂν σύνεσις γένοιτο μὴ ἐφαπτομένοις; Πῶς δ' ἂν ἐφαψαίμεθα τοῖς ἀλλοτρίοις; Δεῖ ἄρα καὶ ἡμῖν μετεῖναι τοῦ αἰῶνος. Ἀλλὰ ἐν χρόνῳ οὖσι πῶς; Ἀλλὰ πῶς ἐν χρόνῳ καὶ πῶς ἐν αἰῶνι ἔστιν εἶναι, γνωσθείη ἂν εὑρεθέντος πρότερον τοῦ χρόνου. Καὶ τοίνυν καταβατέον ἡμῖν ἐξ αἰῶνος ἐπὶ τὴν ζήτησιν τοῦ χρόνου καὶ τὸν χρόνον· ἐκεῖ μὲν γὰρ ἦν ἡ πορεία πρὸς τὸ ἄνω, νῦν δὲ λέγωμεν ἤδη οὐ πάντῃ καταβάντες, ἀλλ' οὕτως, ὥσπερ κατέβη χρόνος. Εἰ μὲν περὶ χρόνου εἰρημένον μηδὲν ἦν τοῖς παλαιοῖς καὶ μακαρίοις ἀνδράσιν, ἐχρῆν τῷ αἰῶνι ἐξ ἀρχῆς συνείραντας τὸ ἐφεξῆς λέγειν τὰ δοκοῦντα περὶ αὐτοῦ, πειρωμένους τῇ ἐννοίᾳ αὐτοῦ ἣν κεκτήμεθα ἐφαρμόζειν τὴν λεγομένην ὑφ' ἡμῶν δόξαν· νῦν δ' ἀναγκαῖον πρότερον λαβεῖν τὰ μάλιστα ἀξίως λόγου εἰρημένα σκοποῦντας, εἴ τινι αὐτῶν συμφώνως ὁ παρ' ἡμῶν ἕξει λόγος. Τριχῇ δ' ἴσως διαιρετέον τοὺς λεγομένους περὶ αὐτοῦ λόγους τὴν πρώτην. Ἢ γὰρ κίνησις ἡ λεγομένη, ἢ τὸ κινούμενον λέγοι ἄν, ἢ κινήσεώς τι τὸν χρόνον· τὸ γὰρ στάσιν ἢ τὸ ἑστηκὸς ἢ στάσεώς τι λέγειν παντά-

[1] The view that time was the movement of the universe (or one of its important parts) was current in the early Academy; cp. the Platonic Ὅροι 411B: *χρόνος ἡλίου κίνησις, μέτρον φορᾶς*; Aristotle, *Physics* Δ 10, 218b1–2; that it was the heavenly sphere (cp. l. 24–25) was a Pythagorean

7. Are we, then, saying this as if we were giving evidence on others' behalf and talking about what is not our own? How could we be? For what understanding could there be [of eternity] if we were not in contact with it? But how could we be in contact with what was not our own? We too, then, must have a share in eternity. But how can we, when we are in time? But what it means to be in time and what it means to be in eternity may become known to us when we have discovered time. So, then, we must go down from eternity to the enquiry into time, and to time, for there our way led us upwards, but now we must come down in our discourse, not altogether, but in the way in which time came down. Now if the blessed men of ancient times had said nothing about time, we should have to take eternity as our starting-point and link up our subsequent account of time with it, stating what we think about it and trying to make the opinion we express accord with the interior awareness of time which we have; but, as it is, we must first take the most important statements about it and consider whether our own account will agree with any of them. Perhaps we can, in the first instance, make a threefold division of the accounts of time which have been given, for either time is movement, as it is called, or one might say that it is what is moved, or something belonging to movement,[1] for to say that it is rest, or what is at rest, or something belonging to rest, would be quite

view; cp. note on ch. 2, and Pseudo-Plutarch, *Plac.* I. 884B 5. That it was something belonging to movement was held in different senses by some Academics, Aristotle, Stoics and Epicureans: see notes below.

πασι πόρρω τῆς ἐννοίας ἂν εἴη τοῦ χρόνου οὐδαμῇ τοῦ αὐτοῦ ὄντος. Τῶν δὲ κίνησιν λεγόντων οἱ μὲν πᾶσαν κίνησιν ἂν λέγοιεν, οἱ δὲ τὴν τοῦ παντός· οἱ δὲ τὸ κινούμενον λέγοντες τὴν τοῦ παντὸς ἂν σφαῖραν λέγοιεν· οἱ δὲ κινήσεώς τι ἢ διάστημα κινήσεως, οἱ δὲ μέτρον, οἱ δ' ὅλως παρακολουθοῦν αὐτῇ· καὶ ἢ πάσης ἢ τῆς τεταγμένης.

8. Κίνησιν μὲν οὐχ οἷόν τε οὔτε τὰς συμπάσας λαμβάνοντι κινήσεις καὶ οἷον μίαν ἐκ πασῶν ποιοῦντι, οὔτε τὴν τεταγμένην· ἐν χρόνῳ γὰρ ἡ κίνησις ἑκατέρα ἡ λεγομένη—εἰ δέ τις μὴ ἐν χρόνῳ, πολὺ μᾶλλον ἂν ἀπείη τοῦ χρόνος εἶναι—ὡς ἄλλου ὄντος τοῦ ἐν ᾧ ἡ κίνησις, ἄλλου τῆς κινήσεως αὐτῆς οὔσης. Καὶ ἄλλων λεγομένων καὶ λεχθέντων ἂν ἀρκεῖ τοῦτο καὶ ὅτι κίνησις μὲν ἂν καὶ παύσαιτο καὶ διαλίποι, χρόνος δὲ οὔ. Εἰ δὲ τὴν τοῦ παντὸς κίνησιν μὴ διαλείπειν τις λέγοι, ἀλλὰ καὶ αὕτη, εἴπερ τὴν περιφορὰν λέγοι, ἐν χρόνῳ τινί· καὶ αὕτη περιφέροιτο ἂν εἰς τὸ αὐτό, οὐκ ἐν ᾧ τὸ ἥμισυ ἤνυσται, καὶ ὁ μὲν ἂν εἴη ἥμισυς, ὁ δὲ διπλάσιος, κινήσεως τοῦ παντὸς

---

[1] Some Stoics: cp. *Stoic. Vet. Fr.* II. 514.

[2] Stoics (Zeno and Chrysippus): cp. *Stoic. Vet. Fr.* II. 509–510.

[3] An Academic view taken up and developed by Aristotle: cp. Ὅροι l.c. Aristotle, *Physics* Δ 10 ff.

[4] Epicureans: cp. *Stobaeus Ecl.* I. 8 [I] 103. 6; Wachsmuth = Usener 294).

[5] Cp. *Stoic. Vet. Fragm.* II. 509–510. It is only among Stoics that the distinction between all movement and ordered movement (the movement of the universe) appears. Zeno

remote from our interior awareness of time, which is never in any way the same. Now of those who say it is movement, some seem to mean that it is all movement,[1] others the movement of the universe; those who say that it is what is moved seem to mean that it is the sphere of the universe; those who say that it is something belonging to movement, that it is the distance covered by the movement [2] or (others of them) the measure,[3] or (others again) that it is in a general way a consequence of movement; [4] and either of all movement or only of ordered movement.[5]

8. It is not possible for it to be movement, whether one takes all movements together and makes a kind of single movement out of them, or whether one takes it as ordered movement, for what we call movement, of either kind, is in time; but if someone says that it is not in time, then it would be still further from being time, since that in which movement is, is something different from movement itself. And, though other arguments can be brought, and have been brought, against this position, this one is enough, and also that movement can stop altogether or be interrupted, but time cannot. But, if someone says that the movement of the universe is not interrupted, this, too (if he means the circuit of the heavens), is in a period of time; and it would go round to the same point not in the time in which half its course was finished, and one would be half, the other double time; each movement would be movement of the

said time was πάσης κινήσεως διάστημα, Chrysippus that it was διάστημα τῆς τοῦ κόσμου κινήσεως (*Stoic. Vet. Fr.* II. 510); other Stoics simply that time was movement (*Stoic. Vet. Fr.* II. 514).

οὔσης ἑκατέρας, τῆς τε εἰς τὸ αὐτὸ ἀπὸ τοῦ αὐτοῦ καὶ τῆς εἰς τὸ ἥμισυ ἡκούσης. Καὶ τὸ ὀξυτάτην δὲ καὶ ταχίστην λέγειν τὴν τῆς ἐξωτάτης σφαίρας κίνησιν μαρτυρεῖ τῷ λόγῳ, ὡς ἕτερον ἡ κίνησις αὐτῆς καὶ ὁ χρόνος. Ταχίστη γὰρ πασῶν δηλονότι τῷ ἐλάττονι χρόνῳ τὸ μεῖζον καὶ τὸ μέγιστον διάστημα ἀνύειν· τὰ δ' ἄλλα βραδύτερα τῷ ἐν πλείονι ἂν καὶ μέρος αὐτοῦ.

Εἰ τοίνυν μηδὲ ἡ κίνησις τῆς σφαίρας ὁ χρόνος, σχολῇ γ' ἂν ἡ σφαῖρα αὐτή, ἣ ἐκ τοῦ κινεῖσθαι ὑπενοήθη χρόνος εἶναι.

Ἆρ' οὖν κινήσεώς τι; Εἰ μὲν διάστημα, πρῶτον μὲν οὐ πάσης κινήσεως τὸ αὐτό, οὐδὲ τῆς ὁμοειδοῦς· θᾶττον γὰρ καὶ βραδύτερον ἡ κίνησις καὶ ἡ ἐν τόπῳ. Καὶ εἶεν ἂν ἄμφω μετρούμεναι αἱ διαστάσεις ἑνὶ ἑτέρῳ, ὃ δὴ ὀρθότερον ἄν τις εἴποι χρόνον. Ποτέρας δὴ αὐτῶν τὸ διάστημα χρόνος, μᾶλλον δὲ τίνος αὐτῶν ἀπείρων οὐσῶν; Εἰ δὲ τῆς τεταγμένης, οὐ πάσης μὲν οὐδὲ τῆς τοιαύτης· πολλαὶ γὰρ αὗται· ὥστε καὶ πολλοὶ χρόνοι ἅμα ἔσονται. Εἰ δὲ τῆς τοῦ παντὸς διάστημα, εἰ μὲν τὸ ἐν αὐτῇ τῇ κινήσει διάστημα, τί ἂν ἄλλο ἢ ἡ κίνησις ἂν εἴη; Τοσήδε μέντοι· τὸ δὲ τοσόνδε

universe, one going from the same place to the same place again, and the other reaching the half-way point. And the statement that the movement of the outermost sphere is the most vigorous and quickest is evidence for our argument that its movement is something different from time. For it is, obviously, the quickest of all the spheres because it covers a greater distance than the others, in fact, the greatest distance, in less time; the others are slower because they cover only a part of the distance [covered by the outermost sphere] in a longer time. If, then, time is not the movement of the sphere, it can hardly be the sphere itself, which was supposed to be time because it is in motion.

Is it, then, something belonging to movement? If it is the distance covered by the movement, first, this is not the same for all movement, not even uniform movement, for movement is quicker and slower, even movement in space. And both these distances covered [by the quicker and the slower movement] would be measured by some one other thing, which would more correctly be called time. Well then, of which of the two of them is the distance covered time, or rather of which of all the movements, which are infinite in number? But if it is the distance covered by the ordered movement, then not by all ordered movement, or by one particular kind of ordered movement, for there are many of these; so that there will be many times at once. But if it is the distance covered by the movement of the universe, if the distance in the movement itself is meant, what would this be other than the movement? The movement, certainly is quantitatively

τοῦτο ἤτοι τῷ τόπῳ, ὅτι τοσόσδε ὂν διεξῆλθε, μετρηθήσεται, καὶ τὸ διάστημα τοῦτο ἔσται· τοῦτο δὲ οὐ χρόνος, ἀλλὰ τόπος· ἢ αὐτὴ ἡ κίνησις τῇ συνεχείᾳ αὐτῆς καὶ τῷ μὴ εὐθὺς πεπαῦσθαι, ἀλλ' ἐπιλαμβάνειν ἀεί, τὸ διάστημα ἕξει. Ἀλλὰ τοῦτο τὸ πολὺ τῆς κινήσεως ἂν εἴη· καὶ εἰ μὲν εἰς αὐτήν τις βλέπων ἀποφανεῖται πολλήν, ὥσπερ ἂν εἴ τις πολὺ τὸ θερμὸν λέγοι, οὐδ' ἐνταῦθα χρόνος φανεῖται οὐδὲ προσπίπτει, ἀλλὰ κίνησις πάλιν καὶ πάλιν, ὡσπερεὶ ὕδωρ ῥέον πάλιν καὶ πάλιν, καὶ τὸ ἐπ' αὐτῷ διάστημα θεωρούμενον. Καὶ τὸ μὲν πάλιν καὶ πάλιν ἔσται ἀριθμός, ὥσπερ δυὰς ἢ τριάς, τὸ δὲ διάστημα τοῦ ὄγκου. Οὕτως οὖν καὶ πλῆθος κινήσεως ὡς δεκάς, ἢ ὡς τὸ ἐπιφαινόμενον τῷ οἷον ὄγκῳ τῆς κινήσεως διάστημα, ὃ οὐκ ἔχει ἔννοιαν χρόνου, ἀλλ' ἔσται τὸ τοσόνδε τοῦτο γενόμενον ἐν χρόνῳ, ἢ ὁ χρόνος οὐκ ἔσται πανταχοῦ, ἀλλ' ἐν ὑποκειμένῳ τῇ κινήσει, συμβαίνει τε πάλιν αὖ κίνησιν τὸν χρόνον λέγειν· οὐ γὰρ ἔξω αὐτῆς τὸ διάστημα, ἀλλὰ κίνησις οὐκ ἀθρόα· τὸ δὲ μὴ ἀθρόα εἰς τὸ ἀθρόον ἐν χρόνῳ. Τὸ μὴ ἀθρόον τίνι διοίσει τοῦ ἀθρόως; ἢ τῷ ἐν χρόνῳ, ὥστε ἡ διεστῶσα κίνησις καὶ τὸ διάστημα αὐτῆς οὐκ αὐτὸ χρόνος, ἀλλ' ἐν χρόνῳ.

determined; but this definite quantity will either be measured by the space, because the space which it has traversed is a certain amount of space, and this will be the distance covered; but this is not time but space; or the movement itself, by its continuity and the fact that it does not stop at once but keeps on for ever, will contain the distance. But this would be the multiplicity of movement; and if one, looking at movement, shows that it is multiple (as if one were to say there was a great deal of heat), time will not appear or come into one's mind but movement which keeps on coming again and again, just like water flowing which keeps on coming again and again, and the distance observed in it. And the " again and again " will be a number, like the number two or three, but distance belongs to magnitude. So the amplitude of movement will be like the number ten or the distance from end to end which appears on what you might call the bulk of the movement, and this does not contain our idea of time, but this definite quantity will be something which came to be in time; otherwise time will not be everywhere but in movement as its substrate, and we are back again at the statement that time is movement, for the distance covered is not outside movement but is movement which does not happen all at once; but the comparison of movement which does not happen all at once with what is all at once [the instantaneous] can only be made in time. In what way will the non-instantaneous differ from the instantaneous? By being in time, so that movement which extends over a distance and the distance covered by it are not the actual thing, time, but are in time. But if someone

Εἰ δὲ τὸ διάστημα τῆς κινήσεως λέγοι τις χρόνον, οὐ τὸ αὐτῆς τῆς κινήσεως, ἀλλὰ παρ' ὃ αὐτὴ ἡ κίνησις τὴν παράτασιν ἔχοι οἷον συμπαραθέουσα ἐκείνῳ, τί δὲ τοῦτό ἐστιν οὐκ εἴρηται. Δῆλον γάρ, ὅτι τοῦτ' ἐστὶν ὁ χρόνος, ἐν ᾧ γέγονεν ἡ κίνησις. Τοῦτο δ' ἦν ὃ ἐξ ἀρχῆς ἐζήτει ὁ λόγος, τί ὤν ἐστι χρόνος· ἐπεὶ ὅμοιόν τε γίνεται καὶ ταὐτὸν οἷον εἴ τις ἐρωτηθεὶς τί ἐστι χρόνος, λέγοι κινήσεως διάστημα ἐν χρόνῳ. Τί οὖν ἐστι τοῦτο τὸ διάστημα, ὃ δὴ χρόνον καλεῖς τῆς κινήσεως τοῦ οἰκείου διαστήματος ἔξω τιθέμενος; Καὶ γὰρ αὖ καὶ ἐν αὐτῇ ὁ τιθέμενος τῇ κινήσει τὸ διάστημα τὴν τῆς ἠρεμίας διάστασιν ποῖ θήσεται, ἄπορος ἔσται. Ὅσον γὰρ κινεῖταί τι, τοσοῦτον ἂν σταίη καὶ ἄλλο, καὶ εἴποις ἂν τὸν χρόνον ἑκατέρου τὸν αὐτὸν εἶναι, ὡς ἄλλον δηλονότι ἀμφοῖν ὄντα. Τί οὖν ἐστι καὶ τίνα φύσιν ἔχει τοῦτο τὸ διάστημα; Ἐπείπερ τοπικὸν οὐχ οἷόν τε· ἐπεὶ καὶ τοῦτό γε ἔξωθέν ἐστιν.

9. Ἀριθμὸς δὲ κινήσεως ἢ μέτρον—βέλτιον γὰρ οὕτω συνεχοῦς οὔσης[1]—πῶς, σκεπτέον. Πρῶτον μὲν οὖν καὶ ἐνταῦθα τὸ πάσης ὁμοίως ἀπορητέον, ὥσπερ καὶ ἐπὶ τοῦ διαστήματος τῆς κινήσεως, εἴ τις τῆς πάσης εἶναι ἐλέγετο. Πῶς γὰρ ἄν τις ἀριθμήσειε τὴν ἄτακτον καὶ ἀνώμαλον; ἢ τίς ἀριθμὸς ἢ μέτρον ἢ κατὰ τί τὸ μέτρον; Εἰ δὲ τῷ αὐτῷ ἑκατέραν καὶ ὅλως πᾶσαν, ταχεῖαν,

[1] συνεχοῦς οὔσης J^{lmg}: συνεχούσης codd.

---

[1] Aristotle uses both terms (ἀριθμὸς κινήσεως, *Physics* Δ 11. 219b2; μέτρον κινήσεως, 12. 221a1) without distinction.

were to say that the distance of movement is time, not in the sense of the distance of movement itself, but that in relation to which the movement has its extension, as if it was running along with it, what this is has not been stated. For it is obvious that time is that in which the movement has occurred. But this was what our discussion was trying to find from the beginning, what time essentially is; since this is like, in fact, the same as, an answer to the question "What is time?" which says that it is distance of movement in time. What, then, is this distance which you call time and put outside the proper distance of the movement? Then, again, on the other side, the person who puts the distance in the movement itself, will be hopelessly perplexed about where to put the interval of rest. For something else could rest for the same space as something was moved, and you would say that the time in each case was the same, as being, obviously, different from both. What, then, is this distance, and what is its nature? For it cannot be spatial, since this also lies outside movement.

9. We must now enquire in what sense it is number of movement or measure [1]—for it is better to call it measure of movement, since movement is continuous. First of all, then, a doubt must arise here, too, about its being the measure of all movement alike, just as it did with the distance of movement, if there was said to be a number or measure of all movement. For how could one number disordered and irregular movement? What would its number or measure be, or what its scale of measurement? But if one uses the same measure for both kinds of movement

βραδεῖαν, ἔσται ὁ ἀριθμὸς καὶ τὸ μέτρον τοιοῦτον, οἷον εἰ δεκὰς εἴη μετροῦσα καὶ ἵππους καὶ βοῦς, ἢ εἰ τὸ αὐτὸ μέτρον καὶ ὑγρῶν καὶ ξηρῶν εἴη. Εἰ δὴ τοιοῦτον μέτρον, τίνων μέν ἐστιν ὁ χρόνος εἴρηται, ὅτι κινήσεων, αὐτὸς δὲ ὅ ἐστιν οὔπω εἴρηται. Εἰ δὲ ὥσπερ δεκάδος ληφθείσης καὶ ἄνευ ἵππων ἔστι νοεῖν τὸν ἀριθμόν, καὶ τὸ μέτρον μέτρον ἐστὶ φύσιν ἔχον τινά, κἂν μήπω μετρῇ, οὕτω δεῖ ἔχειν καὶ τὸν χρόνον μέτρον ὄντα· εἰ μὲν τοιοῦτόν ἐστιν ἐφ' ἑαυτοῦ οἷον ἀριθμός, τί ἂν τοῦδε τοῦ ἀριθμοῦ τοῦ κατὰ τὴν δεκάδα ἢ ἄλλου ὁτουοῦν διαφέροι μοναδικοῦ; Εἰ δὲ συνεχὲς μέτρον ἐστί, ποσόν τι ὂν μέτρον ἔσται, οἷον τὸ πηχυαῖον μέγεθος. Μέγεθος τοίνυν ἔσται, οἷον γραμμὴ συνθέουσα δηλονότι κινήσει. Ἀλλ' αὕτη συνθέουσα πῶς μετρήσει τὸ ᾧ συνθεῖ; Τί γὰρ μᾶλλον ὁποτερονοῦν θάτερον; Καὶ βέλτιον τίθεσθαι καὶ πιθανώτερον οὐκ ἐπὶ πάσης, ἀλλ' ᾗ συνθεῖ. Τοῦτο δὲ συνεχὲς δεῖ εἶναι, ἢ ἐφέξει ἡ συνθέουσα. Ἀλλ' οὐκ ἔξωθεν δεῖ τὸ μετροῦν λαμβάνειν οὐδὲ χωρίς, ἀλλὰ ὁμοῦ κίνησιν μεμετρημένην. Καὶ τί τὸ μετροῦν ἔσται; Ἢ μεμετρημένη μὲν ἡ κίνησις ἔσται, μεμετρηκὸς δ' ἔσται μέγεθος. Καὶ ποῖον αὐτῶν ὁ χρόνος ἔσται; Ἡ κίνησις ἡ μεμετρημένη,

[regular and irregular] and in general for all movement, quick and slow, the number and measure will be like the ten which counts both horses and cows, or like the same measure for liquids and solids. Now, if it is a measure of this kind, then it has been said what time is a measure of, that it is a measure of movements, but we have not yet been told what it is itself. But if, just as when one takes the ten even without the horses it is possible to think of the number, and the measure is a measure, with a certain nature, even if it is not yet measuring, so time, too, must have its own nature since it is a measure, and if it is a thing of this kind on its own like number, how can it differ from this number we were considering in the case of the ten, or from any other number made up of abstract units? But if it is a continuous measure, then it will be a measure because it is of a certain size, like a length of one cubit. It will be a magnitude, then, like a line which will obviously run along with movement. But how will this line running along measure that with which it runs? Why should one of them measure the other rather than the other the one? And it is better and more plausible to assume that it is not the measure of all movement but of the movement it runs along with. But this must be something continuous, or the line which runs with it will stop. But one ought not to take what measures as something coming from outside or separate but to consider the measured movement as a whole. And what will the measurer be? Movement will be measured, and the measurer will be magnitude. And which of them will be time? The measured movement or the measuring magnitude?

ἢ τὸ μέγεθος τὸ μετρῆσαν; Ἢ γὰρ ἡ κίνησις ἔσται ἡ μεμετρημένη ὑπὸ τοῦ μεγέθους ὁ χρόνος, ἢ τὸ μέγεθος τὸ μετρῆσαν, ἢ τὸ τῷ μεγέθει χρησάμενον, ὥσπερ τῷ πήχει πρὸς τὸ μετρῆσαι ὅση ἡ κίνησις. Ἀλλ᾽ ἐπὶ μὲν πάντων τούτων ὑποθέσθαι, ὅπερ εἴπομεν πιθανώτερον εἶναι, τὴν ὁμαλὴν κίνησιν· ἄνευ γὰρ ὁμαλότητος καὶ προσέτι μιᾶς καὶ τῆς τοῦ ὅλου ἀπορώτερον τὸ τοῦ λόγου τῷ θεμένῳ ὁπωσοῦν μέτρον γίνεται. Εἰ δὲ δὴ μεμετρημένη κίνησις ὁ χρόνος καὶ ὑπὸ τοῦ ποσοῦ μεμετρημένη, ὥσπερ τὴν κίνησιν, εἰ ἔδει μεμετρῆσθαι, οὐχὶ ὑπ᾽ αὐτῆς ἔδει μεμετρῆσθαι, ἀλλ᾽ ἑτέρῳ, οὕτως ἀνάγκη, εἴπερ μέτρον ἕξει ἄλλο ἢ κίνησις παρ᾽ αὐτήν, καὶ διὰ τοῦτο ἐδεήθημεν τοῦ συνεχοῦς μέτρου εἰς μέτρησιν αὐτῆς, τὸν αὐτὸν τρόπον δεῖ καὶ τῷ μεγέθει αὐτῷ μέτρου, ἵν᾽ [ᾗ] ἡ[1] κίνησις, τοσοῦδε γεγενημένου τοῦ καθ᾽ ὃ μετρεῖται ὅση, μετρηθῇ. Καὶ ὁ ἀριθμὸς τοῦ μεγέθους ἔσται τῇ κινήσει παρομαρτοῦντος ἐκεῖνος ὁ χρόνος, ἀλλ᾽ οὐ τὸ μέγεθος τὸ συνθέον τῇ κινήσει. Οὗτος δὲ τίς ἂν εἴη ἢ ὁ μοναδικός; Ὃς ὅπως μετρήσει ἀπορεῖν ἀνάγκη. Ἐπεί, κἂν τις ἐξεύρῃ ὅπως, οὐ χρόνον εὑρήσει μετροῦντα, ἀλλὰ τὸν τοσόνδε χρόνον· τοῦτο δὲ οὐ ταὐτὸν χρόνῳ. Ἕτερον γὰρ

[1] ἡ Kirchhoff: ᾗἡ wxy: ᾗ Q.

---

[1] Aristotle points out that only a uniform movement can be considered a single movement in *Physics* E4. 228b15 ff.; but for him time is the measure of absolutely any kind of movement (*Physics* Δ 14, 223a20 ff.); though the most uniform

For either the movement which is measured by the magnitude will be time, or the magnitude which measures, or what uses the magnitude, as one uses the cubit to measure how much the movement is. But in all these cases one must assume (which we said was more plausible), uniform movement, for unless there is uniformity, and, besides that, the movement is single, and a movement of the whole thing,[1] the way of proof becomes still more obstructed for whoever holds that time is in any sense a measure. But now, if time is a measured movement, and one measured by quantity; just as the movement, if it had to be measured, could not be measured by itself but by something else, so it is necessary, if the movement is to have another measure besides itself, and this was the reason why we needed the continuous measure for measuring it—in the same way there is need of a measure for the magnitude itself, in order that the movement, by the fixing at a certain length of that by which it is measured as being a certain length, may itself be measured. And the number of the magnitude which accompanies the movement, but not the magnitude which runs along with the movement, will be that time which we were looking for. But what could this be except number made up of abstract units? And here the problem must arise of how this abstract number is going to measure. Then, even if one does discover how it can, one will not discover time measuring but a certain length of time; and this is not the same thing as time. It is

movement, the circular movement of the heavens, is the standard by which in fact we measure other movements and time itself (223b).

εἰπεῖν χρόνον, ἕτερον δὲ τοσόνδε χρόνον· πρὸ γὰρ τοῦ τοσόνδε δεῖ ὅ τί ποτ' ἐστὶν εἰπεῖν ἐκεῖνο, ὃ τοσόνδε ἐστίν. Ἀλλ' ὁ ἀριθμὸς ὁ μετρήσας τὴν κίνησιν ἔξωθεν τῆς κινήσεως ὁ χρόνος, οἷον ἡ δεκὰς ἐπὶ τῶν ἵππων οὐ μετὰ τῶν ἵππων λαμβανόμενος. Τίς οὖν οὗτος ὁ ἀριθμός, οὐκ εἴρηται, ὃς πρὸ τοῦ μετρεῖν ἐστιν ὅπερ ἐστίν, ὥσπερ ἡ δεκάς. Ἢ οὗτος, ὃς κατὰ τὸ πρότερον καὶ ὕστερον τῆς κινήσεως παραθέων ἐμέτρησεν. Ἀλλ' οὗτος ὁ κατὰ τὸ πρότερον καὶ ὕστερον οὔπω δῆλος ὅστις ἐστίν. Ἀλλ' οὖν κατὰ τὸ πρότερον καὶ ὕστερον μετρῶν εἴτε σημείῳ εἴθ' ὁτῳοῦν ἄλλῳ πάντως κατὰ χρόνον μετρήσει. Ἔσται οὖν ὁ χρόνος οὗτος ὁ μετρῶν τὴν κίνησιν τῷ προτέρῳ καὶ ὑστέρῳ ἐχόμενος τοῦ χρόνου καὶ ἐφαπτόμενος, ἵνα μετρῇ. Ἢ γὰρ τὸ τοπικὸν πρότερον καὶ ὕστερον, οἷον ἡ ἀρχὴ τοῦ σταδίου, λαμβάνει, ἢ ἀνάγκη τὸ χρονικὸν λαμβάνειν. Ἔστι γὰρ ὅλως τὸ πρότερον καὶ ὕστερον τὸ μὲν χρόνος ὁ εἰς τὸ νῦν λήγων, τὸ δὲ ὕστερον ὃς ἀπὸ τοῦ νῦν ἄρχεται. Ἄλλο [1] τοίνυν ἀριθμοῦ τοῦ κατὰ τὸ πρότερον καὶ ὕστερον μετροῦντος τὴν κίνησιν οὐ μόνον ἡντινοῦν, ἀλλὰ καὶ τὴν τεταγμένην, ὁ χρόνος. Ἔπειτα διὰ τί ἀριθμοῦ μὲν προσγεγενημένου εἴτε κατὰ τὸ μεμετρημένον εἴτε κατὰ τὸ μετροῦν· ἔστι γὰρ αὖ [2]

[1] ἄλλο A^{pc} aliud Ficinus, ἄλλο H–S: ἀλλὰ A^{ac}ExyQ.
[2] ἔστι γὰρ αὖ H–S: ἔστι γὰρ ἂν codd.

---

1 Plotinus assumes here his own view that number has a separate substantial existence prior to the things which it numbers: see VI. 6 [34] 5.

one thing to say " time " and another to say " a certain length of time "; for before saying " a certain length of time " one ought to say what it is that is of a certain length. But perhaps the number which measures the movement from outside the movement is time, like the ten which counted the horses taken apart from the horses. Well, then, in this version it has not been said what this number is which is what it is before it begins to measure, like the ten.[1] Perhaps it is the number which runs beside the movement and measures it by the sequence of " before " and " after." [2] But it is not yet clear what this number which measures by the sequence of " before " and " after " is. And then, too, anyone who measures by " before " and " after," either with a point or with anything else, will in any case be measuring according to time. So, then, this time of theirs which measures movement by " before " and " after " is bound to time and in contact with time in order to measure. For one either takes " before " and " after " in a spatial sense, like " the beginning of the race-track," or else one must take them in a temporal sense. For in general, " before " and " after " mean, " before," the time which stops at the " now," and " after," the time which begins from the " now." Time, then, is something different from the number which measures by " before " and " after " not only any kind of movement but even ordered movement. Then, why, when number is added to movement, either on the measured or the measuring side—for there is the

[2] Aristotle defines time as *ἀριθμὸς κινήσεως κατὰ τὸ πρότερον καὶ ὕστερον* (*Physics* Δ 4. 219b2–3).

τὸν αὐτὸν καὶ μετροῦντα καὶ μεμετρημένον εἶναι—ἀλλ' οὖν διὰ τί ἀριθμοῦ μὲν γενομένου χρόνος ἔσται, κινήσεως δὲ οὔσης καὶ τοῦ προτέρου πάντως ὑπάρχοντος περὶ αὐτὴν καὶ τοῦ ὑστέρου οὐκ ἔσται χρόνος; Ὥσπερ ἂν εἴ τις λέγοι τὸ μέγεθος μὴ εἶναι ὅσον ἐστίν, εἰ μή τις τὸ ὅσον ἐστὶ τοῦτο λάβοι. Ἀπείρου δὲ τοῦ χρόνου ὄντος καὶ λεγομένου πῶς ἂν περὶ αὐτὸν ἀριθμὸς εἴη; Εἰ μή τις ἀπολαβὼν μέρος τι αὐτοῦ μετροῖ, ἐν ᾧ συμβαίνει εἶναι καὶ πρὶν μετρηθῆναι. Διὰ τί δὲ οὐκ ἔσται πρὶν καὶ ψυχὴν τὴν μετροῦσαν εἶναι; Εἰ μή τις τὴν γένεσιν αὐτοῦ παρὰ ψυχῆς λέγοι γίνεσθαι. Ἐπεὶ διά γε τὸ μετρεῖν οὐδαμῶς ἀναγκαῖον εἶναι· ὑπάρχει γὰρ ὅσον ἐστί, κἂν μή τις μετρῇ. Τὸ δὲ τῷ μεγέθει χρησάμενον πρὸς τὸ μετρῆσαι[1] τὴν ψυχὴν ἄν τις λέγοι· τοῦτο δὲ τί ἂν εἴη πρὸς ἔννοιαν χρόνου;

10. Τὸ δὲ παρακολούθημα λέγειν τῆς κινήσεως, τί ποτε τοῦτό ἐστιν οὐκ ἔστι διδάσκοντος οὐδὲ εἰρηκέ τι,[2] πρὶν εἰπεῖν τί ἐστι τοῦτο τὸ παρακολουθοῦν· ἐκεῖνο γὰρ ἂν ἴσως εἴη ὁ χρόνος. Ἐπισκεπτέον δὲ τὸ παρακολούθημα τοῦτο εἴτε ὕστερον εἴτε ἅμα εἴτε πρότερον, εἴπερ τι ἔστι τοιοῦτον παρακολούθημα· ὅπως γὰρ ἂν λέγηται, ἐν χρόνῳ λέγεται. Εἰ τοῦτο, ἔσται ὁ χρόνος παρακολούθημα κινήσεως ἐν χρόνῳ.

Ἀλλ' ἐπειδὴ οὐ τί μή ἐστι ζητοῦμεν ἀλλὰ τί

possibility that the same number could be both measured and measuring—why should time result from its presence, though when movement exists and, certainly, has a "before" and "after" belonging to it, there will be no time? This is like saying that a magnitude would not be the size it is unless someone understood that it was that size. But again, since time is, and is said to be, unbounded, how could it have a number? Unless, of course, someone took off a piece of it and measured it, but time would be in the piece before it was measured, too. But why can time not exist before the soul which measures it? Unless perhaps one is going to say that it originated from soul. But this is not in any way necessary because of measuring it, for it exists in its full length, even if no one measures it. One might say that the soul is what uses magnitude to measure time; but how could this help us to form the concept of time?

10. As for calling it an accompaniment of movement, this does not explain at all what it is, nor has the statement any content before it is said what this accompanying thing is, for perhaps just this might turn out to be time. But we must consider whether this accompaniment comes after movement, or at the same time as it, or before it—if there is any kind of accompaniment which comes before, for whichever may be said, it is said to be in time. If this is so, time will be an accompaniment of movement in time.

But, since we are not trying to find what time is not

---

[1] μετρῆσαι Kirchhoff, H–S: μετρῆσαν codd.
[2] εἴρηκέ τι Page, H–S[2]: εἰρηκέναι codd.

ἐστιν, εἴρηταί τε πολλὰ πολλοῖς τοῖς πρὸ ἡμῶν καθ' ἑκάστην θέσιν, ἃ εἴ τις διεξίοι, ἱστορίαν μᾶλλον ἂν ποιοῖτο, ὅσον τε ἐξ ἐπιδρομῆς εἴρηταί τι περὶ αὐτῶν, ἔστι δὲ καὶ πρὸς τὸν λέγοντα μέτρον κινήσεως τοῦ παντὸς ἐκ τῶν ἤδη εἰρημένων ἀντιλέγειν τά τε ἄλλα ὅσα νῦν περὶ μέτρου κινήσεως εἴρηται—χωρὶς γὰρ τῆς ἀνωμαλίας πάντα τὰ ἄλλα, ἃ καὶ πρὸς αὐτούς, ἁρμόσει—εἴη ἂν ἀκόλουθον εἰπεῖν, τί ποτε δεῖ νομίζειν τὸν χρόνον εἶναι.

11. Δεῖ δὴ ἀναγαγεῖν ἡμᾶς αὐτοὺς πάλιν εἰς ἐκείνην τὴν διάθεσιν ἣν ἐπὶ τοῦ αἰῶνος ἐλέγομεν εἶναι, τὴν ἀτρεμῆ ἐκείνην καὶ ὁμοῦ πᾶσαν καὶ ἄπειρον ἤδη ζωὴν καὶ ἀκλινῆ πάντῃ καὶ ἐν ἑνὶ καὶ πρὸς ἓν ἑστῶσαν. Χρόνος δὲ οὔπω ἦν, ἢ ἐκείνοις γε οὐκ ἦν, γεννήσομεν δὲ χρόνον λόγῳ καὶ φύσει τοῦ ὑστέρου. Τούτων δὴ οὖν ἡσυχίαν ἀγόντων ἐν αὐτοῖς, ὅπως δὴ πρῶτον ἐξέπεσε χρόνος, τὰς μὲν Μούσας οὔπω τότε οὔσας οὐκ ἄν τις ἴσως καλοῖ εἰπεῖν τοῦτο· ἀλλ' ἴσως, εἴπερ ἦσαν καὶ αἱ Μοῦσαι τότε, αὐτὸν δ' ἄν τις τάχα τὸν γενόμενον χρόνον, ὅπως ἐστὶν ἐκφανεὶς καὶ γενόμενος. Λέγοι δ' ἂν περὶ αὐτοῦ ὧδέ πως· ὡς πρότερον, πρὶν τὸ πρότερον δὴ τοῦτο γεννῆσαι καὶ τοῦ

---

[1] I.e. those who say simply that time is the measure of movement.

[2] One of the most curious examples of adaptation of a Homeric tag to Platonic purposes. In *Iliad* XVI. 112–113 we have

ἔσπετε νῦν μοι, Μοῦσαι Ὀλύμπια δώματ' ἔχουσαι,
ὅππως δὴ πρῶτον πῦρ ἔμπεσε νηυσὶν Ἀχαιῶν.

but what it is, and since a great deal has been said by a great many of our predecessors on every theory of its nature, and if one went through it all one would be making a historical rather than a philosophical enquiry; and since we have already made a cursory survey of some of their arguments, and it is possible from what has been said already to refute the philosopher who says that time is the measure of the movement of the All by using all our arguments about the measure of movement—for apart from the argument from irregularity all the others, which we used against them [1] too, will fit his case—it would be in order to say what one ought to think time is.

11. We must take ourselves back to the disposition which we said existed in eternity, to that quiet life, all a single whole, still unbounded, altogether without declination, resting in and directed towards eternity. Time did not yet exist, not at any rate for the beings of that world; we shall produce time by means of the form and nature of what comes after. If, then, these beings were at rest in themselves, one could hardly, perhaps, call on the Muses, who did not then yet exist, to tell us " how time first came out ": [2] but one might perhaps (even if the Muses did exist then after all) ask time when it has come into being to tell us how it did come into being and appear. It might say something like this about itself; that before, when it had not yet, in fact, produced this

In *Republic* VIII. (545D8E1), Plato, about to describe the decadence of the ideal states, says *ἢ βούλει ὥσπερ Ὅμηρος, εὐχώμεθα ταῖς Μούσαις εἰπεῖν ἡμῖν ὅπως δὴ πρῶτον στάσις ἔμπεσε;* from this, rather than directly from Homer, Plotinus's playful variation is derived.

ὑστέρου δεηθῆναι, σὺν αὐτῷ ἐν τῷ ὄντι ἀνεπαύετο χρόνος οὐκ ὤν, ἀλλ' ἐν ἐκείνῳ καὶ αὐτὸς ἡσυχίαν ἦγε. Φύσεως δὲ πολυπράγμονος καὶ ἄρχειν αὐτῆς βουλομένης καὶ εἶναι αὐτῆς καὶ τὸ πλέον τοῦ παρόντος ζητεῖν ἑλομένης ἐκινήθη μὲν αὐτή, ἐκινήθη δὲ καὶ αὐτός, καὶ εἰς τὸ ἔπειτα ἀεὶ καὶ τὸ ὕστερον καὶ οὐ ταὐτόν, ἀλλ' ἕτερον εἶθ' ἕτερον κινούμενοι, μῆκός τι τῆς πορείας ποιησάμενοι αἰῶνος εἰκόνα τὸν χρόνον εἰργάσμεθα. Ἐπεὶ γὰρ ψυχῆς ἦν τις δύναμις οὐχ ἥσυχος, τὸ δ' ἐκεῖ ὁρώμενον ἀεὶ μεταφέρειν εἰς ἄλλο βουλομένης, τὸ μὲν ἀθρόον αὐτῇ πᾶν παρεῖναι οὐκ ἤθελεν· ὥσπερ δ' ἐκ σπέρματος ἡσύχου ἐξελίττων αὐτὸν ὁ λόγος διέξοδον εἰς πολύ, ὡς οἴεται, ποιεῖ, ἀφανίζων τὸ πολὺ τῷ μερισμῷ, καὶ ἀνθ' ἑνὸς ἐν αὐτῷ οὐκ ἐν αὐτῷ τὸ ἓν δαπανῶν εἰς μῆκος ἀσθενέστερον πρόεισιν, οὕτω δὴ καὶ αὐτὴ κόσμον ποιοῦσα αἰσθητὸν μιμήσει ἐκείνου κινούμενον κίνησιν οὐ τὴν ἐκεῖ, ὁμοίαν δὲ τῇ ἐκεῖ καὶ ἐθέλουσαν εἰκόνα ἐκείνης εἶναι, πρῶτον μὲν ἑαυτὴν ἐχρόνωσεν ἀντὶ τοῦ αἰῶνος τοῦτον ποιήσασα· ἔπειτα δὲ καὶ τῷ γενομένῳ ἔδωκε δουλεύειν χρόνῳ, ἐν χρόνῳ αὐτὸν πάντα ποιήσασα εἶναι, τὰς τούτου διεξόδους ἁπάσας ἐν αὐτῷ περιλαβοῦσα· ἐν ἐκείνῃ γὰρ

---

1 "We," because it is soul which moves and produces time, and we are souls, parts of universal soul and already present in it as it moves out from eternity. This may possibly be the

"before" or felt the need of the "after," it was at rest with eternity in real being; it was not yet time, but itself, too, kept quiet in that. But since there was a restlessly active nature which wanted to control itself and be on its own, and chose to seek for more than its present state, this moved, and time moved with it; and so, always moving on to the "next" and the "after," and what is not the same, but one thing after another, we [1] made a long stretch of our journey and constructed time as an image of eternity. For because soul had an unquiet power, which wanted to keep on transferring what it saw there to something else, it did not want the whole to be present to it all together; and, as from a quiet seed the formative principle, unfolding itself, advances, as it thinks, to largeness, but does away with the largeness by division and, instead of keeping its unity in itself, squanders it outside itself and so goes forward to a weaker extension; [2] in the same way Soul, making the world of sense in imitation of that other world, moving with a motion which is not that which exists There, but like it, and intending to be an image of it, first of all put itself into time, which it made instead of eternity, and then handed over that which came into being as a slave to time, by making the whole of it exist in time and encompassing all its ways with time. For since the world of sense moves in Soul—

significance of the first person in γεννήσομεν above (l. 5); but this may be simply the lecturer's "we."

[2] One of the most vivid expressions in the *Enneads* of the deep and constant conviction of Plotinus that the beginning of a process of development is more perfect than the end, that simplicity, concentration and rest is better than large-scale expansion into a multiplicity of activities.

κινούμενος—οὐ γάρ τις αὐτοῦ τοῦδε τοῦ παντὸς τόπος ἢ[1] ψυχή—καὶ ἐν τῷ ἐκείνης αὖ ἐκινεῖτο χρόνῳ. Τὴν γὰρ ἐνέργειαν αὐτῆς παρεχομένη ἄλλην μετ' ἄλλην, εἶθ' ἑτέραν πάλιν ἐφεξῆς, ἐγέννα τε μετὰ τῆς ἐνεργείας τὸ ἐφεξῆς καὶ συμπροῄει μετὰ διανοίας ἑτέρας μετ' ἐκείνην τὸ μὴ πρότερον ὄν, ὅτι οὐδ' ἡ διάνοια ἐνεργηθεῖσα ἦν οὐδ' ἡ νῦν ζωὴ ὁμοία τῇ πρὸ αὐτῆς. Ἅμα οὖν ζωὴ ἄλλη καὶ τὸ «ἄλλη» χρόνον εἶχεν ἄλλον. Διάστασις οὖν ζωῆς χρόνον εἶχε καὶ τὸ πρόσω ἀεὶ τῆς ζωῆς χρόνον ἔχει ἀεὶ καὶ ἡ παρελθοῦσα ζωὴ χρόνον ἔχει παρεληλυθότα. Εἰ οὖν χρόνον τις λέγοι ψυχῆς ἐν κινήσει μεταβατικῇ ἐξ ἄλλου εἰς ἄλλον βίον ζωὴν εἶναι, ἆρ' ἂν δοκοῖ τι λέγειν; Εἰ γὰρ αἰών ἐστι ζωὴ ἐν στάσει καὶ τῷ αὐτῷ καὶ ὡσαύτως καὶ ἄπειρος ἤδη, εἰκόνα δὲ δεῖ τοῦ αἰῶνος τὸν χρόνον εἶναι, ὥσπερ καὶ τόδε τὸ πᾶν ἔχει πρὸς ἐκεῖνο, ἀντὶ μὲν ζωῆς τῆς ἐκεῖ ἄλλην δεῖ ζωὴν τὴν τῆσδε τῆς δυνάμεως τῆς ψυχῆς ὥσπερ ὁμώνυμον λέγειν εἶναι καὶ ἀντὶ κινήσεως νοερᾶς ψυχῆς τινος μέρους κίνησιν, ἀντὶ δὲ ταὐτότητος καὶ τοῦ ὡσαύτως καὶ μένοντος τὸ μὴ μένον ἐν τῷ αὐτῷ, ἄλλο δὲ καὶ ἄλλο ἐνεργοῦν, ἀντὶ δὲ ἀδιαστάτου καὶ ἑνὸς εἴδωλον τοῦ ἑνὸς τὸ

[1] ἢ Ficinus: ἡ codd.

---

[1] The juxtaposition of *αὐτοῦ* and *τοῦδε τοῦ παντὸς* here is extremely odd. Kirchhoff and Dodds would read *αὐτῷ* (sc. *τῷ Πλάτωνι*) "there is no other place of this universe for Plato than soul," which is an attractive emendation. Alternatively,

there is no other place of it (this universe)[1] than Soul —it moves also in the time of Soul. For as Soul presents one activity after another, and then again another in ordered succession, it produces the succession along with activity, and goes on with another thought coming after that which it had before, to that which did not previously exist because discursive thought was not in action, and Soul's present life is not like that which came before it. So at the same time the life is different and this " different " involves a different time. So the spreading out of life involves time; life's continual progress involves continuity of time, and life which is past involves past time. So would it be sense to say that time is the life of soul in a movement of passage from one way of life to another? Yes, for if eternity is life at rest, unchanging and identical and already unbounded, and time must exist as an image of eternity (in the same relation as that in which this All stands to the intelligible All), then we must say that there is, instead of the life There, another life having, in a way of speaking, the same name as this power of the soul, and instead of intelligible motion that there is the motion of a part of Soul; and, instead of sameness and self-identity and abiding, that which does not abide in the same but does one act after another, and, instead of that which is one without distance or separation, an image of

τοῦδε τοῦ παντός may be bracketed as a gloss. (This was tentatively suggested in H–S², and has now been done by Theiler, with Schwyzer's agreement.) But there remains the possibility that it may be a carelessly added amplification or explanation of αὐτοῦ by Plotinus himself; and therefore, with Henry-Schwyzer, I print and translate the MSS text.

ἐν συνεχείᾳ ἕν, ἀντὶ δὲ ἀπείρου ἤδη καὶ ὅλου τὸ εἰς ἄπειρον πρὸς τὸ ἐφεξῆς ἀεί, ἀντὶ δὲ ἀθρόου ὅλου τὸ κατὰ μέρος ἐσόμενον καὶ ἀεὶ ἐσόμενον ὅλον. Οὕτω γὰρ μιμήσεται τὸ ἤδη ὅλον καὶ ἀθρόον καὶ ἄπειρον ἤδη, εἰ ἐθελήσει ἀεὶ προσκτώμενον εἶναι ἐν τῷ εἶναι· καὶ γὰρ τὸ εἶναι οὕτω τὸ ἐκείνου μιμήσεται. Δεῖ δὲ οὐκ ἔξωθεν τῆς ψυχῆς λαμβάνειν τὸν χρόνον, ὥσπερ οὐδὲ τὸν αἰῶνα ἐκεῖ ἔξω τοῦ ὄντος, οὐδ' αὖ παρακολούθημα οὐδ' ὕστερον, ὥσπερ οὐδ' ἐκεῖ, ἀλλ' ἐνορώμενον καὶ ἐνόντα καὶ συνόντα, ὥσπερ κἀκεῖ ὁ αἰών.

12. Νοῆσαι δὲ δεῖ καὶ ἐντεῦθεν, ὡς ἡ φύσις αὕτη χρόνος, τὸ τοιούτου μῆκος βίου ἐν μεταβολαῖς προϊὸν ὁμαλαῖς τε καὶ ὁμοίαις ἀψοφητὶ προϊούσαις, συνεχὲς τὸ τῆς ἐνεργείας ἔχον. Εἰ δὴ πάλιν τῷ λόγῳ ἀναστρέψαι ποιήσαιμεν τὴν δύναμιν ταύτην καὶ παύσαιμεν τοῦδε τοῦ βίου, ὃν νῦν ἔχει ἄπαυστον ὄντα καὶ οὔποτε λήξοντα, ὅτι ψυχῆς τινος ἀεὶ οὔσης ἐστὶν ἐνέργεια, οὐ πρὸς αὐτὴν οὐδ' ἐν αὐτῇ, ἀλλ' ἐν ποιήσει καὶ γενέσει—εἰ οὖν ὑποθοίμεθα μηκέτι ἐνεργοῦσαν, ἀλλὰ παυσαμένην ταύτην τὴν ἐνέργειαν καὶ ἐπιστραφὲν καὶ τοῦτο τὸ μέρος τῆς ψυχῆς πρὸς τὸ ἐκεῖ καὶ τὸν αἰῶνα καὶ ἐν ἡσυχίᾳ μένον, τί ἂν ἔτι μετὰ αἰῶνα εἴη; Τί δ' ἂν ἄλλο καὶ ἄλλο πάντων ἐν ἑνὶ μεινάντων; Τί δ' ἂν ἔτι πρότερον; Τί δ' ἂν ὕστερον ἢ μέλλον;[1] Ποῦ δ'

[1] μέλλον Page, H–S: μᾶλλον codd.

unity, that which is one in continuity; and instead of a complete unbounded whole, a continuous unbounded succession, and instead of a whole all together a whole which is, and always will be, going to come into being part by part. For this is the way in which it will imitate that which is already a whole, already all together and unbounded, by intending to be always making an increase in its being, for this is how its being will imitate the being of the intelligible world. But one must not conceive time as outside Soul, any more than eternity There as outside real being. It is not an accompaniment of Soul nor something that comes after (any more than eternity There) but something which is seen along with it and exists in it and with it, as eternity does There [with real being].

12. We must understand, too, from this that this nature is time, the extent of life of this kind which goes forward in even and uniform changes progressing quietly, and which possesses continuity of activity. Now if in our thought we were to make this power turn back again, and put a stop to this life which it now has without stop and never-ending, because it is the activity of an always existing soul, whose activity is not directed to itself or in itself, but lies in making and production—if, then we were to suppose that it was no longer active, but stopped this activity, and that this part of the soul turned back to the intelligible world and to eternity, and rested quietly there, what would there still be except eternity? What would " one thing after another " mean when all things remained in unity? What sense would " before " still have, and what " after " or " future "? Where could the soul now fix its

ἂν ἔτι ψυχὴ ἐπιβάλλοι εἰς ἄλλο ἢ ἐν ᾧ ἐστι; Μᾶλλον δὲ οὐδὲ τούτῳ· ἀφεστήκοι γὰρ ἂν πρότερον, ἵνα ἐπιβάλῃ. Ἐπεὶ οὐδ᾽ ἂν ἡ σφαῖρα αὐτὴ εἴη, ἣ οὐ πρώτως ὑπάρχει· [χρόνος][1] ἐν χρόνῳ γὰρ καὶ αὕτη καὶ ἔστι καὶ κινεῖται, κἂν στῇ, ἐκείνης ἐνεργούσης, ὅση ἡ στάσις αὐτῆς, μετρήσομεν, ἕως ἐκείνη τοῦ αἰῶνός ἐστιν ἔξω. Εἰ οὖν ἀποστάσης ἐκείνης καὶ ἑνωθείσης ἀνῄρηται χρόνος, δῆλον ὅτι ἡ ταύτης ἀρχὴ πρὸς ταῦτα κινήσεως καὶ οὗτος ὁ βίος τὸν χρόνον γεννᾷ. Διὸ καὶ εἴρηται ἅμα τῷδε τῷ παντὶ γεγονέναι, ὅτι ψυχὴ αὐτὸν μετὰ τοῦδε τοῦ παντὸς ἐγέννησεν. Ἐν γὰρ τῇ τοιαύτῃ ἐνεργείᾳ καὶ τόδε γεγένηται τὸ πᾶν· καὶ ἡ μὲν χρόνος, ὁ δὲ ἐν χρόνῳ. Εἰ δέ τις λέγοι χρόνους λέγεσθαι αὐτῷ καὶ τὰς τῶν ἄστρων φορὰς, ἀναμνησθήτω, ὅτι ταῦτά φησι γεγονέναι πρὸς δήλωσιν καὶ διορισμὸν χρόνου καὶ τὸ ἵνα ᾖ μέτρον ἐναργές. Ἐπεὶ γὰρ οὐκ ἦν τὸν χρόνον αὐτὸν τῇ ψυχῇ ὁρίσαι οὐδὲ μετρεῖν παρ᾽ αὐτοῖς ἕκαστον αὐτοῦ μέρος ἀοράτου ὄντος καὶ οὐ ληπτοῦ καὶ μάλιστα ἀριθμεῖν οὐκ εἰδόσιν, ἡμέραν καὶ νύκτα ποιεῖ, δι᾽ ὧν ἦν δύο τῇ ἑτερότητι λαβεῖν, ἀφ᾽ οὗ ἔννοιά, φησιν, ἀριθμοῦ. Εἶθ᾽ ὅσον τὸ ἀπ᾽ ἀνατολῆς εἰς τὸ πάλιν λαμβάνουσιν ἦν ὅσον χρόνου διάστημα, ὁμαλοῦ ὄντος τοῦ τῆς κινήσεως εἴδους ὅτῳ ἐπερειδόμεθα, ἔχειν καὶ οἷον μέτρῳ

[1] χρόνος del. H–S.

---

[1] Cp. *Timaeus* 38B6. [2] Cp. *Timaeus* 38C6.
[3] Cp. *Timaeus* 39B2. [4] Cp. *Epinomis* 978D1–6.

gaze on something other than that in which it is? Rather, it could not even fix its gaze on this, for it would have to stand away from it first in order to do so. For the heavenly sphere itself would not be there, since its existence is not primary, for it exists and moves in time, and, if it comes to a stop we shall measure the duration of its stop by the activity of soul, as long as soul is outside eternity. If, then, when soul leaves this activity and returns to unity time is abolished, it is clear that the beginning of this movement in this direction, and this form of the life of soul, generates time. This is why it is said that time came into existence simultaneously with this universe,[1] because soul generated it along with this universe. For it is in activity of this kind that this universe has come into being; and the activity is time and the universe is in time. But if someone wants to say that Plato also calls the courses of the stars " times " he should remember that he says that they have come into existence for the declaring and " division of time,"[2] and his " that there might be an obvious measure."[3] For since it was not possible for the soul to delimit time itself, or for men by themselves to measure each part of it since it was invisible and ungraspable, particularly as they did not know how to count, the god made day and night, by means of which, in virtue of their difference, it was possible to grasp the idea of two, and from this Plato says, came the concept of number.[4] Then, by taking the length of the interval between one sunrise and the next, since the kind of movement on which we base our calculations is even, we can have an interval of time of a certain length, and we use this kind of

χρώμεθα τῷ τοιούτῳ· μέτρῳ δὲ τοῦ χρόνου· οὐ γὰρ ὁ χρόνος αὐτὸς μέτρον. Πῶς γὰρ ἂν καὶ μετροῖ καὶ τί ἂν λέγοι μετρῶν τοσοῦτον εἶναι, ὅσον ἐγὼ τοσόνδε; Τίς οὖν ὁ «ἐγώ»; Ἢ καθ' ὃν ἡ μέτρησις. Οὐκοῦν ὤν, ἵνα μετρῇ, καὶ μὴ μέτρον; Ἡ οὖν κίνησις ἡ τοῦ παντὸς μετρουμένη κατὰ χρόνον ἔσται, καὶ ὁ χρόνος οὐ μέτρον ἔσται κινήσεως κατὰ τὸ τί ἐστιν, ἀλλὰ κατὰ συμβεβηκὸς ὢν ἄλλο τι πρότερον παρέξει δήλωσιν τοῦ ὁπόση ἡ κίνησις. Καὶ ἡ κίνησις δὲ ληφθεῖσα ἡ μία ἐν τοσῷδε χρόνῳ πολλάκις ἀριθμουμένη εἰς ἔννοιαν ἄξει τοῦ ὁπόσος παρελήλυθεν· ὥστε τὴν κίνησιν καὶ τὴν περιφορὰν εἴ τις λέγοι τρόπον τινὰ μετρεῖν τὸν χρόνον, ὅσον οἷόν τε, ὡς δηλοῦσαν ἐν τῷ αὐτῆς τοσῷδε τὸ τοσόνδε τοῦ χρόνου, οὐκ ὂν λαβεῖν οὐδὲ συνεῖναι ἄλλως, οὐκ ἄτοπος τῆς δηλώσεως. Τὸ οὖν μετρούμενον ὑπὸ τῆς περιφορᾶς—τοῦτο δέ ἐστι τὸ δηλούμενον—ὁ χρόνος ἔσται, οὐ γεννηθεὶς ὑπὸ τῆς περιφορᾶς, ἀλλὰ δηλωθείς· καὶ οὕτω τὸ μέτρον τῆς κινήσεως τὸ μετρηθὲν ὑπὸ κινήσεως ὡρισμένης, καὶ μετρούμενον ὑπὸ ταύτης ἄλλο ὂν αὐτῆς· ἐπεὶ καὶ εἰ μετροῦν ἄλλο ἦν, καὶ ᾗ [1] μετρούμενον ἕτερον, μετρούμενον δὲ κατὰ [2] συμβεβηκός. Καὶ οὕτως ἂν ἐλέγετο, ὡς εἰ τὸ μετρούμενον ὑπὸ πήχεως λέγοι

[1] ᾗ Kirchhoff, H–S²: εἰ codd.
[2] κατὰ Kirchhoff, H–S²: καὶ codd.

interval as a measure;[1] but a measure of time, for time itself is not a measure. For how could it measure, and what could it say while it was measuring? "This is as large as such and such a part of myself?" Who, then, is the "I" here? Presumably, that by which the measuring is being done. Then surely, if it is going to measure, it is not a measure? So, then, it will be the movement of the universe which will be measured by time, and time will not be a measure of movement essentially, but it will incidentally, being something else first, afford a clear indication of how long the movement is. And by taking one movement in a certain length of time and counting it again and again we shall arrive at an idea of how much time has passed; so that if one were to say that the movement and the heavenly circuit in a way measure time, as far as possible, in that the circuit shows by its extent the extent of time, which it would not be possible to grasp or understand otherwise, his explanation would not be out of place. So what is measured by the circuit—that is, what is shown—will be time, which is not produced by the circuit but manifested; and so the measure of motion is that which is measured by a limited motion, and since it is measured by this, is other than it, since, even if it was measuring it would be something else, and in so far as it is measured it is different (but it is [only] measured incidentally). This would have the same meaning as if one said that what is measured

[1] Here Plotinus uses some observations of Aristotle on the way in which, in fact, we measure time as the basis of an argument against Aristotle's own definition of time: cp. *Physics* Δ 12. 220b13–221a9.

τις τὸ μέγεθος εἶναι ὅ τί ποτ᾽ ἐστὶν ἐκεῖνο μὴ λέγων, μέγεθος ὁριζόμενος, καὶ οἷον εἴ τις τὴν κίνησιν αὐτὴν οὐ δυνάμενος τῷ ἀόριστον εἶναι δηλῶσαι λέγοι τὸ μετρούμενον ὑπὸ τόπου· λαβὼν γὰρ τόπον τις, ὃν ἐπεξῆλθεν ἡ κίνησις, τοσαύτην ἂν εἶπεν εἶναι, ὅσος ὁ τόπος.

13. Χρόνον οὖν ἡ περιφορὰ δηλοῖ, ἐν ᾧ αὕτη. Δεῖ δὲ αὐτὸν χρόνον μηκέτι τὸ ἐν ᾧ ἔχειν, ἀλλὰ πρῶτον αὐτὸν εἶναι ὅς ἐστιν, ἐν ᾧ τὰ ἄλλα κινεῖται καὶ ἕστηκεν ὁμαλῶς καὶ τεταγμένως, καὶ παρὰ μέν τινος τεταγμένου ἐμφαίνεσθαι καὶ προφαίνεσθαι εἰς ἔννοιαν, οὐ μέντοι γίνεσθαι, εἴτε ἑστῶτος εἴτε κινουμένου, μᾶλλον μέντοι κινουμένου· μᾶλλον γὰρ κινεῖ εἰς γνώρισιν καὶ μετάβασιν ἐπὶ τὸν χρόνον ἡ κίνησις ἤπερ ἡ στάσις καὶ γνωριμώτερον τὸ ὁπόσον κεκίνηταί τι ἢ ὅσον ἕστηκε. Διὸ καὶ κινήσεως ἠνέχθησαν εἰς τὸ εἰπεῖν μέτρον ἀντὶ τοῦ εἰπεῖν κινήσει μετρούμενον, εἶτα προσθεῖναι τί ὂν κινήσει μετρεῖται καὶ μὴ κατὰ συμβεβηκὸς γινόμενον περί τι αὐτοῦ εἰπεῖν καὶ ταῦτα ἐνηλλαγμένως. Ἀλλ᾽ ἴσως ἐκεῖνοι οὐκ ἐνηλλαγμένως, ἡμεῖς δὲ οὐ συνίεμεν, ἀλλὰ σαφῶς λεγόντων μέτρον κατὰ τὸ μετρούμενον οὐκ ἐτυγχάνομεν τῆς ἐκείνων γνώμης. Αἴτιον δὲ τοῦ μὴ συνιέναι ἡμᾶς, ὅτι τί ὂν εἴτε μετροῦν εἴτε μετρούμενον οὐκ ἐδήλουν[1] διὰ τῶν συγγραμμάτων

[1] ἐδήλουν H–S: ἐκδηλοῦν A^{ac}Exy: ἐκδηλοῦσι A^{pc}.

by a cubit was the length, not saying what length was in itself but simply determining how long it was, and if one was not able to explain what movement itself was because of its indefiniteness and said it was what is measured by space, for one could take a space through which the movement went and say that the movement was as long as the space.

13. The heavenly circuit, therefore, shows time, in which it is. But time itself cannot have something in which it is, but it must first of all be itself what it is, that in which the other things move and stand still evenly and regularly; it can be manifested to us by something set in order, and exhibited to our minds so that we form a concept of it, but it cannot be brought into existence by the ordered thing, whether it is at rest or in motion; but a thing in motion will give a better idea of it, for motion more effectively moves our minds to get to know time and to form a concept of it by analogy than rest, and it is easier to know how long something has been moving than how long it has stood still. This is why people were brought to call time the measure of movement, instead of saying that it was measured by movement and then adding what it is that is measured by movement, and not only mentioning something which applies incidentally to a part of it, and getting that the wrong way round. But perhaps they did not get it the wrong way round but we do not understand them, but, when they clearly meant " measure " in the sense of " what is measured," we missed the point of their thought. The reason why we do not understand is that they did not make clear what it is that either measures or is measured in their

ὡς εἰδόσι καὶ ἠκροαμένοις αὐτῶν γράφοντες. Ὁ μέντοι Πλάτων οὔτε μετροῦν εἴρηκεν οὔτε μετρούμενον ὑπό τινος τὴν οὐσίαν αὐτοῦ εἶναι, ἀλλὰ εἰς δήλωσιν αὐτοῦ τὴν περιφορὰν ἐλάχιστόν τι εἰλῆφθαι πρὸς ἐλάχιστον αὐτοῦ μέρος, ὡς ἐντεῦθεν γινώσκειν δύνασθαι, οἷον καὶ ὅσον ὁ χρόνος. Τὴν μέντοι οὐσίαν αὐτοῦ δηλῶσαι θέλων ἅμα οὐρανῷ φησι γεγονέναι κατὰ[1] παράδειγμα αἰῶνος καὶ εἰκόνα κινητήν, ὅτι μὴ μένει μηδ᾽ ὁ χρόνος τῆς ζωῆς οὐ μενούσης, ᾗ συνθεῖ καὶ συντρέχει· ἅμα οὐρανῷ δέ, ὅτι ζωὴ ἡ τοιαύτη καὶ τὸν οὐρανὸν ποιεῖ καὶ μία ζωὴ οὐρανὸν καὶ χρόνον ἐργάζεται. Ἐπιστραφείσης οὖν ζωῆς ταύτης εἰς ἕν, εἰ δύναιτο, ὁμοῦ καὶ χρόνος πέπαυται ἐν τῇ ζωῇ ὢν ταύτῃ καὶ οὐρανὸς τὴν ζωὴν ταύτην οὐκ ἔχων. Εἰ δέ τις τῆσδε μὲν τῆς κινήσεως τὸ πρότερον καὶ τὸ ὕστερον λαμβάνων χρόνον λέγοι—εἶναι γάρ τι τοῦτο—τῆς δ᾽ ἀληθεστέρας κινήσεως τὸ πρότερον καὶ τὸ ὕστερον ἐχούσης μὴ λέγοι τι εἶναι, ἀτοπώτατος ἂν εἴη, κινήσει μὲν ἀψύχῳ διδοὺς ἔχειν τὸ πρότερον καὶ ὕστερον καὶ χρόνον παρ᾽ αὐτήν, κινήσει δέ, καθ᾽ ἣν καὶ αὕτη ὑφέστηκε κατὰ μίμησιν, μὴ διδοὺς τοῦτο, παρ᾽ ἧς καὶ τὸ πρότερον καὶ τὸ ὕστερον πρώτως ὑπέστη αὐτουργοῦ οὔσης κινήσεως καὶ ὥσπερ τὰς ἐνεργείας αὐτῆς ἑκάστας

[1] κατὰ Kirchhoff, H–S²: καὶ codd.

---

[1] Cp. *Timaeus* 39B–C.

writings, since they were writing for those who knew and had heard their lectures. Plato, however, has neither described the essential nature of time as measuring nor as measured by something else, but has said that, to show time, the heavenly circuit has put a least part of itself in relation with a least part of time, so that from this we can come to know the quality and quantity of time.[1] But when he wants to declare its essential nature he says that it came into existence along with heaven according to the pattern of eternity,[2] and as its moving image,[3] because time does not stand still since the life with which it keeps pace in its course does not stand still; it comes into existence with heaven because this kind of life makes heaven, too, and one life produces heaven and time. So when this life—if it could—turned back to unity, time would come to a stop with it, since it exists in this life, and so would heaven, if it did not have this life. But if someone were to take the " before " and " after " of this movement here and call it time—on the ground that this is something real—but though the truer movement [of soul] has a " before " and " after," were to deny this any reality, he would be quite unreasonable, in that he would be granting that soulless movement has " before " and " after " and time accompanying it, but denying this to the movement in imitation of which this [soulless] movement has come into existence, to the movement from which " before " and " after " first came into existence, since it is spontaneous and, as it generates its own individual activities,

[2] *Timaeus* 38B6–C2.
[3] *Timaeus* 37D4–C7.

γεννώσης, οὕτω καὶ τὸ ἐφεξῆς, καὶ ἅμα τῇ γεννήσει καὶ τὴν μετάβασιν αὐτῶν. Διὰ τί οὖν ταύτην μὲν τὴν κίνησιν τὴν τοῦ παντὸς ἀνάγομεν εἰς περιοχὴν ἐκείνης καὶ ἐν χρόνῳ φαμέν, οὐχὶ δέ γε καὶ τὴν τῆς ψυχῆς κίνησιν τὴν ἐν αὐτῇ ἐν διεξόδῳ οὖσαν ἀιδίῳ; Ἢ ὅτι τὸ πρὸ ταύτης ἐστὶν αἰὼν οὐ συμπαραθέων οὐδὲ συμπαρατείνων αὐτῇ. Πρώτη οὖν αὕτη εἰς χρόνον καὶ χρόνον ἐγέννησε καὶ σὺν τῇ ἐνεργείᾳ αὐτῆς ἔχει. Πῶς οὖν πανταχοῦ; Ὅτι κἀκείνη οὐδενὸς ἀφέστηκε τοῦ κόσμου μέρους, ὥσπερ οὐδ' ἡ ἐν ἡμῖν οὐδενὸς ἡμῶν[1] μέρους. Εἰ δέ τις ἐν οὐχ ὑποστάσει ἢ ἐν οὐχ ὑπάρξει τὸν χρόνον λέγοι, δηλονότι ψεύδεσθαι καταθετέον,[2] ὅταν λέγῃ « ἦν » καὶ « ἔσται »· οὕτω γὰρ ἔσται καὶ ἦν, ὡς τὸ ἐν ᾧ λέγει αὐτὸν ἔσεσθαι. Ἀλλὰ πρὸς τοὺς τοιούτους ἄλλος τρόπος λόγων. Ἐκεῖνο δὲ ἐνθυμεῖσθαι δεῖ πρὸς ἅπασι τοῖς εἰρημένοις, ὡς, ὅταν τις τὸν κινούμενον ἄνθρωπον λαμβάνῃ ὅσον προελήλυθε,[3] καὶ τὴν κίνησιν λαμβάνει ὅση, καὶ ὅταν τὴν κίνησιν οἷον τὴν διὰ σκελῶν, ὁράτω[4] καὶ τὸ πρὸ τῆς κινήσεως ταύτης ἐν αὐτῷ κίνημα ὅτι τοσοῦτον ἦν, εἴ γε ἐπὶ τοσοῦτον συνεῖχε τὴν κίνησιν τοῦ σώματος. Τὸ μὲν δὴ σῶμα τὸ κινούμενον τὸν τοσόνδε χρόνον ἀνάξει ἐπὶ τὴν κίνησιν τὴν τοσήνδε—αὕτη γὰρ αἰτία—καὶ τὸν χρόνον ταύτης, ταύτην δὲ ἐπὶ τὴν

[1] ἡμῶν Kirchhoff, H–S²: ἡμῖν wBJy: om.R.
[2] καταθετέον nunc Schwyzer: καὶ τὸ θεὸν αὐτὸν codd, H–S.
[3] προελήλυθε Kirchhoff, H–S²: προσελήλυθε codd.
[4] ὁράτω Dodds, H–S²: ὁρᾷ τῷ codd.

so it generates their succession, and, along with their generation, the transition from one of them to another. Why, then, do we trace back the origin of this movement of the All to that which encompasses it, and say that it is in time, but do not say that the movement of soul, which goes on in it in everlasting progression, is in time? It is because what is before the movement of soul is eternity, which does not run along with it or stretch out with it. This movement of soul was the first to enter time, and generated time, and possesses it along with its own activity. How, then, is time everywhere? Because Soul, too, is not absent from any part of the Universe, just as the soul in us is not absent from any part of us. But if someone were to say that time is in something insubstantial or unreal, it must be stated that he is telling an untruth whenever he says that he "was" or "will be"; for he "will be" and "was" in the same sense as that in which he says he "will be." But against people like this we need another style of argument.

But, besides all that has been said, one must consider this further point, that, when one observes the distance that a moving man has advanced, he also observes the quantity of his movement, and when he observes the movement, for instance, made by his legs, let him notice also that the movement in the man himself which preceded this movement was of a certain quantity, on the assumption that he kept the movement of his body within certain limits. Now the body moved for a certain time will take us back to a certain extent—for this is the cause—and its time, and this to the movement of the soul, which is

τῆς ψυχῆς κίνησιν, ἥτις τὰ ἴσα διειστήκει. Τὴν οὖν κίνησιν τῆς ψυχῆς εἰς τί; Εἰς ὃ γὰρ ἐθελήσει, ἀδιάστατον ἤδη. Τοῦτο τοίνυν τὸ πρώτως καὶ τὸ ἐν ᾧ τὰ ἄλλα· αὐτὸ δὲ οὐκέτι ἔν τῳ·[1] οὐ γὰρ ἕξει [τοῦτο τοίνυν τὸ πρώτως].[2] Καὶ ἐπὶ τῆς ψυχῆς τοῦ παντὸς ὡσαύτως. Ἆρ' οὖν καὶ ἐν ἡμῖν χρόνος; Ἢ ἐν ψυχῇ τῇ τοιαύτῃ πάσῃ καὶ ὁμοειδῶς ἐν πάσῃ καὶ αἱ πᾶσαι μία. Διὸ οὐ διασπασθήσεται ὁ χρόνος· ἐπεὶ οὐδ' ὁ αἰὼν ὁ κατ' ἄλλο ἐν τοῖς ὁμοειδέσι πᾶσιν.

[1] ἔν τῳ Dodds, H–S²: ἐν ᾧ codd.
[2] τοῦτο . . . πρώτως del. Kirchhoff, H–S.

divided into equal intervals. To what, then, will the movement of soul take us back? For that to which one will want to take it back is already without intervals. This, then [the movement of soul] is that which exists primarily and in which the others are; but it is not any more in anything, for it will have nothing to be in. And the same is true also of the Soul of the All. Is time, then, also in us? It is in every soul of this kind, and in the same form in every one of them, and all are one. So time will not be split up, any more than eternity, which, in a different way, is in all the [eternal] beings of the same form.

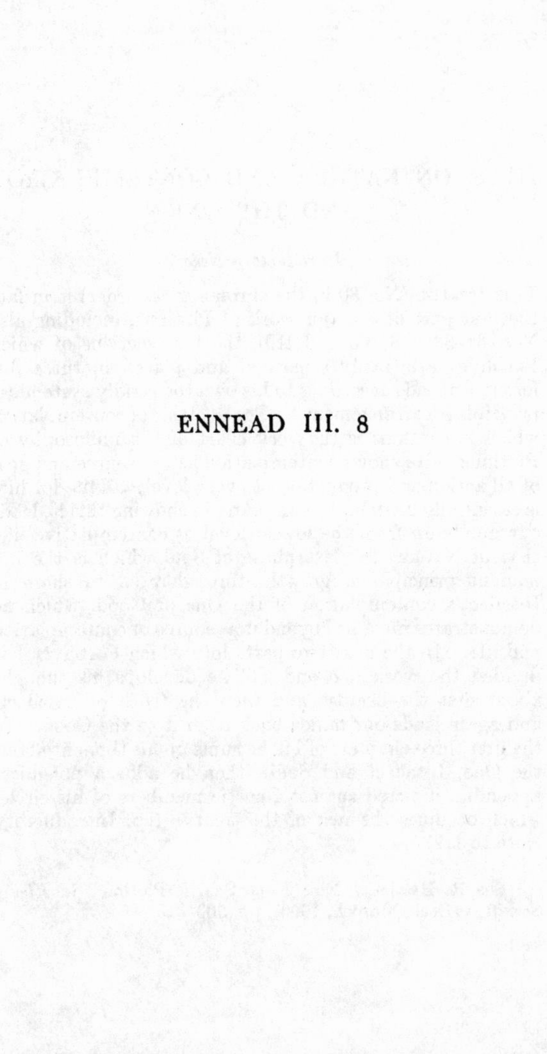

ENNEAD III. 8

III. 8. ON NATURE AND CONTEMPLATION AND THE ONE

Introductory Note

THIS treatise (No. 30 in the chronological order) is in fact the first part of a major work of Plotinus, including also Nos. 31–33 (V8, V5 and II9), the four sections of which Porphyry arbitrarily separated and placed in three different Enneads according to his own too rigidly systematic principles of arrangement.[1] The doctrine of contemplation which it contains is the very heart of the philosophy of Plotinus. He shows contemplation as the source and goal of all action and production at every level: all life for him is essentially contemplation. And in showing this he leads our minds up from the lowest level of contemplative life, that of Nature, the last phase of Soul which is the immanent principle of growth, through Soul to share in Intellect's contemplation of the One or Good, which he demonstrates must lie beyond it as source of contemplation and life. In the next two parts into which Porphyry has divided the work (V8 and V5) he develops his thought about first the beauty, and then the truth of Intellect, and again leads our minds back from it to the Good. In the first three chapters of II9 he sums up his thought about the One, Intellect and Soul; then he adds a polemical appendix, directed against Gnostic members of his circle, which occupies the rest of the treatise (cp. Introductory Note to II9).

[1] See R. Harder, "Eine Neue Schrift Plotins" in *Kleine Schriften* (Beck, Munich, 1960), pp. 303–313.

ON NATURE AND CONTEMPLATION

Synopsis

Let us play with the idea that all things contemplate, even plants and the earth from which they grow (ch. 1). How Nature makes things, and how contemplation underlies its making (chs. 2–3). Plotinus makes Nature speak and comments on what it says, showing how its dreamlike contemplation is the last and weakest, and how weak contemplation leads to action (ch. 4). Contemplation, action and production on the level of Soul, and in human life (chs. 5–6). Contemplation is always the goal of action (ch. 7). The perfect identity of contemplation and object contemplated in Intellect; all life is a kind of thought and the truest life is the truest thought, that of Intellect (ch. 8). Why Intellect is many and not one, and being many cannot be the first, but must have something beyond it, the absolutely simple Good, which we know by immediate awareness of its presence to us (chs. 8–9). The Good is the one productive power of all things (ch. 10). Intellect needs the Good, always desiring it and always attaining; but the Good needs nothing (ch. 11).

III. 8. (30) ΠΕΡΙ ΦΥΣΕΩΣ ΚΑΙ ΘΕΩΡΙΑΣ ΚΑΙ ΤΟΥ ΕΝΟΣ

1. Παίζοντες δὴ τὴν πρώτην πρὶν ἐπιχειρεῖν σπουδάζειν εἰ λέγοιμεν πάντα θεωρίας ἐφίεσθαι καὶ εἰς τέλος τοῦτο βλέπειν, οὐ μόνον ἔλλογα ἀλλὰ καὶ ἄλογα ζῷα καὶ τὴν ἐν φυτοῖς φύσιν καὶ τὴν ταῦτα γεννῶσαν γῆν, καὶ πάντα τυγχάνειν καθ' ὅσον οἷόν τε αὐτοῖς κατὰ φύσιν ἔχοντα, ἄλλα δὲ ἄλλως καὶ θεωρεῖν καὶ τυγχάνειν καὶ τὰ μὲν ἀληθῶς, τὰ δὲ μίμησιν καὶ εἰκόνα τούτου λαμβάνοντα—ἆρ' ἄν τις ἀνάσχοιτο τὸ παράδοξον τοῦ λόγου; Ἢ πρὸς ἡμᾶς αὐτοῦ γινομένου κίνδυνος οὐδεὶς ἐν τῷ παίζειν τὰ αὐτῶν γενήσεται. Ἆρ' οὖν καὶ ἡμεῖς παίζοντες ἐν τῷ παρόντι θεωροῦμεν; Ἢ καὶ ἡμεῖς καὶ πάντες ὅσοι παίζουσι τοῦτο ποιοῦσιν ἢ τούτου[1] γε παίζουσιν ἐφιέμενοι. Καὶ κινδυνεύει, εἴτε τις παῖς εἴτε ἀνὴρ παίζει ἢ σπου-

[1] ἢ τούτου H–S²: ἢ τοῦτο A^{ac}Exy: καὶ τούτου Ficinus, A^{pc}.

---

[1] Perhaps there is a reminiscence in this introduction of Plato, *Laws* IV. 712B1–2 (where the old gentlemen imagining their city are called παῖδες πρεσβῦται), and VII 803C–D (where man is a plaything of god and his highest and most serious activity is to play before him: for another reminiscence of this passage, see III. 2[47]15). In any case, the tone of humorous half-apology in which a doctrine which Plotinus

III. 8. ON NATURE AND CONTEMPLATION AND THE ONE

1. Suppose we said, playing [1] at first before we set out to be serious, that all things aspire to contemplation, and direct their gaze to this end—not only rational but irrational living things,[2] and the power of growth in plants, and the earth which brings them forth—and that all attain to it as far as possible for them in their natural state, but different things contemplate and attain their end in different ways, some truly, and some only having an imitation and image of this true end—could anyone endure the oddity of this line of thought? Well, as this discussion has arisen among ourselves, there will be no risk in playing with our own ideas. Then are we now contemplating as we play? Yes, we and all who play are doing this, or at any rate this is what they aspire to as they play. And it is likely that, whether a child or a man is playing or being serious, one plays and

takes extremely seriously is introduced is entirely in the spirit of Plato.

[2] Cp. Aristotle, *Nicomachean Ethics* K.2 1172b10 (Eudoxus thought that pleasure was the good because all things, rational and irrational, aspired to it). Plotinus is taking Aristotle's conception of *θεωρία* (K.6 and K.7) as the starting-point of his discussion, and is perhaps deliberately indicating by this phrase that his own conception of it is much more universal than Aristotle's.

δάζει, θεωρίας ἕνεκεν ὁ μὲν παίζειν, ὁ δὲ σπουδάζειν, καὶ πρᾶξις πᾶσα εἰς θεωρίαν τὴν σπουδὴν ἔχειν, ἡ μὲν ἀναγκαία καὶ ἐπιπλέον τὴν θεωρίαν ἕλκουσα πρὸς τὸ ἔξω, ἡ δὲ ἑκούσιος λεγομένη ἐπ᾽ ἔλαττον μέν, ὅμως δὲ καὶ αὕτη ἐφέσει θεωρίας γινομένη. Ἀλλὰ ταῦτα μὲν ὕστερον· νῦν δὲ λέγωμεν περί τε γῆς αὐτῆς καὶ δένδρων καὶ ὅλως φυτῶν τίς αὐτῶν ἡ θεωρία, καὶ πῶς τὰ παρ᾽ αὐτῆς ποιούμενα καὶ γεννώμενα ἐπὶ τὴν τῆς θεωρίας ἀνάξομεν ἐνέργειαν, καὶ πῶς ἡ φύσις, ἥν ἀφάνταστόν φασι καὶ ἄλογον εἶναι, θεωρίαν τε ἐν αὐτῇ ἔχει καὶ ἃ ποιεῖ διὰ θεωρίαν ποιεῖ, ἣν οὐκ ἔχει, [καὶ πῶς].[1]

2. Ὅτι μὲν οὖν οὔτε χεῖρες ἐνταῦθα οὔτε πόδες οὔτε τι ὄργανον ἐπακτὸν ἢ σύμφυτον, ὕλης δὲ δεῖ, ἐφ᾽ ἧς ποιήσει, καὶ ἣν ἐνειδοποιεῖ,[2] παντί που δῆλον. Δεῖ δὲ καὶ τὸ μοχλεύειν ἀφελεῖν ἐκ τῆς φυσικῆς ποιήσεως. Ποῖος γὰρ ὠθισμὸς ἢ τίς μοχλεία χρώματα ποικίλα καὶ παντοδαπὰ καὶ σχήματα ποιεῖ; Ἐπεὶ οὐδὲ οἱ κηροπλάσται [ἢ κοροπλάθαι],[3] εἰς οὓς δὴ καὶ βλέποντες ᾠήθησαν τὴν τῆς φύσεως δημιουργίαν τοιαύτην εἶναι,

1 καὶ πῶς del. Müller, H–S^2.
2 ἐνειδοποιεῖ nunc Henry et Schwyzer: ἐν εἴδει ποιεῖ codd, H–S.
3 ἢ κοροπλάθαι del. Müller, H–S^2.

---

1 The Stoics used the terms φύσις ἀφάνταστος and νοερὰ φύσις to distinguish between "nature" in the sense of the Aristotelian growth-principle and in their own sense of the all-pervading divine reason: cp. *Stoic. Vet. Fragm.* II. 1016.

the other is serious for the sake of contemplation, and every action is a serious effort towards contemplation; compulsory action drags contemplation more towards the outer world, and what we call voluntary, less, but, all the same, voluntary action, too, springs from the desire of contemplation. But we will discuss this later: but now let us talk about the earth itself, and trees, and plants in general, and ask what their contemplation is, and how we can relate what the earth makes and produces to its activity of contemplation, and how nature, which people say has no power of forming mental images [1] or reasoning, has contemplation in itself and makes what it makes by contemplation, which it does not have.

2. Well, then, it is clear, I suppose, to everyone that there are no hands here or feet, and no instrument either acquired or of natural growth, but there is need of matter on which nature can work and which it forms. But we must also exclude levering from the operation of nature. For what kind of thrusting or levering can produce this rich variety of colours and shapes of every kind? [2] For the wax-modellers—people have actually looked at them and thought that nature's workmanship was like

[2] Cp. V. 8 [31] 7. 10–11, and V. 9 [5] 6. 22, 23. It is part of Plotinus's consistent effort to eliminate materialistic and spatial conceptions from our ideas of spiritual existence and activity that he insists frequently that soul and nature are not to be thought of as forming the material world with hands and tools and machines. He seems to have in mind the sort of crude Epicurean criticism of Plato which we find in Cicero *De Natura Deorum* I. 8.19 *quae molitio? quae ferramenta? qui vectes? quae machinae?*

χρώματα δύνανται ποιεῖν μὴ χρώματα ἀλλαχόθεν ἐπάγοντες οἷς ποιοῦσιν. Ἀλλὰ γὰρ ἐχρῆν συννοοῦντας, ὡς καὶ ἐπὶ τῶν τὰς τέχνας τὰς τοιαύτας μετιόντων, [ὅτι][1] δεῖ τι ἐν αὐτοῖς μένειν, καθ' ὃ μένον διὰ χειρῶν ποιήσουσιν ἃ αὐτῶν ἔργα, ἐπὶ τὸ τοιοῦτον ἀνελθεῖν τῆς φύσεως καὶ αὐτοὺς καὶ συνεῖναι, ὡς μένειν δεῖ καὶ ἐνταῦθα τὴν δύναμιν τὴν οὐ διὰ χειρῶν ποιοῦσαν καὶ πᾶσαν μένειν. Οὐ γὰρ δὴ δεῖται τῶν μὲν ὡς μενόντων, τῶν δὲ ὡς κινουμένων—ἡ γὰρ ὕλη τὸ κινούμενον, αὐτῆς δὲ οὐδὲν κινούμενον—ἢ ἐκεῖνο οὐκ ἔσται τὸ κινοῦν πρώτως, οὐδὲ ἡ φύσις τοῦτο, ἀλλὰ τὸ ἀκίνητον τὸ ἐν τῷ ὅλῳ. Ὁ μὲν δὴ λόγος, φαίη ἄν τις, ἀκίνητος, αὕτη δὲ ἄλλη παρὰ τὸν λόγον καὶ κινουμένη. Ἀλλ' εἰ μὲν πᾶσαν φήσουσι, καὶ ὁ λόγος· εἰ δέ τι αὐτῆς ἀκίνητον, τοῦτο καὶ ὁ λόγος. Καὶ γὰρ εἶδος αὐτὴν δεῖ εἶναι καὶ οὐκ ἐξ ὕλης καὶ εἴδους· τί γὰρ δεῖ αὐτῇ ὕλης θερμῆς ἢ ψυχρᾶς; Ἡ γὰρ ὑποκειμένη καὶ δημιουργουμένη ὕλη ἥκει τοῦτο φέρουσα, ἢ γίνεται τοιαύτη ἡ μὴ ποιότητα ἔχουσα λογωθεῖσα. Οὐ γὰρ πῦρ δεῖ προσελθεῖν, ἵνα πῦρ ἡ ὕλη γένηται, ἀλλὰ λόγον· ὃ καὶ σημεῖον οὐ μικρὸν τοῦ ἐν τοῖς ζῴοις καὶ ἐν τοῖς φυτοῖς τοὺς λόγους εἶναι τοὺς ποιοῦντας καὶ τὴν φύσιν εἶναι λόγον, ὃς ποιεῖ λόγον ἄλλον

[1] ὅτι del. Ficinus, H–S².

theirs—cannot make colours unless they bring colours from elsewhere to the things they make. But those who make this comparison ought to have considered also that even with those who practise crafts of this kind there must be something in themselves, something which stays unmoved, according to which they will make their works with their hands; they should have brought their minds back to the same kind of thing in nature, and understood that here, too, the power, all of it, which makes without hands, must stay unmoved. For it certainly has no need to have some unmoving and some moving parts—matter is what is in motion, and no part of nature is in motion—otherwise its unmoving part will not be the primary mover, nor will nature be this, but that which is unmoved in the universe as a whole. But someone might say that the rational forming principle is unmoved, but nature is different from the forming principle and is in motion. But if they are going to say that nature as a whole is in motion, then so will the forming principle be; but if any part of it is unmoved, this, too, will be the forming principle. In fact, of course, nature must be a form, and not composed of matter and form; for why should it need hot or cold matter? For matter which underlies it and is worked on by it comes to it bringing this [heat or cold] or rather becomes of this quality (though it has no quality itself) by being given form by a rational principle. For it is not fire which has to come to matter in order that it may become fire, but a forming principle; and this is a strong indication that in animals and plants the forming principles are the makers and nature is a forming principle, which

γέννημα αὐτοῦ δόντα μέν τι τῷ ὑποκειμένῳ, μένοντα δ' αὐτόν. Ὁ μὲν οὖν λόγος ὁ κατὰ τὴν μορφὴν τὴν ὁρωμένην ἔσχατος ἤδη καὶ νεκρὸς καὶ οὐκέτι ποιεῖν δύναται ἄλλον, ὁ δὲ ζωὴν ἔχων ὁ τοῦ ποιήσαντος τὴν μορφὴν ἀδελφὸς ὢν καὶ αὐτὸς τὴν αὐτὴν δύναμιν ἔχων ποιεῖ ἐν τῷ γενομένῳ.

3. Πῶς οὖν ποιῶν καὶ οὕτω ποιῶν θεωρίας τινὸς ἂν ἐφάπτοιτο; Ἤ, εἰ μένων ποιεῖ καὶ ἐν αὐτῷ μένων καί ἐστι λόγος, εἴη ἂν αὐτὸς θεωρία. Ἡ μὲν γὰρ πρᾶξις γένοιτ' ἂν κατὰ λόγον ἑτέρα οὖσα δηλονότι τοῦ λόγου· ὁ μέντοι λόγος καὶ αὐτὸς ὁ συνὼν τῇ πράξει καὶ ἐπιστατῶν οὐκ ἂν εἴη πρᾶξις. Εἰ οὖν μὴ πρᾶξις ἀλλὰ λόγος, θεωρία· καὶ ἐπὶ παντὸς λόγου ὁ μὲν ἔσχατος ἐκ θεωρίας καὶ θεωρία οὕτως ὡς τεθεωρημένος, ὁ δὲ πρὸ τούτου πᾶς ὁ μὲν ἄλλος ἄλλως, ὁ μὴ ὡς φύσις ἀλλὰ ψυχή, ὁ δ' ἐν τῇ φύσει καὶ ἡ φύσις. Ἆρά γε καὶ αὐτὸς ἐκ θεωρίας; Πάντως μὲν ἐκ θεωρίας. Ἀλλ' εἰ καὶ αὐτὸς τεθεωρηκὼς αὑτόν; ἢ πῶς; ἔστι μὲν γὰρ ἀποτέλεσμα θεωρίας καὶ θεωρήσαντός τινος. Πῶς δὲ αὕτη ἔχει θεωρίαν; Τὴν μὲν δὴ ἐκ λόγου οὐκ ἔχει· λέγω δ' ἐκ λόγου τὸ σκοπεῖσθαι περὶ τῶν ἐν αὐτῇ. Διὰ τί οὖν ζωή τις οὖσα καὶ λόγος καὶ

---

1 This is a good example of the variety of meaning which the word λόγος can have in Plotinus. The logical subject of the sentence is λόγος in the special sense which it often bears in the *Enneads*, combining the ideas of intelligence, intelligibility and formative activity, which I translate by "rational principle" or "rational formative principle"; it is a λόγος in this sense which does not have contemplation ἐκ λόγου in the ordinary sense of "reasoning," "discursive thinking."

makes another principle, its own product, which gives something to the substrate, but stays unmoved itself. This forming principle, then, which operates in the visible shape, is the last, and is dead and no longer able to make another, but that which has life is the brother of that which makes the shape, and has the same power itself, and makes in that which comes into being.

3. How then, when it makes, and makes in this way, can it attain to any sort of contemplation? If it stays unmoved as it makes, and stays in itself, and is a forming principle, it must itself be contemplation. For action must take place according to a rational principle, and is obviously different from the principle; but the principle itself, which accompanies and supervises the action, cannot be action. If, then, it is not action but rational principle, it is contemplation; and in every rational principle its last and lowest manifestation springs from contemplation, and is contemplation in the sense of being contemplated; but the manifestation of the principle before this is universal, one part in a different way, the part which is not nature but soul; the other is the rational principle in nature, and is nature. Then is this itself, too, the result of contemplation? Yes, it is altogether the result of contemplation. But is it so because it has itself contemplated itself, or how? For it is a result of contemplation, and something has been contemplating. But how does this, nature, possess contemplation? It certainly does not have the contemplation that comes from reasoning:[1] I mean by " reasoning " the research into what it has in itself. But why [should it not have it] when it is a

δύναμις ποιοῦσα; Ἆρ᾽ ὅτι τὸ σκοπεῖσθαί ἐστι τὸ μήπω ἔχειν; Ἡ δὲ ἔχει, καὶ διὰ τοῦτο ὅτι ἔχει καὶ ποιεῖ. Τὸ οὖν εἶναι αὐτῇ ὅ ἐστι τοῦτό ἐστι τὸ ποιεῖν αὐτῇ καὶ ὅσον ἐστὶ τοῦτό ἐστι τὸ ποιοῦν. Ἔστι δὲ θεωρία καὶ θεώρημα, λόγος γάρ. Τῷ οὖν εἶναι θεωρία καὶ θεώρημα καὶ λόγος τούτῳ καὶ ποιεῖ ᾗ ταῦτά ἐστιν. Ἡ ποίησις ἄρα θεωρία ἡμῖν ἀναπέφανται· ἔστι γὰρ ἀποτέλεσμα θεωρίας μενούσης θεωρίας οὐκ ἄλλο τι πραξάσης, ἀλλὰ τῷ εἶναι θεωρία ποιησάσης.

4. Καὶ εἴ τις δὲ αὐτὴν ἔροιτο τίνος ἕνεκα ποιεῖ, εἰ τοῦ ἐρωτῶντος ἐθέλοι ἐπαίειν καὶ λέγειν, εἴποι ἄν· « Ἐχρῆν μὲν μὴ ἐρωτᾶν, ἀλλὰ συνιέναι καὶ αὐτὸν σιωπῇ, ὥσπερ ἐγὼ σιωπῶ καὶ οὐκ εἴθισμαι λέγειν. Τί οὖν συνιέναι; Ὅτι τὸ γενόμενόν ἐστι θέαμα ἐμόν, σιωπώσης,[1] καὶ φύσει γενόμενον θεώρημα, καί μοι γενομένῃ ἐκ θεωρίας τῆς ὡδὶ τὴν φύσιν ἔχειν φιλοθεάμονα ὑπάρχειν. Καὶ τὸ θεωροῦν μου θεώρημα ποιεῖ, ὥσπερ οἱ γεωμέτραι θεωροῦντες γράφουσιν· ἀλλ᾽ ἐμοῦ μὴ γραφούσης, θεωρούσης δέ, ὑφίστανται αἱ τῶν σωμάτων γραμμαὶ ὥσπερ ἐκπίπτουσαι. Καί μοι τὸ τῆς μητρὸς καὶ τῶν γειναμένων ὑπάρχει πάθος· καὶ

[1] σιωπώσης Coleridge (secundum Dodds) et nunc Henry et Schwyzer: σιώπησις codd., H–S.

---

[1] Though this is not a precise allusion to anything in Plato, Plotinus is thinking in terms of something like the construction of the regular solids which are the figures of the

life and a rational principle and a power which makes? Is it because research means not yet possessing? But nature possesses, and just because it possesses, it also makes. Making, for it, means being what it is, and its making power is coextensive with what it is. But it is contemplation and object of contemplation, for it is a rational principle. So by being contemplation and object of contemplation and rational principle, it makes in so far as it is these things. So its making has been revealed to us as contemplation, for it is a result of contemplation, and the contemplation stays unchanged and does not do anything else but makes by being contemplation.

4. And if anyone were to ask nature why it makes, if it cared to hear and answer the questioner it would say: " You ought not to ask, but to understand in silence, you, too, just as I am silent and not in the habit of talking. Understand what, then? That what comes into being is what I see in my silence, an object of contemplation which comes to be naturally, and that I, originating from this sort of contemplation have a contemplative nature. And my act of contemplation makes what it contemplates, as the geometers draw their figures while they contemplate. But I do not draw, but as I contemplate, the lines which bound bodies come to be as if they fell from my contemplation.[1] What happens to me is what happens to my mother and the beings that

primary bodies in *Timaeus* 53C–55C. But the intuitive spontaneity of the process here, as contrasted with the careful and deliberate mathematical planning in Plato's symbolical description, brings out clearly an important difference in the mentality of the two philosophers.

γὰρ ἐκεῖνοί εἰσιν ἐκ θεωρίας καὶ ἡ γένεσις ἡ ἐμὴ ἐκείνων οὐδὲν πραξάντων, ἀλλ᾽ ὄντων μειζόνων λόγων καὶ θεωρούντων αὐτοὺς ἐγὼ γεγέννημαι.»

Τί οὖν ταῦτα βούλεται; Ὡς ἡ μὲν λεγομένη φύσις ψυχὴ οὖσα, γέννημα ψυχῆς προτέρας δυνατώτερον ζώσης, ἡσυχῇ ἐν ἑαυτῇ θεωρίαν ἔχουσα οὐ πρὸς τὸ ἄνω οὐδ᾽ αὖ ἔτι πρὸς τὸ κάτω, στᾶσα δὲ ἐν ᾧ ἔστιν, ἐν τῇ αὑτῆς στάσει καὶ οἷον συναισθήσει, τῇ συνέσει ταύτῃ καὶ συναισθήσει τὸ μετ᾽ αὐτὴν εἶδεν ὡς οἷόν τε αὐτῇ καὶ οὐκέτι ἐζήτησεν ἄλλα θεώρημα ἀποτελέσασα ἀγλαὸν καὶ χάριεν. Καὶ εἴτε τις βούλεται σύνεσίν τινα ἢ αἴσθησιν αὐτῇ διδόναι, οὐχ οἵαν λέγομεν ἐπὶ τῶν ἄλλων τὴν αἴσθησιν ἢ τὴν σύνεσιν, ἀλλ᾽ οἷον εἴ τις τὴν καθύπνου[1] τῇ[2] ἐγρηγορότος προσεικάσειε. Θεωροῦσα γὰρ θεώρημα αὐτῆς ἀναπαύεται γενόμενον αὐτῇ ἐκ τοῦ ἐν αὐτῇ καὶ σὺν αὐτῇ μένειν καὶ θεώρημα εἶναι· καὶ θεωρία ἄψοφος, ἀμυδροτέρα δέ. Ἑτέρα γὰρ αὐτῆς εἰς θέαν ἐναργεστέρα, ἡ δὲ εἴδωλον θεωρίας ἄλλης. Ταύτῃ δὴ καὶ τὸ γεννηθὲν ὑπ᾽ αὐτῆς ἀσθενὲς παντάπασιν, ὅτι ἀσθενοῦσα θεωρία ἀσθενὲς θεώρημα ποιεῖ· ἐπεὶ καὶ ἄνθρωποι, ὅταν ἀσθενήσωσιν εἰς τὸ θεωρεῖν, σκιὰν θεωρίας καὶ λόγου τὴν πρᾶξιν ποιοῦνται. Ὅτι γὰρ μὴ ἱκανὸν αὐτοῖς τὸ τῆς θεωρίας ὑπ᾽ ἀσθενείας ψυχῆς,

[1] καθύπνου nunc Henry et Schwyzer: τοῦ ὕπνου codd., H–S.
[2] τῇ H–S: τοῦ wxUS: om. C.

generated me,[1] for they, too, derive from contemplation, and it is no action of theirs which brings about my birth; they are greater rational principles, and as they contemplate themselves I come to be."

What does this mean? That what is called nature is a soul, the offspring of a prior soul with a stronger life; that it quietly holds contemplation in itself, not directed upwards or even downwards, but at rest in what it is, in its own repose and a kind of self-perception, and in this consciousness and self-perception it sees what comes after it, as far as it can, and seeks other things no longer, having accomplished a vision of splendour and delight. If anyone wants to attribute to it understanding or perception, it will not be the understanding or perception we speak of in other beings; it will be like comparing the consciousness of someone fast asleep to the consciousness of someone awake. Nature is at rest in contemplation of the vision of itself, a vision which comes to it from its abiding in and with itself and being itself a vision; and its contemplation is silent but somewhat blurred. For there is another, clearer for sight, and nature is the image of another contemplation. For this reason what is produced by it is weak in every way, because a weak contemplation produces a weak object. Men, too, when their power of contemplation weakens, make action a shadow of contemplation and reasoning. Because contemplation is not enough for them, since their souls are weak and they are not able to grasp the

[1] "my mother" = the higher soul: "the beings that generated me" = the λόγοι in soul which are the immediate expressions of the Forms in Intellect.

λαβεῖν οὐ δυνάμενοι τὸ θέαμα ἱκανῶς καὶ διὰ τοῦτο οὐ πληρούμενοι, ἐφιέμενοι δὲ αὐτὸ ἰδεῖν, εἰς πρᾶξιν φέρονται, ἵνα ἴδωσιν, ὃ μὴ νῷ ἐδύναντο. Ὅταν γοῦν ποιῶσι, καὶ αὐτοὶ ὁρᾶν βούλονται αὐτὸ καὶ θεωρεῖν καὶ αἰσθάνεσθαι καὶ τοὺς ἄλλους, ὅταν ἡ πρόθεσις αὐτοῖς ὡς οἷόν τε πρᾶξις ᾖ. Πανταχοῦ δὴ ἀνευρήσομεν τὴν ποίησιν καὶ τὴν πρᾶξιν ἢ ἀσθένειαν θεωρίας ἢ παρακολούθημα· ἀσθένειαν μέν, εἰ μηδέν τις ἔχοι μετὰ τὸ πραχθέν, παρακολούθημα δέ, εἰ ἔχοι ἄλλο πρὸ τούτου κρεῖττον τοῦ ποιηθέντος θεωρεῖν. τίς[1] γὰρ θεωρεῖν τὸ ἀληθινὸν δυνάμενος προηγουμένως ἔρχεται ἐπὶ τὸ εἴδωλον τοῦ ἀληθινοῦ; Μαρτυροῦσι δὲ καὶ οἱ νωθέστεροι τῶν παίδων, οἳ πρὸς τὰς μαθήσεις καὶ θεωρίας ἀδυνάτως ἔχοντες ἐπὶ τὰς τέχνας καὶ τὰς ἐργασίας καταφέρονται.

5. Ἀλλὰ περὶ μὲν φύσεως εἰπόντες ὃν τρόπον θεωρία ἡ γένεσις, ἐπὶ τὴν ψυχὴν τὴν πρὸ ταύτης ἐλθόντες λέγωμεν, ὡς ἡ ταύτης θεωρία καὶ τὸ φιλομαθὲς καὶ τὸ ζητητικὸν καὶ ἡ ἐξ ὧν ἐγνώκει ὠδὶς καὶ τὸ πλῆρες πεποίηκεν αὐτὴν θεώρημα πᾶν γενομένην ἄλλο θεώρημα ποιῆσαι· οἷον ἡ

[1] τίς A^{pc} et nunc Henry et Schwyzer: τί A^{ac}Exy, H–S.

---

[1] This distinction between the action which is a substitute for contemplation and that which naturally issues from it is a valuable one, and the description of the way in which weakness in contemplation leads through dissatisfaction to substitute activities (ll. 33–36) is a good piece of psychological observation. But there is a certain confusion of thought in the passage. There is no real reason why the kind of action

vision sufficiently, and therefore are not filled with it, but still long to see it, they are carried into action, so as to see what they cannot see with their intellect. When they make something, then, it is because they want to see their object themselves and also because they want others to be aware of it and contemplate it, when their project is realised in practice as well as possible. Everywhere we shall find that making and action are either a weakening or a consequence of contemplation;[1] a weakening, if the doer or maker had nothing in view beyond the thing done, a consequence if he had another prior object of contemplation better than what he made. For who, if he is able to contemplate what is truly real will deliberately go after its image? The duller children, too, are evidence of this, who are incapable of learning and contemplative studies and turn to crafts and manual work.

5. But, now that we have said, in speaking of nature, in what way coming into being is contemplation, we must go on to the soul prior to nature and say how its contemplation, its love of learning and spirit of enquiry, its birth-pangs from the knowledge it attains and its fullness, make it, when it has itself become all a vision, produce another vision; it is

which is a consequence of contemplation should imply any weakness in the contemplation itself (however imperfectly it may represent it); and the activity of nature in forming the material world is an activity of this sort. But Plotinus is so deeply convinced of the inferiority of the material world that he has to represent the activity of soul in forming material things as an activity of the lowest form of soul and due to its weakness in contemplation; hence the comparison with the substitute activities of uncontemplative men.

τέχνη ποιεῖ· ὅταν ἑκάστη πλήρης ᾖ, ἄλλην οἷαν μικρὰν τέχνην ποιεῖ ἐν παιγνίῳ[1] ἴνδαλμα ἔχοντι ἁπάντων· ἄλλως μέντοι ταῦτα ὥσπερ ἀμυδρὰ καὶ οὐ δυνάμενα βοηθεῖν ἑαυτοῖς θεάματα καὶ θεωρήματα· τὸ πρῶτον [τὸ λογιστικὸν][2] οὖν αὐτῆς ἄνω πρὸς τὸ ἄνω ἀεὶ πληρούμενον καὶ ἐλλαμπόμενον μένει ἐκεῖ, τὸ δὲ τῇ τοῦ μεταλαβόντος πρώτῃ μεταλήψει μεταλαμβάνον πρόεισι· ⟨πρόεισι⟩[3] γὰρ ἀεὶ ζωὴ ἐκ ζωῆς· ἐνέργεια[4] γὰρ πανταχοῦ φθάνει καὶ οὐκ ἔστιν ὅτου ἀποστατεῖ. Προιοῦσα μέντοι ἐᾷ τὸ πρότερον [τὸ ἑαυτῆς πρόσθεν] μέρος[5] οὗ καταλέλοιπε μένειν· ἀπολιποῦσα γὰρ τὸ πρόσθεν οὐκέτι ἔσται πανταχοῦ, ἀλλ' ἐν ᾧ τελευτᾷ μόνον. Οὐκ ἴσον δὲ τὸ προιὸν τῷ μείναντι. Εἰ οὖν πανταχοῦ δεῖ γίνεσθαι καὶ μὴ εἶναι ὅπου μὴ τὴν ἐνέργειαν τὴν αὐτὴν ἀεί τε τὸ πρότερον ἕτερον τοῦ ὑστέρου, ἥκει δὲ ἡ ἐνέργεια ἐκ θεωρίας ἢ πράξεως, πρᾶξις δὲ οὔπω ἦν—οὐ γὰρ οἷόν τε πρὸ θεωρίας—ἀνάγκη ἀσθενεστέραν μὲν ἑτέραν ἑτέρας εἶναι, πᾶσαν δὲ θεωρίαν· ὥστε τὴν κατὰ τὴν θεωρίαν πρᾶξιν δοκοῦσαν εἶναι τὴν ἀσθενεστάτην θεωρίαν εἶναι·

[1] παιγνίῳ Theiler et nunc Henry et Schwyzer: παιδίῳ codd., H–S.

[2] τὸ λογιστικὸν del. Kirchhoff et nunc Henry et Schwyzer.

[3] ⟨πρόεισι⟩ Theiler et nunc Henry et Schwyzer.

[4] ἐνέργεια wy et nunc Henry et Schwyzer: ἐνεργεία: ἐνεργείᾳ H–S.

[5] τὸ ἑαυτῆς πρόσθεν, del. Dodds.

---

[1] The argument of Dodds (in his *Notes on Ennead III viii, Studi Italiani di Filologia Classica Vol. xxvii–viii*, Florence 1956, p. 109) against the received text here, though not accepted by

like the way in which art produces; when a particular art is complete, it produces a kind of another little art in a toy which possesses a trace of everything in it. But, all the same, these visions, these objects of contemplation, are dim and helpless sorts of things. The first part of soul, then, that which is above and always filled and illuminated by the reality above, remains There; but another part, participating by the first participation of the participant goes forth, for soul goes forth always, life from life; for actuality reaches everywhere, and there is no point where it fails. But in going forth it lets its prior part remain where it left it,[1] for if it abandoned what is before it, it would no longer be everywhere, but only at the last point it reached. But what goes forth is not equal to what remains. If, then, it must come to be everywhere, and there must be nowhere without its activity; and if the prior must always be different from that which comes after; and if activity originates from contemplation or action, and action did not exist at this stage—for it cannot come before contemplation—then all activity of soul must be contemplation, but one stage weaker than another. So what appears to be action according to contemplation is really the weaker form

Henry-Schwyzer, seems to me irrefutable. As the text stands, it makes Plotinus say that the soul allows its higher part to remain where it left it (in the intelligible world), *for* if it left its higher part the soul would lose its omnipresence (which it does not do). This does not really make sense. I therefore follow Dodds in bracketing τὸ ἑαυτῆς πρόσθεν, as a gloss on τὸ πρότερον, designed to show that the priority is in the order of being, not temporal. τὸ πρόσθεν (l. 16) can then refer, as it should, to Intellect.

ὁμογενὲς γὰρ ἀεὶ δεῖ τὸ γεννώμενον εἶναι, ἀσθενέστερον μὴν τῷ ἐξίτηλον καταβαῖνον γίγνεσθαι. Ἀψοφητὶ μὲν δὴ πάντα, ὅτι μηδὲν ἐμφανοῦς καὶ τῆς ἔξωθεν θεωρίας ἢ πράξεως δεῖται, καὶ ψυχὴ δὲ ἡ θεωροῦσα καὶ τὸ οὕτω θεωρῆσαν ἅτε ἐξωτέρω καὶ οὐχ ὡσαύτως τῷ πρὸ αὐτῆς τὸ μετ' αὐτὴν ποιεῖ· καὶ θεωρία τὴν θεωρίαν ποιεῖ. Καὶ γὰρ οὐκ ἔχει πέρας ἡ θεωρία οὐδὲ τὸ θεώρημα. Διὰ τοῦτο δὲ [ἢ καὶ διὰ τοῦτο][1] πανταχοῦ· ποῦ γὰρ οὐχί; Ἐπεὶ καὶ ἐν πάσῃ ψυχῇ τὸ αὐτό. Οὐ γὰρ περιγέγραπται μεγέθει. Οὐ μὴν ὡσαύτως ἐν πᾶσιν, ὥστε οὐδὲ ἐν παντὶ μέρει ψυχῆς ὁμοίως. Διὸ ὁ ἡνίοχος τοῖς ἵπποις δίδωσιν ὧν εἶδεν, οἱ δὲ λαβόντες δῆλον ὅτι ὀρέγοιντο ἂν ὧν εἶδον· ἔλαβον γὰρ οὐ πᾶν. Ὀρεγόμενοι δὲ εἰ πράττοιεν, οὗ ὀρέγονται ἕνεκα πράττουσιν. Ἦν δὲ θεώρημα καὶ θεωρία ἐκεῖνο.

6. Ἡ ἄρα πρᾶξις ἕνεκα θεωρίας καὶ θεωρήματος· ὥστε καὶ τοῖς πράττουσιν ἡ θεωρία τέλος, καὶ οἷον ἐξ εὐθείας ὃ μὴ ἠδυνήθησαν λαβεῖν τοῦτο περιπλανώμενοι ἑλεῖν ζητοῦσι. Καὶ γὰρ αὖ ὅταν τύχωσιν οὗ βούλονται, ὃ γενέσθαι ἠθέλησαν, οὐχ

[1] ἢ καὶ διὰ τοῦτο del. Kirchhoff et nunc Henry et Schwyzer.

---

[1] θεωρία has now received its full extension of meaning, going far beyond the Aristotelian conception from which the treatise started. It is for Plotinus the whole activity of soul,

of contemplation, for that which is produced must always be of the same kind as its producer, but weaker through losing its virtue as it comes down. All goes on noiselessly, for there is no need of any obvious and external contemplation or action; it is soul which contemplates, and makes that which comes after it, that which contemplates in a more external way and not like that which precedes it: and contemplation makes contemplation. Contemplation and vision have no limits.[1] This is why soul makes everywhere, for where does it not? Since the same vision is in every soul. For it is not spatially limited. It is, of course, not present in the same way in every soul, since it is not even in a like way in every part of the soul. That is why the charioteer gives the horses a share of what he sees;[2] and they in taking it obviously would have desired what they saw, for they did not get it all. And if in their longing they act, they act for the sake of what they long for; and that was vision and contemplation.

6. Action, then, is for the sake of contemplation and vision, so that for men of action, too, contemplation is the goal, and what they cannot get by going straight to it, so to speak, they seek to obtain by going round about. For, again, when they reach what they want, the thing which they wished to exist, not so that they should not know it but so that they

of which production is the inseparable other side: and for Plotinus, as for Plato, nothing exists which is not the product of soul's activity.

[2] The ambrosia and nectar with which the charioteer feeds his horses in the *Phaedrus* myth (247E5–6) are interpreted as the share which the lower parts of the soul can receive of the divine vision of the higher.

ἵνα μὴ γνῶσιν, ἀλλ' ἵνα γνῶσι καὶ παρὸν ἴδωσιν ἐν ψυχῇ, δῆλον ὅτι κείμενον θεατόν. Ἐπεὶ καὶ ἀγαθοῦ χάριν πράττουσι· τοῦτο δὲ οὐχ ἵνα ἔξω αὐτῶν, οὐδ' ἵνα μὴ ἔχωσιν, ἀλλ' ἵνα ἔχωσι τὸ ἐκ τῆς πράξεως ἀγαθόν. Τοῦτο δὲ ποῦ; Ἐν ψυχῇ. Ἀνέκαμψεν οὖν πάλιν ἡ πρᾶξις εἰς θεωρίαν· ὃ γὰρ ἐν ψυχῇ λαμβάνει λόγῳ οὔσῃ, τί ἂν ἄλλο ἢ λόγος σιωπῶν εἴη; Καὶ μᾶλλον, ὅσῳ μᾶλλον. Τότε γὰρ καὶ ἡσυχίαν ἄγει καὶ οὐδὲν ζητεῖ ὡς πληρωθεῖσα, καὶ ἡ θεωρία ἡ ἐν τῷ τοιούτῳ τῷ πιστεύειν ἔχειν εἴσω κεῖται. Καὶ ὅσῳ ἐναργεστέρα ἡ πίστις, ἡσυχαιτέρα καὶ ἡ θεωρία, ᾗ μᾶλλον εἰς ἓν ἄγει, καὶ τὸ γινῶσκον ὅσῳ γινώσκει—ἤδη γὰρ σπουδαστέον—εἰς ἓν τῷ γνωσθέντι ἔρχεται. Εἰ γὰρ δύο, τὸ μὲν ἄλλο, τὸ δὲ ἄλλο ἔσται· ὥστε οἷον παράκειται, καὶ τὸ διπλοῦν τοῦτο οὔπω ᾠκείωσεν, οἷον ὅταν ἐνόντες λόγοι ἐν[1] ψυχῇ μηδὲν ποιῶσι. Διὸ δεῖ μὴ ἔξωθεν τὸν λόγον εἶναι, ἀλλ' ἑνωθῆναι τῇ ψυχῇ τοῦ μανθάνοντος, ἕως ἂν οἰκεῖον εὕρῃ. Ἡ μὲν οὖν ψυχή, ὅταν οἰκειωθῇ καὶ διατεθῇ, ὅμως προφέρει καὶ προχειρίζεται—οὐ γὰρ πρώτως εἶχε—καὶ καταμανθάνει, καὶ τῇ προχειρίσει οἷον ἑτέρα αὐτοῦ γίνεται, καὶ διανοουμένη βλέπει ὡς ἄλλο ὂν ἄλλο· καίτοι καὶ αὕτη λόγος ἦν καὶ οἷον νοῦς, ἀλλ' ὁρῶν ἄλλο. Ἔστι

[1] λόγοι ἐν A^pc, H–S: λέγοιεν A^ac Exy.

should know it and see it present in their soul, it is, obviously, an object set there for contemplation. This is so, too, because they act for the sake of a good; but this means, not that the good arising from their action should be outside them, or that they should not have it, but that they should have it. But where do they have it? In their soul. So action bends back again to contemplation, for what someone receives in his soul, which is rational form—what can it be other than silent rational form? And more so, the more it is within the soul. For the soul keeps quiet then, and seeks nothing because it is filled, and the contemplation which is there in a state like this rests within because it is confident of possession. And, in proportion as the confidence is clearer, the contemplation is quieter, in that it unifies more, and what knows, in so far as it knows—we must be serious now—comes into unity with what is known. For if they are two, the knower will be one thing and the known another, so that there is a sort of juxtaposition, and contemplation has not yet made this pair akin to each other, as when rational principles present in the soul do nothing. For this reason the rational principle must not be outside but must be united with the soul of the learner, until it finds that it is its own. The soul, then, when it has become akin to and disposed according to the rational principle, still, all the same, utters and propounds it—for it did not possess it primarily—and learns it thoroughly and by its proposition becomes other than it, and looks at it, considering it, like one thing looking at another; and yet soul, too, was a rational principle and a sort of intellect, but an intellect seeing

γὰρ οὐ πλήρης, ἀλλὰ ἐλλείπει τῷ πρὸ αὐτῆς· ὁρᾷ μέντοι καὶ αὐτὴ ἡσύχως ἃ προφέρει. Ἃ μὲν γὰρ εὖ[1] προήνεγκεν, οὐκέτι προφέρει, ἃ δὲ προφέρει, τῷ ἐλλιπεῖ προφέρει εἰς ἐπίσκεψιν καταμανθάνουσα ὃ ἔχει. Ἐν δὲ τοῖς πρακτικοῖς ἐφαρμόττει ἃ ἔχει τοῖς ἔξω. Καὶ τῷ μὲν μᾶλλον ἔχειν ᾗ ἡ φύσις ἡσυχαιτέρα, καὶ τῷ πλέον θεωρητικὴ μᾶλλον, τῷ δὲ μὴ τελέως ἐφιεμένη μᾶλλον ἔχειν τὴν τοῦ θεωρηθέντος καταμάθησιν καὶ θεωρίαν τὴν ἐξ ἐπισκέψεως. Καὶ ἀπολείπουσα δὲ καὶ ἐν ἄλλοις γινομένη, εἶτ᾽ ἐπανιοῦσα πάλιν, θεωρεῖ τῷ ἀπολειφθέντι αὐτῆς μέρει· ἡ δὲ στᾶσα ἐν αὐτῇ ἧττον τοῦτο ποιεῖ. Διὸ ὁ σπουδαῖος λελόγισται ἤδη καὶ τὸ παρ᾽ αὐτοῦ πρὸς ἄλλον ἀποφαίνει· πρὸς δὲ αὐτὸν ὄψις. Ἤδη γὰρ οὗτος πρὸς τὸ ἓν καὶ πρὸς τὸ ἥσυχον οὐ μόνον τῶν ἔξω, ἀλλὰ καὶ πρὸς αὐτόν, καὶ πάντα εἴσω.

7. Ὅτι μὲν οὖν πάντα τά τε ὡς ἀληθῶς ὄντα ἐκ θεωρίας καὶ θεωρία, καὶ τὰ ἐξ ἐκείνων γενόμενα θεωρούντων ἐκείνων καὶ αὐτὰ θεωρήματα, τὰ μὲν αἰσθήσει τὰ δὲ γνώσει ἢ δόξῃ, καὶ αἱ πράξεις τὸ τέλος ἔχουσιν εἰς γνῶσιν καὶ ἡ ἔφεσις γνώσεως καὶ αἱ γεννήσεις ἀπὸ θεωρίας εἰς ἀποτελεύτησιν

[1] εὖ Theiler et nunc Henry et Schwyzer: οὐ codd., H–S.

something else. For it is not full, but has something wanting in relation to what comes before it; yet it itself sees also quietly what it utters. For it does not go on uttering what it has uttered well already, but what it utters, it utters because of its deficiency, with a view to examining it, trying to learn thoroughly what it possesses. But in men of action the soul fits what it possesses to the things outside it. And because the soul possesses its content more completely it is quieter than nature, and because it has a greater content it is more contemplative; but because it does not have perfect possession it desires to learn more thoroughly what it has contemplated and gain a fuller contemplation, which comes from examining it. And when it leaves itself and comes to be among other things, and then returns again, it contemplates with the part of itself it left behind; but the soul at rest in itself does this less. The truly good and wise man, therefore, has already finished reasoning when he declares what he has in himself to another; but in relation to himself he is vision. For he is already turned to what is one, and to the quiet which is not only of things outside but in relation to himself, and all is within him.

7. That all things come from contemplation and are contemplation, both the things which truly exist and the things which come from them when they contemplate and are themselves objects of contemplation, some by sense-perception and some by knowledge or opinion; and that actions have their goal in knowledge and their driving-force is desire of knowledge; and that the products of contemplation are directed to the perfecting of another form and object

εἴδους καὶ θεωρήματος ἄλλου, καὶ ὅλως μιμήματα ὄντα ἕκαστα τῶν ποιούντων θεωρήματα ποιεῖ καὶ εἴδη, καὶ αἱ γινόμεναι ὑποστάσεις μιμήσεις ὄντων οὖσαι ποιοῦντα δείκνυσι τέλος ποιούμενα οὐ τὰς ποιήσεις οὐδὲ τὰς πράξεις, ἀλλὰ τὸ ἀποτέλεσμα ἵνα θεωρηθῇ, καὶ τοῦτο καὶ αἱ διανοήσεις ἰδεῖν θέλουσι καὶ ἔτι πρότερον αἱ αἰσθήσεις, αἷς τέλος ἡ γνῶσις, καὶ ἔτι πρὸ τούτων ἡ φύσις τὸ θεώρημα τὸ ἐν αὐτῇ καὶ τὸν λόγον ποιεῖ ἄλλον λόγον ἀποτελοῦσα—τὰ μὲν ἦν αὐτόθεν λαβεῖν, τὰ δ' ὑπέμνησεν ὁ λόγος—δῆλόν που. Ἐπεὶ κἀκεῖνο δῆλον, ὡς ἀναγκαῖον ἦν τῶν πρώτων ἐν θεωρίᾳ ὄντων καὶ τὰ ἄλλα πάντα ἐφίεσθαι τούτου, εἴπερ τέλος ἅπασιν ἡ ἀρχή. Ἐπεὶ καί, ὅταν τὰ ζῷα γεννᾷ, οἱ λόγοι ἔνδον ὄντες κινοῦσι, καὶ ἔστιν ἐνέργεια θεωρίας τοῦτο καὶ ὠδὶς τοῦ πολλὰ ποιεῖν εἴδη καὶ πολλὰ θεωρήματα καὶ λόγων πληρῶσαι πάντα καὶ οἷον ἀεὶ θεωρεῖν· τὸ γὰρ ποιεῖν εἶναί τι εἶδός ἐστι ποιεῖν, τοῦτο δέ ἐστι πάντα πληρῶσαι θεωρίας. Καὶ αἱ ἁμαρτίαι δέ, αἵ τε ἐν τοῖς γινομένοις αἵ τε ἐν τοῖς πραττομένοις, θεωρούντων εἰσὶν ἐκ τοῦ θεωρητοῦ παραφορᾷ· καὶ ὅ γε κακὸς τεχνίτης ἔοικεν αἰσχρὰ εἴδη

[1] This is one of the fundamental principles of Greek philosophical thought, here given a special application. By making *θεωρία* the end of all perception and action Plotinus abolishes, no doubt consciously and deliberately, Aristotle's distinction between *πρακτικὴ* and *θεωρητικὴ ἐπιστήμη* or *διάνοια* (cp.

of contemplation; and that in general all active things, which are representations, make objects of contemplation and forms; and that the realities which have come into existence, which are representations of real beings, show that their makers had as their goal in making, not makings or actions, but the finished object of contemplation; and that this is what processes of reasoning want to see, and, even before them, acts of sense perception, whose goal is knowledge; and that before them again nature makes the object of contemplation and the rational principle in itself, perfecting another rational principle; all these points are, I suppose, clear—some of them were self-evident, and the discussion brought others to mind. What follows, too, is clear; that it was necessary, since the first principles were engaged in contemplation, for all other things to aspire to this state, granted that their originative principle is, for all things, the goal.[1] For when living things, too, produce, it is the rational principles within which move them, and this is an activity of contemplation, the birthpain of creating many forms and many things to contemplate and filling all things with rational principles, and a kind of endless contemplation, for creating is bringing a form into being, and this is filling all things with contemplation. And failures, too, both in what comes into being and what is done, are failures of contemplators who are distracted from their object of contemplation; and the bad workman is the sort of person who makes ugly

Nicomachean Ethics A.3, 1095a5; Z.2, 1139a21–b4; K.10, 1179a35 ff.), and makes the whole life, not only of man but the universe, philosophy in Aristotle's sense.

ποιοῦντι. Καὶ οἱ ἐρῶντες δὲ ἰδόντων καὶ πρὸς εἶδος σπευδόντων.

8. Ταῦτα μὲν οὕτω. Τῆς δὲ θεωρίας ἀναβαινούσης ἐκ τῆς φύσεως ἐπὶ ψυχὴν καὶ ἀπὸ ταύτης εἰς νοῦν καὶ ἀεὶ οἰκειοτέρων τῶν θεωριῶν γιγνομένων καὶ ἑνουμένων τοῖς θεωροῦσι καὶ ἐπὶ τῆς σπουδαίας ψυχῆς πρὸς τὸ αὐτὸ τῷ ὑποκειμένῳ ἰόντων τῶν ἐγνωσμένων ἅτε εἰς νοῦν σπευδόντων, ἐπὶ τούτου δηλονότι ἤδη ἓν ἄμφω οὐκ οἰκειώσει, ὥσπερ ἐπὶ τῆς ψυχῆς τῆς ἀρίστης, ἀλλ' οὐσίᾳ καὶ τῷ ταὐτὸν τὸ εἶναι καὶ τὸ νοεῖν εἶναι. Οὐ γὰρ ἔτι ἄλλο, τὸ δ' ἄλλο· πάλιν γὰρ αὖ ἄλλο ἔσται, ὃ οὐκέτι ἄλλο καὶ ἄλλο. Δεῖ οὖν τοῦτο εἶναι ἓν ὄντως ἄμφω· τοῦτο δέ ἐστι θεωρία ζῶσα, οὐ θεώρημα οἷον τὸ ἐν ἄλλῳ. Τὸ γὰρ ἐν ἄλλῳ ζῶν δι' ἐκεῖνο,[1] οὐκ αὐτοζῶν. Εἰ οὖν ζήσεταί τι θεώρημα καὶ νόημα, δεῖ αὐτοζωὴν εἶναι οὐ φυτικὴν οὐδὲ αἰσθητικὴν οὐδὲ ψυχικὴν τὴν ἄλλην. Νοήσεις μὲν γάρ πως καὶ ἄλλαι· ἀλλ' ἡ μὲν φυτικὴ νόησις, ἡ δὲ αἰσθητική, ἡ δὲ ψυχική. Πῶς οὖν νοήσεις; Ὅτι λόγοι. Καὶ πᾶσα ζωὴ νόησίς τις, ἀλλὰ ἄλλη ἄλλης ἀμυδροτέρα, ὥσπερ

[1] ζῶν δι'ἐκεῖνο, Dodds; ζῶν τι, Kirchhoff H–S: ζῶντι, Cr; codices inter ζῶν τι et ζῶντι non distinguunt.

---

[1] Plotinus is here alluding to Parmenides fr. B3DK, which he quotes accurately at V. 1 [10] 8. 17, and uses explicitly, as he does here implicitly, in support of his doctrine that the intelligible objects are not outside intellect.

forms. And lovers, too, are among those who see and press on eagerly towards a form.

8. This, then, is so. But, as contemplation ascends from nature to soul, and soul to intellect, and the contemplations become always more intimate and united to the contemplators, and in the soul of the good and wise man the objects known tend to become identical with the knowing subject, since they are pressing on towards intellect, it is clear that in intellect both are one, not by becoming akin, as in the best soul, but substantially, and because "thinking and being are the same."[1] For there is not still one thing and another, for if there is, there will be something else again, which is not any more one thing and another. So this must be something where both are really one. But this is living contemplation, not an object of contemplation like that in something else. For that which is in something else is alive because of that other, not in its own right.[2] If, then, an object of contemplation and thought is to have life, it must be life in its own right [absolute and unqualified life], not the life of growth or sense-perception or that which belongs to the rest of the soul. For the other lives are thoughts in a way, but one is a growth-thought, one a sense-thought, and one a soul-thought. How, then, are they thoughts? Because they are rational principles. And every life is a thought, but one is dimmer than another, just as life [has degrees of clarity and strength].

[2] Like E. R. Dodds (art. cit., p. 111) I can make no sense of *ἐκεῖνο* with the received text, and therefore follow him in reading *ζῶν δι᾽ἐκεῖνο* for *ζῶν τι ἐκεῖνο*, which gives a good and appropriate sense.

καὶ ζωή. Ἡ δὲ ἐναργεστέρα·[1] αὕτη καὶ πρώτη ζωὴ καὶ πρῶτος νοῦς εἷς. Νόησις οὖν ἡ πρώτη ζωὴ καὶ ζωὴ δευτέρα νόησις δευτέρα καὶ ἡ ἐσχάτη ζωὴ ἐσχάτη νόησις. Πᾶσα οὖν ζωὴ τοῦ γένους τούτου καὶ νόησις. Ἀλλὰ ζωῆς μὲν ἴσως διαφορὰς τάχ' ἂν λέγοιεν[2] ἄνθρωποι, νοήσεων δὲ οὐ λέγουσιν, ἀλλὰ τὰς μέν, τὰς δ' ὅλως οὐ νοήσεις, ὅτι ὅλως τὴν ζωὴν ὅ τι ποτέ ἐστιν οὐ ζητοῦσιν. Ἀλλ' ἐκεῖνό γε ἐπισημαντέον, ὅτι πάλιν αὖ ὁ λόγος πάρεργον ἐνδείκνυται θεωρίας τὰ πάντα ὄντα. Εἰ τοίνυν ἡ ζωὴ ἡ ἀληθεστάτη νοήσει ζωή ἐστιν, αὕτη δὲ ταὐτὸν τῇ ἀληθεστάτῃ νοήσει, ἡ ἀληθεστάτη νόησις ζῇ καὶ ἡ θεωρία καὶ τὸ θεώρημα τὸ τοιοῦτο ζῶν καὶ ζωὴ καὶ ἓν ὁμοῦ τὰ δύο. Ἓν οὖν ὂν τὰ δύο πῶς αὖ πολλὰ τοῦτο τὸ ἕν; Ἢ ὅτι οὐχ ἓν θεωρεῖ. Ἐπεὶ καὶ ὅταν τὸ ἓν θεωρῇ οὐχ ὡς ἕν· εἰ δὲ μή, οὐ γίνεται νοῦς. Ἀλλὰ ἀρξάμενος ὡς ἓν οὐχ ὡς ἤρξατο ἔμεινεν, ἀλλ' ἔλαθεν ἑαυτὸν πολὺς γενόμενος, οἷον βεβαρημένος, καὶ ἐξείλιξεν αὑτὸν πάντα ἔχειν θέλων—ὡς βέλτιον ἦν αὐτῷ μὴ ἐθελῆσαι τοῦτο, δεύτερον γὰρ ἐγένετο—οἷον γὰρ κύκλος ἐξελίξας αὑτὸν γέγονε καὶ σχῆμα

[1] ἐναργεστέρα, Ficinus, H–S: ἐνεργεστέρα codd.
[2] λέγοιεν Müller, H–S: λέγοιμεν codd.

[1] For the doctrine that Intellect in its contemplation of the One necessarily sees it as many and so becomes a multiplicity-in-unity, cp. V. 3 [49] 11; VI. 7 [38] 15. The view, however,

But this life is clearer; this is first life and first intellect in one. So the first life is thought, and the second life thought in the second degree, and the last life thought in the last degree. All life, then, belongs to this kind and is thought. But perhaps men may speak of different kinds of life, but do not speak of different kinds of thought but say that some are thoughts, but others not thoughts at all, because they do not investigate at all what kind of thing life is. But we must bring out this point, at any rate, that again our discussion shows that all things are a by-product of contemplation. If, then, the truest life is life by thought, and is the same thing as the truest thought, then the truest thought lives, and contemplation, and the object of contemplation at this level, is living and life, and the two together are one. So, if the two are one, how is this one many? Because what it contemplates is not one. For when it contemplates the One, it does not contemplate it as one:[1] otherwise it would not become intellect. But beginning as one it did not stay as it began, but, without noticing it, became many, as if heavy [with drunken sleep], and unrolled itself because it wanted to possess everything—how much better it would have been for it not to want this, for it became the second!—for it became like a circle unrolling itself,

taken here of the generation of Intellect as a fall due to the desire for self-expression on a lower plane (cp. l. 34–36) is unusual for Plotinus in its pessimistic tone. Though Intellect is for him always inferior to the One he usually thinks and speaks of it as altogether good and does not emphasise that its generation is a fall or declension, as he does in speaking of the generation of Soul from Intellect (cp., e.g., III. 7 [45] 11).

καὶ ἐπίπεδον καὶ περιφέρεια καὶ κέντρον καὶ γραμμαὶ καὶ τὰ μὲν ἄνω, τὰ δὲ κάτω· βελτίω μὲν ὅθεν, χείρω δὲ εἰς ὅ. Τὸ γὰρ εἰς ὃ[1] οὐκ ἦν τοιοῦτον οἷον τὸ ἀφ᾿ οὗ καὶ εἰς ὅ, οὐδ᾿ αὖ τὸ ἀφ᾿ οὗ καὶ εἰς ὃ οἷον τὸ ἀφ᾿ οὗ μόνον. Καὶ ἄλλως δὲ ὁ νοῦς οὐχ ἑνός τινος νοῦς, ἀλλὰ καὶ πᾶς· πᾶς δὲ ὢν καὶ πάντων. Δεῖ οὖν αὐτὸν πάντα ὄντα καὶ πάντων καὶ τὸ μέρος αὐτοῦ ἔχειν πᾶν καὶ πάντα· εἰ δέ μή, ἕξει τι μέρος οὐ νοῦν, καὶ συγκείσεται ἐξ οὐ νῶν, καὶ σωρός τις συμφορητὸς ἔσται ἀναμένων τὸ γενέσθαι νοῦς ἐκ πάντων. Διὸ καὶ ἄπειρος οὕτως καί, εἴ τι ἀπ᾿ αὐτοῦ, οὐκ ἠλάττωται, οὔτε τὸ ἀπ᾿ αὐτοῦ, ὅτι πάντα καὶ αὐτό, οὔτε ἐκεῖνος ὁ ἐξ οὗ ὅτι μὴ σύνθεσις ἦν ἐκ μορίων.

9. Οὗτος μὲν οὖν τοιοῦτος· διὸ οὐ πρῶτος, ἀλλὰ δεῖ εἶναι τὸ ἐπέκεινα αὐτοῦ, οὗπερ χάριν καὶ οἱ πρόσθεν λόγοι, πρῶτον μέν, ὅτι πλῆθος ἑνὸς ὕστερον· καὶ ἀριθμὸς δὲ οὗτος, ἀριθμοῦ δὲ ἀρχὴ καὶ τοῦ τοιούτου τὸ ὄντως[2] ἕν· καὶ οὗτος νοῦς καὶ νοητὸν ἅμα, ὥστε δύο ἅμα. Εἰ δὲ δύο, δεῖ τὸ πρὸ τοῦ δύο λαβεῖν. Τί οὖν; Νοῦς μόνον; Ἀλλὰ παντὶ νῷ συνέζευκται τὸ νοητόν· εἰ οὖν δεῖ μὴ συνεζεῦχθαι τὸ νοητόν, οὐδὲ νοῦς ἔσται. Εἰ οὖν μὴ νοῦς, ἀλλ᾿ ἐκφεύξεται τὰ δύο, τὸ πρότερον τῶν

[1] εἰς ὃ Dodds, H–S²: ἀφ᾿ οὗ codd.
[2] ὄντως Kirchhoff: οὕτως codd.

---

[1] Cp. Plato, *Republic* 509B9.

shape and surface and circumference and centre and radii, some parts above and some below. The better is the " whence," the worse the " whither." For the " whither " is not of the same kind as the " whence-and-whither," nor, again, the " whence-and-whither " the same kind as the " whence " by itself. And, to put it another way, Intellect is not the intellect of one individual, but is universal; and being universal, is the Intellect of all things. So, if it is universal and of all things, its part must possess everything and all things: otherwise it will have a part which is not intellect, and will be composed of non-intellects, and will be a heap casually put together waiting to become an intellect made up of all things. Therefore, too, it is unbounded in this way and, if anything comes from it, there is no diminution, neither of what comes from it, because it, too, is all things, nor of that from which it comes, because it is not something made out of pieces put together.

9. This, then, is what Intellect is like: and for this reason it is not the first, but what is beyond it [1] must exist (that to which our discussion has been leading), first of all, because multiplicity comes after unity; and Intellect is a number, but the principle of number, of this kind of number too, is that which is really one; and it is intellect and intelligible at one, so that it is two things at once. But if it is two, one must understand what comes before the two. What is it, then? Intellect only? But with every intellect its intelligible is coupled; if, then, it must not have its intelligible coupled with it, it will not be intellect. If, then it is not intellect, and is going to get out beyond the two, that which comes before

δύο τούτων ἐπέκεινα νοῦ εἶναι. Τί οὖν κωλύει τὸ νοητὸν αὐτὸ εἶναι; Ἢ ὅτι καὶ τὸ νοητὸν συνέζευκτο τῷ νῷ. Εἰ οὖν μήτε νοῦς μήτε νοητὸν εἴη, τί ἂν εἴη; Ἐξ οὗ ὁ νοῦς καὶ τὸ σὺν αὐτῷ νοητὸν φήσομεν. Τί οὖν τοῦτο καὶ ποῖόν τι αὐτὸ φαντασθησόμεθα; Καὶ γὰρ αὖ ἢ νοοῦν ἔσται ἢ ἀνόητόν τι. Νοοῦν μὲν οὖν νοῦς, ἀνόητον δὲ ἀγνοήσει καὶ ἑαυτό· ὥστε τί σεμνόν; Οὐδὲ γάρ, εἰ λέγοιμεν τὸ ἀγαθὸν εἶναι καὶ ἁπλούστατον εἶναι, δῆλόν τι καὶ σαφὲς ἐροῦμεν τὸ ἀληθὲς λέγοντες, ἕως ἂν μὴ ἔχωμεν ἐπὶ τί ἐρείδοντες τὴν διάνοιαν λέγομεν. Καὶ γὰρ αὖ τῆς γνώσεως διὰ νοῦ τῶν ἄλλων γινομένης καὶ τῷ νῷ νοῦν γινώσκειν δυναμένων ὑπερβεβηκὸς τοῦτο τὴν νοῦ φύσιν τίνι ἂν ἁλίσκοιτο ἐπιβολῇ ἀθρόᾳ; Πρὸς ὃν δεῖ σημῆναι, ὅπως οἷόν τε, τῷ ἐν ἡμῖν ὁμοίῳ φήσομεν. Ἔστι γάρ τι καὶ παρ᾽ ἡμῖν αὐτοῦ· ἢ οὐκ ἔστιν, ὅπου μὴ ἔστιν, οἷς ἐστι μετέχειν αὐτοῦ. Τὸ γὰρ πανταχοῦ παρὸν στήσας [1] ὁπουοῦν τὸ δυνάμενον ἔχειν ἔχεις ἐκεῖθεν· ὥσπερ εἰ φωνῆς κατεχούσης ἐρημίαν ἢ καὶ μετὰ τῆς ἐρημίας καὶ ἀνθρώπους ἐν ὁτῳοῦν τοῦ ἐρήμου στήσας οὓς τὴν φωνὴν κομιεῖ πᾶσαν καὶ αὖ οὐ πᾶσαν. Τί οὖν ἐστιν ὃ κομιούμεθα νοῦν παραστησάμενοι; Ἢ δεῖ τὸν νοῦν οἷον εἰς τοὐπίσω

[1] τὸ codd.: τῷ Kirchhoff, H–S[2]: παρὸν στήσας Theiler: παραστήσας codd., H–S[2]. τὸ γὰρ πανταχοῦ παρὸν στήσας nunc Henry et Schwyzer.

these two must be beyond intellect. What then, prevents it from being the intelligible? The fact that the intelligible also is coupled with intellect. If, then, it is neither intellect nor intelligible, what can it be? We shall assert that it is that from which Intellect and the intelligible with it come. What, then, is this, and what kind of thing shall we imagine it to be? For certainly it will be either a thinking being or something unthinking. Well, if it is thinking it will be an intellect, but if it is unthinking, it will be ignorant even of itself; so what will be grand about it? For even if we say that it is the Good and absolutely simple, we shall not be saying anything clear and distinct, even though we are speaking the truth, as long as we do not have anything on which to base our reasoning when we speak. For, again, since knowledge of other things comes to us from intellect, and we are able to know intellect by intellect, by what sort of simple intuition could one grasp this which transcends the nature of intellect? We shall say to the person to whom we have to explain how this is possible, that it is by the likeness in ourselves. For there is something of it in us too; or rather there is nowhere where it is not, in the things which can participate in it. For, wherever you are, it is from this that you have that which is everywhere present, by setting to it that which can have it; just as if there was a voice filling an empty space, or with the empty space, men too, and by setting yourself to listen at any point in the empty space, you will receive the whole voice, and yet not the whole. What is it, then, which we shall receive when we set our intellect to it? Rather, the intellect

ἀναχωρεῖν καὶ οἷον ἑαυτὸν ἀφέντα τοῖς εἰς ὄπισθεν αὐτοῦ ἀμφίστομον ὄντα, κἀκεῖ[να],[1] εἰ ἐθέλοι ἐκεῖνο ὁρᾶν, μὴ πάντα νοῦν εἶναι. Ἔστι μὲν γὰρ αὐτὸς ζωὴ πρώτη, ἐνέργεια οὖσα ἐν διεξόδῳ τῶν πάντων· διεξόδῳ δὲ οὐ τῇ διεξιούσῃ, ἀλλὰ τῇ διεξελθούσῃ. Εἴπερ οὖν καὶ ζωή ἐστι καὶ διέξοδός ἐστι καὶ πάντα ἀκριβῶς καὶ οὐχ ὁλοσχερῶς ἔχει—ἀτελῶς γὰρ ἂν καὶ ἀδιαρθρώτως ἔχοι—ἔκ τινος ἄλλου αὐτὸν εἶναι, ὃ οὐκέτι ἐν διεξόδῳ, ἀλλὰ ἀρχὴ διεξόδου καὶ ἀρχὴ ζωῆς καὶ ἀρχὴ νοῦ καὶ τῶν πάντων. Οὐ γὰρ ἀρχὴ τὰ πάντα, ἀλλ᾽ ἐξ ἀρχῆς τὰ πάντα, αὕτη δὲ οὐκέτι τὰ πάντα οὐδέ τι τῶν πάντων, ἵνα γεννήσῃ τὰ πάντα, καὶ ἵνα μὴ πλῆθος ᾖ, ἀλλὰ τοῦ πλήθους ἀρχή· τοῦ γὰρ γεννηθέντος πανταχοῦ τὸ γεννῶν ἁπλούστερον. Εἰ οὖν τοῦτο νοῦν ἐγέννησεν, ἁπλούστερον νοῦ δεῖ αὐτὸ εἶναι. Εἰ δέ τις οἴοιτο αὐτὸ τὸ ἓν καὶ τὰ πάντα εἶναι, ἤτοι καθ᾽ ἓν ἕκαστον τῶν πάντων ἐκεῖνο ἔσται ἢ ὁμοῦ πάντα. Εἰ μὲν οὖν ὁμοῦ πάντα συνηθροισμένα, ὕστερον ἔσται τῶν πάντων· εἰ δὲ πρότερον τῶν πάντων, ἄλλα μὲν τὰ πάντα, ἄλλο δὲ αὐτὸ ἔσται τῶν πάντων· εἰ δὲ ἅμα καὶ αὐτὸ καὶ τὰ πάντα, οὐκ ἀρχὴ ἔσται. Δεῖ δὲ αὐτὸ ἀρχὴν εἶναι

[1] κἀκεῖ Kirchhoff, H–S[1]: κἀκεῖνα codd.: † κἀκεῖνα H–S[2].

---

[1] Plotinus could hardly make it clearer than he does in this passage that he is not a pantheist. He is arguing here either against the Stoics, for whom the visible universe was both the totality of being and the supreme unity and divinity, or against

must return, so to speak, backwards, and give itself up, in a way, to what lies behind it (for it faces in both directions); and there, if it wishes to see that First Principle, it must not be altogether intellect. For it is the first life, since it is an activity manifest in the way of outgoing of all things; outgoing not in the sense that it is now in process of going out but that it has gone out. If, then, it is life and outgoing and holds all things distinctly and not in a vague general way—for [in the latter case] it would hold them imperfectly and inarticulately—it must itself derive from something else, which is no more in the way of outgoing, but is the origin of outgoing, and the origin of life and the origin of intellect and all things. For all things [together, the totality of being] are not an origin, but they came from an origin, and this is no more all things, or one of them;[1] [if it is, it will not be of such a kind] that it can generate all things, and not be a multiplicity, but the origin of multiplicity; for that which generates is always simpler than that which is generated. If this, then, generated Intellect, it must be simpler than Intellect. But if anyone should think that the One itself is also all things, then either it will be each one taken separately or all of them together. If, then, it is all of them collected together, it will be posterior to all things; but if it is prior to all things, all things will be other than it, and it will be other than all things, but if it and all things are simultaneous, then it will not be an origin. But it must be an origin, and exist before

Platonists who accepted the identification of the totality of being with Intellect, but did not see the need for the transcendent One.

καὶ εἶναι πρὸ πάντων, ἵνα ᾖ μετ' αὐτὸ καὶ τὰ πάντα. Τὸ δὲ καθ' ἕκαστον τῶν πάντων πρῶτον μὲν τὸ αὐτὸ ἔσται ὁτιοῦν ὁτῳοῦν, ἔπειτα ὁμοῦ πάντα, καὶ οὐδὲν διακρινεῖ. Καὶ οὕτως οὐδὲν τῶν πάντων, ἀλλὰ πρὸ τῶν πάντων.

10. Τί δὴ ὄν; Δύναμις τῶν πάντων· ἧς μὴ οὔσης οὐδ' ἂν τὰ πάντα, οὐδ' ἂν νοῦς ζωὴ ἡ πρώτη καὶ πᾶσα. Τὸ δὲ ὑπὲρ τὴν ζωὴν αἴτιον ζωῆς· οὐ γὰρ ἡ τῆς ζωῆς ἐνέργεια τὰ πάντα οὖσα πρώτη, ἀλλ' ὥσπερ προχυθεῖσα αὐτὴ οἷον ἐκ πηγῆς. Νόησον γὰρ πηγὴν ἀρχὴν ἄλλην οὐκ ἔχουσαν, δοῦσαν δὲ ποταμοῖς πᾶσαν[1] αὐτήν, οὐκ ἀναλωθεῖσαν τοῖς ποταμοῖς, ἀλλὰ μένουσαν αὐτὴν ἡσύχως, τοὺς δὲ ἐξ αὐτῆς προεληλυθότας πρὶν ἄλλον ἄλλῃ ῥεῖν ὁμοῦ συνόντας ἔτι, ἤδη δὲ οἷον ἑκάστους εἰδότας οἷ ἀφήσουσιν αὐτῶν τὰ ῥεύματα· ἢ ζωὴν φυτοῦ μεγίστου διὰ παντὸς ἐλθοῦσαν ἀρχῆς μενούσης καὶ οὐ σκεδασθείσης περὶ πᾶν αὐτῆς οἷον ἐν ῥίζῃ ἱδρυμένης. Αὕτη τοίνυν παρέσχε μὲν τὴν πᾶσαν ζωὴν τῷ φυτῷ τὴν πολλήν, ἔμεινε δὲ αὐτὴ οὐ πολλὴ οὖσα, ἀλλ' ἀρχὴ τῆς πολλῆς. Καὶ θαῦμα οὐδέν. Ἢ καὶ θαῦμα, πῶς τὸ πλῆθος τῆς ζωῆς ἐξ οὐ πλήθους ἦν, καὶ οὐκ ἦν τὸ πλῆθος, εἰ μὴ τὸ πρὸ τοῦ πλήθους ἦν ὃ μὴ πλῆθος ἦν. Οὐ γὰρ μερίζεται εἰς τὸ πᾶν ἡ

[1] πᾶσαν Mras et nunc Henry et Schwyzer: πᾶσιν codd., H–S.

---

[1] For the application of the word δύναμις to the One as principle of all things, cp. IV. 8 [6] 6. 11, and VI. 9 [9] 5. 36. It should not be misunderstood as meaning "potentiality" in the

all things, in order that all things, too, may exist after it. But as for its being each one taken separately, first, any one of them will be the same as any other, then all will be confounded together and there will be no distinction [between them]. And so it is not one of all things, but is before all things.

10. What is it, then? The productive power of all things;[1] if it did not exist, neither would all things, nor would Intellect be the first and universal life. But what is above life is cause of life; for the activity of life, which is all things, is not first, but itself flows out, so to speak, as if from a spring. For think of a spring which has no other origin, but gives the whole of itself to rivers, and is not used up by the rivers but remains itself at rest, but the rivers that rise from it, before each of them flows in a different direction, remain for a while all together, though each of them knows, in a way, the direction in which it is going to let its stream flow; or of the life of a huge plant, which goes through the whole of it while its origin remains and is not dispersed over the whole, since it is, as it were, firmly settled in the root. So this origin gives to the plant its whole life in its multiplicity, but remains itself not multiple but the origin of the multiple life. And this is no wonder. Or, yes, it is a wonder how the multiplicity of life came from what is not multiplicity, and the multiplicity would not have existed, if what was not multiplicity had not existed before the multiplicity. For the origin is not divided up into the All, for if it were divided up

Aristotelian sense: it is rather (as translated here) "productive power," supremely active, not passive, a formlessness productive of forms, not a formlessness which submits to forms.

ἀρχή· μερισθεῖσα γὰρ ἀπώλεσεν ἂν καὶ τὸ πᾶν, καὶ οὐδ᾽ ἂν ἔτι γένοιτο μὴ μενούσης τῆς ἀρχῆς ἐφ᾽ ἑαυτῆς ἑτέρας οὔσης. Διὸ καὶ ἡ ἀναγωγὴ πανταχοῦ ἐφ᾽ ἕν. Καὶ ἐφ᾽ ἑκάστου μέν τι ἕν, εἰς ὃ ἀνάξεις, καὶ τόδε πᾶν εἰς ἓν τὸ πρὸ αὐτοῦ, οὐχ ἁπλῶς ἕν, ἕως τις ἐπὶ τὸ ἁπλῶς ἓν ἔλθῃ· τοῦτο δὲ οὐκέτι ἐπ᾽ ἄλλο. Ἀλλ᾽ εἰ μὲν τὸ τοῦ φυτοῦ ἕν—τοῦτο δὲ καὶ ἡ ἀρχὴ ἡ μένουσα—καὶ τὸ ζῴου ἓν καὶ τὸ ψυχῆς ἓν καὶ τὸ τοῦ παντὸς ἓν λαμβάνοι, λαμβάνει ἑκασταχοῦ τὸ δυνατώτατον καὶ τὸ τίμιον· εἰ δὲ τὸ τῶν κατ᾽ ἀλήθειαν ὄντων ἕν, τὴν ἀρχὴν καὶ πηγὴν καὶ δύναμιν, λαμβάνοι, ἀπιστήσομεν καὶ τὸ μηδὲν ὑπονοήσομεν; Ἢ ἔστι μὲν τὸ μηδὲν τούτων ὧν ἐστιν ἀρχή, τοιοῦτο μέντοι, οἷον, μηδενὸς αὐτοῦ κατηγορεῖσθαι δυναμένου, μὴ ὄντος, μὴ οὐσίας, μὴ ζωῆς, τὸ ὑπὲρ πάντα αὐτῶν εἶναι. Εἰ δὲ ἀφελὼν τὸ εἶναι λαμβάνοις, θαῦμα ἕξεις. Καὶ βαλὼν πρὸς αὐτὸ καὶ τυχὼν ἐντὸς[1] αὐτοῦ ἀναπαυσάμενος συννόει μᾶλλον τῇ προσβολῇ συνείς, συνορῶν δὲ τὸ μέγα αὐτοῦ τοῖς μετ᾽ αὐτὸ δι᾽ αὐτὸ οὖσιν.

11. Ἔτι δὲ καὶ ὧδε· ἐπεὶ γὰρ ὁ νοῦς ἐστιν ὄψις τις καὶ ὄψις ὁρῶσα, δύναμις ἔσται εἰς ἐνέργειαν ἐλθοῦσα. Ἔσται τοίνυν τὸ μὲν ὕλη, τὸ δὲ εἶδος αὐτοῦ—[οἷον καὶ ἡ κατ᾽ ἐνέργειαν ὅρασις][2]—

[1] ἐντὸς αὐτοῦ H–S²: ἐν τοῖς αὐτοῦ codd., H–S¹: ἐντὸς σαυτοῦ Dodds.

[2] οἷον . . . ὅρασις del. Theiler et nunc Henry et Schwyzer.

it would destroy the All too; and the All could not any more come into being if the origin did not remain by itself, different from it. Therefore, too, we go back everywhere to *one.* And in each and every thing there is some *one* to which you will trace it back, and this in every case to the *one* before it, which is not simply one, until we come to the simply one; but this cannot be traced back to something else. But if we take the *one* of the plant—this is its abiding origin—and the *one* of the animal and the *one* of the soul and the *one* of the universe, we are taking in each case what is most powerful and really valuable in it; but if we take the *one* of the beings which truly exist, their origin and spring and productive power, shall we lose faith and think of it as nothing? It is certainly none of the things of which it is origin; it is of such a kind, though nothing can be predicated of it, not being, not substance, not life, as to be above all of these things. But if you grasp it by taking away being from it, you will be filled with wonder. And, throwing yourself upon it and coming to rest within it, understand it more and more intimately, knowing it by intuition and seeing its greatness by the things which exist after it and through it.[1]

11. And again, consider it this way, for since Intellect is a kind of sight, and a sight which is seeing, it will be a potency which has come into act. So there will be a distinction of matter and form in it, but the matter will be [the kind that

[1] The repeated συν– in this sentence defies translation: it suggests the intimate presence of the One both with the Forms which spring from it and the contemplating mind.

ὕλη δὲ ἐν νοητοῖς· ἐπεὶ καὶ ἡ ὅρασις ἡ κατ' ἐνέργειαν διττὸν ἔχει· πρὶν γοῦν ἰδεῖν ἦν ἕν. Τὸ οὖν ἓν δύο γέγονε καὶ τὰ δύο ἕν. Τῇ μὲν οὖν ὁράσει ἡ πλήρωσις παρὰ τοῦ αἰσθητοῦ καὶ ἡ οἷον τελείωσις, τῇ δὲ τοῦ νοῦ ὄψει τὸ ἀγαθὸν τὸ πληροῦν. Εἰ γὰρ αὐτὸς τὸ ἀγαθόν, τί ἔδει ὁρᾶν ἢ ἐνεργεῖν ὅλως; Τὰ μὲν γὰρ ἄλλα περὶ τὸ ἀγαθὸν καὶ διὰ τὸ ἀγαθὸν ἔχει τὴν ἐνέργειαν, τὸ δὲ ἀγαθὸν οὐδενὸς δεῖται· διὸ οὐδέν ἐστιν αὐτῷ ἢ αὐτό. Φθεγξάμενος οὖν τὸ ἀγαθὸν μηδὲν ἔτι προσνόει· ἐὰν γάρ τι προσθῇς, ᾧ προσέθηκας ὁτιοῦν, ἐνδεὲς ποιήσεις. Διὸ οὐδὲ τὸ νοεῖν, ἵνα μὴ καὶ ἄλλο, καὶ ποιήσῃς δύο, νοῦν καὶ ἀγαθόν. Ὁ μὲν γὰρ νοῦς τοῦ ἀγαθοῦ, τὸ δ' ἀγαθὸν οὐ δεῖται ἐκείνου· ὅθεν καὶ τυγχάνων τοῦ ἀγαθοῦ ἀγαθοειδὲς γίνεται καὶ τελειοῦται παρὰ τοῦ ἀγαθοῦ, τοῦ μὲν εἴδους τοῦ ἐπ' αὐτῷ παρὰ τοῦ ἀγαθοῦ ἥκοντος ἀγαθοειδῆ ποιοῦντος. Οἷον δὲ ἐνορᾶται ἐπ' αὐτῷ ἴχνος τοῦ ἀγαθοῦ, τοιοῦτον τὸ ἀρχέτυπον ἐννοεῖν προσήκει τὸ ἀληθινὸν ἐκείνου ἐνθυμηθέντα ἐκ τοῦ ἐπὶ τῷ νῷ ἐπιθέοντος ἴχνους. Τὸ μὲν οὖν ἐπ' αὐτοῦ ἴχνος αὐτοῦ τῷ νῷ ὁρῶντι ἔδωκεν ἔχειν· ὥστε ἐν μὲν τῷ νῷ ἡ ἔφεσις καὶ ἐφιέμενος ἀεὶ καὶ ἀεὶ τυγχάνων, ἐκεῖ⟨νος⟩[1] δὲ οὔτε ἐφιέμενος—τίνος γάρ;— οὔτε τυγχάνων· οὐδὲ γὰρ ἐφίετο. Οὐ τοίνυν

[1] ἐκεῖ⟨νος⟩ Theiler et nunc Henry et Schwyzer: ἐκεῖ codd., H–S.

exists in] the intelligible world:[1] since actual seeing, too, has a doubleness in it, it was, certainly, one before seeing. So the one has become two and the two one. For seeing, then, fulfilment and a kind of completion comes from the object perceived, but it is the Good which brings fulfilment to the sight of Intellect. For if it was itself the Good, why would it have to see, or to be active at all? For other things have their activity about the Good and because of the Good, but the Good needs nothing; therefore it has nothing but itself. Therefore, when you have said " The Good " do not add anything to it in your mind, for if you add anything, you will make it deficient by whatever you have added. Therefore you must not even add thinking, in order that you may not add something other than it and make two, intellect and good. For Intellect needs the Good, but the Good does not need it; hence, too, when it attains the Good it becomes conformed to the Good[2] and is completed by the Good, since the form which comes upon it from the Good conforms it to the Good. A trace of the Good is seen in it, and it is in the likeness of this that one should conceive its true archetype, forming an idea of it in oneself from the trace of it which plays upon Intellect. The Good, therefore has given the trace of itself on Intellect to Intellect to have by seeing, so that in Intellect there is desire, and it is always desiring and always attaining, but the Good is not desiring—for what could it desire?—or attaining, for it did not desire [to attain anything]. So it is not even Intellect.

[1] For matter in the intelligible world, cp. II. 4 [12] 3–5.

[2] Cp. *Republic* 509A3.

οὐδὲ νοῦς. Ἔφεσις γὰρ καὶ ἐν τούτῳ καὶ σύννευσις πρὸς τὸ εἶδος αὐτοῦ. Τοῦ δὴ νοῦ καλοῦ ὄντος καὶ πάντων καλλίστου, ἐν φωτὶ καθαρῷ καὶ αὐγῇ καθαρᾷ κειμένου καὶ τὴν τῶν ὄντων περιλαβόντος φύσιν, οὗ καὶ ὁ καλὸς οὗτος κόσμος σκιὰ καὶ εἰκών, καὶ ἐν πάσῃ ἀγλαΐᾳ κειμένου, ὅτι μηδὲν ἀνόητον μηδὲ σκοτεινὸν μηδ' ἄμετρον ἐν αὐτῷ, ζῶντος ζωὴν μακαρίαν, θάμβος μὲν ἂν ἔχοι τὸν ἰδόντα καὶ τοῦτον καὶ ὡς χρὴ εἰς αὐτὸν εἰσδύντα καὶ αὐτῷ[1] γενόμενον ἕνα. Ὡς δὴ ὁ ἀναβλέψας εἰς τὸν οὐρανὸν καὶ τὸ τῶν ἄστρων φέγγος ἰδὼν τὸν ποιήσαντα ἐνθυμεῖται καὶ ζητεῖ, οὕτω χρὴ καὶ τὸν νοητὸν κόσμον ὃς ἐθεάσατο καὶ ἐνεῖδε καὶ ἐθαύμασε τὸν κἀκείνου ποιητὴν τίς ἄρα ὁ τοιοῦτον ὑποστήσας ζητεῖν, [ἢ ποῦ][2] ἢ πῶς, ὁ τοιοῦτον παῖδα γεννήσας νοῦν, κόρον καλὸν καὶ παρ' αὐτοῦ γενόμενον κόρον. Πάντως τοι οὔτε νοῦς ἐκεῖνος οὔτε κόρος, ἀλλὰ καὶ πρὸ νοῦ καὶ κόρου· μετὰ γὰρ αὐτὸν νοῦς καὶ κόρος, δεηθέντα καὶ κεκορέσθαι καὶ νενοηκέναι· ἃ πλησίον μέν ἐστι τοῦ ἀνενδεοῦς καὶ τοῦ νοεῖν οὐδὲν δεομένου, πλήρωσιν δὲ ἀληθινὴν καὶ νόησιν ἔχει, ὅτι πρώτως ἔχει. Τὸ δὲ πρὸ αὐτῶν οὔτε δεῖται οὔτε ἔχει· ἢ οὐκ ἂν τὸ ἀγαθὸν ἦν.

[1] αὐτῷ Dodds, H–S²: αὐτοῦ codd.
[2] ἢ ποῦ del. Dodds, H–S².

For in Intellect there is desire and a movement to convergence with its form. Intellect is, certainly, beautiful, and the most beautiful of all; its place is in pure light and pure radiance [1] and it includes the nature of real beings; this beautiful universe of ours is a shadow and image of it; and it has its place in all glory, because there is nothing unintelligent or dark or unmeasured in it, and it lives a blessed life; so wonder would possess him [2] who saw this too, and, as he should, entered it and became one with it. As certainly, one who looks up to the sky and sees the light of the stars thinks of their maker and seeks him, so the man who has contemplated the intelligible world and observed it closely and wondered at it must seek its maker, too, and enquire who it is who has brought into being something like this, and how, he who produced a son like Intellect, a beautiful boy filled full from himself.[3] He is most certainly neither Intellect nor fullness, but before Intellect and fullness. For Intellect and fullness came after him; they needed to come into their fulfilment and intelligence; they are near to that which needs nothing and has no necessity to think, but have true fulfilment and true thinking, because they have them at first hand. But that which is before them neither needs nor has; or it would not be the Good.

[1] *Phaedrus* 250C4.

[2] An oddly inappropriate verbal reminiscence of *Iliad* III. 342.

[3] There is an untranslateable word-play here on κόρος (boy) and κόρος (satiety, fulness).

ENNEAD III. 9

III. 9. VARIOUS CONSIDERATIONS

Introductory Note

THIS odd little collection of notes (No. 13 in Porphyry's chronological order, but the numbering must be quite arbitrary: the notes are unlikely all to have been written at about the same time), which Porphyry found among his master's papers and put together to make a ninth " treatise" to complete his Third Ennead, on the whole adds little to our understanding of the thought of Plotinus. They are quite disconnected, and each of them deals with a point discussed more fully elsewhere in the Enneads. The first and longest is, however, of some interest. In it we find Plotinus reflecting on a problem much discussed in his school, that of the relationship of Intellect to the Forms, which arises in the interpretation of *Timaeus* 39E. 7–9. And in the course of his discussion of it (l. 15 ff.) he appears to be considering with some sympathetic interest the possibility of a subdivision of Intellect very like that which is reported to have been taught by Amelius,[1] and which he decisively rejects in his treatise *Against the Gnostics*: [2] he certainly does not, however, commit himself to this, and at the end of the note seems to be putting forward his usual view that there are three, and only three, hypostases without subdivisions.

Synopsis

The correct interpretation of *Timaeus* 39E. 7–9: does it require a subdivision of Intellect, or can we interpret it in

[1] Proclus, *In Tim.* I. 306.1–3. [2] II. 9 [33] 1.25 ff.

terms of a single Intellect and Soul? (Note 1). We must unite ourselves as subjects of study are united in one discipline and direct our united selves to the higher world (Note 2). Universal Soul is not in place and unmoving; but individuals move and change, in a sense, and in so doing make their bodily images (Note 3). The One is everywhere and nowhere (Note 4). The soul is matter in relation to Intellect (Note 5). Intellect at rest exists before our self-thinking (Note 6). The One is beyond motion and rest, and transcends thinking (Note 7). Act and potency in compounded and uncompounded beings (Note 8). The Good does not think, and is not conscious of itself (Note 9).

III. 9. (13) ΕΠΙΣΚΕΨΕΙΣ ΔΙΑΦΟΡΟΙ

1. Νοῦς, φησιν, ὁρᾷ ἐνούσας ἰδέας ἐν τῷ ὅ ἐστι ζῷον· εἶτα διενοήθη, φησίν, ὁ δημιουργός, ἃ ὁ νοῦς ὁρᾷ ἐν τῷ ὅ ἐστι ζῷον, καὶ τόδε τὸ πᾶν ἔχειν. Οὐκοῦν φησιν ἤδη εἶναι τὰ εἴδη πρὸ τοῦ νοῦ, ὄντα δὲ αὐτὰ νοεῖν τὸν νοῦν; Πρῶτον οὖν ἐκεῖνο, λέγω δὲ τὸ ζῷον, ζητητέον εἰ μὴ νοῦς, ἀλλ' ἕτερον νοῦ· τὸ γὰρ θεώμενον νοῦς· τὸ τοίνυν ζῷον αὐτὸ οὐ νοῦς, ἀλλὰ νοητὸν αὐτὸ φήσομεν καὶ τὸν νοῦν ἔξω φήσομεν αὐτοῦ ἃ ὁρᾷ ἔχειν. Εἴδωλα ἄρα καὶ οὐ τἀληθῆ ἔχει, εἰ ἐκεῖ τἀληθῆ. Ἐκεῖ γὰρ καὶ τὴν ἀλήθειάν φησιν εἶναι ἐν τῷ ὄντι, οὗ αὐτὸ ἕκαστον. Ἤ, κἂν ἕτερον ἑκάτερον, οὐ χωρὶς ἀλλήλων, ἀλλ' ἢ μόνον τῷ ἕτερα. Ἔπειτα οὐδὲν κωλύει ὅσον ἐπὶ τῷ λεγομένῳ ἓν εἶναι ἄμφω, διαιρούμενα δὲ τῇ νοήσει, εἴπερ μόνον ὡς ὂν τὸ μὲν νοητόν, τὸ δὲ νοοῦν· ὃ γὰρ καθορᾷ οὔ φησιν ἐν ἑτέρῳ πάντως, ἀλλ' ἐν αὐτῷ τῷ ἐν αὐτῷ τὸ

[1] *Timaeus* 39E, 7–9.

[2] This view, which Plotinus here and elsewhere consistently opposes, was at one time held by Porphyry (cp. *Life*, ch. 18, 11, and Proclus, *In Tim.* I. 322. 22–4). It differs from that of

III. 9. VARIOUS CONSIDERATIONS

1. "Intellect," Plato says, "sees the Ideas existing in the real living creature" then, he says, "the Maker planned that, what Intellect sees in the real living creature, this universe too should have.[1]" Does he, then, say that the Forms exist already before Intellect, and that Intellect thinks them when they [already] exist? First of all, then, we must investigate that reality (I mean the living creature), to see if it is not Intellect, but something other than Intellect; for that which contemplates it is Intellect; so we shall say that the living creature is not Intellect, but intelligible, and that Intellect has what it sees outside itself.[2] So, then, it has images and not true realities, if the true realities are there [in the living creature]. For there, Plato says, is truth too, in real being, where each and every thing in itself is.[3] Now, even if the two are different from each other, they are not separate from each other except in so far as they are different. Further, there is nothing in the statement against both being one, but distinguished by thought, though only in the sense that one is intelligible object, the other intelligent subject; for Plato does not say that what it sees is in something absolutely different, but in it,

Longinus, who made the Forms not only outside, but posterior to, the Demiurge (Proclus, l.c.).

[3] Cp. *Phaedrus* 247C–E.

νοητὸν ἔχειν. Ἢ τὸ μὲν νοητὸν οὐδὲν κωλύει καὶ νοῦν εἶναι ἐν στάσει καὶ ἑνότητι καὶ ἡσυχίᾳ, τὴν δὲ τοῦ νοῦ φύσιν τοῦ ὁρῶντος ἐκεῖνον τὸν νοῦν τὸν ἐν αὑτῷ ἐνέργειάν τινα ἀπ᾽ ἐκείνου, ᾗ ὁρᾷ ἐκεῖνον· ὁρῶντα δὲ ἐκεῖνον οἷον [ἐκεῖνον][1] εἶναι νοῦν ἐκείνου, ὅτι νοεῖ ἐκεῖνον· νοοῦντα δὲ ἐκεῖνον καὶ αὐτὸν νοῦν καὶ νοητὸν ἄλλως εἶναι τῷ μεμιμῆσθαι. Τοῦτο οὖν ἐστι τὸ "διανοηθέν," ἃ ἐκεῖ ὁρᾷ, ἐν τῷδε τῷ κόσμῳ ποιῆσαι ζῴων γένη τέσσαρα. Δοκεῖ γε μὴν τὸ διανοούμενον ἐπικεκρυμμένως ἕτερον ἐκείνων τῶν δύο ποιεῖν. Ἄλλοις δὲ δόξει τὰ τρία ἓν εἶναι, τὸ ζῷον αὐτὸ ὅ ἐστιν, ὁ νοῦς, τὸ διανοούμενον. Ἢ, ὥσπερ ἐν πολλοῖς, προτείνων ἄλλως, ὁ δὲ ἄλλως νοεῖ τρία εἶναι. Καὶ τὰ μὲν δύο εἴρηται, τὸ δὲ τρίτον τί, ὃ διενοήθη τὰ ὁρώμενα ὑπὸ τοῦ νοῦ ἐν τῷ ζῴῳ κείμενα αὐτὸ ἐργάσασθαι καὶ ποιῆσαι καὶ μερίσαι; Ἢ δυνατὸν τρόπον μὲν ἄλλον τὸν νοῦν εἶναι τὸν μερίσαντα, τρόπον δὲ ἕτερον τὸν μερίσαντα μὴ τὸν νοῦν εἶναι· ᾗ μὲν γὰρ παρ᾽ αὐτοῦ τὰ μερισθέντα, αὐτὸν εἶναι τὸν μερίσαντα, ᾗ δ᾽ αὐτὸς ἀμέριστος μένει, τὰ δ᾽ ἀπ᾽ αὐτοῦ ἐστι τὰ μερισθέντα—ταῦτα δέ ἐστι ψυχαί—ψυχὴν εἶναι τὴν μερίσασαν εἰς πολλὰς ψυχάς. Διὸ

[1] ἐκεῖνον del. Volkmann, H–S².

---

[1] This may be a misinterpretation, or careless reading, of *Timaeus* 30C7–8.

[2] *Timaeus* 39E10–40A2. The "four kinds" are gods,

in that it has the intelligible object in itself.[1] Or there is nothing against [this solution]; the intelligible object is also an intellect at rest and in unity and quietness, but the nature of the intellect which sees that intellect which remains within itself is an activity proceeding from it, which sees that [static] intellect; and by seeing that intellect it is in a way the intellect of that intellect, because it thinks it; but that thinking intellect itself too is intelligent subject and intelligible object in a different way, by imitation. This, then, is that which "planned" to make in this universe the four kinds of living creatures [2] which it sees in the intelligible. Plato seems, nevertheless, to be making, obscurely, the intending principle something other than those two. But to others it will seem that the three are one, the living creature which exists in itself, the intellect, and the planning principle. Just as in many other questions, different people understand "being three" in different ways because they formulate the problem differently. We have dealt with the two, but what is the third, which "planned" itself to construct and make and divide into parts the things seen by Intellect in the living creature? Now it is possible that in one way it may be Intellect that divides, but in another way the divider may not be Intellect; for in so far as the things divided into parts come from it, it is itself the divider, but in so far as it remains undivided itself, and it is the things which come from it which are divided—and these are souls—it is Soul which makes the division into many souls. This

birds, fishes and land animals, one kind for each of the elements, fire, air, water and earth.

καί φησι τοῦ τρίτου εἶναι τὸν μερισμὸν καὶ ἐν τῷ τρίτῳ, ὅτι διενοήθη, ὃ οὐ νοῦ ἔργον—ἡ διάνοια—ἀλλὰ ψυχῆς μεριστὴν ἐνέργειαν ἐχούσης ἐν μεριστῇ φύσει.

2. *Οἷον γὰρ μιᾶς ἐπιστήμης τῆς ὅλης ὁ μερισμὸς εἰς τὰ θεωρήματα τὰ καθέκαστα οὐ σκεδασθείσης οὐδὲ κατακερματισθείσης, ἔχει δὲ ἕκαστον δυνάμει τὸ ὅλον, οὗ τὸ αὐτὸ ἀρχὴ καὶ τέλος, καὶ οὕτω χρὴ παρασκευάζειν αὐτόν, ὡς τὰς ἀρχὰς τὰς ἐν αὐτῷ καὶ τέλη εἶναι καὶ ὅλα καὶ πάντα εἰς τὸ τῆς φύσεως ἄριστον· ὁ γενόμενός ἐστιν ἐκεῖ· τούτῳ γὰρ τῷ ἀρίστῳ αὐτοῦ, ὅταν ἔχῃ, ἅψεται ἐκείνου.*

3. *Ἡ πᾶσα ψυχὴ οὐδαμοῦ ἐγένετο οὐδὲ ἦλθεν· οὐδὲ γὰρ ἦν ὅπου· ἀλλὰ τὸ σῶμα γειτονῆσαν μετέλαβεν αὐτῆς· διὸ οὐκ ἐν τῷ σώματι οὐδ' ὁ Πλάτων φησί που, ἀλλὰ τὸ σῶμα εἰς αὐτήν. Αἱ δ' ἄλλαι ἔχουσιν ὅθεν—ἀπὸ γὰρ ψυχῆς—καὶ εἰς ὅ, καὶ κατελθεῖν καὶ μετελθεῖν· ὅθεν καὶ ἀνελθεῖν. Ἡ δ' ἀεὶ ἄνω ἐν ᾧ πέφυκεν εἶναι ψυχή· τὸ δὲ ἐφεξῆς τὸ πᾶν, οἷον τὸ πλησίον ἢ τὸ ὑφ' ἡλίῳ.*

---

[1] Plotinus is here very freely interpreting *Timaeus* 35A. Porphry held that Soul was the Demiurge, and believed that this interpretation agreed with that of Plotinus (Proclus, *In Tim.* I 306. 32–307, 2); this passage gives him some support, and, though elsewhere (II. 3 [52] 18. 15, and V. 9 [5] 3. 26) Plotinus identifies the Demiurge with Intellect, he makes it clear that it is Soul which actually makes the visible universe. Intellect is only "the true demiurge and maker" in the sense that it supplies Soul with the forms according to which it makes.

[2] Cp. *Timaeus* 36D9–E1.

is the reason why Plato also says that the division belongs to the third and is in the third, because it "planned," this—planning—is not the work of Intellect, but of Soul, which has a divided activity in a divided nature.[1]

2. Just as one discipline which is a whole is not scattered or broken into pieces by the division into the single subjects of study, but each of these contains potentially the whole, which has the same principle and goal; in the same way, too, a man must prepare himself so that the principles in him are also his goals, and each as a whole and all together are directed to the best of his nature; when he has become this, he is there [in the higher world]; for with this best of him, when he possesses it, he will grasp that [higher reality].

3. Universal Soul did not come to be anywhere or come to any place, for there was no place; but the body came near to it and participated in it; for this reason Plato, too, does not say anywhere that it is in the body, but that the body was put into it.[2] But the other souls have somewhere they come from—for they come from [universal] Soul and somewhere to go to, and a going down and going about: consequently also a going up. But the [universal] Soul is always above, where it is natural for it to be: that which comes next to it is the All [the physical universe] both the immediately neighbouring part and that which is beneath the sun.[3] The partial soul,

[3] This extremely puzzling remark may possibly be meant to exclude the literal, spatial meaning of "above" and to indicate that all parts of the universe, the lower as well as the upper, are "next" to soul.

Φωτίζεται μὲν οὖν ἡ μερικὴ πρὸς τὸ πρὸ αὐτῆς φερομένη—ὄντι γὰρ ἐντυγχάνει—εἰς δὲ τὸ μετ᾿ αὐτὴν εἰς τὸ μὴ ὄν. Τοῦτο δὲ ποιεῖ, ὅταν πρὸς αὐτήν· πρὸς αὐτὴν γὰρ βουλομένη τὸ μετ᾿ αὐτὴν ποιεῖ εἴδωλον αὐτῆς, τὸ μὴ ὄν, οἷον κενεμβατοῦσα καὶ ἀοριστοτέρα γινομένη· καὶ τούτου τὸ εἴδωλον τὸ ἀόριστον πάντη σκοτεινόν· ἄλογον γὰρ καὶ ἀνόητον πάντη καὶ πολὺ τοῦ ὄντος ἀποστατοῦν. Εἰς δὲ τὸ μεταξύ ἐστιν ἐν τῷ οἰκείῳ, πάλιν δὲ ἰδοῦσα οἷον δευτέρᾳ προσβολῇ τὸ εἴδωλον ἐμόρφωσε καὶ ἡσθεῖσα ἔρχεται εἰς αὐτό.

4. Πῶς οὖν ἐξ ἑνὸς πλῆθος; Ὅτι πανταχοῦ· οὐ γάρ ἐστιν ὅπου οὔ. Πάντα οὖν πληροῖ· πολλὰ οὖν, μᾶλλον δὲ πάντα ἤδη. Αὐτὸ μὲν γὰρ εἰ μόνον πανταχοῦ, αὐτὸ ἂν ἦν τὰ πάντα· ἐπεὶ δὲ καὶ οὐδαμοῦ, τὰ πάντα γίνεται μὲν δι᾿ αὐτόν, ὅτι πανταχοῦ ἐκεῖνος, ἕτερα δὲ αὐτοῦ, ὅτι αὐτὸς οὐδαμοῦ. Διὰ τί οὖν οὐκ αὐτὸς μόνον πανταχοῦ καὶ αὖ πρὸς τούτῳ καὶ οὐδαμοῦ; Ὅτι δεῖ πρὸ πάντων ἓν εἶναι. Πληροῦν οὖν δεῖ αὐτὸν καὶ ποιεῖν πάντα, οὐκ εἶναι τὰ πάντα, ἃ ποιεῖ.

5. Τὴν ψυχὴν αὐτὴν δεῖ ὥσπερ ὄψιν εἶναι, ὁρατὸν δὲ αὐτῇ τὸν νοῦν εἶναι, ἀόριστον πρὶν ἰδεῖν, πεφυκυῖαν δὲ νοεῖν· ὕλην οὖν πρὸς νοῦν.

6. Νοοῦντες αὐτοὺς βλέπομεν δηλονότι νοοῦσαν φύσιν, ἢ ψευδοίμεθα ἂν τὸ νοεῖν. Εἰ οὖν νοοῦμεν

then, is illuminated when it goes towards that which is before it—for then it meets reality—but when it goes towards what comes after it, it goes towards non-existence. But it does this, when it goes towards itself, for, wishing to be directed towards itself it makes an image of itself, the non-existent, as if walking on emptiness and becoming more indefinite; and the indefinite image of this is every way dark: for it is altogether without reason and unintelligent and stands far removed from reality. Up to the time between it is in its own world, but when it looks at the image again, as it were directing its attention to it a second time, it forms it and goes into it rejoicing.

4. How then does multiplicity come from one? Because it is everywhere, for there is nowhere where it is not. Therefore it fills all things; so it is many, or rather it is already all. Now if it itself were only everywhere, it would itself be all things; but since it is also nowhere, all things come into being through him, because he is everywhere, but are other than him, because he is nowhere. Why, then, is he not only everywhere, and is also, besides being everywhere, nowhere? Because there must be one before all things. Therefore he must fill all things and make all things, not be all the things he makes.

5. The soul itself must be like sight, and what it sees must be Intellect; before it sees it is indeterminate, but naturally adapted to intellection: so it is matter in relation to intellect.

6. When we are thinking ourselves we are, obviously, looking at a thinking nature, or our statement that there is thinking would be false. If, then, we

καὶ ἑαυτοὺς νοοῦμεν, νοερὰν οὖσαν φύσιν νοοῦμεν· πρὸ ἄρα τῆς νοήσεως ταύτης ἄλλη ἐστὶ νόησις οἷον ἥσυχος. Καὶ οὐσίας δὴ νόησις καὶ ζωῆς νόησις· ὥστε πρὸ ταύτης τῆς ζωῆς καὶ οὐσίας ἄλλη οὐσία καὶ ζωή. Ταῦτα ἄρα εἶδεν, ὅσα ἐνέργειαι. Εἰ δὲ νόες αἱ ἐνέργειαι αἱ κατὰ τὸ νοεῖν οὕτως ἑαυτούς, τὸ νοητὸν ἡμεῖς οἱ ὄντως. Ἡ δὲ νόησις ἡ αὐτῶν τὴν εἰκόνα φέρει.

7. Τὸ μὲν πρῶτον δύναμίς ἐστι κινήσεως καὶ στάσεως, ὥστε ἐπέκεινα τούτων· τὸ δὲ δεύτερον ἕστηκέ τε καὶ κινεῖται περὶ ἐκεῖνο· καὶ νοῦς δὲ περὶ τὸ δεύτερον· ἄλλο γὰρ ὂν πρὸς ἄλλο ἔχει τὴν νόησιν, τὸ δὲ ἓν νόησιν οὐκ ἔχει. Διπλοῦν δὲ τὸ νοοῦν, κἂν[1] αὐτὸν νοῇ, καὶ ἐλλιπές, ὅτι ἐν τῷ νοεῖν ἔχει τὸ εὖ, οὐκ ἐν τῇ ὑποστάσει.

8. Τὸ ἐνεργείᾳ παντὶ τῷ ἐκ δυνάμεως εἰς ἐνέργειαν ὅ ἐστι ταὐτὸν ἀεί, ἕως ἂν ᾖ· ὥστε καὶ τὸ τέλειον καὶ τοῖς σώμασιν ὑπάρχει, οἷον τῷ πυρί· ἀλλ᾽ οὐ δύναται ἀεὶ εἶναι, ὅτι μεθ᾽ ὕλης· ὃ δ᾽ ἂν ἀσύνθετον ὂν ἐνεργείᾳ ᾖ, ἀεὶ ἔστιν. Ἔστι δὲ τὸ αὐτὸ ἐνεργείᾳ ὂν δυνάμει κατ᾽ ἄλλο εἶναι.

9. Ἀλλ᾽ οὐ νοεῖ[2] τὸ πρῶτον ἐπέκεινα ὄντος·[3] ὁ δὲ νοῦς τὰ ὄντα, καὶ ἔστι κίνησις ἐνταῦθα καὶ στάσις. Περὶ οὐδὲν γὰρ αὐτὸ τὸ πρῶτον, τὰ ἄλλα

[1] κἂν H–S: καὶ codd.
[2] νοεῖ Inge, H–S: θεοὶ wxy.
[3] ὄντος Vitringa, H–S: ὄντες wxy.

think, and think ourselves, we think a nature which is thinking; then before this thinking there is another which is, so to speak, at rest. And there is, certainly, a thinking of substance and a thinking of life; so that before this life and substance there is another substance and life. These, then, all the things which are activities saw. But if the activities engaged in thinking themselves in this way are intelligences, then our real selves are their intelligible object. But their thinking brings [only] the image of it.

7. The First is the power which causes motion and rest, so that it is beyond them; but the Second is at rest and also in motion around the First; and Intellect is in the sphere of the Second,[1] for it is one thing and has its thought directed to another, but the One does not have thought. So that which thinks is double, even if it thinks itself, and defective, because it has its good in its thinking, not in its being.

8. Being in act is, for everything which passes from potency to act, that which is always the same as long as the thing exists; so that completion exists for bodies too, fire, for instance; but they cannot always exist, because they are compounded with matter; but that which is uncompounded and in act always exists. But it is possible for the same thing which is in act to be in potency in another respect.

9. But the First beyond being does not think: Intellect is the real beings, and there is movement here and rest. The First itself is not related to anything, but the other things are related to it, staying

[1] Cp. Plato, *Second Letter* 312E3.

δὲ περὶ αὐτὸ ἀναπαυόμενα ἕστηκε καὶ κινεῖται· ἡ γὰρ κίνησις ἔφεσις, τὸ δὲ οὐδενὸς ἐφίεται· τίνος γὰρ τό γε ἀκρότατον; Οὐ νοεῖ οὖν οὐδὲ ἑαυτό; Ἢ ᾗ ἔχει ἑαυτό, καὶ νοεῖν ὅλως λέγεται; Ἢ τῷ ἔχειν ἑαυτὸ οὐ νοεῖν λέγεται, ἀλλὰ τῷ πρὸς τὸ πρῶτον βλέπειν. Ἔστι δὲ πρώτη ἐνέργεια καὶ αὐτὴ ἡ νόησις. Εἰ οὖν αὕτη πρώτη, οὐδεμίαν δεῖ προτέραν. Τὸ οὖν παρέχον ταύτην ἐπέκεινα ταύτης· ὥστε δευτέρα ἡ νόησις μετ᾽ ἐκεῖνο. Οὐδὲ γὰρ τὸ πρώτως σεμνὸν ἡ νόησις· οὔκουν οὐδὲ πᾶσα, ἀλλ᾽ ἡ τοῦ ἀγαθοῦ· ἐπέκεινα ἄρα νοήσεως τἀγαθόν. Ἀλλ᾽ οὐ παρακολουθήσει αὑτῷ. Τί οὖν ἡ παρακολούθησις αὑτῷ; Ἀγαθοῦ ὄντος ἢ οὔ; Εἰ μὲν γὰρ ὄντος, ἤδη ἐστὶ πρὸ τῆς παρακολουθήσεως τἀγαθόν· εἰ δ᾽ ἡ παρακολούθησις ποιεῖ, οὐκ ἂν εἴη πρὸ ταύτης τὸ ἀγαθόν· ὥστε οὐδ᾽ αὐτὴ ἔσται μὴ οὖσα ἀγαθοῦ. Τί οὖν; Οὐδὲ ζῇ; Ἢ ζῆν μὲν οὐ λεκτέον, εἴπερ δέ, ζωὴν δίδωσι. Τὸ δὲ παρακολουθοῦν ἑαυτῷ καὶ τὸ νοοῦν αὐτὸ δεύτερον· παρακολουθεῖ γάρ, ἵνα τῇ ἐνεργείᾳ ταύτῃ συνῇ αὐτό. Δεῖ οὖν, εἰ καταμανθάνει αὐτό, ἀκαταμάθητον τετυχηκέναι εἶναι αὑτοῦ καὶ τῇ αὐτοῦ φύσει ἐλλιπὲς εἶναι, τῇ δὲ νοήσει τελειοῦσθαι. Τὸ ἄρα κατανοεῖν ἐξαιρετέον· ἡ γὰρ προσθήκη ἀφαίρεσιν καὶ ἔλλειψιν ποιεῖ.

around it in their rest, and moving around it, for movement is desire, but it desires nothing, for what could it desire, it which is the highest? Does it not, then, even think itself? Is it not said in a general way to think in that it possesses itself? It is not by possessing itself that anything is said to think, but by looking at the First. But thinking itself is also the first actuality. If, then, this is the first, there is no need of anything before it. That, then, which produces this is beyond it, so thinking is second after that. For thinking is also not the primarily venerable; all thinking is certainly not venerable, only thinking about the Good, so the Good is beyond thinking. But the Good will not be conscious of itself. What, then, would its consciousness of itself be? A consciousness of itself as being good or not? Well, then, if it is of itself as being good, the Good exists already before the consciousness; but if the consciousness makes it good, the Good would not exist before it, so that the consciousness itself would not exist, since it is of the Good. What then? Is it not alive either? No, it cannot be said to live, but if it can, [only in the sense that] it gives life. That which is conscious of itself and thinks itself comes second, for it is conscious of itself in order that in this actuality of consciousness it may understand itself. Therefore, if it becomes acquainted with itself, it must have been unacquainted with itself and deficient in its own nature, and is completed by its thinking. So, then, thinking must be excluded from the Good, for the addition causes diminution and defect.